GEOPOLITICS AND EMPIRE

Cultivated Landscapes of Middle America on the Eve of Conquest
Thomas W. Whitmore and B. L. Turner II

Worlds of Food
Place, Power, and Provenance in the Food Chain
Kevin Morgan, Terry Marsden, and Jonathan Murdoch

The Nature of the State
Excavating the Political Ecologies of the Modern State
Mark Whitehead, Rhys Jones, and Martin Jones

Decolonizing the Colonial City
Urbanization and Stratification in Kingston, Jamaica
Colin Clarke

Industrial Transformation in the Developing World
Michael T. Rock and David P. Angel

The Globalized City
Economic Restructuring and Social Polarization in European Cities
Edited by Frank Moulaert, Arantxa Rodriguez, and Erik Swyngedouw

Conflict, Consensus, and Rationality in Environmental Planning
An Institutional Discourse Approach
Yvonne Rydin

Globalization and Urban Change
Capital, Culture, and Pacific Rim Mega-Projects
Kris Olds

Cultivated Landscapes of Native Amazonia and the Andes
William M. Denevan

Poliomyelitis
A World Geography: Emergence to Eradication
Matthew Smallman-Raynor and Andrew Cliff

War Epidemics
An Historical Geography of Infectious Diseases in Military Conflict
and Civil Strife, 1850–2000
Matthew Smallman-Raynor and Andrew Cliff

Social Power and the Urbanization of Water
Flows of Power
Erik Swyngedouw

Geopolitics and Empire

The Legacy of Halford Mackinder

Gerry Kearns

OXFORD
UNIVERSITY PRESS

*This book has been printed digitally and produced in a standard specification
in order to ensure its continuing availability*

OXFORD
UNIVERSITY PRESS

Great Clarendon Street, Oxford OX2 6DP
Oxford University Press is a department of the University of Oxford.
It furthers the University's objective of excellence in research, scholarship,
and education by publishing worldwide in

Oxford New York

Auckland   Cape Town Dar es Salaam   Hong Kong   Karachi
Kuala Lumpur Madrid Melbourne Mexico City   Nairobi
New Delhi Shanghai Taipei Toronto
With offices in
Argentina Austria Brazil Chile Czech Republic France Greece
Guatemala Hungary Italy Japan South Korea Poland Portugal
Singapore Switzerland Thailand Turkey Ukraine Vietnam

Oxford is a registered trade mark of Oxford University Press
in the UK and in certain other countries

Published in the United States
by Oxford University Press Inc., New York

© Gerry Kearns 2009

ISBN 978-0-19-923011-2

EDITORS' PREFACE

Even as processes of globalization expand in range and scale, the world remains marked by huge inequalities, social divisions and environmental degradation. We continue to live in a world marked by inequality and injustice; torn apart by poverty, war, and disputes over the right to own, control, and use resources, and by religious, ethnic, and racialized conflicts; and marked by differences in living standards and quality of life both within and between societies, based on class, gender, age, and other social distinctions. This series is driven by the desire to explore and explain these inequalities, as well as to investigate the possibilities of socio-spatial justice and environmental sustainability.

The key issues of our times are interwoven spatial issues. Climate change, global warming, the inequitable use of resources by the world's richest nations, the global movement of capital and labour, the development of new technologies, pandemics and new diseases that may jump the species gap, are transforming and remaking spatial divisions within and between power blocs, nation-states, regions, and communities.

New theoretical responses to these changes are also emerging both within and beyond geography as the practices, technologies, and significance of spatial difference are being addressed in a range of disciplines. The ubiquitous rhetoric of globalization and the uncritical division between the local and the global are being critically examined across disciplinary and academic borders and older versions of internationalism, social justice, and environmental management are being rethought by geographers and others in work that insists on the articulation of the local within larger frameworks as both an intellectual and an ethical project.

The Oxford Geography and Environmental Studies series aims to reflect these new approaches and interdisciplinary work, as well as to continue to publish the best original research in geography and environmental studies.

Gordon L. Clark
Diana Liverman
Linda McDowell
David Thomas
Sarah Whatmore

PREFACE

In a recent novel, *The Mission Song*, John le Carré refers to a US-sponsored coup in the Eastern Congo as promoted by '[b]old conceptual thinkers [...]. A-list neo-conservatives, geopoliticians on the grand scale. The sort of fellows who meet in ski resorts and decide the fate of nations'.[1] Geopolitics is a strategic view of the world in terms of environments, spaces, contiguities, and influences. It appears also in George Orwell's *1984*, the novel in which a dystopian vision of 1948 is projected into the near future and where the world is divided into three zones: Oceania, Eurasia, and Eastasia. At any one time, Oceania is at war with one or other of the other two powers. This opposition between sea-power (Oceania) and land-power (Eurasia and Eastasia) recalls one of the most important geopolitical visions, that of Halford Mackinder. As Thomas Pynchon notes in his Foreword to a recent edition of Orwell's 1949 novel, '[g]eopolitical thinking in those days was enchanted with the "World-Island" idea of British geographer Halford Mackinder—meaning Europe, Asia and Africa considered as a single landmass surrounded by water, the "pivot of history", whose heartland was *1984*'s "Eurasia". "Who rules the Heartland commands the World-Island", as Mackinder had put, and "Who rules the World-island commands the World", a pronouncement not lost on Hitler and other theoreticians of realpolitik'.[2] The enchantment extends to Pynchon's own recent novel, *Against the Day*, where, in a novel of doubling and splitting, the geopolitical argument is distributed between the English professor, Renfrew, and his mirror-opposite, the German, Werfner. Renfrew adds the frozen lands of the Arctic to the World Island and insists that 'you can see that it all makes one great mass, doesn't it? Eurasia, Africa, America, With Inner Asia at its heart. Control Inner Asia, therefore, and you control the planet'.[3] Renfrew describes Werfner as a devotee of land-power, 'obsessed with railway lines, history emerges from geography of course, but for him the primary geography of the planet is the rails, [...] capital made material—and flows of power as well, expressed, for example, in massive troop movements, now and in the futurity'.[4] Reflecting the antagonism between the German and the English professors, the narrator insists, with evident and heavy irony, that '[t]he professors' manoeuvrings had at least the grace to avoid the mirrorlike—if symmetries arose now and then, it was written off to accident, "some predisposition to

[1] le Carré, *Mission Song*, 206–7.
[2] Pynchon, 'Foreword', xiv.
[3] Pynchon, *Against the Day*, 242. The novel is set in the period 1893–1923.
[4] Pynchon, *Against the Day*, 242.

the echoic", as Werfner put it, "perhaps built into the nature of Time", added Renfrew'.[5]

This fictional reach of Geopolitics from the turn of the twentieth century in Pynchon's novel, to the years following the Second World War in Orwell's, and on to the present in le Carré's, reflects historical realities. Indeed, Pynchon's novel points to the echoes today of the affairs of a century earlier, with terrorism, 'unrestrained corporate greed, false religiosity, moronic feck-lessness, [. . .] evil intent in high places', and, yes, Geopolitics.[6] The literary historian Christopher GoGwilt treats Geopolitics as a 'powerful fiction that has dominated the twentieth century'.[7] GoGwilt argues that in the nineteenth century, many Europeans believed that Enlightenment values would diffuse from Europe overseas, that European history was an integral part, the leading edge, of a universal history. He suggests that in the late nineteenth century, the anti-colonial challenge of insurgent nationalisms abroad raised in a most direct way the question of European privilege. Geopolitics, for GoGwilt, is the discourse that emerges as the idea of universal history is abandoned and Europeans identify instead with a West that has a history quite its own, and represents a set of values that are under threat such that Geopolitics can be the discourse of 'geography in the service of an expansionist, imperialist politics'.[8] The West is not only set apart, but its future is under threat if it does not accept an imperial mission to control the chaos without. This link between Geopolitics and Imperialism is at the heart of GoGwilt's argument and, like Pynchon, he traces these relations back to the work of Mackinder.

In this book, I document and reflect upon the continuities, repetitions, and echoes in the links between Geopolitics and Empire. My argument is that the style of geographical reasoning developed by Mackinder in the early twentieth century serves imperialism very well, making the projection of force abroad seem not only natural, but unavoidable. However, I want also to question this naturalizing of Empire. I return to Mackinder's ideas and their original intellectual context in order to recover the contestability of these views. The hegemonic discourse of Geopolitics incorporates a view of the world as a force field upon which states contend for supremacy or mere survival. Mackinder insisted that this was the international reality, however much fantasists might hope instead for a world organized by law, justice, and legitimate international bodies, mere ideals he sniffed. This denigration of non-violence and non-state agents is open to challenge. It ignores an alternative set of ideas that describe the world in quite different ways and

---

[5] Pynchon, *Against the Day*, 227.
[6] Pynchon, '[Promotional blurb for *Against the Day*]'. The modern lesson is only more evident with Pynchon's own disclaimer in this early promotional material for the book, that '[n]o reference to the present day is intended or should be inferred'.
[7] GoGwilt, *Fiction of Geopolitics*, 1.
[8] GoGwilt, *Fiction of Geopolitics*, 22.

while views very like those of Mackinder can be found among groups such as the 'realists' of International Relations and the 'Neo-conservatives' so prominent in the United States, a contrary stance can be elaborated from the writings of some of Mackinder's contemporaries, particularly those sympathetic to socialist and anarchist politics. I identify, then, a Progressive Geopolitics that I oppose to the Conservative Geopolitics of Mackinder and 'cadres of spellbound familiars and enslaved disciples'.[9] Progressive Geopolitics could, and still can, point to features of international relations that are simply not conjured by the philosophy of the rival tradition. My book finishes by describing some of these hopeful dimensions of our modern world, the reality of non-violence, justice, and cooperation.

I first gave a paper on these ideas thirty years ago and ever since I have accumulated debts in pursuit of this project. Derek Gregory, Graham Smith, Mike Heffernan, and Stuart Corbridge were involved almost from the start, when I was a graduate student at Cambridge. I am sorry that Graham did not live to give the book the friendly and acerbic reading that would have eliminated its waffle and sharpened its politics. Derek, Mike, and Stuart have ever been generous when they had much better things to do, like their own work. Derek has repeatedly interrupted my work with urgent intellectual questions that involve me in further reading, first of all of his own work.

At Liverpool, I learned much from Andy Charlesworth, Bill Marsden, Bob Woods, David Siddle, Dick Lawton, Graham Mooney, John Dickenson, John Peel, Mansell Prothero, Naomi Williams, Paul Laxton, and Robert Lee. Paul has been a constant support and read the whole manuscript at a point when it really needed some independent discipline. My first work on the history of Geography was encouraged by Walter Freeman, who sent me long letters and patiently nursed my prose towards clarity. Peter Taylor, Linda McDowell, Gerard Toal, and John Agnew have repeatedly brought me back to Mackinder with invitations to write essays that are distant cousins of some of the work in this book. Gerard has been a good friend and intellectual sparring partner in many contexts. All who work on the history of British Geography owe a massive debt to Brian Blouet who was the first to place Geography in its political context. Brian has continued to provide generous advice and suggestions, even though we read Mackinder in very different ways. At Madison, Wisconsin, I was very lucky to have my ideas sharpened by Bill Cronon, Bob Sack, Martin Lewis, Paul Plummer, and Yi-Fu Tuan.

When I realized that I wanted to develop a book-length argument about Mackinder, the British Academy provided vital funds that enabled me to spend further time in the archives in Oxford, London, and Cambridge. They also funded an intelligent, efficient, and cheerful research assistant, Millie Glennon. Millie's care, curiosity, and diligence helped me organize

---

[9] Pynchon, *Against the Day*, 227.

the materials so that I retained the broad view of the project, thank you Millie. David Livingstone, John Agnew, John Cornwell, Karen Till, Linda McDowell, Patrick Joyce, and Stuart Corbridge helped me to turn my ideas into a book proposal. A good deal of the writing was done while I was a Visiting Fellow at the Institute for Advanced Study at the University of Minnesota-Minneapolis and I thank Ann Waltner, Susannah Smith, Karen Kinoshita, and Angie Hoffmann-Walter for taking care to make my stay so productive.

Karen Till's editorial skills are quite extraordinary and there is not a paragraph here that is not better, and very different, for her attention. She has lived with this book for the past two years enriching both the work and its very grateful author. I love you Karen and I know how lucky I am. While Karen worked hard to expunge the passive voice, Paul Laxton likewise did sterling service to evict the first person. Neither is possible, at least for me.

It seems appropriate that a work begun as a graduate student at Cambridge should be finished while lecturing in the same place. At Cambridge, Amanda Fitzgerald, Andy Tucker, David Nally, Duncan Bell, Hannah Weston, Jay Levy, Jim Duncan, Juliet Mitchell, John Cornwell, Nancy Duncan, Nick Megoran, Nick Ray, Peter Garnsey, Phil Howell, Richard Smith, Rory Gallagher, Simon Reid-Henry, and Steve Legg have each helped me improve my argument and its exposition. Andy, David, and Steve have been exceptionally generous, reading draft chapters at short notice to meet my unreasonable haste and along with Amanda, Hannah, Jay, Simon, and Rory, remind me how lucky I am to see my students turn into friends and colleagues. The professionalism and cheerful cooperativeness of Ian Agnew, Owen Tucker, and Phil Stickler in the Cartography Unit of the Department of Geography have added greatly to the appearance of this book. The generosity of Richard Smith in taking on the role of Head of Department has underlined for me just how important and fragile is staff morale and what a vital but intangible part it plays in my own intellectual ambition. Thank you Richard.

Many of my friends and advisors are part of the diffuse network sustained by conferences, article-refereeing, and emails. This book has been enriched by the advice and enthusiasm of many people including Andy Wood, Anna Secor, Bruce Braun, David Harvey, David Newman, Eric Sheppard, Fabrizio Eva, George Henderson, Helga Leitner, James Sidaway, Joe Schwartzberg, John Morrissey, John Rogers, Mary Thomas, Matthew Gandy, Mat Coleman, Matt Hannah, Mike Sammers, Neil Smith, Patricia Ehrkamp, Phillipe Pelletier, Simon Dalby, Sue Roberts, Ulf Strohmayer, and Vinay Gidwani. John Morrissey deserves special thanks for sharing his own work and entering fully into the argument of mine.

I am grateful for permission to quote from private papers held in various libraries: the Bodleian Library for permission to quote from the papers of James Bryce, Alfred Milner, and Michael Sadler; the Syndics of Cambridge University Library for the papers of Benjamin Kidd and Alfred Hugh Fisher;

the Master and Fellows of Churchill College, Cambridge for the papers
of Winston Churchill; London School of Economics for the papers of
Martha Woolley; National Archives for papers of the Cabinet, the Foreign
Office, and Mackinder; the Keeper of Rhodes House for Mackinder's Kenya
Notebooks; the Royal Geographical Society for the minutes of the RGS
Council and for letters of Peter Kropótkin, Mackinder, and H. R. Mill; the
School of Geography at the University of Oxford for the papers of
E. W. Gilbert and Mackinder; and West Sussex Record Office for the papers
of Leo Maxse. Without the kindness of librarians, I would rarely find what
I am looking for, thank you. In addition to the illustrations produced
specifically for this book, I am grateful to the following for permission to
use photographs in their possession: London School of Economics for
photographs of Mackinder (Figures 2.1 and 4.3); the Syndics of Cambridge
University Library for the photographs of Mary Kingsley (Figure 4.1) and of
'H.M.S. King Edward VII' (Cover and Figure 6.2); and James Spottiswoode
for the photograph of Bonnie Mackinder (Figure 4.2). Some elements of
the arguments here have been published in different places and I am grateful
for permission to rework them: the Royal Geographical Society for permission to use material in Chapter 3 that first appeared in the *Geographical
Journal* (2004) and material in Chapter 4 that was published in the *Transactions of the Institute of British Geographers* (1997); Pion Limited for material
in Chapter 5, including Table 5.1, that was published first in *Environment and
Planning D: Society and Space* (1984); and Taylor & Francis for material
in Chapter 8 that appeared first in *Geopolitics* (2006).

   Finally, I would like to thank my family for the care and love that sustains
my belief in myself: thank you Chris and Kevin, my parents; thank you to
my brother and sister, Adrian and Anita; and thank you also to my best
friend, lover, and wife, Karen. I know that my sister Denise would have
been inordinately proud of me for finishing anything this grand even if it
took three decades, and I am bitterly sorry that her early death robbed me
of the delight I would feel in her pride.

CONTENTS

LIST OF FIGURES

Cover. "The battleship, Hugh Fisher, 'H.M.S. King Edward VII'", used by kind permission of Cambridge University Library

LIST OF TABLES

ABBREVIATIONS

BAAS   British Association for the Advancement of Science
CEO   Chief Executive Officer
CIS   Commonwealth of Independent States
EU   European Union
GDP   Gross Domestic Product
LSE   London School of Economics
MP   Mackinder Papers, School of Geography, University of Oxford
NATO   North Atlantic Treaty Organization
NGOs   Non-governmental Organizations
NSS   The National Security Strategy of the United States of America
OPEC   Organization of the Petroleum Exporting Countries
RGS   Royal Geographical Society
TNCs   Transnational Corporations
TRIPs   Trade Related Aspects of Intellectual Property
UK   United Kingdom
UN   United Nations
US   United States
WASP   White Anglo-Saxon Protestant

Introduction: A Return to Empire

In the United States, Empire is the order of the day. A search of the *New York Times* for the eight years that Bill Clinton was President (1993–2000) retrieves an article mentioning the 'American Empire' about once every ten weeks. During the first seven years of the presidency of George W. Bush (2001–), they appeared one week in three. In 2003, there were three articles a fortnight, largely in response to President Bush's publication of *The National Security Strategy of the United Sates of America* (NSS) in September 2002.

The historian of the Cold-War foreign policy of the United States, John Lewis Gaddis, suggested that the NSS might be 'the most important reformulation of U.S. grand strategy in over half a century'.[1] In this document, the Bush Administration insisted that: to 'prevent [. . .] hostile acts by our adversaries, the United States will, if necessary, act preemptively'; and to avoid 'complications in our military operations', it would ensure that its military were 'not impaired by the potential for investigations, inquiry, or prosecution by the International Criminal Court'.[2] The NSS asserted the United States' military pre-eminence and its right to use this power to defend 'democracy and freedom', both at home and abroad. It proposed that today's security challenge comes not from other Great Powers, but from failed states and the terrorist groups that sit like cuckoos within these spaces. Pre-emption was to be extended, and the justificatory notion of imminent threat broadened, to include intention of attack, even in cases where 'uncertainty remains as to the time and place of the enemy's attack'.[3]

Whereas Gaddis was broadly sympathetic to the US agenda, giving several reasons why the rest of the world might grow to accept 'American hegemony', other commentators were more critical.[4] One of the editors of *Le Monde Diplomatique*, Ignacio Ramonet, noted that '[t]he world's geopolitical architecture now has at its apex a single hyperpower, the US', and Europeans should realize that '[a]n empire does not have allies, it has only vassals'.[5] While the US administration disavowed in public any imperial designs, some

---

[1] Gaddis, 'Grand Strategy', 56.

[2] *National Security Strategy 2002* [NSS 2002], 15, 31.

[3] NSS 2002, 15.

[4] Gaddis, 'Grand Strategy', 52. Many use the term 'America', as Gaddis does here, when they mean in fact the United States. I realize that this is offensive to all the other Americans, who live to the north and south of the United States, and I try to avoid it myself.

[5] Ramonet, 'Servile States'.

of its senior figures are occasionally less coy as when, in 2002, one senior aide, widely believed to be Karl Rove, Senior Advisor (2001–7) to President Bush, chided Ron Suskind of the *Wall Street Journal*: '[w]e're an empire now, and when we act, we create our own reality'.[6] Critics, of both the Left and of the Right have attacked on precisely these grounds.[7]

In the current debate about Empire, US imperialism is largely understood through comparisons with the British Empire of a century earlier. Truckling to the vanities of the British with his best-selling trade book, *Empire: How Britain Made the Modern World*, the war historian, Niall Ferguson, reissued the same book in the United States with a subtitle more accommodating to American proclivities, *Empire: The Rise and Demise of the British World Order and the Lessons for Global Power*.[8] Ferguson argued that the British strove to spread their liberal values when they enjoyed global economic and military hegemony, and, with a far greater advantage, the United States might now do the same. In contrast, the naval historian, Paul Kennedy argued twenty years ago that the United States would be unable to resist the temptations of Empire and that, through 'imperial overextension', its global economic and thus political hegemony would slip away.[9] Many theorists of international relations repeat Kennedy's claims, including Eric Hobsbawm, the respected Marxist economic historian, who argued that comparing the empires of Great Britain and the United States reveals the greater danger of the unprecedented hubris of current American imperialism.[10]

Indeed, if the use of the concept 'Empire' has become well established as a means to understand the foreign policy of the United States, its features have come to include the reliance upon unilateral force to spread (American) 'democratic' values. In making this point, commentators have again reached for comparable cases in history to understand this apparent imperial turn in policy, including Ancient Rome; the Soviet Union; and the Mongolian, Ottoman, and Ming Empires. Withstanding this range of examples, the most common foil for understanding the nature, dynamics, and likely resolution of the so-called American Empire remains the global empire established by the British in the nineteenth century. These attempts to use the historical British experience to clarify the dilemmas of Empire for modern imperialists comprise, in the main, the study of imperial ambitions in economic, political, and ideological terms.

Comparisons may be drawn between the United States today and Britain a century earlier, not only in the matter of imperial ambition, but also with respect to their economic, political, and even territorial strategies. Imperial

---

[6] R. Suskind, 'Faith, Certainty and Bush'.

[7] B. Porter, 'We Don't Do Empire'; Johnson, *The Sorrows of Empire*; Buchanan, *A Republic, not an Empire*.

[8] N. Ferguson, *Empire: How Britain Made the Modern World*; idem, *Empire: The Rise and Demise of the British World Order and the Lessons for Global Power*. The book was the basis for a television series on the British Channel Four, and '[i]n 2004 Time magazine named him as one of the world's hundred most influential people': 'Niall Ferguson: Biography'.

[9] Kennedy, *Rise and Fall*.

[10] Hobsbawm, 'The United States'. See also: Eland, *The Empire Strikes Out*; Lind, 'The Tragic Costs'.

ideologies have a significant geographical element, a geopolitical imaginary, and those contemplating the gest of Empire must be sensitive to the relations between states and the geostrategic relations of states to the constitution of empires. No nation state, nor even empire, rises and falls in isolation, for they are embedded within networks and systems of states, empires, and various other transnational bodies. Empires comprise mutually defensible parts and, for all their civilizing claims, they rest upon resources, and this means that some parts of the earth are more highly prized than others. They must keep order within and resist challenge from without, and this means that empires must deploy forces into spaces to limit rivals' access to strategically significant places and economically significant resources. The challenge and possibility of projecting power overseas remains a question of spatial relations, the links between strategy and economics, a matter of Geopolitics. British imperialists then and US imperialists now seem to have learned the same lessons in Geography.

As this book argues, there are striking parallels between the geopolitical ideas animating those who advocate the consolidation or even extension of the global influence of the United States today, and those who a century ago took up a similar stance on behalf of Great Britain. I show that the ideologies for justifying Empire, both in the British experience and in the current-day US case, are homologous on a number of quite specific points, including: a sense of contemporary crisis as a newly interdependent world renders obsolete an isolationist stance; a racist account of civilizational difference; a masculinist understanding of the unavoidability and justice of force in international relations; an exceptionalist view of the global hegemon as uniquely democratic and peace-loving; and, finally, a staggering confidence in the possibility of perpetuating global domination. This set of attitudes, this geopolitical imaginary of Empire, orders, in both time and space, the economies, cultures, and polities of the global system as a material field of opportunities and threats.

Such strategic thinking can be thought of as Geography aiding statecraft, or Geopolitics.[11] This perspective can be found in the writings of a number of commentators from the turn of the twentieth century but among them the one whose ideas resonate most loudly in today's debates is Halford Mackinder, a British geographer who, a century ago, proposed ways for the British to maintain their empire in the face of challenges from newer imperial powers. Mackinder's view of the world was not unique but he expressed with particular clarity the geopolitical dilemmas of Empire and set out a clear strategy for containing rivals.

The Roots of Geopolitics

Geopolitics cohered between 1890 and 1920 around the works of four thinkers: the naval strategist from the United States, Alfred Mahan

---

[11] Teggart, 'Geography as an Aid to Statecraft'.

(1840–1914), on sea-power; the German geographer, Friedrich Ratzel (1844–1904), on *Lebensraum*; Halford Mackinder (1861–1947) on land-power; and Rudolf Kjellén (1864–1922), a Swedish political scientist, on regional blocs. All four were passionately interested in the territorial struggles between states and in the rise and fall of empires.

Mahan lectured on military warfare at the Naval War College in Newport, Rhode Island. From his 1890 study of the way that Britain established global supremacy in the eighteenth century and his work of two years later on how Britain defended its hegemony against revolutionary and Napoleonic France, Mahan proposed that 'the use and control of the sea is and has been a great factor in the history of the world'.[12] He argued that the mobility of naval force, if used intelligently, could support the landing of soldiers wherever needed and could also contain the aggression of an opposing army by preventing it putting to sea. For these reasons, he examined the British Empire as a series of coaling stations and friendly harbours that enabled the British to bring their force to bear wheresoever they wished, while denying a comparable mobility to any rival.[13]

Ratzel understood the state as an organism, requiring an expansion of territory in order to thrive and proposed that each state was a union, 'one part humanity and one part earth'.[14] A German patriot, Ratzel believed that war was good for the national soul and that emigration and colonialism were essential for the health of the German state. He argued that the true basis of national wealth was its relation to the land through agriculture.[15] From his articles of the 1890s, on the biogeographical basis of the spatial limits of political communities, Ratzel elaborated in 1901 a theory of the struggle between states for living-space, or *Lebensraum*.[16]

Mackinder was a close reader of Ratzel and shared his organic conception of the state.[17] Drawing upon 'Captain Mahan', Mackinder acknowledged the significance of 'the geographical condition of ultimate unity in the command of the sea', but argued that sea-power applied to an era that was now passing.[18] In an article of 1904, he noted that the mobilization of land-based resources via the railway promised to redress the balance between sea- and land-power in favour of the latter.[19] The railroad meant a new, more fully integrated world, wherein land-based power might achieve the global reach of a world empire. Mackinder suggested that the 'Heartland' for an emergent

---

[12] Mahan, *Sea Power*, iii.

[13] Russell, 'Mahan and American Geopolitics'.

[14] Rumley, Minghi, and Grimm, 'Ratzel's "Politische Geographie" ', 272.

[15] Wanklyn, *Ratzel*, 10, 23; Smith, 'Ratzel and the Origins of Lebensraum'.

[16] Ratzel, 'Der Lebensraum'; *idem, Die Erde und das Leben*.

[17] In 1895, surveying how much British had to yet to learn from German Geography, Mackinder noted in particular Ratzel's 'anthropogeography', suggesting that the 'anthropogeographer is in some sense the most typical and complete of geographers'. He referred to Ratzel's *Anthropogeographie* in *Britain and the British Seas*, to clarify the meanings of globe, world, and ecumene. Mackinder, 'Modern Geography', 375; *idem, Britain and the British Seas*, 13; Ratzel, *Anthropogeographie*.

[18] Mackinder, 'Geographical Pivot', 432–3.

[19] Mackinder, 'Geographical Pivot', 433.

global land-power could be anchored in the tremendous collection of natural resources in and around Western Russia, wherefrom suzerainty could be established over vast regions stretching eastwards across the steppelands and forests of Eurasia. From this Heartland, the whole of the 'World Island' (continental Europe, Asia, and Africa) might be dominated and World Empire realized. He had the wit to give the pith of his doctrine urgent clarity: 'Who rules East Europe commands the Heartland: | Who rules the Heartland commands the World-Island: | Who rules the World-Island commands the World'.[20]

Kjellén is credited with first using the term *Geopolitik*.[21] His work expanded Ratzel's description of the state as a unity of people and land, and proposed that this union produced two state imperatives: to manage people, *Ethnopolitik*, and to manage territorial expansion, *Geopolitik*.[22] Ratzel wrote of the advantages of large and expansive political units in both the second volume of *Anthropogeographie* (1891) and in the second edition of *Politische Geographie* (1903). Chicago geographer Ellen Churchill Semple (1863–1932) summarized Ratzel's argument: '[t]he earlier a state fixes its frontier without allowance for growth, the earlier comes the cessation of its development'; the truly dynamic polity 'advance[s] from a small, self-dependent community to interdependent relations with other peoples, then to ethnic expansion or union of groups to form a state or empire'.[23] Kjellén developed from Ratzel's work a theory about the ideal scale of political integration for modern times. Blocs of states, rather than individual nation states, were now required and he urged that the choice facing Central Europe was whether it would accept German rule or would suffer Russian domination.[24]

Geopolitics is a useful term to describe the world views of these four thinkers and their understanding of states as divided between land- and sea-powers, as engaged in territorial competition, and as becoming empires through war, trade, and protection. In recent years, there has been a return to these discourses about how states and empires are shaped by strategic conflict over territory and resources. Thus, alongside the renewed interest in the question of Empire has come a fresh concern with Geopolitics, and in the revival of Geopolitics the ideas of Mackinder have been central, with at least two intellectual think tanks trading under his name. The Mackinder Forum promises to meet the 'geopolitical challenge' whereas the London School of Economics Mackinder Centre will 'promote new approaches to and improved methods for research on that class of geopolitical issues—long wave events—which pose some of the greatest challenges to the 21st century'.[25]

---

[20] Mackinder, *Democratic Ideals and Reality*, 104. References in the notes are to the original 1919 British edition from Constable, which may be accessed at: http://ia341234.us.archive.org/1/items/democraticideals00mackiala/democraticideals00mackiala.pdf.

[21] Kjellén, 'Sveriges Politiska Gränser'.

[22] Natter, 'Geopolitics in Germany'; Tunander, 'Swedish-German Geopolitics'.

[23] Semple, *Influences of Geographic Environment*, 197.

[24] Kjellén, *Stormakterna*; idem, *Stormakterna och Världskrisen*; Tunander, 'Swedish-German Geopolitics', 460.

[25] 'Mackinder Forum, Mission Statement'; 'London School of Economics Mackinder Centre for the Study of Long Wave Events'.

The Revival of Geopolitics

In 1999, the journalist Charles Clover described Geopolitics as an ideology, 'romantically obscure, [...] intellectually sloppy, and [...] likely to start a third world war'.[26] He was referring to the re-emergence of Geopolitics in Russia, a discourse distinguishing between continental and maritime styles of civilization and identifying the resources and strategies to help the continental Russians eject from Eurasia all Atlanticist (US) influence. As Clover noted, both these themes were taken from the work of Halford Mackinder. In 2004, the *U.S. Army War College Guide to National Security and Policy* stated that '[g]eopolitical analysis is best known in the West as refracted by Halford Mackinder's heartland concept', and went on to note that: '[a] striking contemporary illustration of the continuing impact of geopolitical perspectives is provided by the heartland power *par excellence*, the Russian Federation, where dillusionment with the gilded promises of globalization and integration with the U.S.-led world economy have led to a rapid and broadly influential revival of geopolitical theory'.[27]

Post-Soviet Russian nationalists had made extensive use of Mackinder.[28] Clover reproduced an illustration from the journalist and Russian nationalist, Aleksandr Dugin (*The Foundations of Geopolitics*, 1997) that is a lightly reworked version of Mackinder's map of the Heartland.[29] Although Mackinder did not use the term 'Geopolitics', Dugin insisted that 'the father of geopolitics remains Mackinder, whose fundamental pattern stood at the bases of all subsequent geopolitical studies'.[30] From his Eurasian perspective, Dugin was highly critical of the Western orientation of Boris Yel'tsin's presidency (1991–9). Vladimir Putin's 'new Eurasian politics' (2000-) has been more to Dugin's liking, as Putin himself declared in 2000 that 'Russia has always seen itself as a Euro-Asiatic nation'.[31] In the 1980s, Dugin was on the anti-Semitic, occultist, and neo-fascist fringe of Russian nationalist politics, but with Putin's presidency Dugin moved to the heart of national debate in Russia. He now 'anchors a weekly [television] broadcast on geopolitics called *Landmarks* (*Vekhi*)', and has 'collaborated on the writing of a work undertaken at the Russian Academy of Sciences entitled, *Atlas of Geopolitical Problems of South Russia*. A key objective of the book is to explain the connections between the territorialization of ethnic groups and the economic realities of the North-Caucasus (e.g. the pipelines)'.[32] His federalist proposals, for retaining the North Caucasus politically (and thus

---

[26] Clover, 'Dreams of the Eurasian Heartland', 9.

[27] Nation, 'Regional Studies', 58; Edwards, 'The New Great Game'.

[28] Bassin and Konstantin, 'Mackinder and the Heartland'; Rangsimaporn, 'Interpretations of Eurasianism'; Shlapentokh, 'Dugin Eurasianism'. G. Smith, 'Masks of Proteus'.

[29] Dugin, *Osnovy Geopolitiki*. Dugin's book also contains extensive extracts from Mackinder's writings: Sedgwick, *Against the Modern World*, 230.

[30] From his own summary of the book: Dugin, 'The Great War of Continents'.

[31] Berman, 'Slouching Toward Eurasia?'.

[32] Laruelle, *Aleksandr Dugin*, 1; *idem*, 'Alexandre Dugin'.

economically) while allowing it to follow a relatively autonomous and trad-itional cultural path, were quite close to Putin's policies for the region.[33]

Since the end of the Cold War, there has been an evident but less explicit revival of Mackinder's ideas among American strategists as well. Here, the dual emphasis is upon natural resources and the need to prevent the emer-gence of a continental hegemon in Eurasia. Political scientist, Clement Henry, argued in 2003 that 'oil [. . .] seems to have reinvigorated Mackinder's geo-political legacy'.[34] For strategists, the crucial issue is Russia, and its access to the oil in the region that Russia calls its near abroad, the South Caucasus and Central Asia. Paul Wolfowitz, who advised Presidents Bush senior and junior, and did much, as Deputy Secretary of State for Defense (2001–5), to devise the current Global War on Terror, is thought to be influenced by Mackinder's work. British journalist, Gerard Killoran, writes that Mackinder 'is said to be the inspiration' for Wolfowitz, while a Swiss journal claims that Wolfowitz 'is known to admire the "geopolitical doctrine" put forward by' Mackinder.[35] Scholars, including the sociologist, John Bellamy Foster, likewise link Wol-fowitz's strategic writings to Mackinder's ideas about the Heartland.[36]

In early 1992, as Under Secretary for Policy at the Pentagon, Wolfowitz prepared a policy intended to guide the Defense Department after the end of the Cold War.[37] Leaked to the *New York Times*, this draft of 18 February 1992 'ma[de] the case for a world dominated by one superpower whose position can be perpetuated by constructive behavior and sufficient military might to deter any nation or group of nations from challenging American primacy'.[38] The threat from the Heartland is evident in the first strategic goal recommended for the United States:

Our first objective is to prevent the re-emergence of a new rival, either on the territory of the former Soviet Union or elsewhere, that poses a threat on the order of that posed formerly by the Soviet Union. This is a dominant consideration underlying the new regional defense strategy and requires that we endeavor to prevent any hostile power from dominating a region whose resources would, under consolidated control, be sufficient to generate global power'.[39]

There was only one Eurasian power that Wolfowitz imagined might es-tablish such a regional hegemony and he consequently warned of the danger of allowing Russia 'to reincorporate [. . .] the newly independent republics of Ukraine, Belarus, and possibly others'.[40] In 1994, he criticized President Clinton's administration for being 'unwilling to challenge Russian actions in its so-called "near-abroad"'.[41]

---

[33] Lucas, *New Cold War*.

[34] Henry, 'Clash of Globalizations', 5–6.

[35] Killoran, '45 minutes'; 'Rumsfeld and His Crew'.

[36] Foster, 'New Geopolitics of Empire'.

[37] This drew upon an earlier briefing on the implications of the end of the Cold War that he had prepared for Cheney in May 1990: Lemann, 'The Next World Order'.

[38] Tyler, 'US Strategy'.

[39] Quoted in 'Excerpts From Pentagon's Plan'.

[40] Henry, 'Clash of Globalizations', 6.   [41] Wolfowitz, 'Clinton's First Year', 41.

The Secretary of Defense for whom Wolfowitz prepared his advice in 1992 was Dick Cheney, and, together, they have continued to influence strategic debate in the United States, both as critics of the Clinton presidency through the Project for a New American Century, and subsequently as senior figures within the administrations of Bush-*fils*.[42] Two ex-members of the Clinton administration have since described the ambition of current US foreign policy as 'hegemonism', the claim that 'America's immense power, and the willingness to wield it, even over the objection of others, is the key to securing America's interests in the world'.[43]

This worry about the emergence of a regional hegemon in Eurasia is a recurring concern among the strategic elite in the United States, as is the association of this doctrine with Mackinder. Zbigniew Brzezinski, the former National Security Advisor to President Carter, echoed Wolfowitz's warnings about Russia in 1994.[44] Brzezinski set out his geopolitical vision very clearly in 1997 when he wrote of Eurasia as 'the decisive geopolitical chessboard': 'Eurasia is the world's axial supercontinent. A power that dominated Eurasia would exercise decisive influence over two of the world's three most economically productive regions, Western Europe and East Asia. A glance at the map also suggests that a country dominant in Eurasia would almost automatically control the Middle East and Africa'.[45] Brzezinski cited Mackinder's dictum that the control of the Heartland would give control of the World Island (Eurasia and Africa) and thus ultimately of the world itself.[46] Henry Kissinger similarly warned, in 1994, that 'Russia regardless of who governs it, sits astride what Halford Mackinder called the geopolitical heartland, and is the heir to one of the most potent imperial traditions'.[47] A few years later, in testimony before the United States Senate, the political scientist and expert on Central Asia, Martha Brill Olcott, again reinforced these connections between geopolitics and resources, suggesting that '[w]hile U.S. policy-makers certainly do not want to see a hegemonic Russia for general geopolitical reasons, the potential costs of such hegemony become far greater if Russia is able to dictate the terms and limit western access to the world's last known vast oil and gas reserves'.[48]

Fixing the new world order that followed the end of the Cold War, these views from Russia and the United States are in fact mirror images of each other. The first sets out a geopolitical strategy for Russia expelling the United States from Eurasia by controlling first the crucial resources of the Heartland. The second seeks to bar Russia from access to the hydrocarbon

---

[42] Unger, *Fall of the House of Bush*.
[43] Daalder and Lindsay, *America Unbound*, 40; see also, Schell, 'Moral Equivalent of Empire'.
[44] Brzezinski, 'The Premature Partnership'.
[45] Brzezinski, 'Geostrategy for Eurasia', 50.
[46] Brzezinski, *The Grand Chessboard*, 38–9.
[47] Kissinger, *Diplomacy*, 814.
[48] Olcott, 'The Central Asian States: An Overview of Five Years of Independence', Testimony before the United States Senate Committee on Foreign Relations, 22 July 1997, quoted in: Seiple, 'Revisiting the Geo-Political Thinking of Sir Halford Mackinder', 161.

resources of its neighbours and, in this way, tries to deny it the opportunity of continental and thus global dominance. These parallel revivals of Geopolitics are indexed by the renewed attention to the ideas of Mackinder. Yet no study to date has explored Mackinder's ideas in their original context in order to explain why his ideas have such purchase today. This book contributes to present-day discussions of Geopolitics, Empire, and international relations through a historical and contextual approach to the emergence and repeated revivals of Mackinder's work. My central claim is that the study of the history of the ways that the relations between Geopolitics and Empire have been theorized can clarify current debates on these issues.

The Legacy of Mackinder

As the following chapter describes, Mackinder's ideas have been revived more than once. Indeed, his ideas have had particular resonance at four historical moments: in late-nineteenth and early-twentieth century Britain, in Nazi Germany, in the United States during the Cold War, and now among both Russian and US strategists. Historically, Mackinder's ideas emerged in response to the threat to the maritime British Empire from a land-based empire and expressed a deep-seated anxiety about the state and future of Britain. The British desire to prevail over other imperial powers sharpened current worries about socialism; the faltering of national economic dynamism; the need for housing and social reform; and, finally, the rise of military rivals in Germany, the United States, Japan, and Russia. Geopolitics was a view of the world as structured by geographical realities that Mackinder believed undermined any attempt to build a global order on the basis of legalism and pacifism. Force was unavoidable.

In the 1930s, his ideas were taken up by Nazi military planners, anxious to give substance to Mackinder's warnings about the prospect of a land-based global empire. The explicit association of Geopolitics with Nazism discredited the term but did not really interrupt the discussion of the geographical relations of force, territorial contest, and strategic opportunities that Mackinder expressed so powerfully. Whereas the Nazis put themselves in the position of the land-power keen to break out of its continental shell, after the Second World War strategists in the United States returned to the other pole of Mackinder's analysis and assumed instead the position of the sea-power determined to confine the new land-power, the Soviet Union. These distinct uses of Mackinder resurfaced in the twenty-first century with the expansionist vision of Russian nationalists and the related containment strategies of the United States.

In these ways, Mackinder's ideas have influenced repeatedly debates over global strategy. Geopolitics was used to: address the dilemma of preserving British supremacy in the face of competition from newly industrializing countries in the late-nineteenth and early-twentieth century; ground a plan for a Nazi land-based empire; inform a policy of containing the Soviet Union during the Cold War; and, finally, project power abroad in the new world order that has followed the end of the Cold War. On each occasion, the currency of Mackinder's ideas has been promoted by contemporary concerns over imperial policy.

The legacy of Mackinder lies in the interrelations between Geopolitics and Empire, and there are several reasons why Mackinder's ideas, and ideas very like his, recur.[49] Mackinder provides a powerful argument for believing that international politics and economics rest ultimately upon force and that projecting force abroad is essential to national survival. Mackinder described the world as dangerously interconnected and dismissed isolationism as unrealistic because, he argued, threats to national survival might now arise from any part of the globe.[50] He rejected international legalism as mere idealism, insisting instead upon the realities of war and trade competition.[51] In other words, imperialism now, as then, combines a view of the world as structured by force with a conception of one's own society as uniquely blessed with virtues that the rest of the world must adopt, at the point of a gun if necessary. For those who believe in it, this combination of force and exceptionalism is justified by a global racial or cultural geography that places civilized 'us' on one side, and barbarian 'them' on the other.

Another reason Mackinder's ideas have recurred in the present day is because some of the physical and geographical features of the world have the same significance as they did about a century ago. States still rely upon hydrocarbon sources of energy and some of the largest reserves remain in the region, identified so emphatically by Mackinder, that runs from the Caspian Basin down to the Persian Gulf. To secure access to these resources and deny rivals access, the Great Powers continue to interest themselves militarily in the internal affairs of the band of countries ranging from the eastern Mediterranean, up to the borders of India, including the very same places in which the British were mired during Mackinder's career: Afghanistan, Iraq, the south Caucasus, and the Caspian Basin.

[49] Where the ideas of Mackinder are cited explicitly, as they often are, I choose to speak of Mackinder's influence. In other cases, ideas that are very similar seem to have been derived either indirectly from or even independently of the works of Mackinder and I term these the echoes of Mackinder. When I discuss the legacy of Mackinder in the present I cover both of these.

[50] The French cultural theorist Paul Virilio, for example, draws upon Mackinder to insist that the world is so integrated spatially that location no longer matters, a conclusion the opposite of Mackinder's: '[t]his [geostrategic] homogenization was already announced in the nineteenth century, notably by the Englishman Mackinder in his theory of the "World-Island", in which Europe, Asia and Africa would compose a single continent to the detriment of the Americas'; Virilio, 'The State of Emergency', 47.

[51] The German legal theorist, Carl Schmitt (1888–1985), shared with Mackinder a view of sovereignty as grounded in a capacity of force and in his own work on the legal territoriality of land and sea, he made specific mention of the fact that he was 'much indebted to geographers, most of all to Mackinder'; Schmitt, *"Nomos" of the Earth*, 37. In some ways, Schmitt owed more to Kjellén and the idea of regional blocs than to Mackinder on land- and sea-power. It is likely that he was introduced to both Mackinder and Kjellén by the German geopolitical literature of the 1930s.

Understanding the context in which Mackinder's ideas first received attention thus helps explain both their initial appeal and their later use to justify economic and political advantage secured by force. But there were, and are, alternatives, for Mackinder's was not the only way to think about global dilemmas. In nineteenth-century Britain, different views for or against Empire were legion, and other geographers and economists, who shared much the same political, cultural, and intellectual world as Mackinder, nevertheless rejected the imperialist imperative.[52] In this book, I examine these differences of opinion in the past as a resource to imagine an alternative to his geopolitical legacy in the future. The question is whether, contra Mackinder and his followers, there is a realistic basis for a global regime of democratic ideals. All too often, the realities of force are celebrated as ideals in themselves. I conclude this book nonetheless by contrasting the ideals and realities of what I call Mackinder's Conservative Geopolitics of forceful and contending states, with what I suggest is a rival tradition and alternative set of ideas and realities, a Progressive Geopolitics based upon legalism, cooperation, and multilateral agencies alongside states.

Outline of the Book

Chapter 1 sets out some of the implications of this recurring set of relations between Geopolitics and Empire and notes that the relationship between imperialism and Geopolitics was widely accepted for Nazi Germany. I am sceptical, however, of the claim that it is only in Nazi Germany that geographical science was placed in service to imperialistic statecraft. There are differences of degree between Nazi Geopolitics, on one hand, and the Political Geography published at about the same time in Britain, France, or the United States, but the arguments made about force, exceptionalism, and the territorial imperative are similar. The chapter then takes up the broader question of the nature of imperialism and proposes that it is best understood as the practice of Empire, by which I mean the ways that powerful states compromise the sovereignty of weaker states. These interferences and interventions may be arranged along a continuum from the heavy hand of Colonial Imperialism to the lighter touch of Liberal Imperialism, and the practice of Empire demonstrates a repeated switching between these poles. The chapter ends by describing the long-term patterns of imperialism within which the recurrence of interest in Geopolitics and Empire takes place.

Chapter 2 examines Mackinder's ideas in terms of discourse, context, and comparison. By discourse, I mean the ways that arguments convince, which includes both the settings as well as the form in which arguments are put, and

---

[52] D. Bell, 'Victorian Visions of Global Order'.

received. Mackinder made his case from Oxford University, from the British Parliament, through government-sponsored innovations in educational curricula, and in textbooks issued by well-established publishing houses. His views on Empire were like a well-used passport, having received many an official stamp. In addition to the importance of setting, arguments convince also because they imply and draw upon other sets of ideas. As Chapter 3 shows, ideas influential in the public domain during the late-nineteenth century, particularly evolutionary Biology, were central to the discipline of Geography and shaped very profoundly Mackinder's own arguments. In both chapters my contextual approach relates the thought of Mackinder to the life out of which the writing emerged.[53] So, for example, I pay close attention to the networks Mackinder established early in life, particularly at the University of Oxford, because these contacts recurred throughout his life and are at the heart of his 'official' career.[54]

Political debate also provided both the occasion and the focus of much of Mackinder's work on Geography and Empire. Chapters 4 through 7 address the significance of and the relations between the fate of the British Empire and the status of Geography. As described in Chapter 4, Mackinder felt impelled to embody his geographical knowledge as an active explorer and not just as a sedentary academic. Through exploration, he advanced the cause of Empire, one that was gendered and yet demonstrated an ever-anxious masculinity. Chapter 5 describes how Mackinder addressed the question of imperial competition, setting out his theory of the Heartland and how this drew upon economic history to establish the guidelines for defending British imperial advantage. Mackinder also attempted to make education relevant to what he saw as the central issues of the day, as outlined in Chapter 6. Finally, in Chapter 7, Mackinder's imperialist adventure in the Heartland itself is described. In 1919, the British government sent him to South Russia, the very area he had identified as pivotal for the future of Britain, to help coordinate the military and political campaigns against the Bolshevik Revolution.

In many ways, then, the life and context of Mackinder help us to understand why he had the intellectual concerns he did, and why he found a ready audience for many of these ruling passions. There was, however, no single view of Empire in Mackinder's Britain. Mackinder's outlook was representative of one significant group of imperialists who did, at certain times, wield influence. It expressed with particular clarity the argument for the projection of force overseas and it has also resounded through to the present day on

---

[53] There are now many contextual histories of Geography, see for example: Driver, *Geography Militant*; Livingstone, *Geographical Tradition*; Stoddart, *Geography, Ideology, and Social Concern*. On the biographical approach in Geography, see: Daniels and Nash, 'Lifepaths'. The comparative approach I take here is rather less well developed in the literature on the history of geographical thought.

[54] On the importance of interpersonal networks, see: Lambert and Lester, 'Introduction'. In stressing the biographical dimension in this study, I have benefited greatly from the work of Leonard Cantor, William Parker, Brian Blouet, Michael Barbour, and James Ryan, although each has rather different emphasis to mine.

occasions when similar policies have been advocated. Rather than dwell upon the diversity of ways Empire was supported, this book complements Mackinder's views with a study of some of the contemporary critics of Empire and each chapter takes up a contested element in the imperial vision; race in Chapter 3, masculinity in Chapter 4, capitalism in Chapter 5, progress in Chapter 6, and democracy in Chapter 7.

Mackinder claimed to draw upon the ideas of Charles Darwin (1809–82) to develop his own vision of Geography and the centrality of race in Mackinder's biological vision of society is detailed in Chapter 3. Yet, the concepts that translated a biological reading of society were essentially contestable, to adapt the helpful formulation of the philosopher, Walter Gallie.[55] His contemporary, Peter Kropótkin (1842–1921), shared the ambition of explaining society in terms of its biological roots, but, unlike Mackinder, Kropótkin stressed cooperation not competition; in place of race as a 'community of fate', Kropótkin celebrated the free association of people in cooperative effort.[56] This is a matter not only of ontology, but of ethics.

Masculinity was central to Mackinder's understanding of Empire and of Geography. To highlight this dimension of his work, Chapter 4 takes up the contrasting case of the geographer and anthropologist, Mary Kingsley (1862–1900), who shared Mackinder's concern with exploration and Empire, but who negotiated differently the shoals of race and masculinity. Some of the gestures of Mackinder were quite unavailable to this enterprising young woman and others were simply distasteful given her gendered and classed social location. Moreover, the personal as well as ideological bases of the relations between masculinity and violence illuminate broader imperialist practices.

Mackinder theorized the relations between imperialism and capitalism by biologizing both, relating them to a common vital root rather than to each other. In Chapter 5, I take John Hobson (1858–1940) as my foil to show how he challenged directly the imperialist apologetics of the likes of Mackinder.[57] At the same time, the organic account of the state that Hobson shared with Mackinder limited his own proposals for social and economic change. This common organicism compromised Hobson's democratic imagination.

The limits of contemporary imagination are again evident in Chapter 6 which considers Mackinder's philosophy of education. He saw education as vital to his imperial mission and wrote many school texts eloquent in their explication of the British imperial purpose. Here, I turn to another great contemporary geographical educator, Élisée Reclus (1830–1905), and elaborate his very different view of the global human community. Mackinder and Reclus read, to a lesser and greater extent, the same body of contemporary geographic, eco-

---

[55] Gallie, 'Essentially Contested Concepts'.
[56] The felicitous phrase 'community of fate' comes from: Heimer, *Reactive Risk*.
[57] Hobson was also very important to the later development of Marxist theories of imperialism through Lenin's use of his work.

nomic, and ethnographic texts, but their conclusions about the nature of Empire were quite different. Mackinder saw global progress as possible only through Empire and the associated diffusion of Anglo-Saxon democracy. Reclus acknowledged the damage that indigenous peoples experienced through colonialism but accepted a sort of civilizational scale that contemplated the possibility of benevolent colonialism, what I call a Liberal Imperialism.

Liberal Imperialism, more broadly, frames Chapter 7, wherein the variety of agendas Mackinder was asked to serve on his mission to South Russia is described. If imperialism, as defined in Chapter 1, is the abridging of the sovereignty of a weaker by a stronger state or by its agents, Mackinder would have had little problem with this notion, as long as the stronger state was British. In different ways, George Curzon (1859–1925) and Winston Churchill (1874–1965), who as Foreign and War Secretaries, respectively, were responsible for sending Mackinder to Russia, shared a similar perspective. Their justifications for denying Russia the opportunity to pursue its communist future were articulated solely in terms of British strategic interests, even if they could not agree upon which of these interests were primary. I call this approach Colonial Imperialism. There was, however, a different argument, set out by the Prime Minister, David Lloyd George (1863–1945), that the British were intervening in the interests of the Russian people since the new Bolshevik regime would not meet the minimal requirements for a state to be accepted into the global family of sovereign states. We see here the inkling of humanitarian intervention, a Liberal Imperialism. It shares a belief in the necessity to compromise the sovereignty of weaker states but its justification is rather different.

Such contentious dimensions of Empire remain relevant today; specifically, and in order, race, gender, capitalism, progress, and democracy. The final chapters of the book consider these modern echoes of Mackinder's ideas and return again to these dimensions and practices of Geopolitics and Empire. Chapter 8 describes some of the main features of modern Conservative Geopolitics, the body of ideas used today in the justification of Empire that I find to be essentially similar to the position set out by Mackinder a century ago. The challenges to Mackinder, described in Chapters 3 through 6, however, do not straightforwardly translate into a full-blown alternative to Conservative Geopolitics. Most obviously, the world has changed significantly since 1900. Moreover, there are serious limits implicit in the biological framework of the late-nineteenth century, including difficulties with Hobson's organicism and Reclus's ethnocentric understanding of social progress. Nevertheless, the final chapter begins with the ideas of Kropótkin, Kingsley, Hobson, and Reclus, but rejects any notion of a single civilizational scale. I argue instead for a Progressive Geopolitics defined by an understanding of global interdependencies, the obligations of human solidarity, and the claims of international human rights.

1

Geopolitics and Empire

During the Second World War, American and British publics were introduced to Geopolitics as the geographical theory behind Nazi imperialism, and to Karl Haushofer (1869–1946), a professor in Geography at the University of Munich, as the brains behind the science. Yet, in *Raumüberwindende Mächte* ('Space-conquering Powers', 1934), Haushofer had written that he owed his geopolitical vision to 'the greatest of all geographic world views', Halford Mackinder's account of the 'Geographical Pivot of History' (1904).[1] The paternity became a popular rumour, as in a sensationalist 1941 article in *Life* magazine, and a slightly more measured 1946 piece in *Time* magazine, where readers were assured that Haushofer's leading ideas were '[a]lmost directly derived from Britain's distinguished geographer, Sir Halford Mackinder'.[2] A political scientist, and refugee from Nazi Germany, Hans Weigert (1902–83), wrote on Mackinder and Haushofer in the popular American *Harper's Magazine* in 1941; the American military took 12,000 copies of the piece.[3] In fact, during the Second World War in 1943, Dorothy Thompson (1893–1961), the renowned American journalist, visited the eighty-one-year-old Mackinder in retirement in Dorset and an American foreign policy journal secured from him his final thoughts on the ideas that had excited Haushofer so much.[4]

Statecraft in the service of projecting power beyond domestic state boundaries was and continues to be informed by a lively academic discourse that circulates internationally. Under pressure of war, human and physical sciences may become militarized, with enduring consequence.[5] Geopolitics, indeed, was confined neither to Germany nor to the 1930s. Wherever the term appears, however, its practitioners seem always to honour the memory of the British geographer. This book uses this legacy of Halford Mackinder to explore modern and historical relations between Geopolitics and Empire. Some commentators argue that Geopolitics is a discredited discourse of state aggression characteristic only of the perverted Political Geography produced

---

[1] Quoted in Weigert, *Generals and Geographers*, 116; Mackinder, 'Geographical Pivot'.

[2] Thorndike, 'The Lurid Career'; 'Haushofer's Heritage'.

[3] Weigert, 'German Geopolitics'; Mackinder to Arthur Hinks, 30 March 1942, Royal Geographical Society (RGS) Archives, Mackinder Correspondence.

[4] 'Mysteries of Geopolitics'; Mackinder, 'Round World'. These views are discussed in detail in Chapter Five.

[5] Pickering, 'Cyborg History'; Barnes and Farish, 'Between Regions'.

in Nazi Germany. Yet such a distinction between Political Geography and Geopolitics serves only to excuse geographers from the ethical questions they aim at Nazi geopoliticians.[6]

The central claim of this book is that there are similarities between the problems addressed by Mackinder on one hand, and by later geopolitical theorists on the other. He continues to be so widely cited and his ideas so resonant in numerous geostrategic debates in a range of distinct contexts that to ignore his legacy would be irresponsible. Mackinder's legacy can be found in at least three forms: the Nazi geopolitics of the 1930s, the US strategy of containment during the Cold War, and the current unipolar intentions of the United States, alongside the continental ambitions of some Russian nationalists.

Geopolitics on Trial

In October 1945 Edmund Walsh (1885–1956), interrogated General Karl Haushofer, founder in 1924 of the *Zeitschrift für Geopolitik*, and the most infamous Nazi geopolitician. Walsh, a Jesuit priest, founder in 1919 of the Georgetown University School of Foreign Service, and then lecturing there on Geopolitics, was Consultant to the US Chief of Counsel at the Nuremberg trials and was asked to determine whether Haushofer should be prosecuted for war crimes.[7] During the interview, Haushofer claimed that his work on Geopolitics developed further the ideas of a number of European and American writers, including Mackinder and the American geographer, Isaiah Bowman (1878–1950).

The Nuremberg trials were held to decide which Nazis had committed crimes against humanity, defined by the London Charter of 8 August 1945, as the 'deliberate planning and launching of an aggressive war, violations of the laws and customs of war [. . ., or] inhumane persecutions of racial, religious, or other groups'.[8] Under the last of these headings medical science was interrogated, some practitioners were tried, and a new Nuremberg Code was promulgated restating the Hippocratic injunction that doctors should do no harm.[9] More broadly, education and research that served 'to channel and shape public opinion in the National Socialist "revolution"' were also considered criminal activity.[10] In particular, planning for aggressive war or inhumane persecutions placed many academic careers in question, from

---

[6] For an insightful account of these difficulties and embarrassments in the case of German Political Geography, see: Lossau, 'Politische Geographe und Geopolitik'.
[7] Walsh, *Total Power*.
[8] Telford, 'Nuremberg War Crimes Trials', 21.
[9] Proctor, *Racial Hygiene*.
[10] Cornwell, *Hitler's Scientists*, 8.

the anthropologists who measured and classified Jewish and Slavic people in occupied Poland, to geographers, such as Walter Christaller (1893–1969), a member of the Nazi Party, whose 'Central Places in the East and their Cultural and Market Domains' (1941) was written while working for Heinrich Himmler (1900–45) at the Reich Commission for the Strengthening of Germandom, and a 'Planning and Soil' unit, that plotted the resettlement of Poland.[11] The geographer, Konrad Meyer (1901–73), who invited Christaller to Berlin, declared his National Socialist allegiance as early as 1932, and was central to the writing of the General Plan East.[12] Beyond the pursuit of the leading war criminals after 1945, there was also an ambitiously conceived, but shortly attenuated, process of denazification whereby the Nazi influence over German culture, education, and research was to be terminated by removing its ideologues from their posts.[13] The process had mixed results. Although Meyer faced trial at Nuremberg, he was not found guilty and continued his academic career at the highest level in post-war Germany.[14]

The academic field of Geopolitics was suspect for both its centrality to Nazi war-plans and for its propagandistic role in popular German nationalism. Through the 1930s, Haushofer supported the Nazi ideology and party as the vehicle for his own vision of German geopolitical destiny for, as Andrew Gyorgy, an American political scientist, described it in 1943, Geopolitics was 'geography in the service of world-wide warfare'.[15] In following this calling, Haushofer explicitly drew upon Mackinder's account of the significance of the Heartland of the World Island (described in Chapter 5), together with Mackinder's observation that German world-domination might follow an alliance with, or a victory over, Russia. Moreover, his influence on Rudolf Hess (1894–1987), Deputy Leader of the Nazi party, is clear. Haushofer became a close friend of Hess, who was a student of Haushofer in Munich. Later, in 1927, Haushofer was one of Hess's two best men at his wedding.[16] The other was Adolf Hitler. When Hess was in prison alongside Hitler in 1923–4, Haushofer visited on a score of Wednesdays, staying all day with them and supervising their reading of classics in German Political Geography, notably the second edition of Friedrich Ratzel's *Political Geography* (with the significant subtitle of 'The Geography of States, of Trade, and of War'), as well as the work *On War* by Carl von Clausewitz (1780–1831).[17] Upon his release from prison in 1924, Hess went to work as Haushofer's research assistant.[18]

[11] Schafft, *From Racism to Genocide*; Hottes, 'Walter Christaller'; Rössler, '"Area Research" and "Spatial Planning"'.
[12] Koehl, *RKFDV*, 71; Rössler, 'Geography and Area Planning', 68.
[13] Remy, *Heidelberg Myth*.
[14] Rössler, 'Geography and Area Planning', 73.
[15] Gyorgy, 'Geopolitics of War', 348.
[16] Hernig, '*Geopolitik*'.
[17] Walsh, *Total Power*, 15; Ratzel, *Politische Geographie*; von Clausewitz, *Vom Kriege*.
[18] Deuel, *People under Hitler*, 103.

At the dawn of the Third Reich, Haushofer popularized Geopolitics through his writings and his radio shows. In 1933, he published an account of *Der nationalsozialistische Gedanke in der Welt* ('National Socialist Thought in the World') for the new German Academy of Sciences to which Hitler had just appointed him President. Haushofer dedicated his *Weltpolitik von Heute* ('World Politics Today', 1934) to Hess, and, in an article of 1937, Haushofer offered his 'scientific geopolitics' to 'those powerful men to whom its findings are of practical interest'.[19] In October 1938 he used an editorial in *Zeitschrift für Geopolitik* to praise the Munich agreement between Britain and Germany, lauding Hitler's 'geopolitical mastery'.[20] Haushofer developed Geopolitics both as a technical aid to German expansionism and as part of the indoctrination of the people in the Nazi policy. His book on National Socialist thought made this clear: '[i]t is necessary that the whole scholarship of a people so deeply moved serve the leaders of such a movement in making understandable their national, political, and supranational aims'.[21] Hitler appears also to have learned his geopolitical lessons well, for there is more than an echo of Mackinder's heartland theory in his speeches, such as this passage from 1936: '[i]f I had the Ural Mountains with their incalculable store of treasures in raw materials, Siberia with its vast forests, and the Ukraine with its tremendous wheat fields, Germany and the National Socialist leadership would swim in plenty'.[22]

Geopolitics versus Political Geography

Some of Haushofer's contemporaries abroad were very critical of his geopolitical theories. Geopolitics was something that happened, or so his critics implied, in Germany alone, and was a consequence of the ways German intellectual life served national ideology rather than universal scholarship. In 1942, the geographer Isaiah Bowman, who was then president of Johns Hopkins University, wrote of German Geopolitics' 'perversion of fact to philosophy', for geographical science had been put at the service of 'the national ambition to conquer and govern', and 'territorial expansion' had been given a 'pseudoscientific justification'.[23] In the same year, Jean Gottmann (1915–94), a geographer of Russian–Jewish origin, in refuge in the United States after fleeing Nazi-occupied France, insisted that 'we [...] distinguish between geopolitics and political geography. The latter is a

---

[19] Heske, 'Haushofter'; Strausz-Hupé, *Geopolitics*, 73.
[20] Hernig, '*Geopolitik*', 233.
[21] Quoted in Weinreich, *Hitler's Professors*, 5.
[22] Quoted in Fifield and Pearcy, *Geopolitics*, 23.
[23] Bowman, 'Geography *vs.* Geopolitics', 656.

respectable discipline with a brilliant past', whereas the former was merely 'a certain amount of scientific trappings in order to plead and facilitate certain national expansions'.[24] Other geographers agreed. George Kiss (1914–89), another émigré from Europe who worked in the United States, was anxious to trace Geopolitics back to Hegel who had, he suggested, reacted to the shame of Napoléon's defeat of Prussia by preaching that Germany's 'eternal mission was one of conquest and domination'.[25] Derwent Whittlesey (1890–1956), at a time when he was President of the Association of American Geographers, proposed that Geopolitics was 'the product of a national habit of mind which reaches far back into German history'.[26] Only in Germany (and Japan), it seemed, could Political Geography degenerate to Geopolitics.

Writing in the immediate post-war period, Walsh, Haushofer's interrogator, argued that the creation of an empire required 'foresight, forethought', and, most importantly, 'geopolitical wisdom'.[27] The prospectus for Walsh's 1942 course on Geopolitics at Georgetown described it as 'one of the most powerful weapons used by the Axis Powers'.[28] Yet Walsh insisted that it was not geopolitical wisdom that Haushofer sought but rather that the Germans had 'discarded objectivity for subjective prejudices and interpreted geographic phenomena mainly in their relationship to the interests of Germany, thereby committing treason against that very scientific credo which Germany has so noisily worshipped as her outstanding creation'.[29] Walsh, then, presented his own work on Geopolitics as reactive not proscriptive: '[d]eciphering the geopolitical strategy of the enemy was his passion and countering their world revolutionary plans his vocation'.[30] The Free World, it would seem, had Political Geography and the Unfree World had Geopolitics, which was Political Geography in the service of Empire.

Such an understanding, however, was a particularly post-war and Cold-War perspective. The relations between Geopolitics and Empire, historically, were already more pervasive than Haushofer's critics allowed. An emphasis on national *Lebensraum* (living-space) was characteristic of German Geography already during the Weimar period, as was the propagandist use of maps to present German claims for more territory.[31] These spatial imaginaries, in other words, were not particular to Nazi ideologists. Certainly, fascist regimes developed, advanced, and borrowed geopolitical concepts for their own agendas. In Italy, for example, the journal *Geopolitica* was started in 1939 and Benito Mussolini told its editor that 'Geopolitics is much more than mere Geography' and that he would himself 'be the most attentive

---

[24] Gottmann, 'Background of Geopolitics', 206, 205.
[25] Kiss, 'Political Geography into Geopolitics', 633.
[26] Whittlesey, *German Strategy*, 58.
[27] From a speech of 1952, quoted in Ó Tuathail, 'Spiritual Geopolitics', 199.
[28] McNamara, *A Catholic Cold War*, 113.
[29] Walsh, 'Geopolitics and International Morals', 26.
[30] Ó Tuathail, 'Spiritual Geopolitics', 199.
[31] Murphy, *Heroic Earth*; Herb, *Under the Map of Germany*.

and assiduous reader of your magazine'.[32] Japanese geographers also set up
their own journal of Geopolitics (*Chiseigaku*) in 1942.[33] Haushofer was very
close to the Japanese geopoliticians, including Saneshige/Tsunekichi Komaki
(1898–1990). Komaki wrote *Nippon Chiseigaku Sengen* ('A Manifesto of
Japanese Geopolitics') in 1940 and promoted ultranationalist and expansionist stances, similar to Haushofer's own, to claim Japanese primacy in
Asia. In his view, because both Europe and the Americas were settled first
by Asians, Japan had those continents as their birthright too, along with all
the world's oceans, more properly in his eyes, the Great Japanese Sea.[34]

There was evidence, then, to support Haushofer's claim that his work in
Geopolitics was developing ideas entertained more generally among geographers, as well as for his further assertion that his work rested upon that of
Ratzel, together with its development by Ellen Churchill Semple in the United
States, and by Rudolf Kjellén in Sweden. He identified as the 'basic inspirers
of my teachings', among others: Alfred Mahan; Brooks Adams (1848–1927),
the American economic historian; Joseph Chamberlain (1836–1914), the
British advocate of economic protectionism; Thomas Holdich (1843–1929),
the British theorist of frontiers; Alfred Kitchener (1850–1916), another British theorist and practitioner of frontiers; and, of course, Mackinder himself.[35]
Haushofer claimed, and again with reason, that political geographers in
Britain and America had developed the teachings of Ratzel 'for the sake of
power expansion'.[36] This was very evident in the case of Semple, who quoted
Ratzel's formulation about the struggle for existence being a fight for space
when she noted the importance of the Spanish-American War of 1898 as
the extension of American influence outside its territorial borders: '[t]he
commercial strength of the American Republic was bound sooner or later
to find a political expression in that international struggle for existence, which
is a struggle for space, going on in Asiatic territory'.[37]

Haushofer claimed to have learned, too, from Bowman, much angering the
object of his praise. In 1930, Haushofer suggested that '[t]he ultimate solution
of Japan's problem of over-population is expansion into spheres of least
resistance'.[38] He suggested that given its own territorial expanse, people in the
United States were unable to understand this biological need for expansion.
However, Haushofer claimed that in the case of Japan, Bowman had accepted
that this nation must 'overflow its boundaries'.[39] In his commentary upon
Nazi Geopolitics, Weigert pounced upon this as a misleading quotation, ex-
postulating that 'Haushofer forgets to say, however, that Bowman added, "if

---

[32] Fifield and Pearcy, *Geopolitics*, 9; Atkinson, 'Geopolitical Imaginations'.
[33] Takeuchi, 'Japanese Imperial Tradition'; *idem*, 'Japanese Geopolitics'.
[34] Padover, 'Japanese Race Propaganda'.
[35] Haushofer, 'Defense of German Geopolitics'.
[36] Quoted in Brodie et al., *Principles of Political Geography*, 7.
[37] Semple, *American History*, 433.
[38] Quoted in Weigert, 'Haushofer and the Pacific', 741.
[39] Bowman, *New World*, 578.

not by people then by exports". This instance of Haushofer's utter disregard of all attempts to solve such problems by international economic cooperation is characteristic'.[40] Bowman was indignant: '[t]he phrase "utter disregard" is much too weak. It is utterly dishonest, unless we believe in constant war, to talk in terms of "population pressure" as a thing to be relieved by theft of territory from a neighbor'.[41] Bowman and Weigert were trying to draw a stark distinction between, on one side, the peaceful, economic interaction favoured by democratic political geographers, and, on the other, the violent process of colonization promoted by aggressive geopoliticians.

Unfortunately for Bowman, his own book went on to discuss the very same solution proposed by Haushofer. Trade, he suggested, was indeed a way for Japan to develop but Bowman added that as trade grew, 'this invited both territorial expansion and the stimulation of industry'.[42] He then turned to alternatives to commerce: '[n]ot by trade alone is empire to be extended. Westward across the Sea of Japan are fair lands thinly populated. Manchuria and Mongolia are empires in geographical extent, far larger than Japan, and in parts of them are fertile plains with a temperate zone climate—a land capable of supporting a dense population and as yet only in a pioneer stage of development'.[43] Indeed, noted Bowman:

Manchuria offers Japan a highly strategic position on the continent. It enables her to secure preferential terms for her manufactured goods; and what is of greatest import-ance, it enables her to control agricultural and mineral resources capable of large exploitation. The coal mines are in Japanese hands. Not only is it a strategic hinter-land to Korea (now definitely annexed to Japan); it was here that Japan learned how important was the possession of Manchuria if the Chinese Eastern Railway and the South Manchurian Railway were not to invite armed hosts to the western shores of the Sea of Japan. China cannot control the region, though sovereignty nominally resides in the Chinese government today. If Japan were to withdraw, this great pioneer region of fertile plains, temperate zone products, rich mines and forests would come under Russian control. The exports to Japan would be in Russian hands, and Russian capital would guide development.[44]

It must be obvious what advice Bowman would offer the Japanese, and it would not be that they should rely upon trade alone.

In other words, it was, and continues to be, misleading to present German Geopolitics as radically detached from a purely academic Political Geog-raphy even in Europe and North America. From 1940, there were proposals to establish within the United States a distinct Geopolitical Institute and in June 1942 'a Geopolitical Section of the Military Intelligence Service was

---

[40] Weigert, 'Haushofer and the Pacific', 742.
[41] Bowman, 'Geography vs. Geopolitics', 655.
[42] Bowman, *New World*, 578.
[43] Bowman, ibid., 582.
[44] Bowman, ibid., 582.

created. The section's objectives were "to study physical, economic, political, and ethnological geography in order to advise on measure of national security and assurance of continued peace in the post-war world, as well as to conduct such studies as may be demanded for the immediate prosecution of the war".[45]

Geopolitics, as the political scientist, and colleague of Bowman at Johns Hopkins, Johannes Mattern (1882–1970), observed in 1942, was a European and American, and not just narrowly German, discourse for 'a great deal has been going on in the past and is going on today everywhere in the world that is plain, unadulterated Geopolitik, though it is not called by that name, even when it has been and is being called obeying Manifest Destiny or assuming the White Man's Burden'.[46]

More recently, historical and political geographers have agreed with such an assessment. Michael Heffernan attributes the broader European origins of Geopolitics to the 'geopolitical panic' of late-nineteenth century Europe, when states responded to the industrial florescence of Germany and the United States, the intensified competition for colonies, and the reorganization of European diplomacy around a common fear of German might.[47] Gearóid Ó Tuathail, also characterizes Geopolitics in terms of a global perspective, observing that it was born of the statecraft of an 'era of imperialist rivalry', 1870–1945.[48]

The point is not that there was no difference between German Geopolitics and geostrategic thinking in other places. Indeed, Haushofer's anti-modernism and his anti-Semitism were both extreme. However, his organicism was widely shared and there was continuity rather than a distinction between German Geopolitics and these other geographical perspectives. In an excellent summary, the historian, Dan Diner, highlights a number of features of what he describes as the German nature of Geopolitics. German Geopolitics, writes Diner, was characterized by 'deterministic biological materialism', expressed 'an ideology legitimizing international domination through putatively natural hence timeless or unchanging principles', and Diner concludes by describing:

[A]pproaches of the time that were virulently narrow in their national and imperial interests. These approaches shared a propensity to balance off imperial realms against one another. The degree of ethnocentrism involved here runs parallel to a second propensity: the justification of a selfish ordering of outwardly directed political claims through a nationalistically amputated international law.[49]

---

[45] Crampton and Ó Tuathail, 'Intellectuals, Institutions and Ideology', 539; Vagts, 'Geography in War and Geopolitics'.
[46] Mattern, *Geopolitik*, 11.
[47] Heffernan, '*Fin de Siècle*', 29.
[48] Ó Tuathail, 'Thinking Critically'; *idem*, 'Part I. Introduction', 15.
[49] Diner, *Beyond the Conceivable*, 27.

In fine, I think this describes an ideal-type of Geopolitics that many geographers seeking to aid statecraft all too often approach.

The Return of Geopolitics

Although the term Geopolitics was not often used by Anglophone contemporaries of Haushofer, reticence waned. In the 1940s, about half-a-dozen books with the term 'Geopolitics' in the title were published in Britain and the United States, the majority of which were about the German school and its relations with Nazi imperialism.[50] None was published in the 1950s, one in the 1960s, and a further half-dozen in the 1970s, mainly about access to oil. By the 1980s, several dozen books were published and since then the trickle has become a torrent. Sloan and Gray date the revival of the term Geopolitics to the initiative of Henry Kissinger, who published the first volume of his memoirs in 1979, peppering the book with references to Geopolitics: 'Kissinger used it as a method of analysis to combat the American liberal politics of idealism [. . . and] as a means of presenting an alternative to the conservative policies of an ideological anti-Communism'.[51] In other words, Kissinger used Geopolitics to refer to the strategic dimensions of his own version of *Realpolitik*, paying less attention to the spatial arrangement of countries than did earlier geopolitical thinkers, and less even than in the contemporary alternative geostrategic vision of states falling to communism in proximate succession as a line of dominos.[52] Kissinger was less concerned with the internal arrangements of states, such as whether they were communist or not, than with their external behaviour and he was criticized, indeed, for the weakening of anti-Communism that resulted.[53]

During the Cold War, Geopolitics was presented by American diplomats as a realistic world view countering two forms of idealism: liberalism and extreme anti-Communism. Military strategists too thought in broadly geopolitical ways, and the political geographer, Leslie Hepple, has detailed the popularity of Geopolitics among Latin American generals, including Augusto Pinochet (1915–2006), who taught Military Geography and Geopolitics in both Chile and Ecuador during the 1950s and 1960s, before becoming head of the Chilean armed forces and leading the coup that replaced the socialist and democratic government of Salvador Allende

---

[50] Based on a search of the Internet catalogues for the Library of Congress (Washington DC) and the British Library (London).

[51] Sloan and Gray, 'Why Geopolitics?', 1.

[52] Kissinger, *White House Years*; Jay, 'Regionalism as Geopolitics'; Howard, 'World According to Henry'; Ninkovich, *Modernity and Power*.

[53] Shulzinger, 'Naïve and Sentimental Diplomat'.

(1908–73) with a military dictatorship.[54] The single appendix to Pinochet's textbook on Geopolitics was a translation of Mackinder's 1904 paper on the Geographical Pivot.[55] The United States Army War College continues to make explicit use of Geopolitics in its own teaching, presenting it in 2004 as an alternative to strategic views based on 'globalization' and 'time–space compression' that leave too 'little space for sticky concern with the intricacies of regional affairs'.[56] There is, it would seem, a revival of Geopolitics, particularly 'among the leadership cadres of the major powers, above all in the United States'.[57]

Mackinder in the United States: Influence and Echoes

While largely ignored in Britain in the 1920s and 1930s, Mackinder was, as noted already, championed in contemporary Germany. The hysterical representations of Nazi Geopolitics in the United States brought renewed attention to his work, and it is clear that both directly, and through the restating of his theories by Nicholas Spykman (1893–1943) and Walter Lippmann (1889–1974), Mackinder's ideas became central to the United States' post-war policy of containing the Soviet Union.[58] However, by 2004, as geographer Nicholas Megoran suggests, some strategists invoked Mackinder more as a talisman to give academic respectability to expansionist ideologies, whereas others see enduring geopolitical realities captured succinctly in Mackinder's theories.[59] In broad terms, it is necessary to distinguish between the explicit use of Mackinder's ideas as his influence, and the articulation of similar ideas without clear evidence of direct influence as echo.

Mackinder's explicit influence is very evident. In the 1970s, Colin Gray, a political scientist in the United States, began referring to the military threat posed by the Soviet Union as that of a heartland power moving to control the rimlands of the World Island.[60] For Gray, Mackinder's theory remains 'far superior to rival conceptions, for understanding the principal international security issues', and Mackinder is 'the first and . . . the greatest of geopolitical theorists'.[61] His colleague Francis Sempa insists that 'statesmen and strategists still operate in Mackinder's world'.[62] Introducing a 1962 reprint of Mackinder's 1919 work, *Democratic Ideals and Reality*, the political scientist, Anthony Pearce argued that in America and England, 'most studies of global

[54] Hepple, 'South American Heartland'; Hewitt, 'Between Pinochet and Kropotkin'.
[55] Pinochet Ugarte, *Introduction to Geopolitics*.
[56] Nation, 'Regional Studies', 57; Owens, 'In Defense of Classical Geopolitics'.
[57] Hepple, 'Revival of Geopolitics'; Klare, 'New Geopolitics', 52.
[58] Spykman, *Geography of the Peace*; Lippmann, *US Foreign Policy*; Gaddis, *Long Peace*.
[59] Megoran, 'Revisiting the "Pivot"'.
[60] Gray, *Geopolitics of the Nuclear Era*; Brown, 'End to Grand Strategy'.
[61] Gray, *Geopolitics of Super Power*, 4; idem, 'In Defence of the Heartland', 32.
[62] Sempa, *Geopolitics*, 21.

strategy or political geography have been based, in whole or in part, upon Mackinder's theories'.[63] In 1996, the President of the National Defense University in Washington D.C., Lieutenant-General Ervin Rokke, prefaced a reprint of the same book with the observation that Mackinder was particularly important in the multi-polar, post-containment world, now that 'regional strategic concerns' were so pressing.[64] A retired professor of National Security Strategy at the same US National Defense University, Stephen Mladineo, in providing an introduction to this reprint, urged the United States to heed Mackinder's warnings, for 'the reality of a resurgent autocratic power seeking hegemony over central Eurasia remains a possibility'.[65]

There were many powerful echoes of Mackinder during the Cold War. The diplomat and geostrategist, George Kennan (1904–2005), for example, is often credited with articulating the containment policy for the Cold-War United States, and his language could not be closer to Mackinder's. In one version of the doctrine, from 1950, he proposed that the United States should ensure that 'no single Continental land power should come to dominate the entire Eurasian land mass[, . . .] become a great sea power as well as land power [. . . ,] and enter [. . .] on an overseas expansion hostile to ourselves and supported by the immense resources of the interior of Europe and Asia'.[66] On the other side of the Atlantic, the language was similar. According to Donald Meinig, '[i]n a secret report to the British Cabinet in early 1948 Foreign Secretary Ernest Bevan had . . . spoken in Mackinderese: "[p]hysical control of the Eurasian landmass and eventual control of the whole World Island is what the Politburo is aiming at—no less a thing than that" '.[67] As late as 1988, Ronald Reagan's National Security Strategy declared that: 'the United States' most basic national interests would be endangered if a hostile state or group of states were to dominate the Eurasian landmass—that part of the globe often referred to as the world's heartland'.[68]

These echoes and influences come down to the present. In the Introduction to this book, I set out some of the evidence for asserting a family resemblance between Mackinder's ideas and the conflicting geopolitical visions of Neo-conservatives within the United States and Russian nationalists within the Russian Federation and I return to the US case in Chapter 8. The rest of the book treats Mackinder's ideas in detail in order to contribute to current debates that seem to replay many of those themes. First, I want to explain why there have been repeated returns both to the works of Mackinder and to ideas very like his own; in 1930s Germany, in Cold-War United States, and today in both the United States and the Russian Federation. The issue that

[63] Pearce, 'Introduction', xxi.
[64] Rokke, 'Preface', vii.
[65] Mladineo, 'Introduction', xxii.
[66] Quoted in Liberman, 'Spoils of Conquest', 128.
[67] Meinig, *The Shaping of America 4*, 352.
[68] Quoted in O'Hara, 'Great Game', 145.

recurs is the question of global empire. Great Powers are tempted by the prospect of a unipolar world and Mackinder's ideas about Heartland, about land- and sea-power, about the inevitability of the use of force in global politics, and about the incompatibility between different civilizations provide a way for one type of state that sees itself as maritime (Britain or the United States) to explain how and why it must contain another type of state (continental) that it sees challenging for global hegemony. In contrast, states that see themselves as continental powers (Germany or the Russian Federation) find in Mackinder's account of geopolitical realities, a blueprint for overturning the contemporary global order and establishing their own suzerainty over the World Island and thus by extension a World Empire. Empire and imperialism shaped the contexts in which Mackinder's ideas evolved and have been revived, so I turn now to these contentious concepts.

Empire

There are clear similarities between the problems addressed, on one hand, by Mackinder and, on the other, by later geopolitical theorists. There is, in short, a continuity of imperial issues. The terms empire, imperialism, and colonialism are used in such interrelated ways that one person's imperialism is another's colonialism. For example, in a work on the geography of early modern Ireland, Willie Smyth defines colonialism 'as a process that involves the intrusion into and conquest of an inhabited territory by representatives of an external power, or as geographer Donald Meinig notes, "the aggressive encroachment of one people upon the territory of another, resulting in the subjugation of the latter people to alien rule"'.[69] Yet, Meinig was giving his own definition of imperialism, not colonialism, as a distinctive 'type of geopolitical relationship'.[70] There is an emotional and ethical charge to the terms colonialism and imperialism and much ink spilled exempting or including this or that case under one or other term; the case of Ireland being perhaps the most notorious example.[71] There are also ambiguities introduced by the nature of the units involved in the relationship, leading the political scientist, Michael Hechter, for example, and again with Ireland in mind, to identify 'internal colonialism'.[72] The Lebanese philosopher and diplomat, Charles Malik, referred to Brazil, the United States, and the Soviet Union as each having an 'internal empire'.[73] Yet there is no clear difference between Hechter's 'internal colonialism' and Malik's 'internal empire'. In 1917, Lenin termed imperialism, the 'latest stage of capitalism', but in writing of the

---

[69] Smyth, *Map-Making*, 9.   [70] Meinig, *The Shaping of America 1*, xviii.
[71] Howe, *Ireland and Empire*; Kearns, 'Ireland after Theory'; McDonough, *Was Ireland a Colony?*.
[72] Hechter, *Internal Colonialism*.   [73] Malik, 'Independence', 76.

relations between rich and poor countries referred to the latter as 'subject countries' including 'more than half the population of the globe' in a series of 'colonies and semi-colonies'.[74] The intellectual historian, Uday Mehta, reflects this ambivalent usage when deciding to 'use the terms *empire* and *colony* and their philological cognates interchangeably'.[75]

Colonialism and Imperialism refer to relations of inequality between politically differentiated units. The first has perhaps a stronger sense of the political about it and the second a greater emphasis on the economic. It is clear, however, that political and economic asymmetries require and feed each other. Lenin recalled that 'Rome, founded on slavery, pursued a colonial policy and achieved imperialism'.[76] By colonies, here, Lenin referred to territories that Rome annexed to its empire and ruled directly. I am going to use the term 'colonial' more generally to describe asymmetric relations that are strongly buttressed by political influence; in other words, where the self-determination of the weaker people is directly compromised by interference from the more powerful people. There is clearly a continuum here, from direct rule through to the sort of steer that can be given by clear 'advice', backed up by the threat of military intervention or economic sanctions were the advice not followed. By imperialism, Lenin intended the ways that the resources (labour, raw materials, effective demand) of the weaker place can be deployed to the benefit of some people from the more powerful place. This inequity is secured through coercively attained property relations (from theft through to what the geographer, David Harvey, terms 'accumulation by dispossession') and unfair terms of trade (what the economist, Arghiri Emmanuel, called 'unequal exchange').[77] Lenin's main point was that these economic instruments of exploitation take on a particular form under capitalism, they are shaped by the disciplines of capital accumulation; which is why a theory of imperialism based solely on trading relations (as is Emmanuel's) is inadequate. Yet, the extra-economic basis of the system remains clear, for the essence of Lenin's 'latest' stage of capitalism was the sway of monopoly forms, and attempts to convert nation-state economic and political power into a protection for some national enterprises from the competition that reduces the profits of their foreign rivals.

There is a continual to-ing and fro-ing between economic and political poles as firms seek free trade to enjoy the advantages they secured in the last round of political or military interventions, or seek new coercive assistance as they try to challenge the advantages of rivals, which they represent as belonging to foreign imperial powers. In this sense, I am content, with the economic historians John Gallagher and Ronald Robinson, to speak of the

---

[74] Lenin, *Imperialism*, 10. I am persuaded that 'latest' was Lenin's settled choice for the imperialist stage of capitalism; rather than 'highest' or even 'last'; 'Notes from the Editors', 1.

[75] Mehta, *Liberalism and Empire*, 2.

[76] Lenin, *Imperialism*, 82.

[77] Harvey, *New Imperialism*; Emmanuel, *Unequal Exchange*.

'imperialism of free trade'.[78] Michael Doyle, an historian of Empire, suggests
that imperialism is 'simply the process or policy of establishing or maintaining an empire'.[79] Doyle also helpfully suggests that 'Empire is a relationship,
formal or informal, in which one state controls the effective political sovereignty of another political society. It can be achieved by force, by political
collaboration, by economic, social or cultural dependence'.[80] The political
scientist, Alejandro Colás, adds that empires are characterized by expansion,
hierarchy, and order.[81]

I also follow the geographer, Neil Smith, in seeing economic imperialism as
more general than political colonialism, since economic exploitation will
occur both during the moments of extra-economic intervention and during
the apparently calmer interludes.[82] A colonial type of imperialism, then, is
where the abridging of the sovereignty of the weaker state is achieved
through direct political control, whereas liberal imperialism covers those
cases where control is achieved by other means, primarily economic ones.
Yet colonial types of imperialism are not an earlier form that was superseded
by indirect, financial, or liberal imperialism. It is telling, I think, that commentators announce new imperialisms in these terms and that the new
imperialism is nearly always seen as involving less direct forms of control
than the old, but it is also striking that this transition has been identified
repeatedly. In 1964, Hamza Alavi worried that the end of 'direct colonial
rule' had not precipitated the crisis in global capitalism that many had
anticipated from their reading of Lenin.[83] Alavi argued that there was a
new imperialism that did not need direct colonial rule since it no longer
sought out cheap labour abroad to engage through its surplus capital, but
rather, now, sought markets for the excess products produced through
capital's renovation of the means of production in the rich countries themselves. This led the economist, Harry Magdoff, to write of 'imperialism
without colonies'.[84]

The argument, however, bears some similarity to arguments about a
'new imperialism' from both early- and late-nineteenth century Britain. The
economic historian, Patrick O'Brien notes that when Britain established
global commercial hegemony after 1815, many British commentators turned
against colonial adventures, making an 'economic case for withdrawal
from empire'.[85] O'Brien refers to the period 1846–1914 as one of 'Liberal
Imperialism'. One hundred years earlier, the English economist, William
Cunningham (1849–1919) went much further than O'Brien, and in 1899
suggested that with the repeal of the Corn Laws in 1846, Britain evolved an
economic policy that was 'not national, but cosmopolitan in character'.[86]

---

[78] Gallagher and Robinson, 'Imperialism of Free Trade'.
[79] Doyle, *Empires*, 45.   [80] Doyle, *Empires*, 45.   [81] Colás, *Empire*, 9.
[82] N. Smith, *Endgame*, 25.   [83] Alavi, 'Imperialism Old and New', 104.
[84] Magdoff, *Imperialism Without Colonies*.
[85] O'Brien, 'Imperialism', 63.   [86] Cunningham, 'English Imperialism', 1.

Britain's role in its colonies was now exercised for the disinterested benefit of all developed nations in keeping markets open and also for the specific advantage of the colonized peoples: 'we gain nothing for ourselves, but we insure such law and order as India has never known before'.[87] Indeed, many British commentators thought that the benefits from direct rule were fast passing. They argued instead for something that some historians now term an 'informal empire' in which 'overt foreign rule is avoided while economic advantages are secured by "unequal" legal and institutional arrangements, and also by the constant threat of political meddling and military coercion'.[88]

Late-nineteenth-century British imperialism, therefore, was 'new' in these two ways: it disavowed national interest and sought influence without the responsibility of direct rule. Its defenders often chose not to speak its name.[89] Mackinder and other geographers were central to these British debates over the New Imperialism.[90] Neil Smith locates a central difference between what he sees as the pessimism of Mackinder in the 1900s, based in a declining empire, and the optimism of Bowman in the 1920s, living at the heart of the rising US empire. For Smith, the difference expressed itself in terms of a contrast between two forms of imperialism, the one based on conceptions of 'absolute space' and thus requiring territorial, that is colonial, control and the other focused on 'relative space', requiring only informal control to pursue the benefits of economic efficiency.[91]

A similar transition between direct and indirect imperial control, between colonial and liberal imperialism, is located by different scholars at diverse points of the past two centuries. Yet instead of a transition, capitalist forms of Liberal Imperialism and Colonial Imperialism should be seen as dialectically constituting and undermining each other across the whole of the last century or so. There was and is no simple sequence of liberal following colonial imperialism.

A disclaimer. Liberal Imperialism is a difficult term because the adjective 'liberal' is so contested and thus ambiguous, and because historically it was used in nineteenth-century Britain to describe one version of the New Imperialism (discussed above). I use it in this book nonetheless because this version of imperialism takes seriously the question of individual liberty, and for this reason is avowedly liberal. From this perspective, imperialism cannot be justified simply in terms of the interests of the colonizer. Liberal Imperialists, moreover, deny that this form of imperialism is colonial by intention; they instead persuade themselves that, without benevolent attention from

---

[87] Cunningham, 'English Imperialism', 4.
[88] Osterhammel, 'Britain and China', 148.
[89] Historian Bernard Porter is one of many modern commentators who see very much the same denial among the current occupants of the White House; Porter, 'We Don't Do Empire'.
[90] Hudson, 'New Geography'.
[91] N. Smith, *American Empire*, 12–28.

more developed peoples, less-developed peoples can never progress.[92] The imperialism of Victorian and Edwardian liberals, for example, followed from a moral geography that divided the world between civilized and barbarian peoples.[93] Liberals, however, were and are uneasy about having to exercise this tutelage and remain open to ready persuasion that less direct forms of influence can be effective. In particular, the liberal belief in individualism in both politics and the economy results in the conviction that free trade can secure more easily some of the gains that colonial rule promises.

While there is a continuum between colonial and liberal forms of imperialism, political and economic relations are twisted together across the full range. Under a strongly colonial form of imperialism, in which there is direct rule, there is also likely to be the deliberate manipulation of production, trade, and markets to serve the immediate interests of the colonial power, as evidenced by English relations with India in the eighteenth century and English relations with Ireland in the seventeenth century. With a more liberal version of imperialism, there are also likely to be legal and property arrangements that dilute local sovereignty in the name of free trade, open markets, and the repatriation of profits by foreign companies. In the period 1945–90, the labelling as communist those attempts by poor countries to control their economies through nationalization, tariffs, and price controls, was just such a threat to political sovereignty.

We can imagine a form of imperialism that could present itself as 'liberal', when and where there is such a gap in economic efficiency and capacity between rich and poor states that even the mildest influence in favour of open markets allows richer states to derive extensive benefit through trade with, and investment in, poorer countries. The United States faced almost the whole of the rest of the world in precisely this way in the years immediately after the Second World War. In these circumstances, free trade favours the strong and can even be presented as drawing the poorer state into a process of economic development by which it might slowly ascend the ladder of relative prosperity.

In contrast, Colonial Imperialism can be very expensive, but if successful it may create an opportunity for converting to its liberal alternative. Liberal Imperialism, on the other hand, can be self-limiting as technologies are copied and rivals develop to compete for their share of the markets and resources of the poorest countries and even to encroach upon the home markets of the world hegemon. The liberal Leviathan may be tempted to use its military superiority to reintroduce an advantage it is losing economically. The two types of imperialism are in a dialectical relationship in ways that mean they repeatedly, but only temporarily, replace and succeed each other.

---

[92] Mehta, *Liberalism and Empire*, ch. 3.
[93] Bell, 'Empire and International Relations'; Bell and Sylvest, 'International Society'.

Without playing down the importance of differences in historical and geographical contexts, I wish to suggest that some of these dilemmas recur in ways that explain the influence and echo of the writings and ideas of one time and place for peoples of another time and place. Figure 1.1 shows the historical experience of Germany, the United Kingdom, and the United States with regard to their changing shares of world's production of wealth and the world's total population.[94] For each of eleven dates in Figure 1.1, the share of global population and of global GDP is plotted and successive data-points are connected for each country; the trajectory of the relationship

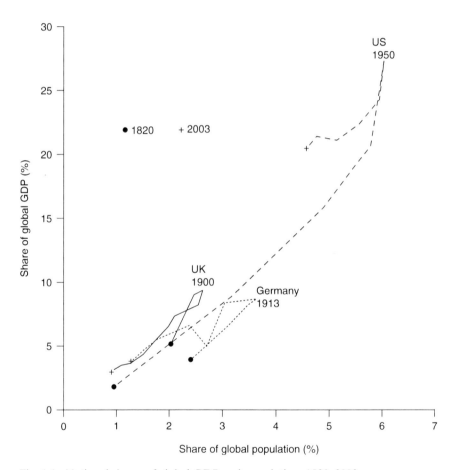

Fig. 1.1. National shares of global GDP and population, 1820–2003

[94] The data are plotted for 1820, 1870, 1900, 1913, 1940, 1950, 1960, 1970, 1980, 1990, and 2003. Data on Gross Domestic Product and population from Maddison, *World Economy*, 638, 641 (supplemented from online tables referred to in the text).

between global population and GDP between 1820 and 2003 is traced out as a line. Thus, for example, in 1820 the United States contained about 1 per cent of the people in the world and produced more than its share (1.8%) of the world's goods and services. Thereafter the United States grew steadily both in demographic and economic terms reaching its peak relative to the rest of the world in 1950, when it accounted for 27 per cent of the world's GDP and 6 per cent of its population. On both counts, it has been declining ever since, and now produces 20.7 per cent of the world's goods and services by value, from about 4.6 per cent of the world's people. Figure 1.1 shows that similar reversals affected at earlier times the United Kingdom (9.4% world GDP and 2.6% world population in 1900) and Germany (8.7% and 3.6%, respectively in 1913).

Figure 1.2 illustrates the share of each country's spending in the total military expenditure of all countries for which there are records.[95] Changes in relative national economic standings are ever central to political debate and prod military insecurity. In the 1880s, British politicians looked nervously at the rise of Germany and the United States. In 1888, the British government set out its two-power standard declaring that it would never allow the British navy to fall below the level of the combined strength of 'any two nations combined'.[96] German politicians believed that their growing economy could steam past the British and that an arms race would weaken the British and leave Germany with a supremacy behind which they might build their own overseas empire, very likely at British expense.[97] The German naval laws of 1898, 1900, 1906, and 1908 triggered the greatest arms race in history with the United States, Germany, and Britain each building unprecedented numbers of large battleships, the Dreadnoughts. In the six years (1899–1904) between the first of the German naval laws and Mackinder's outline of the 'Geographical Pivot of History', German military spending rose by 19 per cent over the average of the previous six years, but that of the United States rose by 38 per cent and Britain's by a staggering 150 per cent.[98] Figure 1.2 sets this arms race in context; the data are also summarized for broad periods in Table 1.1.

For the nineteenth century, the curves for France, Russia, and the United Kingdom wander around each other with clear national peaks associated

---

[95] 'National Material Capabilities (v3.02)'. The dataset is described in: Singer, Bremer, and Stuckey, 'Capability Distribution, Uncertainty, and Major Power War'; Singer, 'Reconstructing the Correlates of War Dataset'. The size of the world system of states grows from twenty in 1815 to 191 in 2001 although in each year there are a few (usually small) states with data missing. I have somewhat anachronistically reported for the period before German unification, figures for the states that were to become Germany. Conversely, the Russia time-series includes all component parts of the Soviet Union for the period 1917–89 but reports only Russia before that and the CIS from 1990.

[96] Woodward, *Great Britain and the German Navy*, 455.

[97] Berghahn, *Germany and the Approach of War*.

[98] The data on military spending are from the Correlates of War project, specifically the dataset, 'National Material Capabilities (v3.02)'.

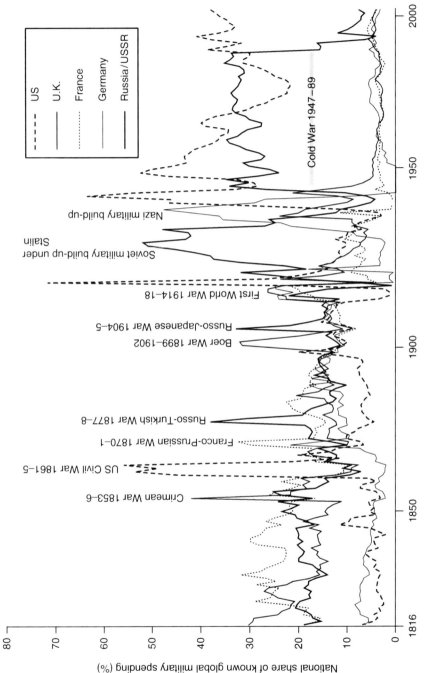

Fig. 1.2. National shares of known global military spending, 1816–2001

Geopolitics and Empire

Table 1.1. National shares (%) of known global military spending

	1816–50	1851–85	1886–1918	1919–45	1946–89	1990–2001
US	4.9	15.3	7.6	35.2	30.1	35.5
U.K.	19.1	14.9	23.8	12.0	3.5	4.5
France	24.5	18.3	19.3	2.4	3.2	4.8
Germany	5.9	7.6	23.1	25.4	4.1	4.6
Russia/USSR	18.8	16.3	12.4	11.5	31.2	9.1

with particular wars (the Crimean war for the United Kingdom in 1854, the Franco-Prussian war of 1870 for France, its war with Turkey in 1877–8 for Russia, the US Civil War, notably in the years 1862–4). As illustrated in Table 1.1, the spending on arms of France, following the end of the Napoleonic Wars in 1815, was broadly comparable with arms spending in the United Kingdom and the Russian Empire. After mid-century, the United States joined this group of big spenders, but the late-nineteenth century highlights the dramatic arms race between Britain and Germany. I have already remarked upon the growth in British spending around the turn of the twentieth century. While Russia, France, Germany and Britain demonstrate dramatic increases leading into the First World War, the response of the economy of the United States to its entry into the war was stupendous, although it was the collapse of rival economies, rather than a further increase in production, that explains how the United States reached 72 per cent of global arms expenditure in 1919, the year following the end of the First World War. Table 1.1 also shows the significance of the arms race between Germany and Britain in the period that straddled the turn of the twentieth century; together these two countries accounted for nearly half of global military spending between 1886 and 1919.

The level of spending during the First World War was soon reduced for most belligerents and, from Figure 1.2, we can see the massive Soviet rearmament in the period 1925–40. The Nazi militarization became evident in 1933, with a British response two years later. The staggering mobilization of US resources began in 1941 and reached its apogee in 1946. After the Second World War, most European powers declined to an unprecedented *insignificance*. The share of global military spending undertaken by the United States did not return to its pre-war levels of around 10 per cent but rather, after a brief decline to 30 per cent, rose again at the start of the Cold War to 50 per cent before falling unsteadily towards about 20 per cent by the end of the 1970s. During the Cold War, the Soviet Union spent up to about 30 per cent of global military expenditure but this was the region that experienced the most dramatic peace-dividend from the end of the Cold War. The last decade of the Cold War witnessed rising military spending in the United States.

What is most striking about Figure 1.2 is that US military spending continued to rise after the Cold War. By 2005, the United States accounted for about 40 per cent of the world's total military spending, as well as perhaps 60 per cent of global arms production.[99] Almost from the end of the Cold War, the United States has, in an ironic echo of the British Dreadnought policy, defined its primary defence posture as being the capacity to prevail in two simultaneous major wars, with or without any military assistance from allies.[100] Table 1.1 indicates the global significance of the military expenditure of the United States during the twentieth century. It accounted for about one-third of global militarization throughout the century, and only in the period of the Cold War did it face a rival that spent anything comparable. From the end of the Cold War, the arms gap behind the United States and the rest of the world is without precedent.

Britain at the start of the twentieth and the United States at the start of the twenty-first century faced very different situations. Nevertheless, these figures demonstrate that both sought to sustain their influence in the world by raising their share of the world's military power at a time when their underlying economy was producing a declining share of the world's wealth. The problem of how to motivate and justify intervention in a world shaped by extreme asymmetries of wealth and power is common to the geopolitical vision of both Mackinder and his modern disciples. These inequalities, at least as regards power, are today even greater, and thus more dangerous, than in the past.

---

[99] Data on military spending from the Stockholm International Peace Research Institute showing Purchasing Power Parity figures for military spending; Stockholm International Peace Research Institute, *SIPRI Yearbook 2006*, Appendix 8A. Data on arms production are from the same SIPRI report (Appendix 9A) and relate to arms production by the world's largest 100 arms companies, 40 of which are in the United States.

[100] Metz, *Revising*.

2

An Imperial Subject

At seventy, Mackinder recalled his first memory of public affairs: as a nine-year-old running home with the news 'which he had learnt from a telegram on the post office door, that Napoleon III and his whole army had surrendered to the Prussians at Sedan'.[1] He had been 'writing a history of the war in a notebook' and with this 'hot news' expected that 'the seniors [in his home] would have to treat me as on their level and no longer a child'.[2]

Mackinder remembered his boyhood games as distinctly paternalist. He would ride about on his pony and play at being the king of some island he had studied in his father's library and, in his imagination, he developed the economy of the island 'and generally civilised its usually backward inhabitants'.[3] War and colonialism framed Mackinder's experiences as well as his view of the world. Mackinder was seven years old when, in 1868, the great campaigns for British imperial unity began, with the founding of the Royal Colonial Society and the publication of Charles Dilke's (1810–69) *Greater Britain*.[4] Mackinder was ten years old when, in an attempt to reassert Tory values against hegemonic Liberalism, Benjamin Disraeli (1804–81), then leader of a Conservative party in opposition, rejected free trade and took up the cause of imperial preference, urging that the British make a tariff barrier

---

[1] Quoted in: Gilbert, 'Mackinder', 94. Mackinder was sharing this early memory of the Franco-Prussian war of 1870 with his colleagues on the Imperial Economic Committee, a group working to promote the marketing in the United Kingdom of goods produced in the British Empire overseas.

[2] Mackinder, 'Early Memoirs', in M. Wilson Woolley, 'The Philosophy of Sir Halford J. Mackinder', 142–60, 150; unpublished MS, London School of Economics, Archives, Mackinder M 1856 (1). This is a piece by Mackinder, found among his papers at his death and sent by his wife, Emilie Catherine Mackinder, to Martha Morse (née Wilson, and later Woolley), an ex-student of Mackinder who worked, for perhaps forty years, on a philosophical and biographical study of Mackinder before sending it (1978), together with publishers' rejection notes, to Michael Wise, professor of Geography at LSE, who later passed it to the LSE Archives.

[3] Mackinder, 'Autobiographical Fragments' [notes for a speech for a dinner to mark his resignation from the chair of the Imperial Economic Committee, 13 May 1931], Mackinder Papers, School of Geography, Oxford University, MP/C/100 [envelope b, i], 2. The papers of Mackinder at the School of Geography are in a trunk, probably one of those he brought back from Kenya (for the trunks containing the so-called 'iron rations', see Chapter 4). They were classified in broad terms by Brian Blouet. I have distinguished in addition between envelopes within each class and then given a number to each piece within the envelopes. These additional references are given in square brackets although I did not make any mark upon either envelopes or pieces. Of course, only if things stay in the same envelopes in the same order will my additional reference prove helpful. These materials should really be placed in the Bodleian Library and catalogued properly.

[4] Tyler, *Struggle for Imperial Unity*.

around, but not within their Empire. Six years later, in 1877, Disraeli, now prime minister, invited Queen Victoria to assume the title Empress of India. Patriotism, war, and Empire were popular enthusiasms and, in 1878, during the Russo-Turkish war, a popular song urged British intervention against Russia and coined an evocative term: 'We don't want to fight, but by jingo if we do, | We've got the ships, we've got the men, we've got the money too!'[5]

As the theme of Empire moved centre stage in British politics, Mackinder attended Oxford University (1880–85). During this time, the historian, John Seeley (1834–95), published *The Expansion of England*, which sold 80,000 copies in its first year, and prompted the founding of the Imperial Federation League in 1884.[6] As Mackinder began his related careers as an educationalist and as a campaigner for the Empire, the cause of Empire shone, never more brightly perhaps than during the Diamond Jubilee of Queen Victoria in 1897, yet it was soon to be tarnished.[7] The Boer War (1899–1902) demonstrated the fragility of the British Empire, almost shaking South Africa free from British rule. South Africa was retained but only through a massive deployment of troops and only after the British had resorted to the appalling expediency of concentration camps to deny the Boer soldiers their support among local residents. This mobilization also revealed the weakness of the British vital capacity, with a very large share of British urban residents unfit to fight; spectres of racial degeneration haunted public debate.[8] The war threw up evidence of incompetence and inefficiency, most notably in the army, but also more widely within British society.[9]

Some historians have concluded that the idea of Empire never recovered the moral high ground after the Boer War, and that it was never as easy again to equate patriotism with imperialism.[10] These anxieties about the security of the British Empire were sharpened by the evidence of anti-colonial struggles within the Empire (in Ireland, Egypt, and India), and by the rise of German militarism without.[11] Mackinder identified with the politicians who argued that imperialism was vital to national survival and that an imperial nation needed also to attend to domestic reform, thereby promoting national efficiency.[12] Mackinder developed his geopolitical theories under the shadow of the questions raised by the Boer War.

---

[5] Cunningham, 'Jingoism'.
[6] Deudney, 'Greater Britain or Greater Synthesis?', 194.
[7] MacKenzie, *Imperialism and Popular Culture*; Morris, *Pax Britannica*.
[8] Nash, 'The Boer War'; Pakenham, *Boer War*; Soloway, 'Counting the Degenerates'.
[9] Funnell, 'National Efficiency'.
[10] Thornton, *The Imperial Idea*; A. Thompson, 'Language of Imperialism'.
[11] Garvin, 'Anatomy of a Nationalist Revolution'; Gershoni and Jankowski, *Egypt, Islam and the Arabs*; Guha, *First Spark of Revolution*; Frederick, 'Anglo-German Rivalry'.
[12] Searle, *National Efficiency*; Semmel, *Imperialism and Social Reform*.

Mackinder as Student

Like some other Oxford students and dons, Mackinder participated in the popular militarism of the day. He joined the Oxford Kriegspiel (War Games) Society shortly after his arrival as an undergraduate in 1880. Spenser Wilkinson (1853–1937), a graduate at Merton College, Oxford, set up the Society in 1875 to imitate the annual war games of the Prussian General Staff.[13] The Chair of the Society was Hereford George (1838–1910), a lecturer in History who gave the only explicit teaching in Geography at Oxford, one lecture a week to historians.[14] George was later to write a *Historical Geography of the British Empire* in which he reassured the school-children for whom the book was intended that '[o]ur empire is not unfair to other nations, as England stands alone in the favourable treatment which she offers to foreigners'; meaning that the British were the best of imperialists.[15] Mackinder also knew George through the Volunteer Force, another military organization for students, dating from threat of French invasion in 1859, and giving volunteers experience of drill, manoeuvre, and marksmanship. Mackinder was 'promoted to lieutenant in 1883', and, during his vacations, 'took every course at Aldershot [and] Wellington [and] Chelsea Barracks which was then open to Volunteers'.[16] At one point Mackinder even considered a military career and shocked his father with the revelation in 1878 that 'I had determined to throw up the scholarship that I had won at Saint Bartholomew's Hospital and to apply for a University Commission in the Army'.[17] Although the scholarship to Christ Church, a college of Oxford University, supervened, the martial and the academic remained intertwined in Mackinder's life. When he applied for membership of the Royal Geographical Society (RGS), in 1886, for example, one of his sponsors was Hereford George.[18]

At the time Mackinder attended, Oxford was dominated by literary and historical studies, particularly Classics, and only one student in twenty took natural sciences. Mackinder's boarding school education at Epsom College, where the sons of medical doctors were sent, helped him win a five-year Junior Studentship in Physical Sciences.[19] Oxford was also dominated by contemporary British politics and at this time about one-quarter of the British House of Commons, and rather more of the House of Lords, had

[13] der Derian, 'The Simulation Syndrome', 192; Wilkinson, *Thirty-Five Years*, 6; Boardman, 'Manchester Tactical Society'.
[14] Symonds, *Oxford and Empire*, 145.
[15] George, *Historical Geography*, 4.
[16] Summers, 'Militarism in Britain'; Blouet, *Mackinder*, 21; Mackinder, 'Autobiographical Fragments' [1944?], MP/C/100 [b, vii].
[17] Mackinder, 'Autobiographical Fragments' [1944?], MP/C/100 [c, vi], 7; Cantor, 'Mackinder', 4.
[18] Blouet, *Mackinder*, 22.
[19] Dr. Draper Mackinder (1818–1912), Halford's father, was a medical doctor in Gainsborough, a small English market town.

graduated from Oxford.[20] Many of these graduates came back to Oxford for meetings with students and still others were virtually present through anecdote and portrait. This political life resonated with Empire. Mackinder's own college had been home to Richard Hakluyt (1552–1616), the chronicler of British exploration, the last person to hold a post in Geography in the University, and a firm believer that 'geographical knowledge could benefit the State'.[21] With the cathedral of the Diocese of Oxford within its grounds, and as the college of William Gladstone (1809–98), Christ Church was not as strongly associated with militaristic imperialism as was Balliol or All Souls, and Mackinder's tastes took him to the famous debating society, the Oxford Union, where he found redder meat.

The *Oxford Magazine* claimed later (1918) that 'it was at the Oxford Union and from the lips of Milner and Parkin that the doctrine of Imperial Federation was first preached'.[22] George Parkin (1846–1922) came to Oxford for six months in 1873. It was then that he spoke at the Union and befriended Alfred Milner (1854–1925), a stellar student and president of the Union. Parkin later campaigned actively for Imperial Preference among his fellow Canadians and, according to his son-in-law, 'never got God and Oxford and the British Empire wholly separated'.[23] In 1919, Milner would pay tribute to Parkin's 'new vision of the future of the British Empire' for recruiting him to the cause of Empire.[24]

Milner became the political attraction around which many imperialists, including Mackinder, circulated. Milner, like Mackinder, was of relatively modest background compared to many of the luminaries of the Union, such as the wealthy aristocrat, and imperialist, who was president when Mackinder arrived, George Curzon, who once told a fellow undergraduate that: '[t]here has never been anything so great in the world's history as the British Empire'.[25] He thought also that support for the Empire was unavoidable for students of Oxford whose graduates 'have carried its name to the corners of the World and stamped their own on the fabric of imperial grandeur'.[26] Both Curzon and Milner studied Classics and then went into colonial service, imperialist agitation, and, later, British government. Mackinder would follow them into the Union, where he too became President (1883), a signal that he was destined to go far in party politics.

This group of imperialists were to owe much to another Oxford student who, significantly, took little part in the party-political debates of the Union. Cecil Rhodes (1853–1902) was a student intermittently from 1873 to 1881,

[20] Symonds, *Oxford and Empire*, 1. The dominance of British politics by Oxford University continued through the twentieth century; B. Harrison, 'Politics'.

[21] Symonds, *Oxford and Empire*, 141.

[22] Quoted in Symonds, *Oxford and Empire*, 18.

[23] Quoted in Symonds, ibid., 243.

[24] Quoted in Nimocks, *Milner's Young Men*, 13.

[25] Quoted in Symonds, *Oxford and Empire*, 36.

[26] Earl of Ronaldshay, *Curzon 1*, 49.

taken away by ill-health and by his business interests in South Africa. Leo Amery (1873–1955) insisted that Rhodes was strongly affected by the Inaugural Lecture (1870) of John Ruskin (1819–1900) as Oxford's Slade Professor of Fine Art.[27] Ruskin commanded his 'still undegenerate' race:

This is what England must do or perish. She must found Colonies as fast and as far as she is able, formed of her most energetic and worthiest men, seizing every piece she can get her feet on and teaching these Colonists that their chief virtue is to be fidelity to their country, and that, though they live in a distant plot of land, they are no more to consider themselves therefore disenfranchised from their native land than the sailors of her fleet do.[28]

Thoughts of mortality, immortality, and his legacy coalesced around Rhodes' desire to leave something that would serve the Empire. In the first (1877) of many versions of his will, he left what he hoped would be a substantial fortune to found a secret society, after the Jesuits, that would promote, by propaganda and diplomacy, political and economic union both within the Empire and between Britain and the United States.[29] Rhodes died in 1902 and left £4 million in trust for imperial purposes which included, in the public realm, the famous scholarships that brought students from the United States and from the four corners of the British Empire to study at Oxford. His secret diplomacy was not neglected and while Parkin managed the scholarship scheme in the United States and the Empire, and Francis Wylie (1865–1952) did likewise in Oxford, Milner was left free to use the funds in any other way he thought useful.

The historian, Richard Symonds, has argued that a crisis of religious faith led many at Oxford to see the Empire as providential, and secular, work replacing holy orders.[30] As a student of Physical Sciences, Mackinder was at the heart of contemporary intellectual as well as political debate. The Darwinian revolution had been given renewed vigour when, in 1871, Charles Darwin published *The Descent of Man* with its definitive rejection of the literal truth of the story of human creation given in the book of Genesis. Among the Darwinists, H. N. Moseley (1844–91), the Linacre Chair of Comparative Anatomy, was of particular importance to Mackinder. Moseley had been on the Challenger expedition (1872–6) and he published his famous account of it just before Mackinder arrived in his lectures.[31] In suggesting the role of random variation and environmental control in natural selection, Moseley taught that geographical distributions had been central to the Darwinian Revolution. He also lectured on Embryology and Palaeontology

[27] Amery, *My Political Life 1*, 181; but for a sceptical note, see: Rotberg and Shore, *The Founder*, 94–5.

[28] Quoted in Symonds, Oxford and Empire, 26–7.

[29] Amery, *My Political Life 1*, 182.

[30] Symonds, *Oxford and Empire*.

[31] Moseley, *Notes by a Naturalist*.

at the Oxford Museum where he collected human skulls.[32] Moseley inspired
students with reports of new scientific breakthroughs but, thought Mackinder, had 'no sense' of the humanities.[33] Having got his First class honours in
Physical Sciences in 1883, Mackinder then 'persuaded my tutor [...] to let me
take an unusual degree, both [s]cientific and [l]iterary' and he then took up the
question of evolution within human society by studying History and attending classes in Anthropology.[34]

The treatment of evolution within the humanities that Mackinder found at
Oxford was broadly Social Darwinist, and it reinforced the assumptions of
racial inequality upon which rested the Empire, with its separation of self-
governing dominions from directly ruled dependencies. These views stayed
with Mackinder throughout his long life, as I describe in Chapter 3. The
Regius Professor of History during the years Mackinder was studying the
subject was E. A. Freeman (1823–92) whom Mackinder thought well enough
of to quote as an authority in his 'Geographical Pivot' paper some twenty
years later. Freeman was openly racist in a manner extreme even for the time.
He saw the Empire as worthy only as regards the unity of English folk.
He referred to African-Americans as 'great black apes' and 'when asked to
sign a protest against pogroms in Russia, he replied that every nation had the
right to wallop its own Jews'.[35] Presumably, Mackinder also attended
George's lectures on Historical Geography although he has left no record
of what he learned. He did recall the lectures of Edward Tylor (1832–1917)
on Anthropology, 'the science which more and more must be the handmaiden of administration in wide areas of our Empire'.[36] On Moseley's
recommendation, Tylor had been appointed in 1883 to organize the collection of artefacts given to the University by Augustus Pitt Rivers (1827–1900),
and which were used to represent the evolution of tools from one civilizational group to the next. Mackinder's first friend at Oxford, Baldwin Spencer
(1860–1929), continued in Anthropology and much later died in South
America, 'whither he had gone,' said Mackinder, 'to explore the mind of
the degenerate Fuegian Tribe'.[37]

The unorthodox mixture of science and humanities in his undergraduate
degree was not an asset in securing a college fellowship. Attempting the final
Honours examination in History after only one and not three years' study,
Mackinder achieved a creditable second-class result. His brilliance at the
Union suggested a political career but he first needed to earn a living. He
prepared for a legal career and qualified as a barrister but even while doing
this he had begun teaching.

[32] Mackinder, 'Autobiographical Fragments' [1944?], MP/C/100 [c, vi].
[33] Mackinder, ibid., MP/C/100 [c, iv].
[34] Mackinder, ibid., MP/C/100 [b, vii].
[35] Symonds, *Oxford and Empire*, 49.
[36] Mackinder, 'Autobiographical Fragments' [1931], MP/C/100 [b, i], 3.
[37] Mulvaney, 'Spencer'. Mackinder, 'Autobiographical Fragments' [1931], MP/C/100 [b, i], 2.

Mackinder as Educator

At the time Mackinder began to teach, Oxford and Cambridge were suspicious of Geography on three grounds: it was new, it was synthetic (rather than scientific), and it was the handmaiden of war. Mackinder's earliest writings on Geography stressed the study of the shaping of the earth's surface as the determining context for human activity, and in 1905 he claimed that Geography's 'chief subject matter is the control of climates by landscapes, and of landscapes by climates, and the control by both of the environment of living beings'.[38] The emphasis on physical processes was in part an attempt to capitalize upon Mackinder's own standing as a physical scientist at Oxford and to claim respectability for the new science. Thus, to answer critics, Mackinder talked up the scientific, narrowly understood, at the expense of the synthetic, nature of Geography.

From 1885, Mackinder was drawn into the Extension lectures, given under the auspices of the Local Examinations Board of the University of Oxford and intended to bring higher education to people who could not come to Oxford as undergraduate students. In this way, the University showed that it was doing something to discharge the national obligations urged upon it both by some of its own dons and, more ominously, by educational reformers in parliament. Arthur Acland (1847–1926) had run the scheme in the early 1880s but his successor Michael Sadler (1861–1943) relaunched it with more purpose in 1885. By 1892, Acland applauded Sadler with the reflection that 'owing to the popularity of Extension operations there is no demand in the country for reform [of Oxford University]'.[39] Sadler, certainly, claimed that the main purpose of providing lectures to working men was to 'break down the barriers and remove the class feeling and the class prejudice which were such dangerous elements in the present state of society'.[40] The extension of the franchise to working men required that they be educated to exercise it. Merely elementary education gave them the ability to read but exercised little control over how they formed opinions. For this reason, Mackinder and Sadler promoted University Extension not only in technical but also in literary and historical subjects for '[t]he study of national history and national literature cannot fail to inspire patriotism' and 'conduces to sobriety of political judgment'.[41]

Sadler's social conscience had been agitated by hearing Ruskin lecture and, in 1886, he promised one of his first two recruits to University Extension,

---

[38] Quoted in Cantor, 'Mackinder', 253.
[39] Goldman, *Dons and Workers*, 35.
[40] Goldman, ibid., 48.
[41] Mackinder and Sadler, *University Extension*, 142. Like Mackinder, Sadler was the son of a physician and, again like Mackinder, he was elected President of the Oxford Union.

G. W. Hudson Shaw (1859–1944), that the enterprise was 'missionary work on a broad basis welcomed by all sects and classes'.[42] Hudson Shaw was another Ruskin disciple and had followed Mackinder as President of the Union, as Mackinder had followed Sadler. With a second-class degree in History and poorer than Sadler and Mackinder, he was able to take up the work of lecturing only when one of his contemporaries, a fellow student at Balliol, made him an anonymous allowance.[43]

When Sadler was offered direction of the programme in 1885, he was disposed to accept, he told Mackinder, 'if Hudson Shaw and I would be his first lecturers'.[44] By the early 1890s, with 192 courses and 20,000 students, eight times as many people were reached by extension lectures in their towns as attended undergraduate lectures in Oxford. The movement was catholic in topics and lecturers; not only imperialists like Mackinder and William Hewins (1865–1931) taught, but so too did opponents such as John Hobson. The anarchist, Peter Kropótkin, applied to teach as well.[45] Extension lectures opened an educational space for subjects poorly represented within British universities, such as Political Economy.[46] After a trial lecture to 400 workmen at the Rotherham Mechanics' Institute in November 1885, Mackinder gave, at Bath, his first course of six lectures on Political Economy in the winter of 1885–6. In May 1886, his appointment as extension lecturer in Natural Science and Economic History recognized the diversity of his responsibilities and, in the winter of 1886–7, when he returned to Bath, 'I determined to talk on Geography and gave to my course of lectures the title of the New Geography'.[47] Mackinder now specialized in Geography and for the next fifteen years travelled, roughly, 10,000 miles each winter, 'visiting almost every corner of England and gradually familiarising intelligent people throughout the country with the idea that geography consisted neither of lists of names nor of travellers' tales'.[48] The printed syllabus for these lectures reached Francis Galton (1822–1911) and, together with conversations with John Scott Keltie (1840–1927), resulted in an invitation from Henry Walter Bates (1825–92) to present the ideas behind the lectures as a paper for a meeting of the RGS in early 1887. His account of the 'main line of geographical argument' focused the establishment thereafter of British Geography both institutionally and intellectually.[49]

[42] Quoted in Goldman, *Dons and Workers*, 64.
[43] Goldman, *Dons and Workers*, 72.
[44] Mackinder, 'Autobiographical Fragments' [1944?], MP/C/100 [c, vi], 22.
[45] Goldman, *Dons and Workers*, 68–9.
[46] Kadish, *Oxford Economists*.
[47] Mackinder, 'Autobiographical Fragments' [1944?], MP/C/100 [c, vi], 29.
[48] Mackinder, ibid., MP/C/100 [c, vi], 36; see the map of 'Towns in which H. J. Mackinder gave lectures, 1885–1893' in Gilbert, *British Pioneers in Geography*, 143.
[49] Mackinder, *A Syllabus*; idem, 'Scope and Methods', 155. On Bates, see: Dickenson, 'Naturalist on the River Amazons'.

In 1887, with RGS funds, Mackinder was appointed to a five-year Readership in Geography at Oxford but the salary was modest, and so he continued with his Extension lectures.[50] Until 1899, with the establishment of a School of Geography and Mackinder as its Director, there was no qualification available in Geography at Oxford, and even then only a diploma. Mackinder insisted that Geography met 'the practical requirements of the statesman and merchant' but he had no success in persuading the government to include it as a compulsory element in civil service examinations.[51] Geography as taught in 1918 was deemed 'too severe and technical' by the civil service but not rigorous enough by Oxford's science dons for it to accede to the place in the Physical Sciences that Mackinder's successor as Reader, Arthur Herbertson (1865–1915), had been anxious to realize.[52] An Honours degree and a Chair in Geography were created finally in 1933 but Mackinder had long since resigned (1905). Geography at Oxford proved a frustrating business but Mackinder had done his best.

Mackinder trimmed his teaching at Oxford to the flutter of students, shifting the emphasis from physical geography for around a dozen scientists to historical geography for audiences of about 100 historians. He also stayed in close contact with schoolteachers. In each winter from 1893 to 1898, he taught a course in Geography to teachers and pupil-teachers at Gresham College, in the City of London. In 1893, prompted by the suggestion of B. B. Dickson, a teacher at Rugby, to the RGS that a borrowing library of slides would help geographical instruction in schools, Mackinder became involved with the creation of a Geographical Association to support teachers.[53] He organized at Oxford the first ever summer schools for schoolteachers (1903–4), and these in Geography. The temporary Readership at Oxford was renewed for a further five years in 1892 but the RGS refused to continue paying its half after 1897.

With the accession of Clements Markham (1830–1916) to the Presidency of the RGS, the explorers retook the Society after a decade of domination by educationalists. As Chapter 4 describes, in 1898, Mackinder decided to gain his explorer's spurs and prepared the attempt to become the first European to climb the second-highest peak in East Africa, Mount Kenya: '[t]o be generally regarded as the complete geographer it was still necessary at that time for me to prove that I could explore as well as teach'.[54] In the summer of 1899 Mackinder went to Kenya, anxious to use the opportunity of a new railway before any German competitor could likewise steal this head-start on the

---

[50] Mackinder was paid £300 per year, of which the RGS met half; Cantor, 'Mackinder', 109. In contrast, when, to establish Indian Studies at Oxford, a Chair of Sanskrit was endowed in 1832, its annual stipend was £1000; Symonds, *Oxford and Empire*, 103.

[51] Mackinder, 'Scope and Methods', 159.

[52] Currie, 'Arts and Social Studies', 117.

[53] Mackinder, 'Autobiographical Fragments' [1944?], MP/C/100 [c, vi], 44–5.

[54] Mackinder, ibid., MP/C/100 [d, x].

ascent. Having got to the top on 13 September, Mackinder telegraphed news
of his success to Keltie at the International Geographical Congress meeting
in Berlin.[55] Keltie was able to announce the triumph to the Congress at the
start of October for this competitive element was an important part of the
imperial context of the expedition, and in this regard the triumph was both
Britain's and Mackinder's.[56] Mackinder's expedition meant that he missed
the opening of the School of Geography that October, but in climbing the
mountain, and, incidentally, naming such features as Markham Downs, he
had given great satisfaction to the explorers at the RGS and not least to their
President.[57]

Seedlings in University Extension took root more quickly. From 1888,
Oxford hosted about 1,000 students each summer for ten days of short
courses followed by three weeks of more intensive supervised study for
about 150 students.[58] These opportunities were meat and drink to the auto-
didacts among working men and middle-class women excluded from formal
higher education.[59] In 1890, the government allocated funds to local authorities for the purpose of higher education in technical topics and University
Extension became one of the main beneficiaries. The densest networks
of extension courses were organized from regional centres and in 1892 one
of these was converted to an extension college complete with its own class-
rooms. Mackinder was offered a fellowship at his undergraduate college,
Christ Church, on condition that he take on the Principalship of the new
college. Mackinder said he could not do so without a salary beyond the small
stipend of a fellowship and his old tutor at Christ Church, Francis Paget
(1851–1911), organized an anonymous annual benefaction for him.[60] In the
spirit of the technical courses funded by local authorities, an agricultural unit
was attached to Reading in 1893.[61] In 1902, with over 200 full-time students
in addition to its part-time evening students, Reading became a University
College in its own right and in 1903 Mackinder resigned, leaving to others the
challenge of converting the College into a University.[62]

Mackinder wanted to change both the recipients and the content of
education. He identified two main audiences for Geography: the elite and
the masses. For the elite, he proposed that Geography might take the place
that Classics held in the training of an earlier generation for 'eminence in

[55] Mackinder, 'Diary', 246.
[56] Parker, *Mackinder*, 22; 'Expedition to Mount Kenya'. This episode is considered in more detail in
Chapter 4.
[57] Blouet, *Mackinder*, 85.
[58] Mackinder and Sadler, *University Extension*, 77.
[59] Rowbotham, 'Travellers in a Strange Country'. There is no mention of working-class women in
any of the studies of University Extension that I have seen.
[60] Mackinder, 'Autobiographical Fragments' [1931], MP/C/100 [b, i], 5.
[61] Blouet, *Mackinder*, 58.
[62] Blouet, ibid., 69.

Church and State'.[63] Geography, he reflected in 1935, brings together specialist knowledge to discern the spatial pattern behind phenomena. To educate citizens, the pattern of public affairs needed to be laid out so that people could reflect in sober judgement on political matters. Chapter 6 examines the popular Geography he developed in his textbooks and pedagogical writings. At its heart lay the Empire, the dream for which, as the geographer and anthropologist, Herbert Fleure (1877–1969) recalled, Mackinder would 'gladly have sacrificed himself'.[64] In a world of incipient and competing empires, Mackinder saw all political problems as global problems but this message would only reach the masses if it were taught in school, for which was needed schoolteachers trained at university.

This emphasis on applied knowledge was evidenced clearly by his work at the London School of Economics (LSE), the academic institution with which he maintained the longest formal relationship (Figure 2.1).[65] With an appointment as part-time Lecturer in Economic Geography, he was there at the birth of the School in 1895. From 1903 to 1908 he directed the School, and returned to part-time lecturing at £300 per annum from 1908 to 1913. Thereafter, although his salary was doubled, he lectured less frequently, accepting the title of Professor in 1923 and retiring in 1925.[66]

The LSE was set up by Sidney Webb (1859–1947), after a bequest of Henry Hunt Hutchinson (d. 1894) for the promotion of the ideals of Webb's Fabian Society. The School taught social and political sciences to people involved in business and public administration. There was common intellectual purpose at the heart of the LSE. To challenge the laissez-faire economics of the Manchester School, hegemonic in British society from the 1840s to the 1890s, the School promoted a historical, institutional, and state-centric approach to political economy. Against functionalism and individualism, the dogma of free trade and the prohibition on state interference with economy and society was questioned. Mackinder reflected much later that the School set itself to 'the tearing to pieces of the old fashioned classical *a priori* political economy and the foundation of a group of specialists aimed at ascertaining the facts in the first place and then a generalisation from them in a really scientific spirit'.[67]

After the socialist, Graham Wallas (1858–1932), refused the Directorship, it was accepted by the imperialist, and extension lecturer, William Hewins.[68]

---

[63] Mackinder, 'Progress of Geography', 12.

[64] Cantor, 'Mackinder', 325.

[65] He was at the LSE for thirty years (1895–1925), compared to twenty-five at Oxford (1880–1905), and eleven at Reading (1892–1903). Figure 2.1 is a studio portrait from about 1910 and was passed to the LSE from the Fabian Society archives. It is used by kind permission of the Library of the London School of Economics and Political Science.

[66] Cantor, 'Mackinder', 185.

[67] Mackinder, 'Autobiographical Fragments' [1944?], MP/C/100 [c, vi], 66.

[68] Hayek, 'London School of Economics', 4.

Fig. 2.1. Halford Mackinder about 1910

Source: Used by kind permission of the Library of the London School of Economics and Political Science.

This coalition of imperialism and social reform, while unstable in various ways, was at the heart of the movement for National Efficiency, with one side stressing global competition and the other domestic needs.[69] Mackinder and the LSE embraced this cause. At the School, Mackinder was charged with lecturing on 'Applications of Geography to definite Economic and Political Problems'.[70] His earliest classes were on 'the influence of geographical conditions on commercial development and trade routes' and were, no doubt, similar to those he gave to the Institute of Bankers on 'The Great Trade Routes' (see Chapter 5).[71] In 1902, 'Economic and Political Geography' was one of the fourteen sections under which the LSE organized its syllabus.[72]

In 1906, by then Director of the LSE, he was approached by Richard Haldane (1856–1928), then Secretary of State for War, and asked to prepare a six-month course in administration for Army officers, which Mackinder did, covering 'such things as the effect of issuing paper money in a country occupied by an advancing army and the proper method of organising a railway'.[73] Dubbed by some wags, Haldane's Mackindergarten, the course was given successfully each year at the LSE until the start of the First World War, 1914.[74] It brought Mackinder into much closer contact with 'the

[69] Searle, *National Efficiency*.
[70] Cantor, 'Mackinder', 160.
[71] Wise, 'First Half Century', 3; Mackinder, 'Great Trade Routes'.
[72] Hayek, 'London School of Economics', 14.
[73] Mackinder, 'Autobiographical Fragments' [1931], MP/C/100 [b, i], 7.
[74] Parker, *Mackinder*, 35; Hudson, 'New Geography'; Stoddart, 'Geography and War'.

Regular Army, and in the years between 1907 and the outbreak of the First World War, he was on several occasions invited to deliver lectures on Geography and Strategy to military audiences'.[75]

Mackinder, then, wanted to reform society by promoting useful knowledge. In 1935, Mackinder claimed that it was time for science, and perhaps Geography in particular, to take up the task of attaching ethical value to discovery, to thus 'steady the mind of the world', and 'bring science into close relation with the values of life'.[76] Geography should serve, in the main, education and not research and provide 'in the mind of the ordinary man [...] a coherent universe tallying with the concrete Universe around' and in this way guide judgement under the 'governing influence [of] the world pattern'.[77] A study like Geography might make the conclusions of science relevant to the 'philosophy of values' for no subject was 'better fitted than geography to take science right up to the gates of philosophy'.[78]

Mackinder recalled that, at Oxford, Geography had been 'criticised as tending to militarism [and] imperialism, in other words was regarded as incipient Geopolitics (a philosophy rather than a science)—the valuation rather than the measurement of geographical facts—the aim being action and not merely thought'.[79] As understood by Mackinder in 1944, the British would value geographical facts differently than the German geopoliticians (discussed in Chapter 1), since, while they understood that 'the Physical Facts of Geography lent themselves to the development of a world despotism', they would resist such material determinism.[80] They would do so because they supported a rival Empire, 'pledged to the defence of liberty', on the basis of 'ingrained ideas', the 'slow growth of a thousand years', and, in sum, concluded Mackinder in 1916 'the defence of Freedom and Democracy in the world at large must rest finally on the strength and, in the days that are coming, on the instant readiness of the British Empire'.[81]

This commitment to the Empire pulled Mackinder between politics and education despite his best efforts to make them serve each other. In a typical letter to Keltie of 1901, Mackinder promised that he was about to give up some of his many responsibilities for: '[w]hat I want to devote the remainder of my working life to is the modernisation of our English education. It appears to me that the whole future of Britain depends ultimately on this.

---

[75] Cantor, 'Mackinder', 179; for example on 'Geography for Soldiers' to the Royal Military College in October and November 1908; *Times*, 24 October 1908, 10d; *Times*, 22 November 1908, 14a.

[76] Mackinder, 'Progress of Geography', 6, 7.

[77] Mackinder, ibid., 8.

[78] Mackinder, ibid., 11.

[79] Mackinder, 'Autobiographical Fragments' [1944?], MP/C/100 [d, ii], 2.

[80] Mackinder, ibid., MP/C/100 [d, ii], 4.

[81] Mackinder, 'The Constitutional Problem', speech to conference of members of the Home and Dominon parliaments, 1916; Milner Papers, Bodleian Library, University of Oxford, MSS Milner dep. 129; X. Films 9/45, f. 272b, f. 273a.

And for this I required a combined basis of geography, administration, politics and writing'.[82] By 1903, Mackinder became even more deeply involved in politics, and gave up his education work at Reading. At the end of his life, he lamented to his old pupil Percy Roxby (1880–1947), as reported in a later letter by the Oxford geographer, Edmund Gilbert (1900–73), that 'he was sorry he did not stick to Geography alone throughout his career, and that he regretted dropping it, at any rate partially, for politics, in or about 1905. It seems that he made it quite clear to Fleure that he wishes he had remained wholly a geographer'.[83] Nevertheless, the cause that took him away from education was the one that was also at the core of his academic mission, the Empire.

Mackinder, the Politician and Economist

In 1916, Mackinder recalled that '[a]s a student fresh from Oxford I threw myself into the 1886 Election' and claimed that he had 'all my life long been consistently a Unionist', believing that Ireland should not separate from Britain, and that, the Union of Britain and Ireland was necessary both to prevent 'tyranny in Ireland by one religion or another' and to ensure that 'Ireland shall in no case be other than true to the Empire'.[84] Gladstone had declared himself in favour of Irish Home Rule in 1885 and this had prompted a group to leave his Liberal Party and identify themselves as a separate group of Liberal Unionists. The Conservatives also declared against Home Rule. Mackinder spent part of the summer of 1886 back home in Gainsborough campaigning for the election of the Conservative Colonel Henry Eyre (1834– 1904), primarily on the policy of opposing Home Rule for Ireland.[85] The religious dimension of Home Rule no doubt meant a lot to a young man whose father was Master of the Gainsborough Lodge of the Freemasons, and Mackinder said frankly that '[t]he Protestants among us fear the pretensions of the Roman Church'.[86] For Mackinder, Empire was placed above the wishes of the Irish people. This matter of imperial unity first brought Mackinder into politics.

---

[82] Mackinder to Keltie, 2 March 1901, Royal Geographical Society [RGS] Archives. Mackinder Correspondence.

[83] Gilbert to Robert Aitken, 1 March 1962, Mackinder Papers, School of Geography, University of Oxford.

[84] *The Official Report, House of Commons, 5th Series* [*Hansard 5th*], 84 (31 July 1916), 2211.

[85] Blouet, *Mackinder*, 141; Cantor, 'Mackinder', 11.

[86] Mackinder to Edmund Dawber, 28 December 1946, Gilbert Papers, School of Geography, Oxford University; *Hansard 5th*, 84 (31 July 1916), 2214. Mackinder treated the religious divide in Ireland as a racial one and consistently opposed Home Rule as a naked attempt to allow the Catholic race to dominate the Protestant (see the discussion of race in the following chapter).

The Empire was strongly associated with Disraeli's Conservatism, the new Liberal Unionists, and also a large group that remained within the Liberal Party. From 1886 to 1892, the President of the Imperial Federation League was Lord Rosebery (Archibald Primrose, 1847–1929), 'the outstanding British spokesman for imperial unity', and a senior member of the Liberal Party.[87] Some Liberals, such as James Bryce (1838–1922) who was chair of the Oxford branch, may have joined, as Bryce said, just to keep the League 'out of Tory hands', but for others the Empire dominated their politics.[88] The League foundered in 1893 on the issue of free trade with some traditional Liberals unwilling to consider its repudiation even in the cause of imperial union. Beyond this, there were many Liberals with a strong aversion to foreign entanglements that might threaten world peace. They were derided as Little Englanders by the imperialists.

In 1900, at the height of the South African [Boer] War, a 'khaki' election was called, turning essentially on support for the war. Rosebery led a section of the Liberal Party, identified as Liberal Imperialist, that viewed the Liberal Party leadership as too conciliatory towards the Boers. This was the first election in which Mackinder was a candidate and it is significant that he stood as a Liberal Imperialist, indicating clearly his fidelity to Empire. He told his electors that he was a Liberal because:

I believe that no other party is sufficiently free to achieve the security of our federal Empire. Without that Empire, little England, however true to herself, would soon be less safe when confronted by the military powers, the rapidly developing resources of whose vast territories will presently enable them to build fleets. No other course is open to us than to bind Britain and her colonies into a league of democracies, defended by a united Navy and an efficient Army.[89]

This was pure Rosebery in its attack on Little England. It was also typical in the vague reference to a democratic Empire, which Mackinder and his auditors would have understood as including the self-governing Dominions, excluding their indigenous peoples. In 1911, he was clear that he intended a 'truly Imperial Government' as 'in some way representative of all the Britains'.[90]

Mackinder lost the 1900 election at Warwick-and-Leamington to a Conservative with very similar pro-War views. In 1902, he was offered but did not take the opportunity to stand for the College Division constituency of Glasgow, confiding to his diary: 'Ludicrous position—in debt and coquetting with Parliament'.[91] He was by now an important figure among young

[87] Jacobson, 'Rosebery and Liberal Imperialism', 84.
[88] Bryce to E. A. Freeman, 24 December 1886; quoted in Kendle, *Colonial and Imperial Conferences*, 3.
[89] Cantor, 'Mackinder', 26–7.
[90] Quoted in Parker, *Mackinder*, 69.
[91] Quoted in Cantor, 'Mackinder', 27. The debt was 'owing to the action of the Foreign Office in exacting reimbursement of the cost of the two expeditions which though I did not ask for were sent to

Liberals and he was involving himself directly in the public advocacy of imperial causes, given renewed spirit by the Boer War. In 1901, he joined the new Victoria League, an organization, primarily of women, that 'hoped to link the self-governing dominions to the "mother country" by the organization of imperial "sentiment" against the rising tide of colonial nationalism'.[92] When, in 1907, the League decided to admit men to its executive, Mackinder was invited. He spoke frequently for the League although not always with the excitement of his 1914 talk to the Industrial Syndicalist Education League when he had 'to contend not only with "a somewhat cynical reception" but also with "a small bomb"'.[93] The League was one of many organizations that promoted education to improve mutual understanding among (British) people in different parts of the Empire, drawing Mackinder further into this work by employing him in 1902 'to give [ten] lectures in large towns at £10 a lecture'.[94] Their most ambitious scheme, the production of slide lectures for diffusion through the Empire, was unsuccessful in its application to the Rhodes Trust, but something very similar was soon after promoted by the Visual Instruction Committee of the Colonial Office, for which Mackinder was retained (1907–9) to write the lectures and direct the taking of appropriate slides illustrating the Empire.[95]

Mackinder was an activist in the interlinked fields of education and in politics. As an educationalist he was recruited to the LSE and thus broadened his political connections. In a draft of his autobiography, he recalled that after one of his evening lectures the politician, Haldane, the playwright, George Bernard Shaw (1856–1950), and Shaw's wife, Charlotte (1859–1943), turned up and took him out to dinner.[96] These were heady days. In the summer of 1901 he was working on *Britain and the British Seas* 'at a farmhouse in Gloucestershire and there I came into contact with Mr. and Mrs. Sidney Webb who were also in rustic quarters at literary work'.[97] The next summer, again in Gloucestershire, Mackinder went cycling around the countryside with the Webbs, visiting churches and he recalls that this was when Beatrice Webb (1858–1943) 'said that she had a number of friends who she thought should meet and indeed she proposed that they should form a Dining Club together[. S]he would be present at the first dinner to which she would invite them all and afterwards would retire, the days of the equality of women had not yet arrived'.[98] Thus was born the Coefficients, originally intended as a brains trust for the interventionist causes of imperialism

my relief at Kenya'; Mackinder, 'Autobiographical Fragments' [1944?], MP/C/100 [c, vi], 73; see Chapter 4.

92   Riedi, 'Victoria League', 573.
93   Riedi, ibid., 578.
94   Greenlee, 'Imperial Studies'; Riedi, 'Victoria League', 589.
95   Ryan, 'Visualizing Imperial Geography'; see Chapter 6.
96   Mackinder, 'Autobiographical Fragments' [1944?], MP/C/100 [c, vi], 66.
97   Mackinder, ibid., MP/C/100 [c, vi], 65.
98   Mackinder, ibid., MP/C/100 [c, vi], 67.

and social reform, but fairly soon a mere dining club where the divisions between social reform and imperialism were played out. Mackinder's position was evident to all. The dinners started in November 1902 with twelve people selected for their specific expertise and, in the report of Leopold Amery, these included: Amery for the Army, Carlyon Bellairs (1871–1955) for the Navy, Clinton Dawkins (1859–1905) for finance, Edward Grey (1862–1933) for foreign policy, Haldane for Law, Hewins for Economics, Leo Maxse (1864–1932) for journalism, Walter Pember Reeves (1857–1932) for the colonial point of view, Bertrand Russell (1872–1970) for Science, Sidney Webb for municipal affairs, and H. G. Wells (1866–1946) for literature.

Amery recorded Mackinder's specialism as 'active Liberal Imperialism'.[99] And active he was. Wells wrote that the liberalism of himself, Reeves, and Russell was deflated by the pragmatism of Maxse, Bellairs, Hewins, Amery, and Mackinder, 'all stung by the small but humiliating tale of disasters in the South African war' and 'profoundly alarmed by the naval and military aggressiveness of Germany'.[100] On the report of Beatrice Webb, Russell thought Mackinder 'brutal' and left the club after one bruising exchange in which 'Hewins, Amery and Mackinder declared themselves fanatical devotees of the Empire'.[101] The Webbs were trying to make an alliance between Liberal Unionists and Liberal Imperialists in favour of projects of social reform but in 1903 Joseph Chamberlain fractured these alliances along the same issue that had earlier broken the Imperial Federation League: protectionism.

From 1895 to 1903, Chamberlain brought to the office of Colonial Secretary immense political prestige and fierce commitment to Empire. He was sure that the 'Anglo Saxon race [was ...] destined to be the predominating force in the future history and civilization of the world' and that this meant bringing the 'great independencies of the British Empire into one supreme and Imperial Parliament', the 'ideal future of the British race'.[102] Chamberlain realized that the demand for imperial union would have to come from the parliaments of the self-governing Dominions and when his proposal for taxation for imperial defence was rejected at the 1902 Colonial Conference, he concluded that union required that the Dominions see the relationship as of immediate commercial benefit. For this reason, he began in 1903 to advocate imperial preference and thought he had persuaded the Conservative Cabinet to make a beginning by retaining the wartime tax on imports of corn against all countries but the Dominions and Dependencies of the British Empire. When, in his absence, the decision was reversed and the Cabinet agreed to a budget that removed the corn tariff entirely, Chamberlain resigned as Colonial Secretary and devoted himself full-time to a crusade

---

[99] Amery, *My Political Life 1*, 224.   [100] Quoted in Parker, *Mackinder*, 31.

[101] Blouet, *Mackinder*, 134; Cantor, 'Mackinder', 34.

[102] Speeches of 1887, 1886, and 1895, respectively; quoted in Kendle, *Colonial and Imperial Conferences*, 20.

for imperial preference. He set up a Tariff Commission to 'provide a scientific basis' for his belief that protection would not destroy British industry.[103]

On 15 May 1903, Chamberlain's explosive declaration in favour of tariff protection for the Empire challenged all sectors of British politics. Some of the Liberal Imperialists were excited and began working for Chamberlain. At precisely this moment, Mackinder announced he would resign from Reading, citing a wish to move into politics.[104] Amery organized a group of Liberal Imperialists and Conservatives, the Stafford House Group, to work on Chamberlain's campaign and drafted for publication in the *Times* a letter supporting Chamberlain's position. It was published on 21 July 1903 urging that tariff protection was 'no longer a matter of possible expediency, but rather one of urgent national necessity', and Mackinder was one of the Liberal Imperialists who signed it.[105] Amery was anxious that the new Tariff Reform League should 'secure a first rate organizing secretary, someone who had the necessary imagination and drive, but who also had a complete grasp of the economic and imperial case we were out to preach. Precisely the right man was available in the shape of Mackinder whom I persuaded to offer his services'.[106] Certainly Mackinder was thrilled at the prospect, writing to Benjamin Kidd (1858–1916), who had also signed Amery's letter, of: '[g]ood *private* news. Hewins will join the Committee if I am Sec[retary]. He proposes going straight to Chamberlain to ask him to intervene. All this quite private. I am now going to Amery to ask him to meet Hewins tonight'.[107] But Mackinder did not become Secretary since the editor of the *Daily Express*, Arthur Pearson (1866–1921), was willing to proselytize for the movement in his paper only if he were Chair of the League and could have as Secretary someone pliable to his will. Amery thought this a disaster for, without Mackinder (and Amery), 'the sheer intellectual and historical case against Free Trade was never made with sufficient vigour and persistency or on a sufficient scale'.[108] Hewins took the post of Secretary to Chamberlain's investigatory Tariff Reform Commission and resigned the Directorship of the LSE on 18 November. Recommended by Haldane and Bernard Shaw, Mackinder took Hewins' place at the LSE in December 1903.[109]

Mackinder was committed to the Tariff Reform League for the full twenty years of its existence and, indeed, resigned from the Liberal Party in October 1903 so that he could work more openly with Chamberlain, a

---

[103] Hayek, 'London School of Economics', 15.

[104] Blouet notes a report in the *Berkshire Chronicle* of 16 May 1903; Blouet, *Mackinder*, 69. This is some months before the Directorship of the LSE was a possibility.

[105] *Times*, 21 July 1903, 5f.

[106] Amery, *My Political Life 1*, 238–9.

[107] Mackinder to Kidd, [n.d., but almost certainly August 1903]; Cambridge University Library, Benjamin Kidd Correspondence and Papers, Add. MS 8069, M49.

[108] Amery, *My Political Life 1*, 239–40. Amery argued that case against Free Trade in: Amery, *Fundamental Fallacies*.

[109] Mackinder, 'Autobiographical Fragments' [1931], MP/C/100 [b, i], 7.

Conservative.[110] This was a significant move for, as Amery recalled, Mackinder was 'at the time regarded as a coming man in the [Liberal] Party'.[111] It was largely on Amery's persuasion that Mackinder decided to join, what Amery presented as, 'a great Imperial movement which might revivify the whole of our political and social life'.[112] Chapter 5 shows how Mackinder's geopolitical views were shaped by the combination of imperialism, protectionism, and social reform that defined Chamberlain's initial vision, but as Chamberlain developed further his propaganda against free trade, several of his supporters thought that the needs of British industry and agriculture were throwing into the shade those of Empire.[113]

To keep the Empire to the fore, a group came together as the Compatriots and, in January 1904, Mackinder was among the small group Amery invited to dine with him to discuss the new society.[114] The Compatriots grew to include over 100 members and Mackinder gave several lectures at meetings organized under their auspices, as in 1907 when he spoke on Canada and imperial preference.[115] In November 1905, Chamberlain floated with Amery the possibility of finding Mackinder a seat to fight as Conservative candidate in the forthcoming election, but, as Blouet notes, 'nothing came of the matter'.[116] A page surviving from Mackinder's diary lists some of his work during the election of January 1906.[117] In the first week he revised an article on 'Money-Power and Man-Power' for publication as a pamphlet and on the next three successive days he spoke in support of Arthur Steel-Maitland (1876–1935) at Rugby, Amery at Wolverhampton, and Alfred Lyttleton (1857–1913) at Leamington. The Conservatives lost the election of 1906 so Mackinder had left his colleagues in the Liberal Party just as they were coming into government.

It is likely that Mackinder felt he could not afford to give up the LSE to try for Parliament in 1906. When given a realistic opportunity to give up his principal education commitment to serve the Empire in politics, Mackinder did not hesitate. The opportunity came in 1908 from Milner via Amery. Milner had discretionary use of the funds of the Rhodes Trust and he was also assiduous in soliciting other private funds for imperial purposes. In 1893, Milner had raised private funds to support Parkin's work beyond the collapse of the Imperial Federation League in that year.[118] When, in February 1897 Milner was appointed Governor of the Cape Colony and High Commissioner to South Africa, he recruited to assist him young men from Oxford whose salaries were paid 'from an anonymous source' so that they

---

[110] Blouet, *Mackinder*, 119.   [111] Amery, *My Political Life 1*, 224.
[112] Amery, ibid., 224.   [113] A. Thompson, 'Tariff Reform'.
[114] Amery, ibid., 264–5.   [115] *Times*, 1 December 1907, 9b.
[116] Blouet, *Mackinder*, 143.
[117] Mackinder, 'Autobiographical Fragments' [page from diary, attached to copy of pamphlet, *Money-power and Man-power*], MP/C/100 [b, ii].
[118] Nimocks, *Milner's Young Men*, 14.

held office 'directly responsible to himself, with no rank in the official hierarchy'.[119] These young men, Milner's kindergarten, were at the heart of campaigns for imperial union hereafter. When he was made a peer in 1901, Milner chose as his motto 'Communis Patria' and this was the origin of the title of the club of imperialists that Amery formed in 1904.[120]

Mackinder recalled that '[a]t the time of the [Colonial] Conference of [1907] the Compatriots were especially active. We entertained at dinner this time among others Mr. [Deakin] the eloquent Prime Minister of Australia'.[121] Alfred Deakin (1856–1919) was in favour of closer imperial union and, like Milner and Amery, thought that the occasional Colonial Conferences (1887, 1897, 1902, 1907) might form the focus for imperial institutions if they were sustained by a 'permanent secretariat' independent of the British Colonial Office.[122] The conservatism of the British civil service and the fierce independence of the Canadians scotched these plans and the Conference merely agreed to meet again in four years and leave the interim administration to the British Colonial Office, widely recognized as having neither the capacity nor the temerity to bring forward proposals for dramatic political or economic union. At this point, Milner and Amery decided that the Compatriots would have to work as an independent secretariat to prepare the way for the next Conference and Mackinder was given his chance to give up education.

In October 1907, and from Rhodes Trust funds, Milner arranged for Amery to be paid £300 per quarter to work establishing Compatriot groups in South Africa. In February 1908, Amery approached Mackinder 'to go into politics and to join in the Imperial Secretariat work'.[123] Mackinder was willing to 'give myself to the Cause of Empire [... and] would do so on [...] condition that the money was not derived from Party funds for I had no desire to become a party hack'.[124] Amery told him that the funds would be anonymous, non-partisan, and administered by Milner as guarantor of probity and independence.[125] Mackinder was 'to devote myself to further to the best of my ability the cause of imperial unity generally, more especially in connexion with the forthcoming Imperial conference'.[126] He would receive £850 per annum for four years. On this basis, Mackinder resigned the Directorship of the LSE and sought a place in Parliament. He went first to promote the Compatriot policy in Canada and when he came back gave

---

[119] Symonds, *Oxford and Empire*, 63.

[120] Nimocks, *Milner's Young Men*, 146.

[121] Mackinder, 'Autobiographical Fragments' [1944?], MP/C/100 [c, vi], 76. I have corrected some spelling mistakes and errors of date in these fragments, which were likely dictated to his sister-in-law and not checked by Mackinder. I place my corrections in square brackets.

[122] Kendle, *Colonial and Imperial Conferences*, 92.

[123] Amery to Milner, 30 March 1908; quoted in Kendle, *Colonial and Imperial Conferences*, 127.

[124] Mackinder, 'Autobiographical Fragments' [1944?], MP/C/100 [c, vi], 76.

[125] In fact Amery was one of the contributors at £250 per year along with Violet Markham, who knew Mackinder through the Victoria League, and three others; Kendle, *Colonial and Imperial Conferences*, 127.

[126] Mackinder to Amery, 22 May 1908, Milner Papers, dep.34, X. Films 9/5, f. 156.

many lectures on the challenges facing those, like himself, who would bind Canada more tightly into the Empire.

In 1909, Mackinder stood as a Unionist in a by-election in Hawick Burghs, in southern Scotland near the border with England. He lost. The victorious Liberal campaigned on free trade and Mackinder had to be satisfied with the *Times*' observation that 'tariff reform has never been more thoroughly expounded before a democratic constituency'.[127] Mackinder was unrepentant and continued to press the policy of protection 'for upon this question, he ventured to say, the future of their country and this Empire depended'.[128] Mackinder was consistent in this view that protection served the Empire and not merely the needs of domestic industry and agriculture, insisting in 1913 that 'the tariff is but the flag by which we know what we believe to be the one and only possible Imperial policy.'[129] In the General Election of January 1910, Mackinder was successful as Unionist candidate for the Camlachie constituency of the Glasgow docklands, where his imperialism mattered on two counts: first, because his opposition to Home Rule for Ireland pleased the ultra-Protestants of the city; and, second, because his support for militarization in the face of German competition promised work for the naval shipyards. As they had in 1906, the Liberals again won the election in 1910 and Mackinder entered the House of Commons as a member of the opposition.

Classical Liberal doctrines of Irish Home Rule, global free trade, and world peace were anathema to Mackinder. On Home Rule, he assured the House of Commons that there were 'only two courses open with regard to Ireland. They could pass legislation which would give prosperity and peace to Ireland, or they could hand Ireland over to the Irish'.[130] He was equally blunt on tariffs, believing free trade required access to markets and that this was only retained by the threat of using force against rivals who would close access. Free trade thus rested upon taxation for the navy. For Mackinder, negotiation with commercial rivals meant having either tariff barriers to barter with, or ships to batter with: '[w]e hold the road to India by fleet power, by adequate fleet power. [And thus w]e hold the markets of Lancashire at the present moment, not by one form of Protection, but by another, and at least as costly'.[131] He was adamant that the world was turned by force not virtue. In proposing a toast to the 'Armed Forces' at a dinner in Glasgow he praised them as needed at home, 'to maintain order in the presence of industrial strife' and abroad as the 'force [that] was behind our diplomacy'.[132] Discharging his obligations to Milner, he tried to pressure

[127] *Times*, 6 March 1909, 12c.   [128] *Times*, ibid., 12c.
[129] Quoted in Thackeray, 'Tariff Reform League', 54.
[130] *Times*, 3 May 1912, 14d.
[131] *Hansard 5th*, 14 (23 February 1910), 322.
[132] *Glasgow Herald*, 12 October 1911; clipping in Mackinder Papers, School of Geography, University of Oxford, MP/C/200, 'Family Letters, Newspaper Cuttings', [i].

the Colonial Office to prepare adequately for the future Imperial Conference of 1911, but it did not.[133]

The Tariff Reform campaign ran out of steam in the years just before the First World War as proponents of a focus on the Empire drifted away from those concentrating on the needs of British producers. Many of the more radical imperialists left but Mackinder stayed. The imperialists worked increasingly through the Round Table, a new group formed around the group of young men that Milner had invited out to South Africa to help him with his administration.[134] In 1911, Mackinder went into business with, in the brief note of his schematic autobiography, 'Lord Selborne, Peddie etc.'[135] This may be the reason why he stayed with the Tariff Reform League as it became focused increasingly on the needs of British industry, becoming President (to Austen Chamberlain's [1863–1937] Chair) of the rump left after the split of 1917.[136]

Mackinder was, however, far from finished with Empire. During the First World War, he was, at Haldane's suggestion, employed by Alfred Kitchener to organize recruiting in Scotland (1915) and, on his own report, later started the scheme of National Savings (1916) that, again, he promoted in Scotland.[137] In December 1916, the Liberal government was replaced by a Coalition under David Lloyd George. Several Conservative imperialists, such as Milner, were gathered in to government and Mackinder wrote immediately to his old friend in terms that suggest he knew the imperialist investment in his career in 1908 had not yielded the expected fruit:

Will you allow me to offer you my services for any special purpose whenever you like to command them? I feel that you have a right to them. It is still in me to do better than I have yet done, [and] I would like to do it for you. [. . .] I would go on any mission for you either continuously or on occasion.[138]

Although the War Cabinet of five also included Curzon, the call to serve did not come. Mackinder was not even included when Amery brought 'together a research staff to work up all the information that could be conceivably required about any country' when it came to the eventual negotiation of the terms for post-war Peace.[139] He was, however, one of the two secretaries of the British Section of the Inter-Allied Parliamentary Committee, a group

[133] *Hansard 5th*, 17 (29 June 1910), 925, 977–83.
[134] Gorman, 'Lionel Curtis'.
[135] Mackinder, 'Autobiographical Fragments' [1944?], MP/C/100 [d, i]; there is an account of Mackinder's business interests in Blouet, *Mackinder*, 154–5.
[136] Thackeray, 'Tariff Reform League', 58.
[137] Mackinder, 'Autobiographical Fragments' [1931], MP/C/100 [b, i], 9, 11; *Times*, 2 November 1915, 9d; *Times*, 9 February 1916, 8b.
[138] Mackinder to Milner, 11 December 1916, Milner Papers dep.353, X. Films 9/159, f. 178.
[139] Amery, *My Political Life 2*, 103. Martha Woolley claimed that 'Mackinder had accompanied the British Delegation to Versailles in the capacity of advisor' ('Philosophy of Mackinder', 258) but I can find no other corroboration of this, although he was in and out of Paris on work for the inter-parliamentary committee, and the British team sent to the peace talks numbered some 400 (Macmillan,

of MPs corresponding on the terms for peace with parliamentarians initially from France and later also from Italy. The British committee included members nominated by the whips of each party. After the war, Lloyd George, the British Prime Minister, asked Mackinder and his associate, Charles Henry (1860–1919), to continue their work, for the Committee had 'rendered very useful services during the war in promoting good understanding with Allied Parliaments'.[140] This was a relatively minor contribution given the ambition of Mackinder's academic interest in questions of war and peace, as explained first in a 1917 article and then in a book.[141]

Alongside the reconstruction of Europe, Britain's politicians were also concerned with Britain's role beyond Europe. I will discuss this in Chapter 7, which focuses on Mackinder's most dramatic imperial mission, his period as High Commissioner to South Russia, 1919–20. In all sorts of ways, Bolshevik Russia was an affront to British imperialism. Under Bolshevik rule, the Russians had sued for peace with Germany leaving Britain's enemy to concentrate all its forces upon its Western front. There were also strategic issues relating both to the oilfields of the Caspian basin and to the security of the overland route to India. Consequently, in the final months of the war, Britain had moved troops into nominally independent Russia in order to reopen an Eastern front against Germany. While bringing troops home from most of the former theatres of war, Winston Churchill and Curzon conspired to displace the Bolshevik regime and secure British influence in the lands called, at the time, the Middle East. Vast quantities of weapons were supplied to the anti-Bolshevik forces and in late 1919 Mackinder was sent to South Russia as High Commissioner to take a broadly political and strategic, and not just military, view of the matter. By the time he arrived, the White Russian army was in retreat and his mission was quickly aborted.

He returned, however, to the consolation of a knighthood, the disappointment of losing his seat at the 1922 election, and, finally, the satisfaction of some imperial work for government as Chair of the Imperial Shipping Committee. Although the periodic Imperial and Colonial Conferences had not evolved into a permanent organ of imperial administration, after the inadequacies of the administration of the Boer War, an ad hoc Committee of Imperial Defence had been set up (1902) to advise the British Cabinet on integrating the Military throughout the Empire. This model of the non-executive committee, that sought a common view and then merely recommended action to sovereign governments, was acceptable to both the conservatives in the civil service and to the nationalists in the Dominions.[142]

Peacemakers, 53), so that it is possible, despite Mackinder never mentioning it in his published or unpublished writings, that he advised in some capacity or other.

[140] Lloyd George to Henry and Mackinder, 19 February 1919, Bryce Papers, Bodleian Library, University of Oxford, Bryce MSS 83, f. 120.

[141] Mackinder, 'Some Geographical Aspects'; *idem, Democratic Ideals and Reality*.

[142] Johnson, *Defence by Committee*.

Amery reported that the Committee of Imperial Defence had performed wonderfully in coordinating military specialization before, and collective action during, the First World War, ensuring victory through the 'immense contribution of every part of the Empire to the common effort'.[143] After the First World War, it was extended from defence to commerce with the appointment of an Imperial Shipping Committee that Mackinder chaired from 1920 to 1939. The Committee took evidence and considered shipping questions referred to it by the governments of the Dominions. It met frequently, sixty times in its first three years according to Mackinder's report to the Imperial Economic Conference of 1923.[144] It made unanimous recommendations on issues such as the basis for insurance rates, necessary improvements for harbours in different parts of Empire, and ways of harmonizing dockyard and shipping practices throughout the British Empire. It was also a way of regulating competition between shipping companies.[145] Mackinder was proud of this quiet work that promoted greater understanding and a sense of common purpose within the Empire.

Mackinder's friend, Leo Amery, was Colonial Secretary during the Imperial Economic Conference of 1923, which 'blessed the work of Mackinder's Imperial Shipping Committee and [...] decided on setting up an Imperial Economic Committee to consider economic and commercial problems submitted to it by any of the Governments concerned'.[146] Mackinder was approached to be its Chair, as he wrote in delight and even relief to Milner:

Fifteen years ago you were good enough to become Trustee of a fund which carried me into public life. The one consideration was that I was to work in the interest of the Empire. The War came before I had secured my footing and I had to serve in such ways as were open to me, some of them uncongenial. Fate seems at last to have put me in a position in complete harmony with what was intended.[147]

It took two years for the Committee to materialize and Mackinder directed it until it was pared back as part of the cuts in government departments during the depression in 1931. Already in 1923, Mackinder referred to the Imperial Shipping Committee as an '[i]mperial instrument of government' and in 1925 as part of an experiment in imperial co-operation 'which I sometimes dream may prove to be the seed of great things in the British Empire'.[148] Mackinder's dream of an imperial parliament directing the economy and defences of a united empire did not come to pass.

[143] Amery, *My Political Life 2*, 33.
[144] *Times*, 18 October 1923, 7c.
[145] Marx, *International Shipping Cartels*.
[146] Amery, *My Political Life 2*, 277.
[147] Mackinder to Milner, 15 November 1923, Milner Papers, dep. 34, X. Films 9/24, f. 76.
[148] *Times*, 3 February 1923, 12d; Mackinder, 'English Tradition', 729.

Mackinder and Geopolitics

In his last years, Mackinder was made aware that his ideas about Empires were being taken up anew. Significantly, this news came to him from the United States and significantly too, it was in Germany that his ideas had renewed currency. On 28 July 1941, Mackinder met in London, the journalist, Dorothy Thompson, who had just published in the *New York Post* (23 July 1941) an article about Haushofer and German war aims as 'fulfilling the warnings of the great British geopolitical scientist Sir Halford John Mackinder'.[149] The next year, Mackinder was writing to Arthur Hinks (1873–1945) at the RGS asking for a copy of his own 1904 paper on 'The Geographical Pivot of History' so that he might send it to Hans Weigert who was publishing a book on Geopolitics in which he 'proposes—so he tells me—to make an important element in his treatment of that subject a discussion of the fundamental difference between Haushofer's way of thinking and mine'.[150] In April 1942, Mackinder wrote again to Hinks with news that *Democratic Ideals and Reality*, was to be republished in the United States and he remarked that: 'Haushofer based himself originally on the "Pivot", but it has become clear to me that I have, with my own eyes, only seen a part, and perhaps a small part, of what he has perverted to his wicked uses from my work!'[151] In July, Mackinder thanked Hinks for the summary of Mackinder's 'Pivot' paper contained in the editorial material in the latest issue of the *Geographical Journal* and commented further on the enthusiasm for his old work in the contemporary United States: '[w]hat an extraordinary folk they are over there! However it seems to be thought that I can shake them out of provincialism into globosity! So it is my duty to play the part. Sea-power in jeopardy apparently goes home to them, and an octogenarian is privileged indeed if a war use has been found for him in propaganda'.[152]

The next year, Mackinder wrote to an American correspondent: 'you ask whether I am aware that controversy is raging over my book on the other side of the ocean. No, I am not aware of any such thing. On what points does the controversy turn, and who are the parties of the debate?'[153] In that same year, Mackinder was induced by the American journal, *Foreign Affairs*, to return once again to his geopolitical ideas.[154] In November of 1943, Isaiah Bowman wrote to him that the American Geographical Society proposed awarding Mackinder its Charles P. Daly medal for a life 'filled with services

---

[149] Mackinder, 'Note on a meeting with Dorothy Thompson' [1941], MP/C/100 [b, v].
[150] Mackinder to Hinks, 30 March 1942, RGS Archives, Mackinder Correspondence. Weigert later that year published *Generals and Geographers*.
[151] Mackinder to Hinks, 23 April 1942, RGS Archives, Mackinder Correspondence.
[152] Mackinder to Hinks, 11 July 1942, RGS Archives, Mackinder Correspondence.
[153] Mackinder, Letter to American 1943, MP/C/100 [c, i].
[154] Mackinder, 'Round World'.

to geography that can fairly be described as unique' and, in particular for 'your courage and foresight in publishing "Democratic Ideals and Reality" at a time when the world in general was beguiling itself with the thought that we had concluded a war to end war'.[155] Mackinder, by now 83, received the medal at the American Embassy in London in April 1944 and began his reply to the Ambassador by referring to his current notoriety:

I am grateful to you, in the first place, for the testimony you have borne to my loyalty to democracy, since absurd as it may seem I have been criticized in certain quarters as having helped to lay the foundation of Nazi militarism. It has, I am told, been rumoured that I inspired Haushofer, who inspired Hess, who in turn suggested to Hitler while he was dictating 'Mein Kampf' certain geo-political ideas which are said to have originated with me. Those are three links in a chain, but of the second and third I know nothing. This however I do know from the evidence of his own pen that whatever Haushofer adapted from me he took from an address I gave before the Royal Geographical Society just forty years ago, long before there was any question of a Nazi Party.[156]

Mackinder was embarrassed by the resonance of his ideas in contemporary Germany. To understand why he had, and would have again during the Cold War, such direct influence on Geopolitics in its relation to the clash of empires, I turn, now, from the biographical details of a life shaped by Empire to the writings themselves.

---

[155] Bowman to Mackinder, 24 November 1943, copy in Mackinder to Hinks, 15 January 1944; RGS Archives, Mackinder Correspondence.
[156] 'Monthly Record'.

3

Making Space for Darwin

'What is Geography', asked Mackinder in an important lecture to the Royal Geographical Society (RGS), in 1887. The question demanded an immediate answer both because the RGS wanted a more prominent place for Geography in the halls of science, and because the fame of the RGS as a place of exciting talks by returning explorers must surely soon wane as 'we are now near the end of the roll of great discoveries'.[1] The subject had been little more than an inventory of the earth and in this form it had excited adults with tales of derring-do vouchsafed by dangerous experience at the very limits of the known world, and bored schoolchildren with endless lists to memorize of capes and bays, mountains and rivers.[2] Geography now needed a newly scientific and useful identity. Exploration, in fact, had not only extended the known world, but had transformed understandings of life itself.

Geographical reasoning was central to the Darwinian revolution in the Life Sciences. According to Mackinder, it was time, now, to turn the same attention to social and economic questions and, in particular, to the challenges facing an imperial people. Mackinder was among many scholars who directed Darwinian Biology towards the study of society. The extension was easy to imagine and the subtitle ('The Preservation of Favoured Races in the Struggle for Life') of Darwin's *Origin of Species* invited it.[3] Herbert Spencer (1820–1903) was only one of the most effective of these many Social Darwinists.[4] Spencer popularized the term, 'survival of fittest', and he also identified the essentially contestable concepts that allowed the lessons of Biology to be taught to society. He recognized that geographical arguments were central to evolutionary reasoning: '[t]here is a distribution of organisms in Space, and there is a distribution of organisms in Time'.[5] With these three dimensions of time, space, and organism, Spencer set out the arguments for believing in evolution. For Spencer, the temporal dimension highlighted the coming and going of distinct organisms as environments changed, while the distributions in space suggested that organisms competed with others for resources by expanding into as much of a suitable niche as they could. The human parallel

---

[1] Mackinder, 'Scope and Methods', 141.
[2] The ideological selection of the places worth memorizing is stressed by: Marsden, 'All in a Good Cause'; J. M. Smith, 'State Formation'.
[3] Darwin, *Origin of Species*.   [4] Peel, *Spencer*.
[5] Spencer, *Principles of Biology*, 395.

was evident: '[t]he tendency which we see in the human race, to overrun and occupy one another's lands, as well as the lands inhabited by inferior creatures, is a tendency exhibited by all classes of organisms in various ways'.[6] He used these concepts to explicate the class structure of his own society, thereby naturalizing social inequality.[7] Mackinder took these same three concepts— recasting time as history, space as environment, and organism as race—and applied them to the understanding of international relations.

To ask '[w]hat is Geography', then, was to reflect on how geographical reasoning, as embedded in evolutionary science, could be applied to human societies. It raised other questions too about the institutions and places where geographical understanding should be developed or applied: in universities, schools, public administration, the armed forces, commerce, and politics. Geography in Imperial Britain was part of what Michel Foucault called a 'discursive formation', a set of practices, institutions, and theories that sustain a particular way of viewing and acting in the world.[8] Noting how Geography has concerned itself with the power relations between states, the political geographer, John Agnew, has identified a geopolitical imagination.[9] This geopolitical imagination is and was contestable.

This chapter begins to develop a critical perspective by paying attention to views quite contrary to Mackinder's, expressed by his contemporary the geographer and political philosopher Peter Kropótkin, who interpreted rather differently the social translation of biology. He shared with Mackinder an evolutionary reading of space, time, and organism but he meant something rather different by each of these. I suggest in this chapter that Mackinder's world view was racist and that this aspect of his work was buttressed by a particular reading of Biology, a reading to which Kropótkin developed an important alternative.

Geography, Exploration, and Evolution

Etymologically, Geography is a writing of the Earth, and there has always been a fascination with the limits of that knowledge; limits that were extended dramatically for Europeans with explorations across the Atlantic and into the Pacific Ocean.[10] With cartographic excitement, new lands were

---

[6] Spencer, *Principles of Biology*, 399.

[7] Spencer, *Principles of Sociology*.

[8] Foucault, *Archaeology of Knowledge*.

[9] Agnew, *Geopolitics*, 23. In stressing the political aspects of international space, a geopolitical imagination is a special case of the 'geographical imaginations' studied by Edward Said and Derek Gregory: Said, *Orientalism*; Gregory, *Geographical Imaginations*.

[10] Romm, *Edges of the Earth*; Taylor, *Tudor Geography*; idem, *Late Tudor and Early Stuart Geography*.

outlined; the physiographic details of known lands were filled in; and the sources of rivers, the heights and alignment of mountain ranges, the depths of lakes and oceans, the limits of glaciers, and the extent of desert and forest were engraved onto fuller and more accurate maps. Exploration displaced ancient cosmographies unbalancing the divine ordering of Asia, Africa, and Europe around the holy city of Jerusalem.[11] As new lands brought a new botany and new bestiary, classifications based on Eurasia were challenged and the biblical account of a single act of Creation was challenged by the sheer diversity of life; a diversity established geographically through exploration, and historically through the study of fossils.[12]

The geographer, David Stoddart, has argued that exploration gave Geography the job of spatial prediction; knowing about the landscapes and life of one part of the world, geographers were invited to speculate about what was likely to lie in the spaces of the map yet to be filled.[13] Environmental correlations became central to these speculations. From his transects through the Andes, Alexander von Humboldt (1769–1859) proposed that there were clear links between altitude and vegetation and in his *Cosmos* (1845–58), he tried to reduce to a system the patterns of global ecology.[14] The delight he took in the harmony of climate, flora, and fauna found echoes in the often pantheistic poetry of Wordsworth and Goethe, and even in the sublime view of nature expressed on occasion by Darwin.[15] Geology also posed significant questions for literal readings of the Bible since it suggested that the earth was much older than could be allowed for by the number of generations referenced in the Old Testament. There was in the geologist, James Hutton's (1726–97), phrase of 1788, 'no vestige of a beginning, no prospect of an end'.[16]

The greatest challenge to established religion came from Darwin's insistence on the mutability of species. Darwin reasoned that, because comparable environments on different islands hosted similar but different species of animal, it was likely that animals in one isolated community evolved in a slightly divergent way to animals in another similar but separate place. Environmental requirements set limits to what could survive, but random variations produced variety far beyond the outcomes of a simple correlation of species and environment. In the conjoint mechanisms of random variation and environmental selection, Darwin had an explanation for the emergence of species and for their extinction, should environmental conditions change. The *Origin of Species* (1859) was a dramatic challenge to Genesis but *The Descent of Man* (1871) with its insistence that the mutability of species

[11] Cosgrove, *Apollo's Eye*.
[12] Greenblatt, *Marvellous Possessions*; Larson, 'Not without a Plan'; Fulford, Lee, and Kitson, *Literature, Science, and Exploration*.
[13] Stoddart, *On Geography*.
[14] Farber, *Finding Order in Nature*.
[15] Eichner, 'The Rise of Modern Science'; Richards, *Romantic Conception*; P. Sloan, 'Sense of Sublimity'.
[16] Hallam, *Great Geological Controversies*, 34.

applied also to humans was an affront that could not be evaded; Christian theology had to reject, adapt, or die.[17] Humans, the very purpose of Divine Creation, were not even made as a species at the start of Creation. They had, instead, evolved from species similar to modern apes.

Geographical reasoning was important to religious scepticism. Geography and related Earth Sciences had been central to successive revolutions in exploration and Biology, both of which pushed religion from the centre of explanations of the world and of our place in it: the geography of seas and continents did not attest to the centrality of the Holy City; the geographical diversity of forms of life questioned the idea of a singular Creation; the environmental regulation of plants suggested a harmony that was automatic and not subject to divine intervention; the age of the earth stretched way back before the start of human occupation; and, finally, species, including humans, evolved rather than being permanent features of the Divine Plan.

The significance of the scientific revolution produced by, or at least attributed to, Darwin lent a prestige to environmental and evolutionary thinking that proceeded by widely accepted analogy.[18] The life cycle concept was applied to landforms in the geomorphology of William Morris Davis (1850–1934).[19] The idea of natural selection was held to justify a eugenic concern with preventing the reproduction of the unfit (since advanced society was shielded from nature by the cushion of culture).[20] To legitimate the scientific status of Geography, the Geographical Section (E) of the British Association for the Advancement of Science (BAAS) presented their colleagues with a choice between the fading prestige of exploration and the rising star of evolution. In 1872, Francis Galton said that 'the career of the explorer [... was] inevitably coming to an end' and Geography had to take up questions of 'principles and relations' rather than mere 'facts'.[21] Many of the people promoting scientific Geography at the BAAS worked in the same cause at the RGS, where Galton himself was a leading figure.

The Council of the RGS, as well as delegations from the BAAS sought to get a foothold for Geography at the universities of Oxford and Cambridge and in so doing raise the quality of teachers at the private schools that recruited among the Oxbridge graduates.[22] In 1884, the RGS appointed for one year the geographer and science journalist, John Scott Keltie, as 'Inspector of Geography', to 'inform himself thoroughly on the state of Geographical Education abroad and at home' and make a collection of the

---

[17] Bowler, *Eclipse of Darwinism*; Moore, *Post-Darwinian Controversies*.

[18] It is, of course, true that some of the biological principles taken up with alacrity preceded Darwin and others owed very little to his scientific work at all: Claeys, 'Survival of the Fittest'; Livingstone, 'Natural Theology'.

[19] W. Davis, 'Geographical Cycle'.

[20] D. MacKenzie, 'Eugenics in Britain'.

[21] Quoted in: Withers, Finnegan, and Higgitt, 'Geography's Other Histories?', 443.

[22] Wise, 'Scott Keltie Report'.

best available teaching aids.[23] Keltie found British school Geography in a parlous state, particularly compared to some other European countries. It was mainly an exercise in rote learning and many considered it to be 'not a "manly" subject, but one fit only for elementary classes'.[24] Using Keltie's report, the RGS would later claim that Geography should not be 'a barren catalogue of names and facts' but 'a science that ought to be taught in a liberal way'.[25]

The RGS's use of the term 'liberal' here had the sense of generous or broadranging, although its use also recognizes the concern that Geography could be too martial, a worry that is not eased by the terms of the memorandum which, in claiming that the 'interests of England are as wide as the world', asserted that it was 'a matter of imperial importance that no reasonable means should be neglected of training her youth in sound geographical knowledge'.[26] The British government's Inspectors of Primary Schools proposed that: 'attention should be called to the English colonies, and their productions, government and resources, and to those climatic and other conditions which render our distant possessions suitable fields for emigration and for honourable enterprise'.[27] Keltie also highlighted the imperial purpose of Geography and, comparing it to the twelve university chairs in Germany and the compulsory teaching of Geography in Germany's military academies, indicated the inadequate status of Geography in Britain. Quoting the address to the American Geographical Society of Chief Justice Charles Daly (1815–99), Keltie explained of the Franco-Prussian War of 1870 that it had been 'fought as much by maps as by weapons'.[28] Copies of Keltie's report were sent to supporters of the cause, including his friend Peter Kropótkin, at that time in prison in France. As his contribution to the campaign, Kropótkin then wrote 'What Geography Ought to Be', which was published in 1885 in the influential journal, *Nineteenth Century*.[29]

In December 1885, the RGS staged an exhibition to display the maps, globes, models, and textbooks that Keltie had brought back from his European trip. After the exhibition, in January 1886, the RGS held a conference to 'consider the place of Geography in Education, and particularly the means by which it can be treated as a mental exercise and raised to a level equal to its importance as an Examination subject'.[30] The exhibition and conference were reported upon in national newspapers and Mackinder, who had

---

[23] RGS Council Minutes, 24 March 1884. RGS Archives.

[24] Keltie, *Geographical Education*, 31. This gendering of Geography is a significant matter that will be engaged in the next chapter.

[25] Keltie, ibid., 80.

[26] Keltie, ibid., 80.

[27] Keltie, ibid., 14.

[28] Keltie, ibid., 35. Daly was president of the American Geographical Society from 1864 to 1899 and the medal given to Mackinder in 1944 was named after him (see Chapter 2).

[29] Kropótkin, 'What Geography Ought to Be'.

[30] RGS Council Minutes, 18 January 1886, RGS Archives.

graduated recently from Oxford and was in London preparing for a legal career, first met Keltie at this exhibition. In the winter following this meeting, Mackinder gave his first course of Extension lectures on The New Geography, a discipline that would capitalize upon its place within evolutionary science to address the challenges of the Age of Empire. The RGS invited Mackinder to speak on the New Geography, which he did at an evening meeting of the RGS on 31 January 1887 that was followed after a fortnight by a discussion of his paper, 'The Scope and Methods of Geography'. The talk and discussion drew press attention and *The Times* asked whether the discipline 'will commit itself to the New Geography or remain behind the age and all other similar societies of the first rank'.[31] Following this, Oxford University agreed to appoint a Reader in Geography, the RGS agreed to pay half the salary, and a joint committee of the RGS and the University chose Mackinder for the position in June 1887.[32] Mackinder gave up his fledgling career in Law and launched himself into Geography.

Mackinder's Geography as Biological Destiny

Darwinian Geography rested upon biological readings of space, time, and organism. Mackinder read space as environment and argued that, over the longer term, the variety of the physical and biotic environments created the pattern for the emergence of different sorts of human societies as races and racialized nations. Over the shorter term, the disposition of land and sea, and of natural resources, provided the strategic setting for the unavoidable struggle between these incompatible races (see Chapter 5). In his 1902 publication, *Britain and the British Seas*, he argued that 'the most important facts of contemporary political geography are the extent of the red patches of British dominion upon the map of the world, and the position of the hostile customs frontiers. They are the cartographical expression of the eternal struggle for existence as it stands at the opening of the twentieth century'.[33] The biological argument was explicit: 'Nature is ruthless, and we must build a Power able to contend on equal terms with other Powers, or step into the rank of States which exist on sufferance'.[34] History, as Mackinder's reading of Darwinian time, catalogued these strategic challenges, choices, and outcomes, and suggested how best to read the current geopolitical situation. Finally, Mackinder understood the organisms as incompatible races (some superior and some inferior) engaged in a struggle over territory that is also a

---

[31] *Times*, 18 February 1887, 14a.   [32] Scargill, 'RGS and Oxford'.
[33] Mackinder, *Britain and the British Seas*, 343.
[34] Mackinder, 'Man-Power', 143.

fight to extinction. Yet, as I argue below, Mackinder's geopolitical imagination, particularly his understanding of race, drew more from the biological theories of Jean-Baptiste Lamarck (1744–1829) than from a faithful reading of Darwin. In this, he was not unlike many other social scientists applying Evolutionary Biology to the study of society including, for all their differences, Peter Kropótkin.

Kropótkin read the lessons of Evolutionary Biology very differently to Mackinder. His central insight was that Darwin could be understood as suggesting that evolutionary selection operated through the struggle of a species against its environmental limitations. He argued, further, that in this struggle the cooperation of individuals within a species was a vital evolutionary advantage. Finally, Kropótkin proposed that organisms were directly affected by their environment so that adaptive mutations were most likely. Such a view of nature grounded a very different account of the biological bases of society. For Kropótkin, society was associational rather than racial, cohering in institutions and ethics, rather than through common blood. While he acknowledged the reality of conflict and competition, he understood war and internecine struggle as sapping the life-giving forces of association and cooperation, the true bases of social vitality.

These central points of controversy between Mackinder and Kropótkin are summarized in Table 3.1 and the rest of this chapter elaborates upon their significance for Geopolitics.

Environment

Mackinder said that Geography was 'the science of distribution, the science, that is, which traces the arrangement of things in general on the earth's surface'; having traced these arrangements, the geographer must then 'pass on to consider what relations hold between the distributions of various sets of features'.[35] In contemplating these sets of relations, 'Geography must be a

Table 3.1. The biological basis of Geography

Biology	Geography	Mackinder	Kropótkin
Space	Environment	Environmental selection	Adaptation (plasticity of organisms)
Time	History	Geostrategy	Association vs. centralization/ competition
Organism	Society	Competing races	Network of cooperatives

[35] Mackinder, 'Scope and Methods', 160.

continuous argument'.[36] In other words, the links of cause and effect could be 'strung together in natural sequence'.[37] Mackinder believed that environments shaped societies very directly, and with at first minor and later major reservations understood Geography as 'the physical basis of history'.[38] This was an important part of his reading of Darwinism. A scientific Geography, he wrote, must 'trace causal relations' and, although Mackinder stated repeatedly that Geography examined 'the interaction of man in society and so much of his environment as varies locally', the main mover for Mackinder was clearly the physical rather the human factor.[39] Geography would examine 'the influence of locality'; 'no *rational* political geography can exist which is not built upon and subsequent to physical geography'.[40] In a vivid, and apparently near verbatim, account of the opening of his last lecture course at the LSE (1923), Martha Woolley (1900–90) recalled Mackinder relating Geography to Medicine in striking and environmentalist terms:

'With doctors the physical is a basic to the health, wealth and happiness of the individual'. (Why not to the health, wealth and happiness of the nation?)
Can the individual hope for mental control, without first physical control? Every doctor knows he cannot?
   Can the nation attain to intellectual discipline without, first, physical discipline? Master of its Space? [. . .]
   When the nation is ailing and unhappy, what should the nation do? If it is wise, and it very seldom is, it should summon the geographer, the doctor of humanity, who *first* looks at the anatomy of the nation before announcing the nature of the trouble and ordering medication.[41]

In this passage, the nation is represented as the body-politic that must be cared for by the national-physician, the geographer. It is in this sense that Mackinder asserted that: '[s]urely the essential characteristic of true statesmanship is foresight, the prevention of social disease'.[42]

   The scope of Geography, for Mackinder, was defined by its method, that is, by 'the main line of geographical argument'.[43] This line of causality, in every example Mackinder cited, ran from the physical environment to the

---

[36] Mackinder, 'Scope and Methods', 154.
[37] Mackinder, ibid., 160.
[38] *Times*, 18 February 1887, 14a.
[39] Mackinder, 'Scope and Methods', 143. I realize that Mackinder's use of the term 'man' to refer to people in general is sexist but peppering historical quotations with '[sic]' is inelegant and anachronistic. In Chapter 4, I address some of the further ways Mackinder's geographical writings and work were gendered.
[40] Mackinder, 'Scope and Methods', 143.
[41] Wilson Woolley, 'The Philosophy of Sir Halford J. Mackinder', 266–7; unpublished MS, London School of Economics, Archives, Mackinder M 1856 (1). This passage appears to be extracts from the lecture notes taken by Woolley. I think that all of this reports Mackinder's words (including the matter in parenthesis), as he moves from truths accepted in Medicine, and asks rhetorically whether they are applicable to society.
[42] Mackinder, *Democratic Ideals and Reality*, 250.
[43] Mackinder, 'Scope and Methods', 155.

patterns of human settlement and interaction. In the last chapters of his proposed geographical syllabus, Mackinder concluded that people alter their environment 'and the action of that environment on [. . .] posterity is changed in consequence'.[44] He also noted that the 'relative importance of physical features varies from age to age according to the state of knowledge and of material civilisation'.[45] However, he immediately qualified these points by putting alongside the possibility of human modification, the 'momentum acquired in the past' for people are 'mainly [. . .] creature[s] of habit'.[46] In other words, while the environment might be changed, the impact of its former state would be preserved through the inertia of human society.

Society and History

Not surprisingly, then, in his 1887 RGS address, 'Scope and Methods', Mackinder said very little about human society, declaring that the analysis of 'man in society [. . .] will be shorter than that of the environment'.[47] However, he suggested that 'communities of men should be looked on as units in the struggle for existence, more or less favoured by their several environments'.[48] This is pure Social Darwinism. Not only communities but also locations were to be considered as in competition and, to explain why one place rather than another should now host a metropolis rather than a village, for example, Mackinder 'would propose the term "geographical selection" for the process on the analogy of "natural selection" '.[49] In his continuous argument, the environment created the possibility for settlement through rainfall and vegetation, and then directed the human community into distinct units by the degree of separation it imposed between these natural regions. Mackinder recognized four types of human community distinguished by scale as 'races, nations, provinces, [and] towns'.[50] Significantly, he added that 'the last two expressions are used in the sense of corporate groups of men'.[51] He believed, in other words, that the first two, races and nations, were somehow more natural, more directly the products of environmental variation.

Although the outlines were clear, Mackinder's views on race and nation were undeveloped in his paper of 1887. They were set out a little more fully in *Britain and the British Seas*, a paradigm of the New Geography, published in

[44] Mackinder, 'Scope and Methods', 157.
[45] Mackinder, ibid., 157.
[46] Mackinder, ibid., 157.
[47] Mackinder, ibid., 143.
[48] Mackinder, ibid., 143.
[49] Mackinder, ibid., 159.
[50] Mackinder, ibid., 157.
[51] Mackinder, ibid., 157; and he did indeed mean 'men', for Mackinder was a settled opponent of votes for women (see the discussion in the following chapter).

1902. The geography of Britain was, for Mackinder, 'the intricate product of a continuous history, geological and human'.[52] Britain, he wrote, contained the remnant of a northern Atlantis in the craggy prospect it offered to the Atlantic, whereas the low and open lands of South and East England were a plain of materials eroded from Atlantis. The 'cosmopolitan' society of the South and East interacted with Europe, received 'stimulus from without' and thus 'avoided stagnation'.[53] The provincial societies of industrial England, Scotland, Wales, and Ireland, in contrast, were more 'rooted'.[54] Mackinder located the 'brain of the Empire' in London, and its brawn and its mineral resources, the 'reserves' of Britain, safely beyond the low country in the fast provinces.[55] In this way, the opposition of North and West to South and East was understood as fundamental both to the geological and to the human history of Britain. For Mackinder, 'the salient geographical attributes of Britain are identical, whether tested by the physical or the historical geographer', and the 'geography of Britain is in fact the intricate product of a continuous history, geological and human'.[56] The elaboration of Physical through Historical Geography led Mackinder to describe the ambition of his geostrategic vision as showing how 'human history [w]as part of the world organism'.[57]

It is striking that, in *Britain and the British Seas*, Mackinder made no clear distinction between race and nation—both were matters of blood, although the one was perhaps more ancient than the other. Having taken about half the book to treat the physical geography of Britain, Mackinder turned to the consequent human geography. He described the peopling of Britain as creating a distinct racial geography. Its main features were, again, the opposition between, on one side, lowland England open to the north European plain and peopled by fair-haired Teutonic people, Danes, Angles, and Saxons; and, on the other, the North and West populated by blond Scandinavians in the East and by dark-haired Mediterranean pre-Celts in the West and in Wales, Ireland, and Scotland. The Teutons displaced these pre-Celtic peoples to the margins setting up a distinct geography of 'nigrescence', or dark-haired-ness, greatest in the West and least in the East (see Figure 3.1).[58]

This racial geography recalled Ratzel's own description of global humanity as exhibiting greatest nigrescence in the tropics, and Mackinder refers explicitly to the economist and ethnologist, William Ripley's (1867–1941), reworking of Ratzel's racial geography in the context of the moral geography

---

[52] Mackinder, *Britain and the British Seas*, 229–30.

[53] Mackinder, ibid., 179.

[54] Mackinder, ibid., 15.

[55] Mackinder, ibid., 312, 314.

[56] Mackinder, ibid., 229–30.

[57] Mackinder, 'Geographical Pivot'.

[58] Mackinder, 'Figure 9.2. The Relative Nigrescence of the British Population', *Britain and the British Seas*, 182.

Fig. 3.1. The relative nigrescence of the British population

Source: From Mackinder, *Britain and the British Seas*.

of Europe.[59] However, while Ratzel related nigrescence to skin colour, and as defining the 'negroid races of the world', Ripley and Mackinder followed the anthropologist, John Beddoe (1826–1911), in reading nigrescence from hair colour, with the same implied hierarchy from civilized light to primitive dark.[60] Beddoe asked people to '[n]ote [...] the preponderance among criminals of dark hair', a trait found also among both 'Negroes' and 'Kelts', and an index too of the racial degeneration of the English: 'I regret the diminution of the old blond [...] stock which has hitherto served England well in many ways, but is apparently doomed to give way to a darker and more mobile type, largely the offspring of the proletariat, and more adapted to the atmosphere of great cities'.[61]

Mackinder drew upon the contrast shown in Figure 3.1, between dark north and west and lighter south and east, to reinforce the fundamental division he saw between provincial and metropolitan Britain. He suggested that, because, '[u]ntil recent times most men lived their lives in the neighbourhood of their birthplace', these racial patterns were passed down in the 'blood of whole regions'.[62] Such 'provincial solidarities' were clearest among the 'humbler classes' for Mackinder, who distinguished nine provincial types denoting the 'dark', and pre-Celtic, as 'mercurial' or 'of emotional temperament'.[63] Mackinder treated the difference between the Catholic Irish and the

[59] Ratzel, *History of Mankind 1*, 35; Winlow, 'Mapping Moral Geographies'.
[60] Semple, *Influences of Geographic Environment*, 1410; Winlow, 'Anthropometric Cartography'.
[61] Beddoe, 'Colour and Race', 237.
[62] Mackinder, *Britain and the British Seas*, 191.
[63] Mackinder, ibid., 192.

Ulstermen as racial, and repeatedly during debates over Home Rule for
Ireland attacked those proposing independence because 'they wish one of
the races in Ireland to control the other'.[64]

The insularity of Britain and Ireland, together with centuries free from
hostile invasion, meant, he believed, that there were no significant infusions
of foreign blood between the Norman Conquest and Mackinder's own time.
For Mackinder, the 'basis of fixation of a local variety into a species is that
the variety shall consist not of so many individuals but of a single blood'.[65]
Mackinder believed that the English plain was a natural region within which
the English people were long settled and little interfered with. Thus this
natural region produced a biological community: 'John Bull is a local variety
of the genus and species, *Homo sapiens*[, and ...] in literal truth there is
today in England a single blood'.[66] The biological argument about environment and race was evident:

[I]n the English Plain we have a typical natural region, so far uniform in climate and
soil as to favour social continuity within, but engirt by such physical features as suffice
to break social continuity around by preventing or greatly impeding intermarriage.
Within this natural region we have the English blood, one fluid, the same down
through the centuries, on loan for the moment in the forty million bodies of the
present generation. John Bull in his insularity is the exemplar of the myriad separate
bloods and saps, each the fluid essence of a local variety or species of animal or
plant.[67]

Mackinder used race and nation in the biological sense of species or subspe-
cies. However, his conception of race is more Lamarckian than Darwinian,
for Mackinder's races embody the lessons of past environmental experience.
The pre-Celtic Ulsterman, for example, was 'not quite Teutonic, however
Protestant'.[68] Mackinder believed that it was the way that people gained a
living that determined basic aspects of their racial character. In one lecture,
he proposed that 'what makes men differ one race from another is [...] their
different daily occupations, the pastoral man from the industrial man
and the agricultural man, and the uplander from the lowlander'.[69] In a
related manner, Mackinder suggested that the 'chief distinction in political
geography seems to be founded on the facts that man travels and man
settles'.[70] People in movement included both true nomads and those engaged
in trade. Astride the oasis-roads between Europe and Asia, for example,
grew up the world's 'first commercial peoples' and these 'Babylonians,

---

[64] *The Official Report, House of Commons, 5th Series* [*Hansard 5th*] 34 (19 February 1912), 365.
[65] Mackinder, 'Human Habitat', 325.
[66] Mackinder, ibid., 326.
[67] Mackinder, ibid., 326.
[68] Mackinder, *Britain and the British Seas*, 192.
[69] Mackinder, 'Historical Geography of Britain (Modern Period)', typescript of lecture, Oxford, 29
May 1906, Mackinder Papers, School of Geography, Oxford University, MP/O/100.
[70] Mackinder, 'Physical Basis', 78.

Phoenicians, Jews, Arabs [. . .] were chiefly of one race; and may we not trace the hereditary commercial aptitudes of that great Semitic race to the necessities and opportunities of their remarkable position?'[71] Culture and genetics are barely distinguishable here, and Mackinder referred often to 'the history imbedded in a people's character and traditions'.[72] He insisted that 'each race exhibits a great variety of initiative, the product, in the main of its past history' and that '[i]n each age certain elements of this initiative are selected for success, chiefly by geographical conditions'.[73]

In Mackinder's biological vision, environmental experience was embodied as blood, carrying national and racial character. In these terms, Mackinder was keen to assert the special qualities of the English: 'the English race, the English blood, is valuable as carrying a certain character. That character is, it seems to me, something physical, and therefore not wholly transferable except with the blood'.[74] The English gift to world civilization was, according to Mackinder, 'Responsible Government', and while this was gifted to each English person as biological birthright it could only be taught very slowly to others, and it was the duty of the British Empire to do this. The Empire, in turn, was needed to protect this vital English bloodline and the masses needed to 'learn to value the Empire as the protection of their manhood. Herein, half consciously, lies the reconciliation of Colonial Liberalism with protection, the exclusion of coloured races, and imperialism'.[75] The protection of this valuable English stock, then, required social reform at home, imperialism abroad, tariffs around imperial production, and racial hygiene throughout.

In capturing biology for a spatial perspective, Mackinder equated territory with sustenance, just as he had equated racialized-nations with species. Each nation 'ultimately depended upon the past and present produce of its own territory, and it must be prepared to defend that territory against the intrusion of covetous neighbours'.[76] Although Mackinder showed that only about one-fifteenth of the British domestic product came from the Empire, he still maintained that it was vital, and that the Empire had to be the focus of British economic survival.[77] The Empire had been gathered in piecemeal, either to enforce a trading monopoly, as in India, or to prevent other nations from doing so. Imperial possessions having been acquired, further territories had to be taken in order to protect access to them: '[t]he career of annexation

---

[71] Mackinder, 'Physical Basis', 82.
[72] Mackinder, ibid., 84.
[73] Mackinder, 'Modern Geography', 376.
[74] Mackinder, 'English Tradition', 726.
[75] Mackinder, 'Man-Power', 143.
[76] Mackinder, *Britain and the British Seas*, 309.
[77] He claimed that the total annual income of Britain was £2,000 million, that the Empire brought £200 million and that it cost perhaps £70 million to defend it; Mackinder, *Britain and the British Seas*, 349–51.

once commenced is for reasons of strategy difficult to check'.[78] A country, such as Britain, with investments abroad, would get drawn into protecting the security of those investments: '[f]or all are ultimately held by naval power. The great creditor nation cannot afford to be weak'.[79] As Chapter 5 will show, the competitive acquisition of colonial properties through the struggle between nations meant, for Mackinder, that the world of the early-twentieth century was becoming one of contending empires rather than of hostile states.

According to Mackinder, the dilemma of earlier empires had been twofold: autocratic methods of rule from the colonies had been brought back to the metropolis, corrupting democracy at home; and colonizers had bred with local peoples, thereby polluting the imperial race. For Mackinder, democratic pressure in Britain gave domestic politics elevated goals, tempering the self-interested vice of commerce with the leaven of responsibility and thus providing 'an education in freedom [for] those who go forth on missions of Imperial rule'.[80] The great distance, geographical and biological, between metropole and colony ensured that colonial administrators would hold themselves apart from the peoples they ruled. In Mackinder's terms, distance 'renders the growth of sympathy difficult' and thereby 'preserves undiluted the chief reservoir of the Imperial man-power'.[81] Democracy thus deterred autocracy, and racial superiority averted miscegenation.

The Empire, in Mackinder's view, consisted of Dominions of British settlement, and other places where the 'Imperial race [... was] settled thinly [... on lands] occupied by vast subject peoples of alien blood'.[82] The settler colonies, then, might be drawn to recognize a common interest in pooling their defence capacities with that of Britain in order that together they might tip the scales against the growing powers of Russia, or the United States, or Germany, or France. This was vital for Britain for 'in this little island we have not productivity sufficient to base an empire which shall hold its own with the great continental empires that are developing'.[83] Indeed, Mackinder's geographical teaching was intended to alert Britons, at home and abroad to the common threat:

All the Britains are threatened by the recent expansion of Europe, and therefore all may be ready to share in the support of the common fleet, as being the cheapest method of ensuring peace and freedom to each. Thus the chief danger [to] the Empire may be averted, and the old Britain, when unable to maintain from her own resources a navy equivalent to those of United States and Russia, after they shall have developed their vast potentialities, may still find secure shelter behind the navy of the Britains.[84]

---

[78] Mackinder, *Britain and the British Seas*, 344.
[79] Mackinder, ibid., 346.
[80] Mackinder, 'Man-Power', 137.
[81] Mackinder, ibid., 137.
[82] Mackinder, ibid., 137.
[83] Mackinder, 'Geographical Conditions', 474.
[84] Mackinder, *Britain and the British Seas*, 351.

For Mackinder, this threat was conceptualized in biological terms—a threat to survival. Mackinder admitted that to teach these lessons was to 'deviate from the impartial views of science' but there was no alternative for 'the practical citizens of an empire which has to hold its place according to the universal law of survival through efficiency and effort'.[85] In a speech, or perhaps lecture, to the House of Commons after the First World War, Mackinder warned that:

If hon. Members will think of this country as a little island, then there is very little future for the working classes of this country. If, however, they will think of this Island as part of a vast estate containing hundreds of thousands of fertile square miles, in Africa say, capable of raising sugar, coffee, tobacco, then you are thinking in quantities which will put the working men of this country on a par with the working men of the United States.[86]

Only by developing the Empire for British benefit was survival imaginable:

We have vast tropical areas in which hundreds of thousands of square miles of fertile soil are to be found. Will this great people now by an imaginative and constructive policy help development? Or shall we construct for the future some old house into which to retire? Or will this great democracy of active workers base themselves on a sound economic and daringly constructive policy and so, out of the death penalty— though a glorious penalty—enable us to bring forth a Britain such as even our forefathers never dreamt of?[87]

The Empire gave Britain the chance to evade the fate of other small nations.

Mackinder, then, thought that the Darwinian revolution in the Life Sciences had clear implications for the understanding of society. As the historian of science, Douglas Lorimer notes, evolutionary ideas were 'part of the fabric of the ideology of empire', that, by making social change a part of the biological order, 'eliminated the historical agency and the moral responsibility of the colonizers and similarly denied the colonized a historical role in determining their own fate'.[88] By putting social change back into nature, evolutionary social science suggested that social change would be slow, incremental, and automatic, rather than revolutionary and by design.

Mackinder's was certainly the dominant reading of the lessons of Biology. He took Darwin as proving the necessity of continual struggle and then allied to this a military and strategic reading of space to produce a geopolitical imagination in the service of the flourishing of the British Empire. However, there were others who rejected the chauvinism of racial superiority and were critical of the violence of Empire, believing anti-colonial movements to be

---

[85] Mackinder, 'Teaching of Geography', 83.
[86] *Hansard 5th* 116 (21 May 1919), 463.
[87] ibid., 465.
[88] Lorimer, 'Victorian Images of Race', 216–7.

justified and progressive.[89] Given how closely evolutionary science was en-
twined with imperial ideology, anti-imperialist arguments had to engage not
only with the dominant views of Empire, but also with prevailing understandings of life itself; they had to take on both History and Biology.
Kropótkin yielded no quarter in his admiration for Darwin and, like Mackinder, thought that the social sciences must learn from Biology, but he
understood those lessons in a very different way.

Kropótkin's Geography of Anarchist Cooperation

Although both Mackinder and Kropótkin were drawn into the campaign to
promote British Geography, they did so with very different ends in view.
Mackinder would never have avowed with Kropótkin that the purpose of
Geography was countering 'national self conceit' so that children might learn
that 'all nationalities are valuable to one another' and that 'political frontiers
are relics of a barbarous past'.[90] Mackinder's understanding of Geography,
including his racism, therefore, cannot so easily be regarded as the inevitable
outcome of the times in which he lived. Through Kropótkin's work I explore
alternatives to the then dominant Social Darwinist understandings of environment and society, and, in particular, to geopolitical imaginaries tied to the
needs of Empire.

    While Kropótkin's background was very different to Mackinder's, their
geographical careers showed many parallels. Kropótkin was born in 1842 to
a wealthy landowner in Russia and was sent as a child to the court of the
Tsar.[91] In 1862, he began a career in the Russian military administration by
electing to serve in Siberia where he hoped that social and political reforms
might be hazarded in what was Russia's newest province. Disillusioned with
the corruption of imperial government, he elected instead to explore Siberia
and made studies of the physiography of remote regions. After five prisoners
were summarily executed in Siberia, Kropótkin resigned from the military in
1866 and from the Russian civil service in 1872. He involved himself increasingly in clandestine working-class and anarchist politics. In 1874, he was
arrested and imprisoned before escaping from a prison hospital in 1876.
He then came to Britain and made his living as a science journalist, with
continual assistance from Keltie. In the absence of a significant anarchist
political movement in Britain, Kropótkin's life lacked its central purpose and
he went to France in 1882 where he was soon arrested on false charges and
imprisoned from December 1882 to January 1886. From prison in France,

[89] Porter, *Critics of Empire*.
[90] Kropótkin, 'What Geography Ought to Be', 942.
[91] The best biography is: Woodcock and Avakumović, *Anarchist Prince*.

Kropótkin continued his science journalism. He returned to Britain in 1886 and stayed there until the excitement of the Bolshevik Revolution drew him to Russia again in 1917 where, although disillusioned with the statism of the Bolsheviks, he remained until his death in 1921.

Both Kropótkin and Mackinder insisted that there were close relations between their political and academic work and yet both disappointed many of their geographical admirers by paying so much attention to politics. Keltie regretted that Kropótkin's 'absorption' in politics 'seriously diminished the services which otherwise he might have rendered to Geography', and had similar fears about Mackinder's commitment to the Tariff Reform crusade.[92] Mackinder, however, assured Keltie of his priorities: '[p]lease don't think from the late mentions of my name in the papers, that I am going to sacrifice my geography [and] to substitute politics for Reading. Despite certain things printed I have no intention, for the present at least, to plunge again into detailed organising, though I am going to keep touch with politics'.[93]

Both Kropótkin and Keltie had long and valued relationships with the RGS. After his arrival in Britain in 1876, Kropótkin, in Keltie's recollection, 'soon made himself at home at our Society'.[94] In 1892, Kropótkin was proposed for a Fellowship of the RGS but declined membership of a Society under royal patronage, yet told one of his sponsors, Douglas Freshfield (1845–1934), that: 'I always take the greatest interest in the Society's work and if I can in any way be useful in aiding it, I shall always be delighted to do so'.[95] Kropótkin was closely involved with the RGS, translating and reporting on Russian Geography, refereeing papers, and writing papers of his own for its *Geographical Journal*. Mackinder, of course, owed his academic career to the sponsorship of the RGS and was long a member of its Council. Mackinder was never elected President of the Society and only received its Patron's Medal in his 84th year. Unlike Mackinder, and even his fellow anarchist, Elisée Reclus, Kropótkin never received a medal from the RGS, although it is his portrait, not Mackinder's, which was commissioned by the RGS in 1904 and remains on display at the Society to this day.[96]

Mackinder and Kropótkin evangelized for Geography, and at one teachers' conference in Oxford (in 1893), Kropótkin presented Geography as precisely the sort of synthetic subject championed by Mackinder, a 'philosophical review of knowledge acquired by different branches of science'.[97] Both men frequently attended meetings of the RGS and must have met

[92] Keltie, 'Kropótkin', 317.
[93] Mackinder to Keltie, 7 August 1903, RGS Archives, Mackinder Correspondence.
[94] Keltie, 'Kropótkin', 318.
[95] Kropótkin to Freshfield, 30 January 1892, RGS Archives, Kropótkin Correspondence.
[96] The painting was by Nellie Heath who, as a child came to Kropótkin's home to play with his daughter, Sasha; Woodcock and Avakumović, *Anarchist Prince*, 222; Kropótkin to W. R. Hinks, 26 September 1913, RGS Archives, Correspondence Block 1911–20, Kozlov, Kropótkin; Potter, 'Kropótkin', 67.
[97] Kropótkin, 'Physiography', 359.

several times, although we know, from published records, of only a few such occasions. In April 1903, for example, Elisée Reclus came to give one of his two lectures to the Society. The paper was about the use of various types of spherical and relief maps in teaching. Mackinder and Kropótkin took part in the discussion, each suggesting that Reclus was too purist in insisting on relief models that used no exaggeration of the vertical scale. Mackinder urged public authorities to spend more on maps and models for geographical education. Mindful perhaps of Mackinder's commitment to building up the British navy, Kropótkin referred directly to defence spending, noting that '[w]hen so much money was spent on useless things such as ironclads and the like, surely they ought to be able to find money for what was absolutely essential in carrying on the work of education'.[98] On another occasion, in February 1904, Kropótkin gave a paper on 'The Dessication of Eur-Asia' to the Research Department of the Society and Mackinder sent a critical letter as contribution to the discussion.[99] Kropótkin's forthcoming work on 'The Russian Empire' was advertised inside the first edition of *Britain and the British Seas*, as part of a new series edited by Mackinder on 'The Regions of the World', a series that was also advertised to include Reclus on 'Western Europe' (neither volume was ever published).[100]

As I have noted already, both wrote papers in response to Keltie's report on Geographical Education. Keltie was in regular correspondence with Kropótkin during the latter's French imprisonment and the letters cover both academic and personal matters. Keltie sent a letter to the *Pall Mall Gazette* (22 November 1882) protesting lies about Kropótkin that were being used to justify expulsion from France, but he was no more successful in moving the French authorities with this letter than with the petition he organized after Kropótkin was imprisoned.[101] Keltie sent Kropótkin books and journals so that he could continue working as a geographer and as a science journalist while in prison. Kropótkin's service to Geography was significant, not least because he placed his article on 'What Geography Ought to Be' in the popular magazine where he had been writing reviews of scientific progress. This journal, *Nineteenth Century* had a circulation of 20,000, and one contributor claimed that to write there was 'to command the attention of the world'.[102] Kropótkin's propaganda for Geography undoubtedly reached many more people than could Mackinder through the *Geographical Journal*.

[98] Reclus, 'On Spherical Maps', 297.

[99] Kropótkin, 'Dessication of Eur-Asia'.

[100] I discuss this venture further in Chapter 6.

[101] The letter is in RGS Archives, Kropótkin correspondence; some details of the extensive academic and journalistic support for the petition are given in: Woodcock and Avakumović, *Anarchist Prince*, 194.

[102] Berry, *Articles of Faith*, 114, 123. In fact, in prison Kropótkin had no choice but to follow purely academic pursuits: '[n]othing dealing with social questions [. . .] was permitted to issue from the prison-walls'; Kropótkin, *In Russian and French Prisons*, 286.

Although the careers of Mackinder and Kropótkin swam together from time to time, the differences between their respective geographical imaginations are striking. Kropótkin's Geography stressed the unity of the cosmos showing that people depended upon complex webs of animal, vegetable, and mineral interactions. In this way Geography might 'awaken in our children the taste for natural science'.[103] Kropótkin further believed that Geography should educate citizens about the similarities between so-called primitive peoples and Europeans and that children must learn respect for people too frequently seen as 'a mere nuisance on the globe'.[104] Geography could impart the global perspective needed in 'our own times of railway civilisation and world traffic', and the understanding of nature adequate for an era that would see 'the further development of industry and science'.[105] While the contrast with Mackinder's imperialist sentiments is clear in such statements, Kropótkin did not simply reject the imperialist vision, he also renegotiated its biological basis. In what follows, I outline his alternative understanding of evolutionary Geography.

Environment

Like Mackinder, Kropótkin believed that the environment exercised a tight control upon social and biological development; his reading of the environmental effect was also more Lamarckian than Darwinian.[106] Darwin rejected teleological readings of evolution and believed that there was no purpose to evolution, it was simply the elimination of unfit, randomly produced mutations and the multiplication, through the successful reproduction and survival of individuals with those variations that enabled them to manage best in the environment. If environments changed, then, so would the conditions for survival. For Darwin, environmental change was neutral in moral terms. There was nothing better about later environments, and thus there was also nothing better about later life forms, that were best adapted to the new circumstances.

Mackinder and Kropótkin both believed that species or races adapted to their environment, rather than were simply selected by it, but beyond this they differed markedly. For Mackinder, races internalized, as inheritable characteristics, certain ways of living; he organized races hierarchically, according to his belief that *environments produced races*: some that marauded and others that innovated. Implicitly, then, there were good environments and bad environments, according to Mackinder, in the sense that the former

---

[103] Kropótkin, 'What Geography Ought to Be', 943.
[104] ibid.
[105] Kropótkin, 'Physiography', 350, 353–4.
[106] Alvaro, 'Kropotkin between Lamarck and Darwin'.

produced morally better races than the latter. Kropótkin's arguments were somewhat different.

Kropótkin suggested that Darwin in fact posited three dimensions to the struggle for life: competition between individuals of the same species, competition of one species against another, and competition of individuals against the environment.[107] More than Mackinder, he stressed the third, but did not, like Darwin, understand mutation as the product of blind chance. He was likewise critical of Lamarck's argument that species consciously adapted and then passed these variations down to their progeny.[108] He believed that variations did not occur randomly but were 'called forth by a changing environment', in that the environment produced appropriate changes mechanistically when acting upon organisms with sufficient plasticity.[109] Evolution proceeded, for Kropótkin, by means of the environment producing the variations needed for survival in individual organisms; these changes became part of the genetic make-up of the organism. There was no need for randomly advantaged individuals to eliminate other members of the species in order to survive to breed a fitter succeeding generation. The pitiless total war, of all against all, was unnecessary. For Kropótkin, then, the first of Darwin's dimensions of the struggle for life—the one he borrowed from Malthus—could be downplayed in favour of direct environmental direction. The environment was an evolutionary agent for Kropótkin.

Like Mackinder, Kropótkin was a holist; they both saw unity in nature but whereas Mackinder arranged this unity as a sequential chain of inorganic cause and organic effect, Kropótkin saw the same organizing principles within each sphere of nature, both organic and inorganic. The whole world consisted of 'vibrations' of different kinds.[110] Even the purely physical world of cosmic dust expressed principles that could be carried through to the normative study of human society. In the first place, purely physical entities, such as stars, went through evolution and decay.[111] Secondly, modern science no longer treated the universe as organized around any central fulcrum, tellular or solar: '[t]he center, the origin of force, formerly transferred from the earth to the sun, now turns out to be scattered and disseminated: it is everywhere and nowhere'.[112] The harmony in the universe was nothing more than the equilibrium established at one point in time by the adventitious arrangement of forces. There was, thus, no natural basis for the static social hierarchies presented as eternal by monarchs, princes, or popes, or as Brecht had Galileo observe, displacing the centrality of the sun 'created a draught which is blowing up the gold-embroidered skirts of the prelates and princes,

---

[107] Kropótkin, 'Theory of Evolution', 122.
[108] Kropótkin, ibid., 120.
[109] Kropótkin, 'Direct Action of Environment and Evolution', 86.
[110] Kropótkin, *Modern Science and Anarchism*, 23.
[111] Kropótkin, *Ethics*, 3.
[112] Kropótkin, *Anarchism*.

revealing the fat and skinny legs underneath, legs like our own'.[113] For Kropótkin, there were certainly no scientific grounds for believing in a universal 'plan pre-established by an intelligent will'.[114]

Kropótkin's scientism drew criticism from some contemporary anarchists, such as Errico Malatesta (1853–1922), who said that 'Kropótkin tended to use science "to support his social aspirations" '.[115] Yet Kropótkin had a more historical view of the environment than many contemporaries, including Mackinder. Mackinder admitted that there could be environmental change, either natural or anthropogenic, but it played little part in his Political Geography. In contrast, environmental history was much more important for Kropótkin and provided a significant stimulus to human adaptation. For example, he developed a theory about the dessication of Eurasia, proposing that at the end of the last Ice Age, the mass of ice over Eurasia gradually melted and drained away, and that, during this melting period, the Eurasian landmass had been covered in lakes. As the climate warmed, these lakes dried up, leaving deserts where there had once been lush valleys, and ghost towns where thriving agrarian cities had been. Farming areas shrank and the peoples who had been settled there were driven out, either raiding or settling among the peoples on the rim of the heartland of Eurasia. Mackinder, who believed in a relatively stable environment with an equivalent consistency of racial character, questioned Kropótkin's claim that invasions of Europe were triggered by climatic change. Instead, he argued that the people in question had always been nomads and were led out into Europe by rulers who saw the 'rich booty' there to be had.[116] For Mackinder, 'Geography should, as I see it, be a physiological and anatomical study rather than a study in development'.[117] Kropótkin disagreed.

Kropótkin saw nature as supremely bountiful, not as a limited resource over which people must fight. There was, for Kropótkin, no need for substantial long-distance trade, and Britain could perfectly well feed all its citizens from domestic resources, provided it adopted intensive scientific farming.[118] The extensive agricultural methods of capitalism squandered resources in pursuit of standard products and monopolistic prices. Kropótkin noted that in the 1850s each Briton could be fed from two acres of land, but by the 1880s it required three acres.[119] Land was going out of cultivation and workers were leaving the land. The most efficient use of the environment would be based on reversing those trends: '[a] dense population, a high development of industry, and a high development of agriculture and horticulture, go hand in hand: they are inseparable'.[120] For Kropótkin, therefore,

[113] Brecht, 'Life of Galileo', 7.
[114] Kropótkin, *Anarchism*.
[115] Miller, 'Introduction', 42.
[116] Kropótkin, 'Dessication of Eur-Asia', 735.
[117] Mackinder, 'Comment on Wooldridge and Smetham', 268.
[118] Kropótkin, 'Revolution and Famine'; *idem*, 'Rocks Ahead'.
[119] Kropótkin, *Fields*, 50.   [120] Kropótkin, ibid., 102–3.

subsistence must be the first goal of any more just society, for the 'right to well-being is the social revolution'.[121] In broadly biological terms, Kropótkin defined Economics as the 'study of the needs of mankind, and the means of satisfying them with the least possible waste of human energy. Its true name should be physiology of society'.[122]

Society and History

Kropótkin, then, had a different account of how the environmental effect operated, a different conception of holism, a different view of environmental change, and a distinctive account of agricultural intensification. Nevertheless, it still makes sense to term both Mackinder and Kropótkin environmentalists. However, whereas Mackinder developed racist explanations for the evolution of human socieites, Kropótkin did not. Rather than refer to national or racial characteristics carried in the blood, Kropótkin instead highlighted the development of the social instinct. He argued that, for humans, the central biological bonds were social rather than genetic, a matter of choice rather than fate.

Kropótkin suggested that humans developed their earliest social rules from observing how packs of animals worked, noting how these higher animals cooperated to get food and rarely killed one of their own. Internal solidarity rather than external hostility drove social development; mutual aid 'is the real foundation of our ethical conceptions'.[123] Ethics began with the veneration of the tribe and this was in turn learned from the social animals.[124] The tribe preceded the family and humanity 'spent tens of thousands of years in the clan or tribal phase, during which [...it] developed all kinds of institutions, habits and customs all much earlier than the institutions of the patriarchal family'.[125] With sedentary agriculture, came the development of the village and the elaboration of local systems of justice based on juries. The strength of these local institutions was reinforced by the brotherhoods that developed within trades and together they 'opened the way for a new way of life: that of the free communes'.[126]

These communes, for Kropótkin, were the basis of the free cities of the Late Middle Ages, until they were threatened by the elaboration of centralized states in the Early Modern period. Pre-empting the judicial functions of the communes and claiming a monopoly of military functions, the early European states fought to subjugate the free towns and the federations into which the towns had organized themselves. The State pillaged the lands of the free villages and in the sixteenth century the 'towns were

---

[121] Kropótkin, 'Conquest of Bread', 30.
[122] Kropótkin, ibid., 159.
[123] Kropótkin, *Mutual Aid*, 298.   [124] Kropótkin, *Ethics*, 60.
[125] Kropótkin, *The State*, 12.   [126] Kropótkin, ibid., 23.

besieged, stormed, and sacked, their inhabitants decimated or deported'.[127] In this sense, history was a cyclical process and 'every time the pattern has been the same, beginning with the phase of the primitive tribe followed by the village commune; then by the free city, finally to die with the advent of the State'.[128] The anarchist movement sought 'the destruction of the States, and new life starting again in thousands of centres on the principle of the lively initiative of the individual and groups and that of free agreement'.[129]

Kropótkin openly criticized the prevailing Social Darwinist reading of Biology, in particular as expressed in the work of Thomas Huxley (1825–95). Huxley saw nature as a cruel, relentless struggle: '[f]rom the point of view of the moralist the animal world is on about the same level as a gladiator's show'.[130] If society took a different route it was 'setting limits to the struggle'.[131] But the organic realities would reassert themselves in a Malthusian check upon population growth, unless the society could steal from its neighbour's table. Kropótkin loathed Huxley's 'atrocious article' and was depressed to find that 'the interpretation of "struggle for life" in the sense of a war-cry of "Woe to the Weak", raised to the height of a commandment of nature revealed by science, was so deeply rooted in this country [Britain] that it had become almost a matter of religion'.[132] Encouraged by Henry Walter Bates and by James Knowles (1831–1908), the editor of the journal, *Nineteenth Century*, that had published Huxley's article, Kropótkin replied to Huxley in a series of articles that were later published as his book on *Mutual Aid*.[133] Bates, whom Kropótkin knew from the RGS, was 'delighted', assuring Kropótkin: '[t]hat is true Darwinism. It is a shame to think of what they have made of Darwin'.[134]

This was the start of a lifelong campaign to establish the naturalistic basis of an ethics of mutual care, which Kropótkin published as two series in *Nineteenth Century*, the first in the last decade of the nineteenth century and then in the second decade of the twentieth, later collected as *Mutual Aid: A Factor of Evolution* (1902) and *Ethics: Origin and Development* (1922), respectively. Kropótkin drew upon his friends in the RGS; for example, thanking Freshfield 'for the facts you kindly communicate' that he promises to use in an 'article on the numberless forms which mutual aid takes in our own times, even though the structure of Society appears to be entirely individualistic'.[135] It is clear, then, that Kropótkin found some colleagues at the RGS sympathetic to his view of Darwin. In 1910, he wrote to Keltie asking:

---

[127] Kropótkin, *The State*, 40.   [128] Kropótkin, ibid., 55.
[129] Kropótkin, ibid., 56.
[130] Huxley, 'Struggle for Existence', 330. Huxley's essay was first published in the journal, *Nineteenth Century*, where Kropótkin's reply also first appeared.
[131] Huxley, 'Struggle for Existence', 331.
[132] Kropótkin, *Memoirs*, 299.   [133] Metcalf, *Knowles*, 328.
[134] Kropótkin, *Memoirs*, 300.
[135] Kropótkin to Freshfield, 30 January 1892, RGS Archives, Kropótkin Correspondence; the article appeared as 'Mutual Aid amongst Ourselves'.

Did you come across my last (Lamarckian) article in the June 'Nineteenth Century'. It may interest you—the editor seems to be very pleased with it—as it tends to show the relatively secondary part of natural selection in Evolution. Or, to speak more correctly—not so much its 'secondary' part, as its part of *selecting whole groups*—not individuals—the most capable of adaptation.[136]

On another occasion he praised Hugh Robert Mill's (1861–1950) *The Realm of Nature* promising him a copy of his own 'What Geography Ought to Be':

[Y]our Physiography pleases me *very* much. The *view* you take upon each fact of Nature, its philosophy so to say,–as well as the manner in which you tell it, simply delights me at places. [. . .] As soon as I find my paper on Geography, I will send it to you and hope that you will approve most of the ideas of it—because most are yours as well.[137]

Some few weeks later, addressing a conference of schoolteachers, Kropótkin again praised Mill's book as using Geography to give schoolchildren a grounding in the basic principles of the physical and biological sciences: '[a]n attempt at conveying such a systematical knowledge has been made in that remarkable work, the "Realm of Nature," by Dr. H. R. Mill. I find no adequate terms to express the pleasure I have myself derived from the philosophical and yet plainly worded definitions of the author'.[138]

Emphasizing the social factor gave Kropótkin a view completely different from Mackinder's of nature and of the natural basis of ethics. Bates, Keltie, Freshfield, and Mill, central to the work of the RGS, shared Kropótkin's aversion to the Social Darwinism of Huxley, and indeed of Mackinder. Others at the RGS would have been more sympathetic to Huxley and Mackinder, such as Francis Galton, the eugenicist, or the geographers Vaughan Cornish (1862–1948) and James Fairgrieve (1870–1953).[139] From this range of perspectives, it is clear, then, that biologizing Geography took several forms, each of which corresponded to particular moral and political choices. These choices were negotiated, at least in part, by contesting the lessons of Biology.

Geography and the Nature of Justice

I have suggested that Mackinder and Kropótkin's understanding of Geography, according to environment, society, and history, led to different geopolitical imaginations. Whereas both grounded their arguments in Darwinist

[136] Kropótkin to Keltie, 20 July 1910, RGS Archives, Kozlov Kropótkin Correspondence; the article was 'The Direct Action of Environment on Plants'.
[137] Kropótkin to Mill, 23 March 1893, RGS Archives, H. R. Mill Correspondence; the book was: Mill, *Realm of Nature*.
[138] Kropótkin, 'Physiography', 353; the talk was on 19 April 1893.
[139] On Galton and Fairgrieve, see the excellent: Marsden, 'Rooting Racism'. On Cornish: Dodds, 'Vaughan Cornish'.

discourse, albeit with distinct readings of Evolutionary Biology, their work naturalized quite different geopolitics. Kropótkin saw the struggle for survival as one waged by groups not individuals. The fitness of the group depended upon social solidarity and not upon the elimination of the weak through internal competition; indeed internal struggle weakened the group as a whole. Selfishness was both a public as well as a private vice. Cooperation gave individuals the security to risk innovation, which was then easily copied by others.[140] Civilization was thus a collective achievement and it was impossible with justice to individualize contributions or justify rewards: 'in recognizing the rights of Sir Such-and-Such over a house in Paris, in London, in Rouen, the law appropriates to him—unjustly—a certain part of the products of the work of all humanity'.[141] Private property and capitalism violated the evolutionary principle, and, alongside the institutions of the State, they were part of an anti-evolutionary principle that repeatedly caused civilization to regress. The struggle of humans against the limitations of their environment was crippled by these antisocial forces.

According to Kropótkin, the social principle spread through voluntary empathy and federation, and the circle of mutual support grew steadily 'from the clan to the tribe, the nation and finally to the international union of nations'.[142] At the same time, the antisocial principle was established by the State, attacking communalism wherever it could, creating new possibilities for private monopolies. For Kropótkin: '[w]hat, then, is the use of talking, with Marx, about the "primitive accumulation"–as if this "push" given to capitalists were a thing of the past? In reality, new monopolies have been granted every year till now by the Parliaments of all nations [. . .]. The State's "push" is, and has ever been, the first foundation of all great capitalist fortunes'.[143] The increasing agglomeration of capital served these monopolistic interests rather than any technical purpose: 'the "concentration" so much spoken of is often nothing but an amalgamation of capitalists for the purpose of *dominating the market*, not for cheapening the technical process'.[144] The representative democracies, he believed, represented little more than the interests of the propertied classes they truly answered to, and civil liberties were 'only respected if the people do not make use of them against the privileged classes. But the day the people begin to take advantage of them to undermine those privileges, then the so-called liberties will be cast overboard'.[145] Modern wars served the same bourgeois interests: '[o]pening

---

[140] Kropótkin, *Mutual Aid*, 14–5.

[141] Kropótkin, *Words of a Rebel*, 159.

[142] Kropótkin, *Ethics*, 17.

[143] Kropótkin, *Modern Science and Anarchism*, 83. In writing, recently, of repeated rounds of 'accumulation by dispossession', David Harvey has also questioned the idea of 'primitive accumulation' as the singular original sin of capitalism: Harvey, *New Imperialism*. Kropótkin's idea would be captured by a concept such as 'accumulation through monopoly'.

[144] Kropótkin, *Fields*, 154.

[145] Kropótkin, *Words of a Rebel*, 42.

new markets, imposing one's own merchandise, whether good or bad, is the basis of all present-day politics—European and continental—and the true cause of nineteenth-century wars'.[146] Imperialism 'succeeded in [...] bribing the better-to-do portion of the working men' for in the exploitation of backward markets 'the worker could be buoyed up by the hope that he, too, would be called upon to appropriate an ever and ever larger share of the booty to himself'.[147]

Like Mackinder, Kropótkin saw a global struggle coming between the imperial powers; yet, he thought that this conflict would begin just when finance capital could no longer make adequate returns from funding expansion: 'if war has not burst forth, it is especially due to influential financiers who find it advantageous that States should become more and more indebted. But the day on which Money will find its interest in fomenting war, human flocks will be driven against other human flocks, and will butcher one another to settle the affairs of the world's master financiers'.[148] Whereas Mackinder wanted Britain to prepare for the coming global struggle, Kropótkin instead urged revolution: 'an overthrow of the injustices accumulated by centuries past, a displacement of wealth and political power'.[149] Mackinder favoured provincial localism as providing an alternative to proletarian class identification and thus averting a dangerous challenge to the authority of the central state: '[f]or my part I do not worship King Demos'.[150] Kropótkin inclined to localism precisely because it would undermine central authority and championed Home Rule for Ireland for the very reasons at which Mackinder quailed; it would undermine the imperial government and might be the start of an 'anti-parliamentary movement'.[151] In the absence of centralized power, social harmony would 'result from an ever-changing adjustment and readjustment of equilibrium between the multitudes of forces and influences, and this adjustment would be the easier to obtain as none of the forces would enjoy a special protection from the state'.[152]

The crucial differences between Mackinder and Kropótkin thus involve their interpretations of history and community. Mackinder saw history as a struggle between races, or racialized-nations. The injunction was to compete or face extinction, or at the very least insignificance. Kropótkin saw history as a struggle between two principles: the social power of association versus the antisocial forces of capitalism and the State. The injunction was to decentralize or face oppression.

[146] Kropótkin, *Words of a Rebel*, 66.
[147] Kropótkin, 'Glimpses into the Labour Movement', 118; Kropótkin, *Anarchism*.
[148] Kropótkin, *Anarchism*.
[149] Kropótkin, 'What Revolution Means', 25.
[150] *Hansard 5th*, 145 (19 February 1921), 369.
[151] Kropótkin, 'Parliamentary Rule', 39.
[152] Kropótkin, 'Anarchism', 234.

Unlike Kropótkin, then, race was central to Mackinder's view of Empire; indeed the British Empire was needed precisely to preserve the British people, or the Anglo-Saxon race, in the global struggle for space and power. This ambivalence between British and Anglo-Saxon reflected two features of Mackinder's thought. First, Mackinder racialized nations so that he belongs to the period before the 'New Race Consciousness', following the First World War.[153] In other words, Mackinder shared a view of the world as having fifty or so races, rather than the three to five that dominated imperial and anti-colonial discourses thereafter. In addition, Mackinder, while drawing a distinction between the English and, for example, the Irish, drew little distinction between English people and the Britons abroad (including both the settler colonies that remained Dominions of the Empire and those in the United States that had, unfortunately and he hoped temporarily, left). In this respect, he was a resolute Atlanticist. The scholar of International Relations, Alfred Zimmern (1879–1957), wrote in 1953 that 'if it can be claimed for any one man that he originated the concept of the Atlantic Community—a concept which so boldly challenges the plain facts of physical geography— that man is Mackinder'.[154] Chapter 5 proposes that there was indeed a strategic basis to this Atlanticism, but it was also, more than that, profoundly racial and genealogical. This trans-Atlantic racialized community was critical to his geopolitical imaginary, a view of the world that Chapter 8 demonstrates continues through to modern Geopolitics.[155]

Kropótkin's alternative version of the social, rather than racial, bonds of communities promoted international federation and cooperation instead of civilizational conflict. Such a vision was considered by some as unnatural and idealistic; responses that indicate the extent to which Nature was—and remains—an important rhetorical resource.[156] However, as I argue in Chapter 8, imperialisms continue to be naturalized through geopolitical visions similar to those developed by Mackinder. For this reason, Kropótkin's challenge retains significance. He demonstrated how Nature could be comprehended as a cooperative force and as a singular evolutionary advantage, particularly of higher mammals. In this sense, Nature was ambivalent, containing both competition and mutual aid. At the very least, this evidence undermined the far more common argument that capitalism, imperialism, and private property were somehow natural imperatives.[157] Mackinder, who was committed to capitalism, private property, and centralized authority, pointed to Nature to justify competition and restrictions on the fertility of the

---

[153] Guterl, 'New Race Consciousness'.

[154] Zimmern, *American Road*, 20.

[155] Kramer, 'Empires, Exceptions, and Anglo-Saxons'; Horsman, *Race and Manifest Destiny*.

[156] Today, for example, new spatial imaginaries, such as the network, have changed certain aspects of current geopolitical imaginations: Castells, *Network Society*.

[157] As David Harvey reminds, social commentators often find in nature precisely those arrangements they want to pronounce desirable in society: Harvey, *Justice, Nature, and the Geography of Difference*, 157ff.

unfit. These biological 'realities' underpinned political and social actions for Mackinder: '[s]tatesmen and diplomatists succeed or fail pretty much as they recognise the irresistible power of these forces'.[158] Free will was important although limited: [t]emporary effects contrary to nature may be within human possibilities, but in the long run nature reasserts her supremacy'.[159] Kropótkin likewise made a strong case for acknowledging a naturalistic basis for empathy, and hence of conscience, solidarity and justice, but he also insisted that these fundamental human qualities could only be realized in social settings.

Mackinder's belief in the singular importance of competition and the struggle for survival sustained not only his racism but also a particular emphasis upon the masculinity of the martial races. The British had to show themselves prepared to defend their ecumene against those who would encroach upon it. The next chapter takes up a rather different intersection of Geography and Exploration and one wherein Mackinder exemplified many of the qualities he attributed to men. There were, moreover, deeper connections between masculinity, knowledge, and force that Mackinder was unable to reflect upon directly, but yet communicated through his actions. For Mackinder, the use of force in the world rested upon notions of masculinity that served as supports both for rationality and for aggression. He believed that the world had to be mastered both physically and intellectually, and that exploration forged a union of these twin purposes, albeit an unstable one. Having told the RGS that with the roll-call of exploration almost done, they must answer urgently the question, 'What is Geography?', Mackinder nevertheless found himself an un-bagged prize and rushed off to claim it in the name of Empire, science, and manliness. In 1899, he went to climb Mount Kenya.

---

[158] Mackinder, 'Physical Basis', 84.
[159] Mackinder, 'Modern Geography', 375.

4

Manly Endeavours

When the question of admitting women to the Fellowship of the Royal Geographical Society (RGS) was debated in the 1880s and 1890s, opponents objected that women were not robust enough to be explorers and scientists.[1] A sympathizer in exasperation reported that: '[o]ne young Fellow told us at a recent meeting that he objected broadly to any woman taking any part in any scientific society whatever'.[2] George Curzon, a member of the Council of the RGS, was equally bold: '[w]e contest *in toto* the general capability of women to contribute to scientific geographical knowledge. Their sex and training render them equally unfitted for exploration'.[3] The result of the RGS debates was that the admission of women Fellows, having begun in 1892, was suspended in 1893 and not resumed until 1913. Such statements and actions indicated a latent anxiety that a discipline suited to women must give up its claims to physicality, plain-speaking, serious-mindedness, and precision. If the making of knowledge in Geography required the use of virile force, geographers of the first rank must be men, while women, instead, might at best aspire to entertain readers with travel writing.[4]

While not virile enough to be admitted into the RGS, women were, nonetheless, central to the project of Empire. The literary critic, Amy Kaplan, described the early-twentieth century Empire as a 'nostalgic' space where men might escape the many domestic challenges to psychic coherence in a place where they could enjoy the pleasures of action unfettered by the challenges of feminism, socialism, or democracy.[5] Other feminist and political scholars of the New Imperial History have noted that gender both shapes and is shaped by geopolitical imaginaries.[6] In other words, Empire was inflected by, and

[1] Bell and McEwan, 'Admission of Women Fellows'.
[2] *Times*, 29 May 1893, 7c.
[3] *Times*, 31 May 1893, 11d. Curzon, himself, was an adventurous explorer although he was dogged through life by a cruel rhyme from his college days, that dubbed him an effeminate snob: 'My name is George Nathaniel Curzon | I am a most superior person | My hair is soft, my face is sleek, | I dine at Blenheim once a week'; Wright, 'Curzon and Persia', 343.
[4] McEwan, *Gender, Geography and Empire*.
[5] Kaplan, 'Romancing the Empire', 660; Allen, 'Men Interminably in Crisis?'.
[6] On the New Imperial History and feminist theories of Empire, see: Wilson, *A New Imperial History*; *idem*, 'Old Imperialisms and New Imperial Histories'; Thompson, 'New Imperial History'; Burton, 'Thinking beyond the Boundaries'; and Janiewski, 'Engendering the Invisible Empire'. On more recent discussions of imperialism and international relations, see: Enloe, *Bananas, Beaches and Bases*; Hooper, *Manly States*; Tickner, 'Gendering a Discipline'.

appealed to, personal and social attachments defined by gender roles. Young working-class women, for example, were invited to settle in the colonies as wives, and, in an address to the Camlachie Women's Unionist Association, Mackinder called the emigration of women to the colonies 'a great imperial work [...] which would make things healthier there and healthier here'.[7] Working-class men were called to the colours as soldiers; middle-class men were addressed as decision-makers and voters; whereas their sisters, mothers, and wives were invited to take an interest and applaud.

The spaces of Empire were also gendered because they were shaped by physical force. For Mackinder, physical force was a male attribute and a national virtue. The 'ethical condition' of the British people comprised 'their energy, knowledge, honesty, and faith' in contrast to effeminate Others.[8] In a world where 'the principle of nationalities has carried the day', Mackinder argued in 1905 that those who 'dream of a general philanthropy which is slowly to efface all frontiers' may find 'the whole conception of permanent struggle [...] repellent' but they would also find themselves ineffective, impotent.[9] He believed that government by majority rested upon the threat that it could be backed up by overwhelming force: '[t]he sanction [...] of party government is that there must be the possibility of civil war'.[10] In that sense: '[a] vote is a cheque or draft on power, and ultimately, on physical power'.[11] Parliament and parties were agreeable conventions that could at any point be reduced to their real foundations: 'I am willing to obey the majority if that majority has all the physical force necessary to coerce me—if it is a considerable majority, if it is a virile majority'.[12]

Elsewhere, Mackinder made the same point using racialized and gendered metaphors. During the First World War, he referred to Britain's responsibilities in Europe: '[w]e are the nation which to-day has in this Europe the maximum of man-power. We have not had to spend our blood in the way France did in defending us at Verdun. Europe is looking to us to hold steady the system at the present time in the last great struggle of Germany which is shaking us'.[13] Dismissing the pacifist tendencies of free-trade, Mackinder exclaimed: '[w]e have had enough of that wishy-washy philanthropy for the last fifty or sixty years'.[14] 'Wishy-washy' was a term originally coined to refer to weak or insubstantial beer or soup, but by the mid-nineteenth century it referred to Chinese laundrymen, with the implication that they were of an

---

[7] *Glasgow Herald*, 12 December 1913, clipping in Mackinder Papers, School of Geography, Oxford University, MP/C/400 [ii]. Camlachie was the district of Glasgow that Mackinder represented in the House of Commons as a member of the Unionist Party (Conservatives).

[8] Mackinder, *Britain and the British Seas*, 358.

[9] Mackinder, 'Man-Power', 141.

[10] *The Official Report, House of Commons, 5th Series* [*Hansard 5th*], 25 (5 May 1911), 761.

[11] *Hansard 5th*, 25 (5 May 1911), 763.

[12] ibid., 34 (19 February 1912), 368.

[13] ibid., 93 (16 May 1917), 1654.

[14] ibid., 93 (16 May 1917), 1656.

effeminate race, neither virile nor decisive.[15] During his travels in Africa, Mackinder also observed that: '[t]he Indians are an effeminate race compared with the Swahilis'.[16] In contrast, Mackinder's praise for the defeated enemy in the First World War bonded race and gender in opposite fashion: 'we should only be cheapening our own achievement if we did not recognize in the North German one of the three or four most virile races of mankind'.[17]

Mackinder understood not only race, but also nation and class in terms of virility and masculinity. When he asked in 1919, for example, whether Britain would act to remain powerful or preferred instead to 'construct for the future some old house into which to retire?', he implied that there was a life cycle of nations and urged the British to remain young and vigorous.[18] Mackinder also used the same language to characterize social classes and in one speech on the folly of free trade and pacifism, he offered the British a vision of themselves as still productive, or becoming, like the Dutch, a nation of lenders: '[y]ou may become a rich, small *bourgeois* nation, or, on the other hand, you may determine that this nation will make its fortune afresh, that the strength of this nation shall lie, not in these fat *bourgeoisie*, living on the fortunes of the past, but in a great, vigorous, magnificent nation of workmen'.[19]

For Mackinder, creating a 'nation of workmen' meant that women belonged to the domestic sphere. Women were to civilize men 'from being the irresponsible creatures that they are by nature', by making clear how women were dependent upon men and, in this respect: 'I regard it as discreditable to us that a large number of our women should be earning their living instead of attending to their homes, and I shall do anything in my power to remove them from that position'.[20] Speaking in the House of Commons opposing extending the franchise to women, Mackinder said he had always 'opposed women's suffrage'.[21] He argued that many, perhaps the majority, of women did not want the vote because they could see that it 'will bring about changes in the whole status of women'.[22] There may come occasions when the majority of men in a constituency would vote one way by a small margin, but the majority of women vote the other way by a much larger margin and, then, the female vote would have triumphed over the male. If

---

[15] The ethnic associations of this term are indexed by the creation of the pantomime version of Aladdin in the mid-nineteenth century. In the earlier *Tales of One Thousand and One Nights*, Aladdin was a Chinese boy abducted to Persia. In adapting the tale for the stage, Aladdin was given a comical mother, Widow Twanky, and an indecisive and ineffectual brother, Wishy-Washy, who worked in the family's laundry.

[16] Mackinder, 'Diary', 55.

[17] Mackinder, *Democratic Ideals and Reality*, 110.

[18] *Hansard 5th*, 116 (21 May 1919), 465.

[19] ibid., 114 (25 March 1919), 333–4.

[20] ibid., 25 (5 May 1911), 764.

[21] ibid., 94 (19 June 1917), 1699. Mackinder persisted in his opposition, voting not only with the majority of Unionists (113 of 200) against referring the Bill to a Second Reading but even with a rump of 29 who refused to consent to the Bill going finally to Committee; *Times*, 14 July 1920, 9b.

[22] *Hansard 5th*, 94 (19 June 1917), 1702.

this happened in enough places, women might determine an election. This would, he suggested, create a crisis because the men would challenge the decision through brute force; 'the great men's unions of the country might set themselves wholly against the decision which would then be forced upon Parliament'.[23] Allowing women to vote would create a system in which votes 'no longer represented real physical sovereignty'.[24]

Gender and masculinity, as these examples indicate, were central to thinking about Geography and Empire, about politics, and about social relations between so-called races, nations, and classes. In particular, gender roles normalized a male monopoly over, and responsibility to use, force for the cause of Empire. The ambitions of Empire allowed for a very signifi-cant militarization of society that, in turn, had significant 'masculinized privileging effects'.[25] These privileges included the right to use force with impunity both because the people upon whom it would be practised were of lesser status, and because this ready resort to force was essential to imperial potency. Describing the 'imperialist character', Hannah Arendt (1906–75) wrote that '[r]ace [...] was an escape into an irresponsibility where nothing human could any longer exist'.[26] Indigenous peoples were assimilated to the local populations of fierce mammals.[27] Racism sanc-tioned masculine violence, and the Empire provided one arena for such manly endeavours.

Of course, the leisure of the nineteenth-century British aristocracy already included a quite staggering amount of killing. Under the pretence of serving their kitchens, men killed prodigious numbers of birds. They stocked their estates with deer and provided dens for foxes to reproduce, only to chase and tear apart these animals. They blooded their children from the dead foxes, initiating them into the aristocratic culture of violent leisure.[28] Yet in the colonies, the animals were bigger, faster, more fierce, and their killing was undiluted by the presence of women, as was the case for fox-hunting in Britain.[29] Men demonstrated their virility by killing wild animals abroad and bringing back trophies of tusks, heads, skins, and photographs to their homes.[30]

Not only did men kill wild animals, they also indulged the adventure of exploration, which came to include mountaineering: 'by the 1890s mountains were added to the list of open questions pursued by exploration'.[31] Climbing mountains taught virtues that made people 'truly *men*: brotherhood, discipline,

[23] *Hansard 5th*, 94 (19 June 1917), 1705.   [24] *Hansard 5th*, 94 (19 June 1917), 1705.
[25] Enloe, *Maneuvers*, 294.   [26] Arendt, 'Imperialist Character', 303.
[27] Haraway, 'Teddy Bear Patriarchy'.
[28] Griffin, *Blood Sport*, 131.
[29] McKenzie, 'Big-Game Hunting'.
[30] Wonders, 'Hunting Narratives'.
[31] Ellis, 'Vertical Margins', 17.

selflessness, fortitude, sang-froid'.[32] In this respect these challenges cultivated 'an assertive masculinity to uphold [the] imagined sense of British imperial power'.[33] Mountaineering could be exploration to the extent that the trip was the first ascent or the first mapping.[34] This was an inter-imperial contest as 'mountains in Europe and further afield became pinnacles of the natural world to be "hunted" and "conquered" by robust and manly British men'.[35]

Few men and fewer women climbed mountains in the cause of Empire, but these somewhat exceptional events amplify relations between masculinity, race, knowledge, and imperial politics that are pervasive but perhaps less evident in more mundane spheres. Below I describe two very different climbs, of Mount Kenya (1899) by Mackinder and of Mount Cameroon (1895) by the anthropologist and well-known writer Mary Kingsley, to highlight distinctive understandings of what was considered socially appropriate for men and women, and to indicate their own personal sense of appropriate action while exploring. Over three months in 1899, Mackinder climbed from about 5,000 feet up to the glaciated summit of Mount Kenya (Donyo Egere, the Striped Mountain; 17,058 feet), the second highest peak in East Africa. In one week in September 1895, Mary Kingsley climbed, from sea level, the unglaciated but tallest mountain in West Africa, Mount Cameroon (Mungo Mah Lobeh, Throne of Thunder; 13,435 feet). Duty was the (gendered) motive provided by both Mackinder and Kingsley to climb; but such a focus ignores the desires and pleasures that animated their excursions. For both Mackinder and Kingsley, the visit to Africa was something of a personal indulgence. After the climb, Mackinder refashioned himself as a virile explorer who had had privileged access to the pleasures involved in the Empire as a sphere of action and spoke of the Kenya expedition as a 'spell of freedom'. Kingsley, a campaigner for mercantile—rather than settler—colonialism, also spoke of her climb in terms of freedom, but from her domestic obligations. It was her second trip to Africa and she had greatly enjoyed her first. After her parents died in 1894, both she and her brother decided to travel abroad: 'there were no more odd jobs any one wanted me to do at home'.[36]

An analysis of both Mackinder's and Kingley's writings, as well as the public circulation and reception of their adventures, demonstrates the ways that heroic acts detached the protagonists from responsibility for the consequences and preconditions of their visit. Indeed, notions of Empire 'as

---

[32] Schama, *Landscape and Memory*, 503.

[33] Hansen, 'Alpine Club', 304. In a very interesting paper, Garth Myers shows how later ambivalence about Empire was reflected in the narrative of a failed attempt to climb Mount Kenya that problematized both imperialism and masculinity: 'Colonial Geography and Masculinity'.

[34] Ellis, 'Vertical Margins', 27.

[35] Ryan, 'Photography, Geography and Empire', 126.

[36] Kingsley, *Studies*, xxi.

adventure' presumed a certain masculinity among imperialists, and these two climbs highlight anxieties about masculinity in very distinctive ways. On one hand, for Mackinder, the New Geography represented a claim to objectivity and science, but his New Geography was also dangerously sedentary compared to the manliness of the earlier explorer tradition. Claiming the mountain for British science and for the Empire would enhance his manly reputation at a time when his scientific practice and (as I shall show later in this chapter) even his private life seemed to call this into question. For Kingsley, the associations between science, climbing, adventure, and masculinity were more unsettling. She presented her contributions to knowledge as precisely avoiding the objectivity, and thus masculinity, of science, yet, because her climbing was not done in front of European men, she was still able to present herself as a representative of a masculine race. Mackinder's and Kingsley's climbs thus illuminate broader issues of masculinity, racism, violence, and science that are at the conjunction of Geopolitics and Empire.

Geography and the Peaks of Imperialism

Reporting on the founding meeting of the RGS in 1831, the *Quarterly Review* noted that Geography was a subject so undemanding that even women might benefit from exposure to its travellers' tales without risk to their constitution.[37] Not all contemporaries, nor even all male geographers, accepted that the female constitution justified disabilities upon women in education and the professions.[38] In 1893, the *Times* editorialized that: '[t]here really does not seem to be anything in the nature of geography which should make it particularly difficult to discuss in the presence of ladies. Strange races have strange customs, sometimes, no doubt, but, as lady travellers visit their countries, and observe their ways, they can neither be shocked nor astonished to hear those ways described'.[39] To the charge that few women were fitted to be explorers, Douglas Freshfield, a member of the RGS Council, replied that while '[s]cientific geographers are employed in the study as well as in the field', 'a comparatively small proportion of our Fellows can be makers of knowledge; most of us are content to be receivers and transmitters only'.[40]

---

[37] 'Royal Geographical Society'.
[38] Smith-Rosenberg and Rosenberg, 'Female Animal'.
[39] *Times*, 29 May 1893, 9d.
[40] *Times*, 6 June 1893, 6e.

Such concerns over female fragility may have had more to do with the standing of Geography in academia; some Fellows of the RGS worried that the mere presence of women at the Society reduced its status.[41] In one debate, Mr. Hicks spoke to this effect when he asked: '[i]s the Society to be a scientific or a pleasure society?'[42] Any subject that women could study must, by that fact, be physically undemanding, unscientific, and trivial. The relations between knowledge and virility are evident in Joseph Conrad's (1857–1924) view that '[o]f all sciences, geography finds its origin in action, and what is more in adventurous action'.[43] Conrad went on to praise the imagination and adventure of early exploration ('Geography Fabulous'), and even the struggle of the period when the world was taken from indigenous peoples for colonial purposes ('Geography Militant'), before it lost all excitement with the 'bloodless' certainties of the 'bored professors' who followed the period after the great discoveries ('Geography Triumphant').[44] Masculinist geographers insisted that Geography relied upon knowledge wrested from unknown parts through dangerous physical exertion, and that such exploration was beyond the physical capacity of women. They believed that the subject matter of Geography was too indelicate to speak of in the presence of women. Women, they claimed, were not serious-minded enough to be scientists and scientific Geography required a precision in the making of observations that was alien to the biology and personality of women.

As noted in Chapters 2 and 3, however, there was an apparent contradiction between understandings of Geography as exploration and Geography as science. In turning away from exploration, the New Geography risked the manly reputation of the discipline and, in compensation, many geographers who emphasized the notion of Geography as science felt compelled to climb. Richard Phillips suggests that 'British masculinity [. . . was] constituted in the geography of adventure'.[45] The masculinity and imperialism of the subject were produced at the same time. Clements Markham, President of the RGS when Mackinder was planning his expedition, argued that exploration fused national and scientific values through the cultivation of physical courage:

Of this splendid courage, which knows no turning back from duty, no fear, no thought of self, our best discoverers and explorers are made. It is with such stuff that the greatness of our country has been built up; as well as by that moral courage which prompts men, in positions of responsibility, to decide upon the right course, which is usually the boldest course.[46]

---

[41] More generally, see: Rose, *Feminism and Geography*.
[42] *Times*, 30 May 1893, 9e.
[43] Conrad, 'Geography and Some Explorers', 2.
[44] This essay has been widely discussed, see, for example: Driver, 'Geography's Empire'.
[45] Phillips, *Mapping Men and Empire*, 55.
[46] Markham, 'Field of Geography', 6.

While Mackinder was making a career as a New Geographer, one who would take the discipline into the post-Exploration era of scientific environmentalism, he nevertheless chased the palm as explorer in 1899.[47] Mackinder wanted to straddle the two latter periods of Conrad's scheme (Geography Militant and Geography Triumphant) and shared Conrad's admiration for knowledge gained through struggle. Mackinder was the first European to climb Mount Kenya and he brought back his spoils: photographic evidence, a transect of his route, sketches of the positions of the main glaciers, altitudinal and meteorological observations, biological and botanic specimens, and, for his own satisfaction, a rock taken from the very top of the mountain. He followed Douglas Freshfield's 1893 version of the RGS's famous *Hints to Travellers*, by keeping notebooks from which he hoped later to write up a full diary of his journey.[48] He wired news of his success to John Scott Keltie, the Secretary of the RGS, and presented the first public account of his expedition to the Society on 22 January 1900.[49] In his reflections of the 1940s, Mackinder appeared explicit about the purpose of his climb: 'it was still necessary at that time for me to prove that I could explore as well as teach'.[50] In the draft Introduction to his Kenya book, probably written in the 1920s, Mackinder recalled that he had been working for ten years at Oxford and Reading and 'it seemed to me that a spell of freedom was desirable. Perhaps too there was the ambition no longer to count as a mere armchair geographer'.[51]

The ostensible motive for Mackinder's expedition was scientific. Upon Mackinder's departure from England in June 1899, the *Times* reported that the party was 'well equipped' by instrument and personnel for 'carrying on scientific work' and from the base camp at an elevation of about 16,000 feet, 'they hope to make a good map of the whole mountain, ascend to its summit, journey all round it, investigate its glaciation and its geology, and make ample collections of animals and plants'.[52] Announcing Mackinder's success to an evening meeting of the RGS, Markham described it as a 'model exploring journey'.[53] When Mackinder gave his account to the RGS, it was in triumphant terms. Noted as present at the talk, were: his wife, Bonnie

---

[47] Part of the answer lies with the internal politics of the RGS. Ellis has noted that when, as President, Clements Markham set out for the RGS the challenges remaining to exploration in 1893, he did not include much about mountaineering but had come to do so by 1896: Ellis, 'Vertical Margins', 85–7.

[48] Freshfield and Wharton, *Hints to Travellers*. On the *Hints*, see Driver, *Geography Militant*. Mackinder's notebooks are now in the Rhodes House Library, Oxford University (Mss. Afr. r.11–28), as is a typescript of the notebooks edited into a diary (Mss. Afr. r.29–30). There is a manuscript and a typescript of parts of a proposed book in the Department of Geography. The typescript version of the diary in Rhodes House Library (Mss. Afr. r.29–30) was edited by Michael Barbour and subsequently published; Mackinder, 'Diary'.

[49] Mackinder, 'A Journey'.

[50] Mackinder, 'Autobiographical Fragments', MP/C/100 [envelope d, x].

[51] Mackinder, 'Diary', 31.

[52] *Times*, 14 June 1899, 8b.

[53] *Times*, 14 November 1899, 3e.

Mackinder (1869–1962); his father-in-law, the biblical scholar, Dr. David Ginsburg (1831–1914); his sister-in-law, Hildegarde Hinde (1871–1959), and her husband, Sidney Hinde (1863–1930); and various knights of the realm and important scientists.[54] He was announced to loud cheering and went on to give an account of the climb that emphasized the distance covered, the ecosystems encountered, and the various heights taken. In concluding, he noted that: '[t]he results of the expedition were a plane-table sketch of the upper part of Kenya, together with rock specimens, two route surveys along lines not previously traversed, a series of meteorological and hypsometrical observations, photographs by the ordinary and by the Ives colour process, collections of mammals, birds and plants, and a small collection of insects'.[55]

Mackinder had to make no apology for climbing a mountain in the cause of science because he had the scientific alibi of survey, observation, and collection. In his notes for the unrealized autobiography, Mackinder described 1899 as 'in some ways the culminating year of my life', 'my Kenya year'.[56] It gave him the aura of a true explorer, a hero. One correspondent wrote to him that: '[m]y Sibyl (aetat: 15) worships you shyly and distantly as a hero. When the long account of your work came out in the "Standard", she insisted on reading it to her governess, "instead of lessons"'.[57] Writing to Mackinder's sister-in-law a decade after his death, a niece asserted that: 'H.J.M. is certainly the hero of the younger generation! Every school boy pricks up his ears at the mention of the name [and] knows his work AND "the man who first climbed Mt. Kenya"!!'[58] Mackinder had proved himself as a geographer, an imperialist, and thus a man. But what did it mean to prove that he could explore and before whom did he want to count?

The relations between masculinity and Empire were particularly evident in Mackinder's ascent of Mount Kenya in 1899. In the 1880s and 1890s, Germany and Britain competed for control of territory in East Africa yet neither had done much to exploit the resources of their putative holdings. Mackinder was always alert to the imperial challenge of Germany and in the draft 'Introduction' for his Kenya Book, he praised the German missionary Johann Ludgwig Krapf (1810–81) for realizing as early as 1860 that East Africa would be essential for the defence of India.[59] He noted that the British government failed to realize the region's importance and that '[t]he region to the west of Zanzibar revealed by the labour of so many British explorers and missionaries was suffered in 1886 [...] to pass into the hands of the Germans. As what appeared mere salvage from the wreck, the area lying further northward between Mombasa and the Victoria Nyanza was left open to

[54] *Times*, 24 January 1900, 4e.
[55] *Times*, 24 January 1900, 4e.
[56] Mackinder, 'Autobiographical Fragments', MP/C/100 [d, x].
[57] Rev. J. G. Bailey to Mackinder, 20 January 1900, MP/F/100, item 88.
[58] Jean Ritchie to Ellie Mackinder, 4 March 1958, MP/D/500.
[59] Mackinder, 'Diary', 30.

British enterprise'.[60] Border conflicts continued and when Mackinder was there, he was told of imperial struggle by local proxies: 'the English Masai are on the way to attack the German Masai and [. . .] the Germans have sent up some troops'.[61] Through this region of modern Uganda and Kenya, the British were building the Uganda railway, which, by 1898, had reached past Nairobi to the Athi Plains.

The German climber, Hans Meyer (1858–1929), who had already become the first European on the summit of the tallest mountain in East Africa, Kilimanjaro, announced in 1898 that he would next try for the second highest, Kenya. Significantly, it was this prospect that provided Mackinder with the official spur for his campaign. As I discuss below, there were perhaps more private and slightly earlier motives. He spent the summer of 1898 training to climb in the Alps but had shown no previous inclination. In August 1898, he got permission from the Foreign Office for the expedition on condition that he follow the local instructions of 'Her Majesty's Commissioner as to whether it will safe to proceed' since the area 'is at present in a disturbed condition'.[62] In January 1899, he solicited the support of the RGS for what he described as a 'visit [to] Mount Kenya next summer, availing of the completion of the Ugandan railway'.[63] The RGS gave him £200 towards the anticipated expenses of £1,200 and Mackinder split the rest between himself and his wife's uncle, Campbell Hausburg (1873–1941). All was done covertly because 'I had no wish to find myself competitor in a race up a virgin peak'.[64] The race with the German, Meyer, was implicit and was understood by Mackinder, at least, as an inter-imperial rivalry. This was exploration for Mackinder, because he was to beat the German to the peak, an outcome he announced to an international Geographical Congress then meeting in Berlin, through his cabled news to Keltie.

Kingsley, in contrast, presented the motives for her trip as a matter of filial duty, of honouring the memory of her father by continuing his studies of religious fetish. Yet she also wished to serve the cause of science by bringing back fish specimens for the British Museum and help her friends the Liverpool merchants by collecting further evidence of the benevolence of purely mercantile imperialism. After her father's death she presented in public the image of the grieving daughter (Figure 4.1), always in black, always dutiful to his revered memory, despite his many peccadilloes.[65] She also spoke with the

---

[60] Mackinder, 'Diary', 31.

[61] Mackinder, 'Diary', 52.

[62] Francis Bertie (for Foreign Secretary, Lord Salisbury) to Mackinder, 13 August 1898, MP/F/100, item 38.

[63] Mackinder to Clements Markham, 18 January 1899, MP/F/100, item 37.

[64] Mackinder, 'Patron's Medal', 231.

[65] Cambridge University Library: Royal Commonwealth Society Library, Portrait of Mary Kingsley, Y3043T. From a letter mounted in the frame, we know that while her younger brother considered this the best picture of her, she 'did not care for this portrait'. It is certainly rather conventional with the parasol, and the flowers both in her hair and scattered artfully at her feet. In one respect, though, it is

Fig. 4.1. A studio portrait of Mary
Kingsley from the 1890s

Source: By kind permission of Cambridge University Library.

authority of experience about the marvellous administration that had been provided to the people of the region by a man she idolized, George Goldie (1846–1925): '[f]or twenty years the natives under the Royal Niger Company have had the firm, wise, sympathetic friendship of a great Englishman, who understood them, and knew them personally'.[66]

She had to admit, though, that while the expedition as a whole could be justified as an obligation, climbing Mount Cameroon was not only about duty for '[t]here's next to no fish on [mountains . . .], and precious little fetish, as the population on them is sparse'.[67] Her excuse was that she felt 'quite sure that no white man has ever looked on the great peak of Cameroon without a desire arising in his mind to ascend it'.[68] The first European recorded as climbing the mountain was Richard Burton (1821–90), a particular hero of Kingsley's and now she 'would be the first Englishman, as she termed herself, to ascend by the south-east face'.[69] Significantly, Kingsley presented herself as an English*man* in accepting the challenge of the mountain; she felt able to assert this while abroad, beyond the immediate censorship of British, male company.

The adventures of Mackinder and Kingsley had a complex relationship with the narratives that ultimately presented them to a wider readership. To a very great extent they acted precisely so that their deeds could be retold; their

an image that Kingsley chose, for she is wearing black, as she did in public from the time of her father's death (George Henry Kingsley, 1827–92).

[66] Kingsley, *Studies*, 307.   [67] Kingsley, *Travels*, 549.
[68] Kingsley, ibid., 550.   [69] Pearce, *Kingsley*, 66.

value was realized in their narration. Telling their tales was in some part a process of subjectivation, for the two climbers both presented and even understood themselves in terms of the different models of personality that each appealed to in their writings.[70] Accounts of climbing presented the climber as a central character regardless of the broader pretensions of the author. These presentations and self-understandings link the world of words to the world of actions; they link the climb to the narratives of the climb.

Following the literary scholar, Mary Louise Pratt, I distinguish three narrations of Empire in these accounts of climbing: the archaic, the objective, and the sentimental.[71] Each type presents the spaces of Empire by implying a particular orientation of the observer towards the scene. Archaism produces and performs a patronizing viewer, objectivity a dispassionate and scientific observer, and sentimentalism an ironic and self-mocking narrator. The archaic and the objective are distanced perspectives deployed particularly by Mackinder, whereas Kingsley wrote largely from a sentimental perspective.

The archaic will be explored in greater detail in Chapter 6 through a discussion of the Orientalism of Mackinder's geographical textbooks. Broadly speaking, the anti-historicism of the archaic mode places the spaces of Empire beyond the realm of autonomous historical change.[72] The Europeans noted, in an archaeological gesture, that the remains of the once great societies had so decayed that the spaces of Empire were left in need of the improving gesture of European cultivation and direction. Travelling towards his goal in Kenya, Mackinder gazed with just such an improving eye: '[i]f only water were available what glorious wheat fields these would make'.[73] The self-proclaimed goals of the New Geography, as described in Chapter 3, presented it through the second distancing rhetoric, objective science, a rhetoric distanced from the third, sentimental writing. Geography as a manly endeavour meant policing the membership as well as the contents of the discipline. The maintenance of those borders ran through the narratives of learning about the spaces of the Empire, dividing (masculinist) objective Geography from (feminized) subjective Travel Writing.[74] Objectivity placed the European actor offstage, as a scientific, detached observer of an external world. The world appeared to the objective surveyor as an exhibition that they had no part in arranging.[75]

Kingsley was fully aware that the 'objective gaze' of the geographer was not a position available to her. In 1895, when Kingsley first addressed the Liverpool Geographical Society, her paper was read for her by a man; although in November 1897 the Society suspended their rules to allow her

---

[70] Foucault, *History of Sexuality*; Kearns, 'History of Medical Geography'.
[71] Pratt, *Imperial Eyes*. I have elaborated upon this in more detail in: Kearns, 'Imperial Subject'.
[72] Said, *Orientalism*; S. Amin, *Eurocentrism*; Young, *White Mythologies*.
[73] Mackinder, 'Diary', 98.
[74] McEwan, 'Cutting Power Lines'.
[75] Mitchell, *Colonising Egypt*; Gregory, *Geographical Imaginations*.

to address them in person.[76] After her first trip to West Africa, she was mentioned as likely to be the first woman to address the RGS. She protested to Keltie: 'I am very vexed to see a paragraph that is going the rounds saying that I am to read a paper before the RGS. I should not if you asked me and you have not asked me'.[77] In 1899, she was asked to support a campaign for admitting women to scientific societies. She demurred, although in terms that made the case for inclusion even as she disavowed it:

I have never had a school education to entitle me to a degree and in science I am only a collector of specimens and as a traveller though I have travelled further in West Africa than any of my countrymen still I have never fixed a point or taken an observation or in fact done any surveying work that entitles me to be called a Geographer.[78]

She was, however, invited to join the Anthropological Society, after she had privately solicited this from Edward Tylor, Professor of Anthropology at Oxford University.[79]

Her distance from the objective and speculative science of Geography was on grounds of gender and she presented herself as someone who 'cares for facts, without theories draping them'.[80] Similarly, in describing her involvement with imperialist politics, she flattered Joseph Chamberlain that, as a woman, she might be good on details but that she left abstract concepts to men such as he.[81] There is also a different spatial model of investigation. Instead of the linear route of the explorer, Kingsley stayed for quite a long time in one place and ventured in 'centripetal fashion' to and from various places that interested her.[82] The geographer, Alison Blunt, identifies this model as an interest in 'positionality' rather than in the 'linear mapping' of contemporary Geography.[83] Geographers produced their knowledge in cartographic terms and aspired to render it objectively by map and survey. Kingsley disowned this method: 'my means of learning are not the scientific ones—Taking observations, Surveying, Fixing points, &c., &c.'[84] Keltie, at least, took her at her word and accepting her denial of pretensions to geographical science yet noted in a review that she still 'proves herself possessed of the geographical instinct in many particulars'.[85]

Kingsley adopted the third narrative strategy of imperial detachment, namely sentimentalism, placing herself at the heart of the story. But, as Pratt brilliantly notes, the protagonist is surrounded 'by an aura not of authority, but of innocence and vulnerability'.[86] The sentimental heroine is subject to all sorts of trials and tribulations but prevails through empathy rather than manly force. Empathy was part of the paternalist manners of the improving philanthropist, as Sara Mills has noted for many upper-class women travellers.[87] The sentimentalist did not cultivate the separation

---

[76] Frank, *Voyage Out.*   [77] Birkett, *Kingsley,* 63.   [78] Birkett, *Kingsley,* 156.
[79] Frank, *Voyage Out.*   [80] Kingsley, *Studies,* viii.
[81] Blunt, *Travel, Gender and Imperialism.*   [82] Pratt, *Imperial Eyes,* 158.
[83] Blunt, 'Mapping Authorship', 61.   [84] Kingsley, *Travels,* 101.
[85] Keltie, 'Kingsley', 324.   [86] Pratt, *Imperial Eyes,* 56.   [87] Mills, *Discourses of Difference.*

from landscape that enabled the objective scientist to procure replicable measurements. Kingsley, for example, described her pleasure at the sight of some rapids, which caused her 'to lose all sense of human individuality, all memory of human life, with its grief and worry and doubt, and become part of the atmosphere'.[88] The female observer had a license to 'aestheticize rather than analyze'.[89]

To thus distinguish instinct from science was part and parcel of Victorian notions of feminine, rather than masculine, knowledges. However, through this subject position, Kingsley was to suffer many injustices from contemporary geographers. In the midst of a broadly sympathetic account of the campaign to include women within the RGS, Hugh Robert Mill, its Librarian, contrasted Isabella Bird Bishop (1831–1904) and Mary Kingsley as lady travellers. He saw Bishop as hungry for recognition, whereas 'Mary Kingsley, on the contrary, asked no favours and never posed as anything but what she was, an ardent, plain-spoken seeker after new experiences, as reluctant to ask for help as she was indifferent to praise'.[90] His compliment, however, was misleading for, in terms of the campaign to admit women, it was Bishop's refusal to speak to an evening meeting of the RGS, while there was a ban on women as Fellows, that produced the initial change in practice in 1892.[91] Kingsley in fact argued that the geographical method produced knowledge of the land but not of its people, that the curiosity of the ethnologist is a surer basis for benevolent rule. The ethnologists were 'not explorers of Africa—because we never exactly know where we go, and we never exactly care'.[92] Moreover, the self-deprecation of Kingsley was integral to a sentimental narrative style discussed below that she cultivated in the shadow of this patronizing treatment on grounds of gender.

In the purposes they could avow, and in the type of knowledge they could claim to have won, Mackinder and Kingsley were divided one from the other by their very different relations to the codes of masculinity. As the geographer, Derek Gregory, has pointed out, there is a distinct spatiality to subjectivity; the distance between the act and the reception of the act was part of what it meant to prove oneself as an explorer.[93] Yet to focus only upon the proclaimed motives and reception of the climb—that is, duty to Geography as science or duty to family and science, and the respective distancing narrative strategies they used—ignores other, more personal, reasons they may have had to climb. In addition to narrative strategies, I examine below their practices and social interactions with local peoples in the field the better to understand imperial desire, while also highlighting the tensions between the creation of their public persona as explorers and their personal lives. Their distinctive narrative strategies and the public personae

[88] Kingsley, *Travels*, 178.   [89] Suleri, *Rhetoric of English India*, 75.
[90] Mill, *Autobiography*, 93.   [91] Bell and McEwan, 'Admission of Women', 297.
[92] Kingsley, *Studies*, 379.   [93] Gregory, *Geographical Imaginations*.

created after their climbs became alibis for actions in the field that may otherwise have been unethical at home. These distancing acts were anticipated; in the field they adopted the persona that would later become a central character in their respective narratives of their climbs. The irresponsibility and impunity of the imperial character highlighted by Arendt figured somewhat differently in accounts by the patronizing observer of the archaic scene, the rational observer of the objective scene, and the ironic observer of the sentimental scene, but were most evident in how the climber-explorers engaged with questions of racial difference.

Desire 'in the field': Knowing Race

The context of the encounter between imperial traveller and colonized local was established by previous relations between Europeans and Africans in the region. Whereas both Kingsley and Mackinder moved in areas over which the British claimed to have established authority, violence still threatened their privileged mobility. Into the area through which Mackinder travelled, a British adventurer, Captain Alfred Haslam (1864–98), had, in 1898, wandered without warning, and had been captured and killed. In retaliation, the British sent soldiers to torch villages and killed some 100 Kikuyu people.[94] As James Clifford remarks more generally of the safety of anthropologists in the field: '[a]ll over the world "natives" learned, the hard way, not to kill whites. The cost, often a punitive expedition against your people, was too high'.[95]

Travelling in Africa depended upon securing assistance from local, indigenous people. That assistance was solicited, directed, and rewarded in ways that combined payment, empathy, and violence. The balance was struck differently by Kingsley and Mackinder. For Kingsley, empathy was a survival strategy that obviated cowardly, and probably ineffective, violence. For Mackinder, violence was the ultimate source of authority and it was necessary only for subordinates to understand the sanction in order that they obey.

Empathy

Kingsley owned that 'I like the African on the whole, a thing I never expected to when I went to the Coast with the idea that he was a degraded, savage, cruel brute; but that is a trifling error you soon get rid of when you know

---

[94] Barbour, 'Introduction', 13.   [95] Clifford, 'Travelling Cultures', 112.

him'.[96] Her knowledge of foreign peoples was gendered insofar as that, as a woman, brute force was a less available form of interaction. Moreover, she found threatening African people with a revolver to be 'utter idiocy', thinking there was 'something cowardly in it'.[97] She claimed to be exasperated with the sensationalist way her travels were received: ' "Oh, Miss Kingsley *how* many *men* did you kill?" *I* who never lost a porter'.[98] She boasted that she had 'never raised hand nor caused hand to be raised against a native'.[99] Instead, Kingsley learned the pidgin English of the coastal traders so that she could talk to her African companions. She thought all men could be bribed in the same way noting that 'whenever you see a man, black or white, filled with a nameless longing, it is tobacco that he requires'.[100] She traded for food, eating what was available locally, and thus came not to require a large safari for carrying her European food into Africa. She compared travelling in Africa to edging along a precipice with 'gulfs of murder looming on each side' and yet there was usually 'sufficient holding ground; not on rock in the bush village inhabited by murderous cannibals, but on the ideas in men's and women's minds; and those ideas, which I think I may say you will always find, give you safety'.[101]

The second way her knowledge of African people was gendered was through the empathetic *insights* she thought being a woman provided her. In a letter to her admired Matthew Nathan (1862–1939), she confided: 'I know those nigs because I am a woman, a woman of a masculine race but a woman still'.[102] In one sense this repeats the patronizing racial hierarchy implicit in Mackinder's distinction between virile and effeminate races. On the other hand, there is an explicit recognition of difference, rather than superiority, in her own position with regard to African people. She set aside cultural arrogance: 'I venture to believe that my capacity to think in black came from my not regarding the native form of mind as "low" or "inferior" or "childlike", or anything like that, but as a form of mind of a different sort to white men's—yet a very good form of mind too, in its way'.[103]

Kingsley was sceptical about European male superiority and she did not believe that Europeans should try to convert Africans to Christian beliefs: '[t]he great difficulty is of course how to get people to understand each other'.[104] If Europeans set aside their sense of innate superiority they might listen to African people and then learn to respect their different way of living. Describing one night of dancing, she reflected: '[a]h me! if the aim of life were happiness and pleasure, Africa should send us missionaries instead of our sending them to her—but fortunately for the work of the world, happiness is not'.[105] Indeed, as she was going back to Africa, to nurse Boers in a British

[96] Kingsley, *Travels*, 653.

[97] Kingsley, *Travels*, 330.

[98] Blunt, *Travel, Gender and Imperialism*, 132.

[99] Kingsley, *Travels*, 503.

[100] Kingsley, *Travels*, 125.

[101] Kingsley, *Travels*, 329.

[102] Birkett, *Kingsley*, 150.

[103] Pearce, *Kingsley*, 145.

[104] Kingsley, *Studies*, xvi.

[105] Kingsley, *Travels*, 201.

hospital, where she would in fact die, Kingsley wrote to the editor of a magazine for black nationalists, of the 'Bushman['s...] native form of religion, a pantheism which I confess is a form of my own religion'.[106] She tried hard to get Europeans to understand practices, such as polygamy, against which they were prejudiced, by showing how they suited the very different circumstances of Africa.

As already mentioned, Kingsley adopted the sentimental form in her accounts of the climb up Mount Cameroon. She coped with desertions and laggards among her African servants but was resolute about keeping the remaining men proceeding onwards and upwards: 'I would not prevent those men of mine from going up that peak above me after their touching conduct today. Oh! no; not for worlds, dear things'.[107] The climb was well short of Alpine in difficulty but it was cold, steep, and blanketed in mist. She described leaving her last two companions wrapped up warm while she clambered on up to the top, where she saw ... actually, very little. Cajoling, giving way, and respecting her servants' right to refuse risks she accepted, she had gone to the top of the mount and come back down again: '[t]he only point I congratulate myself on is having got my men up so high and back again, undamaged; but, as they said, I was a Father and a Mother to them, and a very stern though kind set of parents I have been'.[108] This 'maternal-paternal' duty was still masterful; race clearly gave her scope to act the male in the distant space of Empire. But this model of African–European relations was inflected with genuine solicitude and did not count African lives as expendable.[109] Her model was in part Mary Slessor (1848–1915) who, in turn, modelled herself after David Livingstone (1813–73).[110]

In contrast to Kingsley's model was that of Henry Stanley (1841–1904) who was closer to Mackinder's practice.[111] George Bernard Shaw may have had the Stanley model in mind when he compared Kingsley, with 'her commonsense and goodwill, with the wild beast-man, with his elephant rifle, and his atmosphere of dread and murder, making his way by mad selfish assassination out of the difficulties created by his own cowardice'.[112] Whereas Kingsley chose commonsense over dread, Mackinder cleaved instead to the example of Stanley.

Force

As an objective, detached 'scientist', force shaped Mackinder the masculine explorer. He understood the local people he met in terms of racial stereotypes. He was told by one local European informant, a bank manager, that

---

[106] Kingsley, *Studies*, xix.   [107] Kingsley, ibid., 580.
[108] Kingsley, ibid., 604.   [109] Kingsley, ibid., 605.
[110] McEwan, 'How the "Seraphic" became "Geographic"'.
[111] Driver, *Geography Militant*.   [112] Pearce, *Kingsley*, 92.

the Swahili were 'undrivable but easy to manage by laughter and joke'.[113] Another, a British official, assured him that '[a]ll the nigger wants [...] is food, drink, his wife, and liberty to raid by way of sport'.[114] His diaries are full of references to 'niggers', some of which Mackinder (or his wife) converted to 'negroes' in preparing the typescript of the diaries.[115] An engineer building the Uganda railway gave him advice about choosing a servant: 'the African boys get to like you, if you talk to them, but Asiatics become familiar and are spoilt'.[116] Mackinder judged by appearance, or perhaps hindsight, in his description of one cooperative chief as nevertheless having 'avarice and cunning written in every line of his face', while an unaccommodating chief was said to have been 'a man of deceitful and repellent countenance'.[117] Unlike Kingsley, Mackinder made little effort to learn local languages, describing the 'loud grunting responses' of his Swahili porters.[118]

Mackinder travelled through part of his way with the approval of Lenana, a local Masai chief.[119] In moving his cattle beyond the prevailing epidemic of rinderpest, and his people beyond the reach of the concurrent smallpox, Chief Lenana had profited from the advice of the local British District Officer, Mackinder's brother-in-law Sidney Hinde, and his assistance to Mackinder was recognition of a debt. Yet force was more evident than reciprocity in Mackinder's strategy. He remarked on the 'fatalism and dislike of responsibility which characterizes the Swahili. He has no morals'.[120] Contradicting his local informant, Mackinder found the Swahili could certainly be driven. Indeed, he described them as natural slaves. Of two Swahili men, he claimed that '[b]oth obey like the faithful dogs they are; though free, slave blood still runs in their veins'.[121] He recorded ordering his safari of 170 naked African people, with about sixty Swahili and 110 Kikuyu, to be whipped at various points for dropping or discarding loads. He described the former as accepting punishment 'with curious submission', whereas the latter 'rebels and struggles', which Mackinder explained as the 'contrast between the freedman and the freeman born'.[122]

Although Mackinder moved through the region during a famine and smallpox crisis, he still felt justified in outfitting his safari by commandeering food, taking hungry men with him as porters, eking out the minimal supplies for the porters, and remarking, when one died of dysentery, that some of the Kikuyu porters were 'mere famine stricken skeletons'.[123] The weight of daily rations for each of the six Europeans on the safari was equivalent to the weight of a fortnight's rations for an African. This 'presented considerable difficulty, since, [...] a porter can do little more than carry his own month's

[113] Mackinder, 'Diary', 41.   [114] Mackinder, ibid., 82.
[115] Dawson, 'Many Minds of Mackinder'.
[116] Mackinder, 'Diary', 87.   [117] Mackinder, 'A Journey', 456.
[118] Mackinder, 'A Journey', 457.   [119] Mackinder, 'Diary', 102.
[120] Mackinder, ibid., 56.   [121] Mackinder, ibid., 200.
[122] Mackinder, ibid., 240.   [123] Mackinder, ibid., 158.

rations, unless his food-stock be replenished every ten days or so from local sources'.[124] The Europeans of course carried nothing, except their guns. African rations had to be bought locally, which was problematic because the region was stripped of the food normally traded out of village stores. Due to the building of the Uganda railway at this time, the region was tasked with feeding 16,000 new workers, while the year before it had been drained to support the 5,000 British soldiers sent upon the Ugandan Relief Expedition. These British actions, Mackinder admitted, had 'indirectly caused the famine'.[125] Mackinder's problem was to get sufficient stores of food both for the Europeans and for the porters for the last leg of the journey, a trip from the railhead through the forest, to the base of the alpine region, in an area largely unpopulated, and thus bare of supplies. For Mackinder, however, the hunger of African people was merely an obstacle in the way of his scientific mission, an obstacle to be overcome by force.

Mackinder 'practised with my Mauser in the afternoon against a tree trunk' and kept discipline within his own group of porters by regularly shooting off rounds from his gun.[126] The 'moral suasion of my Mauser' was for Mackinder an effective physical representation of the social contract on safari: '[i]t was a strange experience to be thus brought face to face with the ultimate sanctions of society'.[127] Mackinder regularly rejected pleas from his porters to stop for the day with the observation that: '[i]n the interests of discipline I determined that my will must prevail'.[128] When Mackinder refused to stop, he noted that 'the whole body of Kikuyu porters tried to desert, and were only checked by a display of firearms'.[129] His notebooks recorded that 'Cam[pbell Hausburg and the Swahili] Sulamani got ropes for a chain gang, I walked about with a loaded revolver, the Swahilis exhibited some 50 firearms, and at length we got the Washensi [Kikuyu] into line'.[130] Another show of force accompanied negotiations for food with a village chief: 'our Swahilis cleaned their rifles ostentatiously and drilled one another'.[131] Elsewhere, a village Chief, Ngombe, was kidnapped and held hostage until their food needs were met. A brother of Ngombe, Wangombe, killed two Swahilis who had been sent on another food foray. '[M]uch against natural impulse', Mackinder refrained from retaliating since he was not sure he had better than 'demoralised' forces and, after all, '[w]e were a scientific expedition, and had reached the scene of our work'.[132]

In addition to the two murders and the death from dysentery, at least eight other porters were 'shot by orders'.[133] We know this by the list supplied by

[124] Mackinder, 'The Ascent', 104.   [125] Mackinder, 'Diary', 95.
[126] Mackinder, ibid., 156.   [127] Mackinder, ibid., 160.
[128] Mackinder, ibid., 111.   [129] Mackinder, 'A Journey', 457.
[130] Mackinder Notebooks, 2 August 1899, Rhodes House Library, University of Oxford, MSS Afr. r. 13, 44v.
[131] Mackinder, 'Diary', 119.   [132] Mackinder, 'Diary', 182.
[133] See the discussion in Barbour, 'Introduction'.

Hausburg to the Zanzibar company, from which Mackinder had hired the Swahilis. One African and three Europeans led groups of Swahili porters at various points and each in difficult circumstances. One group of thirty-five porters was sent with their headman down to Naivasha. Edward Saunders (1848–1910), who had come on the trip as a collector of biological specimens for the British Museum led one desperate march down from the edge of the forest back to Naivasha to ferry food back up to Mackinder and his starving porters. Saunders took thirty Swahili and twenty-eight Kikuyu porters on a week's safari. Mackinder waved them off: '[t]wo or three were hobbling along with the aid of bamboos, but all seemed hopeful'.[134] On the first day one porter deserted. On the third day, Saunders threatened the leaders of the Kikuyus with a whipping if the men did not come along more quickly. On the fourth day, the Swahili porters dawdled. The next day, the porters kept asking to go back 'until, losing my patience, I set about those nearest me with my fists. The effect was really marvellous'.[135] 'Marvellous' or not, the porters claimed to be starving and Saunders gave them a few of the biscuits from the European food reserves but threatened that he would 'shoot' any porter who tried to steal more of the European food. On the seventh day, another porter absconded. On the eighth, they arrived at Naivasha and Saunders sent twenty-one of the Kikuyu back to Kikuyu Fort Smith from whence forty-six had been hired.

Hausburg, together with a Captain Gorges, took the majority of the remaining porters, fifty, down from the forest to Naivasha after Saunders and Gorges had come back up with food for Mackinder's final spell on the mountain. It must have been a horrifying trip as they had only sixty pounds of rice for fifty porters, equivalent to about one-tenth of the food needed for the eight-day journey. In a newspaper article some thirty years after the event, Hausburg recorded dryly that '[b]y dint of forced marches we got to Naivasha more dead than alive'.[136] It is possible that the eight were killed along this famished road and, certainly, the notebooks, but not the typescript, record Hausburg using violence earlier in the expedition. Both Hausburg and Claude Camburn shot after one African person they took mistakenly to be 'a deserter from our own number', and, a little later, in an attempt to stop their hungry porters thieving sugar from the fields through which they were moving, 'Hausburg lashed at the men vigorously today as we went through the plantation'.[137] It is also notable that the notebooks, but not the typescript, record that Mackinder had been told that 'porters should be treated kindly.–Europeans should never strike them—Headman should administer punishment by order of leader'.[138]

---

[134] Mackinder, 'Diary', 180.

[135] Mackinder, ibid., 211. This part of the book consists of extracts from Saunders' diary.

[136] Mackinder, ibid., 255.

[137] Mackinder Notebooks, 5 August 1899, Rhodes House, MSS Afr. r. 14, 9r; *op. cit.*, 12 August 1899; Rhodes House, MSS Afr. r. 29, 298. This last is based on a brief record in the notebooks, but the sentence is deleted in the typescript and is thus missing from Barbour's published edition.

[138] Mackinder Notebooks, 30 June 1899, Rhodes House, MSS Afr. r. 11, 42v.

Mackinder's own journey down from the mountain, after the exhilaration of the final assault on the summit, was equally desperate. He had twenty-five African men (fourteen of the Swahilis from Zanzibar, an interpreter and two tent boys hired at Mombasa, and eight Kikuyus hired from Kikuyu Fort Smith) and four Europeans with him. During this part of the journey he reflected that 'I could not help comparing the Swahili to a human camel'.[139] Mackinder had to cope with porters who, to conserve their strength, threw away part of their load. He ordered twenty lashes for one Swahili who 'had thrown away a bottle of specimens in spirit', adding that 'there was an epidemic of this'.[140] On another day, two men collapsed and had to be 'forced' to continue, and Mackinder said that the 'day had been spoiled by the sick man'.[141] He recorded that he 'did not like this slave driving, for that is what it really was'.[142]

His two alibis at this point were local custom and necessity: '[i]t was all done according to the *dasturi* (= custom) of the African safari, and we could not stay, for supplies were running short'.[143] His threats perhaps escalated for he noted that the 'Swahili [...] did not cling to life'.[144] A few days later, he found that three-quarters of the botanical specimens had been thrown on the fire to save carrying them further. This time he ordered a number of *kiboko* (lashes with a leather whip) unspecified, uniquely, in the typescript but given in the notebooks as thirty, the highest recorded.[145] The lashings were for Musa, a Swahili who could speak French and that Mackinder trusted with a gun despite his not having been hired as a soldier, or *askiri*. Mackinder felt betrayed, referring to the culprit with surprise as 'the trusted Musa'.[146] Musa was one of the porters recorded as 'shot by orders'.[147]

Existing historical documents do not explicitly specify who killed the eight porters. Both Saunders and Mackinder recorded themselves as issuing death threats. Saunders and Hausburg were in sole charge of groups of porters for days at a time. Mackinder had been ordering whippings and firing off his pistol for weeks. There are, however, two further shreds of circumstantial evidence. First, Hausburg annotated his list of the porters to be returned with

---

[139] Mackinder, 'Diary', 236.   [140] Mackinder, ibid., 239.
[141] Mackinder, ibid., 240.   [142] Mackinder, ibid., 241.
[143] Mackinder, ibid., 241.   [144] Mackinder, ibid., 241.
[145] Mackinder Notebooks, 25 September 1899, Rhodes House, MSS Afr. r. 26, 33r.
[146] Mackinder, 'Diary', 242.
[147] This is a list of Swahili porters supplied from Zanzibar by Messrs Boustead, Ridley and Company; MP/D/100. The list is dated 5 July 1899 and it is annotated by Hausburg who was left responsible for returning the porters, which he did in two batches. He brought down to Mombasa the porters he had led down from the mountain. He then waited in Mombasa for Saunders to bring on from Naivasha those that Mackinder had retained. His notes indicate seventeen porters with a tick, including the eight noted as 'shot by orders'. Mackinder claimed only to have fourteen with him, Hausburg certainly had many more than seventeen with him. The recording of names is not always consistent in the typescript but one of those murdered by Wangombe is given as Feruzi (p. 177) and there is only one porter with a name given as anything similar to that. He is among those with a tick. We know that Mackinder was liable to lose part of his deposit for each porter not returned safely and perhaps the ticks are those absent when Hausburg returned the Swahilis in his care.

seventeen ticks, as well as the notes about the eight who were shot. If the seventeen were those missing in Mombasa, then, Hausburg's list may have included the fourteen with Mackinder, the two killed by Wangombe, and the one who died of dysentery. Significantly, perhaps, the eight he recorded as shot were among this number. If this was the case, they were shot on Mackinder's orders between the mountain and Naivasha, or on Saunders' orders between Naivasha and the railhead. Once they arrived at Naivasha, the starvation that was behind the malingering and discarding of loads would certainly have been alleviated.

The second piece of purely circumstantial evidence concerns Mackinder's precipitate departure. Mackinder left his safari on 29 September 1899, just shy of reaching Naivasha. Shortly before Mackinder's arrival, Hausburg had left Naivasha to return to Mombasa with the majority of the Swahili porters.[148] On arriving at Naivasha, Mackinder telegrammed his wife that he would get back to Marseilles on 14 November, and this was in fact when the other Europeans got there, but the day after sending the telegram, Mackinder instead began a furious dash to the coast and arrived in Marseilles on 29 October. He was surely eager to get back to Oxford since he was in dereliction of his academic duties but, perhaps, he recalled the small print of the contract for hiring the porters. It allowed that in 'a case of "grave emergency" ', the leader of the caravan might go beyond flogging to what-ever was required by 'the safety of the caravan or the members of the caravan'. However, it also reserved the right that 'a competent Court may be called upon to decide whether [the leader had] improperly exercised their discretion'.[149] Four months later at the triumphant talk to the RGS, Sidney Hinde remarked in the discussion that he had yet to talk to Mackinder about the expedition and its difficulties, although he had met Mackinder when the latter arrived at the railhead, a few hours ahead of the rest of his safari, left in the charge of Saunders.[150]

Mackinder may or may not have been a murderer but, in pursuit of the prize, he was certainly willing to use force, beatings, threats, and kidnapping against African people. According to his notebooks, he appears to have been unmoved by the death of porters that he placed in jeopardy.

Empire and Masculinity: Private and Public Lives

Scholars including Blunt and Frank, have noted the way Kingsley's persona seemed to change between England and Africa.[151] Movement creates the possibility of being framed in one way in one place and in another somewhere

---

[148] Mackinder, 'Diary', 246 (fn. by Barbour).   [149] Mackinder, ibid., 267.
[150] Mackinder, ibid., 247.   [151] Blunt, *Travel*; Frank, *Voyage Out*.

else; there may, then, be a 'formative psychological splitting *en route*'.[152] In an important sense, the spaces of Empire gave Kingsley access to manly forms of behaviour that she felt constrained to disavow at home. A felt sense of racial superiority refurbished insecurities produced by a sense of gender and class inferiority at home.

Kingsley went to great lengths to show how obedient she was to gender codes in England. She stressed that, even on safari, she never dressed in manly trousers; a dress code that contemporary women cyclists in Britain were already defying. In public, she appeared in black, mourning weeds appropriate to a woman presenting her travels as filial duty to the memory of a beloved father. In the privacy of her flat, however, Kingsley wore African bangles and smoked cigarettes.[153] Her mother had been a servant and her own accent reflected those origins. Alongside the disability imposed by femininity in England, she was made also to feel the 'hidden injuries of class'.[154] You can hear this in the self-deprecation of one letter to a friend about a speaking engagement: '[d]o you see the nasty things they say about me at the Women's Writers Dinner for dropping my g's—just as if it were not all I could do to hold to the h's'.[155]

For this intelligent, independent, and adventurous woman, exploring proved the injustice of the immoveable disabilities imposed in English public life by gender and class. Perhaps, some sense of those injustices lay behind her refusal of the full arrogance of racial superiority. As we have seen, she was more likely to present the African people as different rather than inferior. Furthermore, when she did comment upon the apparent backwardness of Africa, which she likened to Europe's civilization in the thirteenth century, she blamed Arab invasions and European slave trading for producing a new Dark Age in Africa.[156] In this regard at least, she moved beyond the detachment of the 'sentimental' mode. Travelling like a man allowed her to learn things that other Europeans did not know and thus gave her a public status as a knowledgeable writer and speaker, yet the reception of that knowledge was still marked by Victorian gendered codes. Her public would stomach the meat of her discoveries only with the sentimental salt of her irony, but, in turn, that very irony and self-deprecation reduced her purchase on seriousness. Only serious knowledge was allowed to address the security dilemmas of nation and empire, and, in holding on to its masculine objectivity, Geography positioned itself as precisely that sort of knowledge.

If Kingsley travelled, in part, to repair class and gendered insults felt at home and to gain access to a more masculine, or simply more gender-neutral, conduct overseas, it might be imagined that Mackinder demonstrated a

---

[152] Arshi et al., 'Why Travel?', 229.
[153] Birkett, *Kingsley*; Frank, *Voyage Out*.
[154] Sennett and Cobb, *Hidden Injuries of Class*.
[155] Blunt, *Travel, Gender and Imperialism*, 130.
[156] Kingsley, *Studies*; McEwan, 'How the "Seraphic" became "Geographic"'.

complete contrast. He was a middle-class man, an Oxford don, and a firm believer in the importance of force in national and imperial politics. Yet Mackinder, too, wanted to get away from felt but unspoken challenges to his manliness in Britain. Within Geography, the work of the study was less heroic, involved less virility, than work in the field. Within Oxford University, he taught a subject that could award no degree, was popular with women students, and offered a background course for historians, but not, as he had wanted, for students of the physical sciences. Since there was not a distinct honours degree in the subject, the experiment of Geography at Oxford was deemed practically a failure among the explorer types at the RGS, impressed only by fortitude in the face of physical danger or by status in the shape of academic equality at Oxford or Cambridge.

Mackinder also failed to cultivate the social bonhomie of the man's man, himself aware of his 'shyness amounting in some cases almost to inhibition'; while when 'certain of [my] ground [. . .] I could be confident and effective', he knew he 'was always ready to fail from shyness'.[157] Sadler thought that Mackinder failed to make the mark many expected because the hard graft of earning a living kept him 'from spending the necessary time in the precinct of the H[ouse] of C[ommons], being "chummy" '.[158] Yet it is not clear, however, that he could be 'chummy'. In 1889, William Hewins had sought for himself the job of organizing the summer school for Extension Studies in Oxford, assuring Sadler that Mackinder was 'not popular at Oxford'.[159] After publishing an article on Mackinder, incorporating some of the biographical details included in Gilbert's tribute, one author was commended by Derwent Whittlesey: 'I particularly enjoyed the personal touches because my two contacts with Mackinder left the impression that he was reserved, to use the mildest term available. You make him out to have been quite a human being'.[160] In 1933, thinking of Mackinder's years at the London School of Economics (LSE), one colleague, Christine Mactaggart (1861–1943), the Secretary to the Director of the LSE, recalled him as 'a very shy man: he used to dash upstairs [. . .] and never look at anybody. His home circumstances were unhappy, and that may have something to do with it'.[161] His own reflections on the roots of his reservedness turned to his childhood. The death of a close brother left him to enter his teens as 'a lonely boy' and his father, who taught him at home, would not allow his outlook to be corrupted by play with the social inferiors of the town. When he went to school, aged

---

[157] MP/C/100 [c, vi], 20.
[158] Diary of Michael Sadler, 22 October 1940, Bodleian Library, University of Oxford, Sadler Papers, Letters 44191, f. 191.
[159] Blouet, *Mackinder*, 53.
[160] Gilbert, 'Introduction'; Kruszewski, 'Pivot of History'; Kruszewski to Lord Halifax, 8 May 1954, MP/D/600.
[161] Blouet, *Mackinder*, 201–2.

thirteen, he claimed that he 'had never [before] played with other boys, and for three years I was mercilessly bullied'.[162]

Thinking of his difficulty in the House of Commons, Mackinder remarked: 'it takes some cheek to address an assembly which has not come there to hear you[,] which in fact would rather not hear you[,] and which it is your business to compel to listen'.[163] Shyness afflicted Mackinder in the debating chamber of the House of Commons, certainly, and in the Senior Common Rooms of Oxford, probably, but not in the lecture theatre. Fleure recalled his 'handsome presence, with flashing eye and gift of oratory', and Hilda Ormsby (1877–1973) portrayed him, having arrived late to lecture, and after pausing to look at the maps hung around 'turning to his audience, [and] deliver[ing] in his sonorous voice, without ever a note, a perfectly argued and presented synthesis'.[164] Martha Woolley described him lecturing at sixty-two, with 'the unmistakable bearing of the Edwardian gentleman and scholar [...] and a certain air of elegance and great dignity'.[165] The difference is, of course, that Mackinder knew the students were compelled to listen and that he could speak with authority. His biographer, William Parker remarks that 'Mackinder's command of the written word was equally assured, and here too a strong and masculine style'.[166] The masculinity of his performance in the classroom and the book did not carry over into other areas of public life. He lacked the social skills to force himself on other men when he needed to approach them as, at best, their equal. The Empire thus gave him, too, a realm where he could act without the social disabilities under which he laboured in England.

Mackinder took the Easter term as a planned leave and returned from Kenya in October 1899, just after the School of Geography received its first students, leaving his wife to write his old tutor at Oxford in September, only after he was on the way back, to say that he would miss his commitments at the start of term.[167] It seems likely that this trip served more than merely academic purpose. Mackinder's private life was unhappy.

In 1889, Mackinder married Emilie Catherine ('Bonnie') Ginsburg (Figure 4.2).[168] Their son was born at the end of 1890 but lived only eleven hours.[169] Mackinder's autobiographical notes record for 1892 only: 'March April

[162] Mackinder, 'Early Memoirs', in Wilson Woolley, 'Philosophy of Mackinder', 151, 153.

[163] MP/C/100 [c, vi], 21.

[164] Fleure, 'Sixty Years', 234; Parker, *Mackinder*, 39.

[165] Wilson Woolley, 'Philosophy of Mackinder', 255.

[166] Parker, *Mackinder*, 249.

[167] F. Paget to Bonnie Mackinder, 28 September 1899, MP/F/100, item 83.

[168] From the Spottiswoode online archive: http://www.jsasoc.com/Family_archive/Archive/Sybil Spottiswoode/emmaline (B) Ginsberg see note 1.JPG; accessed 20 October 2007. The Mackinders lived at number 1 Bradmore Road and their house is one of seven in the street designed by Frederick Codd; *Kelly's Directory of Oxfordshire 1895*, 204; Hinchcliffe, *North Oxford*. I am grateful to Jack Langton for help in identifying the house in the photograph.

[169] Mackinder's autobiographical notes record 'Bonnie ill' for 31 December 1890; MP/C/100 [d, i]. Blouet reports that Mackinder registered the baby as born on 1 January 1891; Blouet, *Mackinder*, 47.

Fig. 4.2. Emilie Catherine (Bonnie) Mackinder, c.1895, 1 Bradmore Road, Oxford

Source: By kind permission of James Spottiswoode.

May. Bonnie ill'.[170] For 1895, Mackinder notes 'Ventnor with Sid'. This was Sidney Hinde, whom Mackinder had earlier helped with an RGS presentation that Hinde thought 'went all right on Monday night'.[171] Hinde's account of his 'Travels' in the Congo came from his time in the service of the Belgian King Leopold II during the so-called Arab Campaign of 1892–4, for which he was awarded medals.[172] Hinde had been second-in-command of an army of native people, 'some of whom were hardly reformed cannibals', according to his obituary.[173] In 1895, he joined the British Foreign Service and provided an account of these 'cannibals' in his narrative of the Arab Campaign in 1897.[174] In 1897, Sidney married Bonnie's sister, Hildegarde, whereas Bonnie left Mackinder to live again with her family.[175] Both that summer and the next, Mackinder 'worked at surveying with Cole of the R. G. S.', and he spent part of the summer of 1898 climbing in the Alps.[176] The climbing expedition began, thus, at the time his wife moved out of their marital home. It was, perhaps, both a wish to heal a wounded ego with a triumph and also an opportunity for conceiving a joint-project that would bring his wife more fully into his professional life.

---

[170] MP/C/100 [d, i].

[171] S. L. Hinde to Mackinder, 7 January 1895; Hinde to Mackinder, 17 January 1895; MP/F/100, items 57 and 58. The paper was later published: 'Three Years Travel in the Congo Free State'. The title had been abbreviated for publication from that chosen by Hinde for his talk: 'Three Years Travel and Fighting in the Congo Free State'; *Times*, 12 March 1895, 9a.

[172] *Times*, 29 April 1896, 14d.　　[173] *Times*, 21 October 1930, 19c. See page 118 below.

[174] Hinde, *Congo Arabs*.　　[175] Blouet, *Mackinder*, 74.

[176] Blouet, 'Mackinder: Some New Perspectives', 13.

In a letter to Sidney, of March 1899, Mackinder had first suggested that Bonnie would come out to Kenya with him.[177] After all, they were taking on the expedition the stepbrother of Bonnie's mother, Campbell Hausburg, as a dab hand with a rifle, and they would be staying with Sidney and Hilde, for Sidney was a District Officer in the British East African Protectorate at Nairobi, not far from the railway head from which Mackinder would launch the attempt on Mount Kenya. The expedition had clearly been planned as a family affair, but Bonnie did not go. Nevertheless, Mackinder sent and received letters from her while in Africa and, indeed, sent her his journals of the trip: 'Halford sent the diary to me from Aden, [and] said he wanted me to turn them into a book'.[178] The diaries, she said, had been dropped in a river and Halford later took them back from her to have a legible copy made.[179] Bonnie assisted her sister with the writing and editing of Hilde-garde's first book as well as a second one her sister published with her husband.[180] When, after Mackinder's death, she turned to the manuscript he had worked on in the 1920s, her verdict was blunt: '[it] falls far short of making the achievement live and there is not a memorable passage in the whole script and the writing is bald and undistinguished'.[181]

Many years later, the wife of Mackinder's younger brother commented about Bonnie, writing to Bonnie's younger sister, Ethel Ritchie: 'I feel very unhappy about her. I fear her life has not been too happy all due to her horrid mother who forced her to marry H[alford]'.[182] Ethel Ritchie (1865–1969) told other family members a similar story: 'She told us [Bonnie] had never been in love with Halford Mackinder but had been coerced by her father to marry him, she had really been in love with Ernest Bell, a student of engineering I think at a college near Virginia Water where they had assigna-tions!'[183] The strain of an unhappy relationship resulted in poor health for both Bonnie and Halford early in 1899. In March, Hausburg wrote that he hoped 'Bonnie is better'.[184] Mackinder's close friend Michael Sadler wrote: '[m]y first impression remains unchanged viz. that if a doctor gives you a clean bill of health to stand with you, you will much enjoy and equally gain

---

[177] Barbour, 'Introduction', 16.

[178] Bonnie Mackinder to Ellie Mackinder, 23 June 1952, MP/D/400.

[179] The notebooks show no evidence of water damage. Many are in clear ink penmanship and others in pencil with ink annotations. Perhaps Mackinder took them back to supervise the production of the significantly sanitized typescript, or perhaps he had wanted Bonnie to read before his return the personal reflections he later edited out in producing the typescript.

[180] Hinde and Hinde, *Last of the Masai*; Hinde, *Masai Language*.

[181] Quoted in Ellie Mackinder to Ethel and Jean Ritchie, 13 December 1950, MP/D/100.

[182] Ellie Mackinder to Ethel Ritchie [née Ginsburg] and Jean Ritchie, 13 January 1953, MP/D/400.

[183] Note of Dinah Spottiswoode to James Spottiswoode, 1979; Bonnie's youngest sister, Sybil, married John Spottiswoode; and her son Raymond married Dinah. Their son, James, has placed many family items on the Internet, including this note; http://www.jsasoc.com/Family_archive/Archive/Mackinder/dinah note on Mackinder & Bee.pdf, accessed 15 June 2007.

[184] Hausburg to Mackinder, 2 December 1899, MP/F/100, item 48.

by the complete change to life, work and surroundings'.[185] A colleague at Reading likewise wrote that: 'I hope that the African turn will result in your being completely restored to health'.[186]

Manly endeavours might repair a challenge to manliness,... perhaps. During the supreme crisis of the expedition, when Mackinder was alone on the glacier with two Swahili porters, hoping anxiously that food might arrive soon and thereby allow the endeavour to move to its pinnacle, he began to read with increasing pleasure Charles Dickens' *Old Curiosity Shop*, a book that Hausburg had brought along. The typescript shows Mackinder's deepening introspection and the importance of reading as a distraction but elided from the typescript, however, were his reflections upon his marriage. After an absence from his notebooks for the two months since he had last written to her (2 July), Bonnie was mentioned at this time of crisis: 'I wonder what Bonnie is doing [and] how she is. Shall I ever see her again?'[187] The next day, contemplating the failure of his adventure, she was again on his mind: '[l]ast night as I lay in bed thinking of the organisation of our retreat, I heard my name in Bonnie's voice with such appalling clearness, that it took me some time to settle down again [and] reason myself into courage again'.[188] In both notebook and typescript, he reflected that in the quiet of the terrifying wait, 'I have realised some things as never before'.[189] The notebook retained custody of the following reflection from the same day:

One result of this journey culminating in the present anxiety [and] solitude, is a determination to take life more calmly, [and] not to miss as I have in no small measure hitherto missed the pleasure of heart intercourse with my Bonnie. If I get home again, I am going to devote myself to compassing her happiness; too much neglected hitherto, not from lack of love, but because I left myself no time or power to devote thought to it—to the ways [and] means of achieving it.[190]

Sufficient food was mustered for a small party to attempt the final climb and, as Hausburg brought away the majority of the porters, Mackinder turned his gaze upwards again. The diary notes become again very brief. A week after the existential crisis, Mackinder records 'Hurrah-Summit. Bar 16.9, Sling dry 40. Boiling point 181.6'.[191] Not much room for introspection in that bald entry, but the next day Mackinder allowed himself a brief reflection:

[185] Sadler to Mackinder, 24 May 1899, MP/F/100, item 79.
[186] W. G. de Burgh (1866–1943) to Mackinder, 4 June 1899, MP/F/100, item 72. He had overlapped with Mackinder at Oxford (1885–9) and had also been a colleague in University Extension before going to Reading in 1896 where he later became Professor of Philosophy (1907–34); Blouet, *Mackinder*, 67.
[187] Mackinder Notebooks, 4 September 1899, Rhodes House, MSS Afr. r. 15, 52r.
[188] ibid., 5 September 1899, Rhodes House, MSS Afr. r. 15, 55r.
[189] ibid., 5 September 1899, Rhodes House, MSS Afr. r. 15, 56v; MSS Afr. r. 30, 479.
[190] ibid., 5 September 1899, Rhodes House, MSS Afr. r. 15, 57r–57v.
[191] ibid., 13 September 1899, Rhodes House, MSS Afr. r. 18, unpaginated entry at back of notebook.

'[h]urrah. Kenya is no longer a virgin peak'.[192] His third cheer appears a few days later: '[w]e start our homeward journey today. Hurrah. We have been very successful [and] are now tired of the business'.[193] There was no further mention of Bonnie and his thoughts turned immediately to academic matters: '[i]dea for a book on E[ast] African problems, history [and] geography, has been in my mind for some days'.[194] He had, it seems, reasoned himself back to courage, manliness, and ambition. Within two years of his return from Kenya, Mackinder and his wife separated for good.

If Mackinder was sick with stress before he went, then, the definitive end to his marriage appears to have produced full depression. In April 1902, he apologized to Hausburg for his failure yet to publish the book on Mount Kenya: '[b]oth volumes should have appeared long ago. But when we were together I had no idea that trouble was coming upon me, of which you have doubtless had one account. Please try to realise how hopeless is the struggle to create a book when the heart is full of sorrow and anxiety'.[195] Hausburg wrote back that he had 'of course heard of your trouble, but know from experience that there are generally two sides to such questions'.[196] As late as August 1900 Hausburg had written to Mackinder inquiring: 'Hope Bonnie is flourishing. My best love to her please'.[197] Yet, this letter also asked: '[h]ave you moved out of the Old Parsonage for good and all? And if so, why?'[198] When, in 1897, Bonnie moved back to live with her parents, Mackinder had given up their family home in Bradmore Road, Oxford, and taken rooms in the Old Parsonage for his Oxford terms. He moved to live in College and noted for 1900 in his sketch of his life: 'Summer in Surrey. [. . .] Xmas at Ch [rist] Ch[urch]'.[199] Writing *Britain and the British Seas* in a 'farm house in Albury in Surrey', Mackinder was at least close enough to Bonnie and her family that Hausburg might expect him to pass on his regards.[200] It is impossible to know what produced the final break, but this was the summer he interrupted his writing to accept the invitation to fight his first (and unsuccessful) campaign for election to parliament.

After spending the winter writing *Britain and the British Seas* while living in his Oxford college, Christ Church, he wrote to Keltie apologizing for his absence from London but promised that 'as soon as you have heard the whole circumstances of recent discontents, we shall very soon see eye to eye again'.[201] In March 1901, he explained further that he had been in

---

[192] Mackinder Notebooks, 13 September 1899, Rhodes House, MSS Afr. r. 19, 65r.
[193] ibid., MSS Afr. r. 26, 1r.
[194] ibid., MSS Afr. r. 26, 10v.
[195] Mackinder to Hausburg, 4 April 1902, MP/F/100, item 33.
[196] Hausburg to Mackinder, 6 April 1902, MP/F/100, item 54.
[197] ibid., 10 August 1900, MP/F/100, item 51.
[198] ibid., 10 August 1900.
[199] MP/C/100 [d, i].
[200] MP/C/100 [c, vi], 63.
[201] Mackinder to Keltie, 27 January 1901, RGS Archives, Mackinder correspondence.

'temporary withdrawal' from 'social life' since only this would allow him to 'wedge a literary achievement [*Britain and the British Seas*] into an administrator's life' and thus meet his obligation to his publisher for the first book in the series on World Regions that he was editing.[202] He added that the 'Kenya book will be ABC work after this. I hope it will be completed this spring, ready for publication in October'.[203] For the sake of *Britain and the British Seas*, 'and because of my wife's recent dangerous illness, I have had to lie so low of late'.[204] The book proved anything but 'ABC' and it was not completed as promised in the spring of 1901, and in April 1902 Mackinder wrote to Hausburg in the despairing terms cited above. By August, he tried to reassure Keltie that he was 'slowly forging ahead with the *Kenya*'.[205] He was moving his centre of gravity from Oxford to London and was perhaps considering moving into the ground floor of George Bernard Shaw's residence in Adelphi Terrace. Shaw asked him in gently mocking terms whether he was still interested or whether he should rent instead to the 'New Reform Club (*ci-devant* Liberal Cowards)'.[206] There may have been a promise of social support at a difficult time in Shaw's closing comment that the Liberal group proposed spending nothing on the apartment and 'will simply go into laager with a married couple to make tea for them'.[207]

As noted in Chapter 2, the summers of 1901 and 1902 were spent in company with the Webbs, in Gloucestershire, and thus a good distance from Bonnie's family. 1901 was spent finishing *Britain and the British Seas* and the *Kenya* book was taken up the next summer, but it was not completed then; it never was. The winter of 1902 saw the start of the Coefficients dinners, the summer of 1903 launched the Imperial Preference campaign, and by the end of 1903 Mackinder was Director of the LSE. Many years later he recalled this period in a letter to his old friend Michael Sadler, indicating some of the helplessness he had felt:

I remember the shelter and comfort that you gave to a shipwrecked man when he came to your door in his despair, and that you sent him on his way, with the courage to face his bleak prospect. If in his trouble he begged for help which you could not give, there is not a trace of the fact in his memory, and you may be assured of this that at that time and for many years afterwards there were influences at work which would have repelled intervention from whatever source it came.[208]

---

[202] Mackinder to Keltie, 2 March 1901, RGS Archives, Mackinder correspondence.

[203] ibid., 2 March 1901.

[204] ibid., 2 March 1901.

[205] ibid., 23 August 1902, RGS Archives, Mackinder correspondence.

[206] Shaw to Mackinder, 11 March 1902, http://www.jsasoc.com/Family_archive/Archive/Mackinder/george bernard shaw to Mackinder 3-11-1902 lores.pdf; accessed 17 June 2007.

[207] Shaw to Mackinder, 11 March 1902.

[208] Mackinder to Sadler, 3 October 1940, Bodleian Library, University of Oxford, Sadler Papers, Letters 44191, f. 188.

When he resigned from the LSE in 1908, he wrote in generous terms to Beatrice Webb:

I shall never forget what I owe to you and Mr. Webb. I came to London at a venture, low in spirit after the one great blow of an otherwise happy career, and I owe it to you and Mr. Webb, more than to anyone else, that I weathered the depression and started afresh. At the School you gave me the new task which I needed, and you welcomed me at your house at a time when that welcome meant more than you knew.[209]

These examples demonstrate how Mackinder repeatedly blamed his failed marriage for blighting what would have been otherwise a glorious career. The pall is evident in the Preface for his unfinished memoirs, where Mackinder promised 'the story not of my life but of my work which has been for me a constant romance'.[210] Shortly after his death, his sister-in-law, Ellie Mackinder, sent to Bonnie 'a piece of H[alford]'s handwriting in which he said his life had been a happy one though of course some dark shadows'.[211] It is not clear how pleased Bonnie was to be described as a 'dark shadow' and, although Ellie hoped Mackinder's letter would let Bonnie 'see how Halford was such a big man', the letter instead 'evidently gave her quite a wrong impression'.[212]

Bonnie Mackinder went to live abroad. By 1909, at least, she was in Davos, Switzerland, from where she wrote to Mackinder's fellow Coefficient, the editor of the *National Review*, Leo Maxse, offering to send for publication essays by an acquaintance.[213] Her mother, Emilie Ginsburg (née Hausburg, 1843–1934) wrote to her in Switzerland, the day after one visit, that 'I long and long to be by your side again, my Precious [...] and trust to a loving Providence to bring us together again soon'.[214] Solicitously, she refers to Bonnie's illness, 'I do hope Darling you are fairly fit [and] are not worrying about anything', and offered the comforting prospect that they should 'set our thoughts on the near coming of our dear Hilde who will cheer [and] help us all round'.[215] She finished by promising that 'I would spend myself if I c[ou]ld bring you health [and] happiness'.[216] The biographical

---

[209] Mackinder to Webb, 21 June 1908, Cantor, 'Mackinder', 42–3.

[210] MP/C/100 [b vi].

[211] Ellie Mackinder to Jean Ritchie, 27 June 1947, MP/D/600.

[212] Ellie Mackinder to Jean Ritchie, 6 April 1947; Ellie Mackinder to Jean Ritchie, 27 June 1947, MP/D/600.

[213] E. C. (Mrs.) Mackinder to Maxse, 3 July 1909, West Sussex Record Office, Maxse Collection 460, f. 288. Davos was an Alpine resort for rich consumptives; indeed a sanatorium at Davos is the setting for Thomas Mann's *Magic Mountain* (1924). There are many references to Bonnie's weakness and her need for a nurse, although the letters contain no explicit mention of tuberculosis.

[214] Emilie Ginsburg to Bonnie Mackinder, 22 July 1909, http://www.jsasoc.com/Family_archive/Archive/Hildegard Hinde/letter from mother 7–22–1909.pdf; accessed 17 June 2007. I think it is clear that these letters are actually to Bonnie and not to Hilde; indeed Hilde is mentioned in passing in several.

[215] ibid., 22 July 1909.

[216] ibid., 22 July 1909.

note of Dinah Spottiswoode says that from about 1912 the two sisters lived together 'both having separated from their husbands'.[217] Sidney Hinde died in 1930 in Haverford West. From 1914 to 1940, Hildegarde, his wife, lived with Bonnie and their mother far away on the Isle of Capri and, when Italy entered the War, the sisters moved to Switzerland, their mother having died in 1934. From the letter of 1909, perhaps Hildegarde moved out to Switzerland in 1909. Certainly, the sisters were together by 1914 for in a letter to Bonnie written a few days after the death of her husband, Emilie Ginsburg sympathized with Bonnie having been left alone while Hildegarde came to England to make the funeral and other arrangements succeeding the death of their father, 'competent Hilda has done everything that I sh[ou]ld otherwise have to do'.[218] Emilie promises now to come and stay with her daughter. She consoles Bonnie with the promise of the speedy return of Hilde which 'will be supplemented in due time by the long-exiled mother who is yearning to take you in her arms. It is indeed a joyful wonder that we may now meet without hindrance'.[219] This is a remarkable statement from a woman who has just buried her husband and it may indicate the 'influences at work' that precluded any reconciliation between Mackinder and his wife.

Mackinder did not live entirely alone. He turned repeatedly to his sister-in-law, Ellie, to whom he left the bulk of his modest estate, 'as a small acknowledgement of her kindness to me on several critical occasions during my life'.[220] She recalled that:

During the First World War, Halford was living with my husband and me, and as his secretary was called up, I helped him with his work. Quickly learning shorthand and typewriting. I took down at his dictation the whole of 'Democratic Ideals and Reality' often after he returned from a long sitting in the House. Working sometimes until 2 a[.]m[.] I actually typed the whole book five times for his corrections.[221]

He continued to rely upon Ellie and appears to have lived with her, in Parkstone, Dorset, or in West Bournemouth for much of his retirement. He also saw a lot of his niece-in-law, Jean Ritchie (1898–1967?), who said that she 'was grounded on his series for children "Our Island Home" etc.',

---

[217] Notes by Dinah Spottiswoode on Hilde Hildegarde's African Journal; http://www.jsasoc.com/Family_archive/Archive/Hildegard Hinde/DMS notes on HH AFrican Journal.pdf; accessed 17 June 2007.

[218] Emilie Ginsburg to Bonnie Mackinder, 17 March 1914, http://www.jsasoc.com/Family_archive/Archive/Hildegard Hinde/letter from mother 3-17-1914.pdf; accessed 17 June 2007.

[219] Emilie Ginsburg to Bonnie Mackinder, 17 March 1914. David Ginsburg had died on 7 March 1914; *Times*, 9 March 1914, 6a.

[220] MP/D/100, copy of Mackinder's will in his own handwriting.

[221] Ellie Mackinder to Jean Ritchie, 29 April 1954, MP/D/600. There is no acknowledgement of her labour in the book as there had been for Bonnie's in *Britain and the British Seas*: 'My gratitude is also due to my Wife [...] for correcting portions of the proof' (p. vii).

Fig. 4.3. Halford Mackinder, Villa
Tragara, Capri, 1938

Source: From Woolley, 'Philosophy of Mackinder',
used by kind permission of the Library of the
London School of Economics and Political Science.

and they became such firm friends that she was named an executrix of his will
and was left a small bequest.[222] Ellie Mackinder wrote generously that:

I am more than glad he made this return for all you have done for him, though I am
sure it does not cover the financial losses involved by your loans. And you have done
so much else for him in ways for which no return can be made, in giving him your care
and affection and in bringing peace and happiness into his life.[223]

In a letter to her, some five years after Mackinder's death, Bonnie sent her
'love if you will have it'.[224]

In 1938, some four years after the death of her mother, Bonnie invited
Mackinder to visit her on Capri, a trip recorded in a fragment for his
memoirs reconstructed from cheque stubs: '13 August. Spent ten days at
Capri'.[225] Mackinder wrote soon afterwards to Sadler: '[t]wo years ago a
miracle happened in my life. My wife asked me to go and see her and I spent

---

[222] Jean Ritchie to Captain Hayes, 18 March 1953, MP/D/400. Like her mother, Jean was a midwife.
Her fiancée died in the Second World War. These biographical details come, in part, from email
correspondence with Rebecca Hobbs, who has created a web site where she has published some of Jean
Ritchie's travel diaries. Her mother was godchild of Jean Ritchie's step-sister, called Ethel (as was
Jean's mother, Ethel Ritchie (née Ginsburg)); Ritchie, 'Travels with Jean'.
[223] Ellie Mackinder to Jean Ritchie, 26 March 1947, MP/D/600.
[224] Bonnie Mackinder to Jean Ritchie, 27 September 1952, MP/D/600.
[225] MP/C/100 [d, iv].

ten happy days with her and her sister at her villa in Capri'.[226] The last
photograph of Mackinder (Figure 4.3) was from this visit to Bonnie and
Hilde at their home, Villa Tragara, in Capri.[227] He visited the next year, too,
in the final days before the start of the Second World War (by which time
with Italy a likely belligerent of Britain, Bonnie had moved to Switzerland).
After the war, in 1946, he visited again and was planning another visit when
he died in 1947.

Anxious Masculinities

The personal details of Kingsley and Mackinder suggest how masculinity
linked public and private personae. Masculinity was not only a guide to
behaviour, it was also an impossible norm. The public and the intimate
could not be held to the same standard, particularly for Mackinder, the
imperialist who believed in and practiced force, yet was a social failure. He
never divorced and being without a wife may have had consequences for his
public career. The political scientist, Cynthia Enloe, has noted the significant
place of wives in the 'masculine' world of diplomacy for: '[b]eing a reliable
husband and a man the state can trust [. . .] appear to be connected'.[228] In
addition, a wife was essential for creating the social environment in which
combative men could cultivate the man-to-man personal respect where 'masculinity nurtures diplomatic trust'.[229] Ellie Mackinder reported a conversa-
tion with a friend of Mackinder's in which she had been told that George
Bernard Shaw 'had a great admiration for H[alford] and said he ought to
have been our Ambassador to America. But he quite saw that without a wife
he could not have been'.[230]

The treatment of international issues as resolvable only through force
elevated masculinity as a public virtue, and yet the violence of masculinity
has to be suspended so that trust can be cultivated among equals, creating an
impossible tension. Diplomats sent to represent a nation might represent
military force but, in the world of diplomacy, they needed a wife to create a
home where a domestic and personal touch might also be cultivated. This
contradiction is evident in Mackinder as imperialist. Like Kingsley, his

---

[226] Mackinder to Sadler, 29 September 1940, Bodleian Library, University of Oxford, Sadler
Papers, Letters 44191, f. 187.
[227] The photograph is in Woolley, 'Philosophy of Mackinder', 274. It is identified as taken in the
garden of the Villa Tragara but the date is given as 1946 when it must have been 1938. The image is
reproduced with the permission of the Library of the London School of Economics and Political
Science.
[228] Enloe, *Bananas*, 10.   [229] Enloe, ibid., 114.
[230] Ellie Mackinder to Jean Ritchie, 25 June 1947, MP/D/600.

behaviour on expedition was predicated on a racialized understanding of his own difference to the African people among whom he moved. In his case, the gendering of this gap meant that he thought force was adequate, and justified, as a way of pursuing his goals. Yet, among equals back in England, he needed to suspend this brutality to court and coax agreement, and at this he was much less adept. Rather than seeing his behaviour as the simple expression of a masculine persona, we might instead see the racialized privilege he assumed abroad as allowing him to enact and shore up a masculinity that was under stress at home for both institutional and personal reasons.

The projection of force abroad, then, worked at both the individual and the social levels. The business of Empire was gendered, classed, and racialized *work*, wherein indulging bloodlust was acceptable. This form of violence was also projected abroad. Following the 'example of the manly British Empire', the self-promotion of Theodore Roosevelt (1858–1919) is a case in point.[231] During the First World War, Roosevelt berated conscientious objectors as no better than 'sexless creatures'.[232] '[S]ubject to humiliating attacks on his manliness early in his political career', Roosevelt bought and repaired to a cattle ranch, where his well-publicized cow-punching and pony-taming allowed him to 'reinvent himself as a man's man'.[233] Roosevelt also followed the British out to Africa where he had himself photographed on safari; allowing him to be presented, in the Theodore Roosevelt Memorial in the American Museum of Natural History, as the epitome of the regeneration of American masculinity through violent, dangerous, manly endeavour.[234] To prove, or reassert, its virility, moreover, a nation should show itself ready to use force. The historian, Kristin Hoganson, has also described how US military intervention in Cuba and the Philippines in the 1890s and early 1900s was repeatedly urged as required by American masculinity.[235] Effete Spanish colonials were described as abusing indigenous women and it was suggested, most loudly by Roosevelt himself, that only unmanly American politicians would refuse their chivalric duty to intervene. The US turn from internal expansion to external empire was as often presented as the cultivation of individual and national strength, as its consequence: '[v]irility is less the means to the end of empire building than is empire the occasion for bodybuilding, an inversion which ideologically effaces the violent conflict with foreign bodies on alien terrain'.[236] The risk that the adventure of Empire might produce military defeat was understood as a threat to masculinity, sometimes understood in clinical terms.[237]

[231] Allen, 'Men Interminably in Crisis?', 198; Schumacher, 'American Way of Empire'.
[232] Kurlansky, *Nonviolence*, 122.
[233] Nagel, 'Masculinity and Nationalism', 249, 250.
[234] Haraway, 'Teddy Bear Patriarchy'.
[235] Hoganson, *Fighting for American Manhood*.
[236] A. Kaplan, 'Romancing the Empire', 663.
[237] Anderson, 'The Trespass Speaks'.

The geopolitical imagination rests upon such correlations between the personal and the political and in this way, a man such as Mackinder, who saw 'who will prevail' as the central question in both personal and national lives, was well placed to project violence into spaces where there were people he cared little about. Yet at home, this blunt manner failed the clubbable test of manliness. The political realm challenged Mackinder. He was quite capable of articulating force but not in ways that showed respect for the conventions of sociability that allowed politicians both to affirm (as policy) and deny (as manner) the violence that was at the heart of imperial practice.

It was against the background of the First World War and the Bolshevik Revolution that Mackinder came closest to the heart of national policy. This is the background to Mackinder's mission to South Russia that I describe in Chapter 7, but it is also the background to one of his most successful interventions in the House of Commons. On 10 November 1915, he gave a long speech about the nature of a war economy. Finally, he had the ear of his fellow Members of Parliament and he told them that, by his calculation, at least one half of the national product had to be devoted to fighting the war. He insisted that the economy be seen in terms of use values not exchange values, as manpower and not mere money-power, and that people think of the economy 'in actual human work, in actual human service to the nation'.[238] Consumption by the rich should be restrained through an appeal to their patriotism and the whole empire must be mobilized. Mackinder had been saying these things for years but he finally struck a chord with his view that force must prevail, and that society and economy should be restructured to that end. The *Morning Post* declared that:

Probably the most remarkable speech was that of Mr. Mackinder, one of the Scottish Unionist members. Mr. Mackinder entered the House some years ago with a great outside reputation as an economist. His friends expected him to do big things in Parliament, but these expectations were not fulfilled. To-night, however, he got his chance, and took it. He spoke with marked eloquence—almost, one might say, with inspiration.[239]

---

[238] *Hansard 5th*, 75 (10 November 1915), 1235.
[239] *Morning Post*, 11 November 1915; cutting in MP/C/400 [ii].

5

Theorizing Imperialism

Lenin dated a new imperialistic form of capitalism to 1898, to the war between Spain and the United States over the control of Cuba. For him, this fight between capitalist states over imperial possessions was symptomatic of a new world order, 'in which the division of all territories of the globe among the biggest capitalist powers has been completed'.[1] At the end of the nineteenth century, as Frederick Jackson Turner (1861–1932) announced the Western frontier closed, political commentators in the United States also debated imperialism.[2] American militarism had served frontier expansion, as contiguous territory was incorporated into an expanding continental United States. But how contiguous were Caribbean islands such as Cuba (under direct rule 1898–1902), a Pacific group of islands such as Hawai'i (annexed in 1898) or a western Pacific archipelago such as the Philippines (under direct rule 1898–1946)? And would these places ever be peopled by such folk as Americans could imagine accepting as fellow citizens? Was the United States about to follow European powers in holding an overseas Empire?[3]

For British commentators, the Boer War raised concerns about whether Britain should or could shoulder the burdens of Empire. It was the first major military mobilization in a generation; not since the Crimean War had so many young men been called to colours and sent overseas to kill and die for their country. The demands of the war also threw light on many unflattering aspects of British society. During 1900, some 8,000 of 11,000 volunteers in Manchester were rejected as unfit, raising questions about racial degeneration that were debated in the popular press and in parliament, and leading to the establishment of an official Inter-Departmental Committee on Physical Degeneration to report on the vitality of the working class in British cities.[4] Yet at most times, the Empire was for many British people at best an occasional enthusiasm rather than a ruling obsession, according to historian Bernard Porter; certainly when, in 1870, John Ruskin called Oxford undergraduates to an imperial crusade (see Chapter 2), he felt he was challenging

---

[1] Lenin, *Imperialism*, 89.
[2] On the spatial metaphor of the closing of the frontier, see: Kearns, 'Closed Space'. On the continuity between the frontier processes and imperialism, see: W. Williams, 'Debate over Philippine Annexation'. On the debate over imperialism in the United States, see: Tompkins, *Anti-imperialism*.
[3] Meinig, *The Shaping of America 3*, 394.
[4] Heggie, 'Lies, Damn Lies'; Soloway, 'Counting the Degenerates'.

students' neglect of Empire, what the historian James Froude (1818–94) referred to in the same year as Britons' 'indifference' to Empire.[5] Joseph Chamberlain's tariff reform campaign from 1903 capitalized upon the renewed awareness of Empire that Froude and Ruskin had a part in creating, and, if ever the British Empire could cross from occasional public enthusiasm to ruling obsession, then the early twentieth century was the time and Mackinder's Oxford University the likely epicentre.

Many feared that the Boer and Spanish-American wars that raised imperialism as an issue in Britain and the United States were but dress rehearsals for worse to come. Looking back across the carnage of the First World War, a conflict in which eight-and-a-half million soldiers died, one might say that these fears were realized. Commenting upon that war, the African-American activist and historian, William E. Burghardt Du Bois (1868–1963), detected 'the real soul of white culture' in the European 'jealousy and strife for the possession of the labor of dark millions, for the right to bleed and exploit the colonies of the world'.[6] With the world carved up, competition between the Great Powers became a game of beggar-thy-neighbour with each trying to defend its own gains yet prise free the claims of its rivals. This was a concern, not only for politicians, but for workers anxious about jobs, and of entrepreneurs seeking markets and investment opportunities: '[t]he upswing in interest in imperialism amongst British businessmen in the late nineteenth century was a product of fear over the threatening implication of colonial expansion by rival powers'.[7]

Historically, treaties and proclamations staked out fences between empires. As early as 1823, the United States had asserted, with the Monroe doctrine, that it would not tolerate any European power establishing new colonies in the Western hemisphere.[8] In Africa and in Asia, Europeans gave mutual recognition to protectorates and colonies claimed by each other.[9] But how effective were the fences and would they really ensure neighbourliness? Should the cake be redivided to recognize the shifting geography of economic growth within Europe? What about European latecomers such as Italy or declining powers such as the Spanish and the Portuguese? What about China? Could any power or group of powers render it a dependency? How far might the ambitions of the United States run in East Asia? What about later industrializers such as Japan and Russia? Would they take colonies for markets as had the pioneers of industrialization?

While commentators agreed that a new imperial age had begun by the 1890s, they disagreed on its implications, fomenting divisions between

---

[5] Porter, *Absent-Minded Imperialists*; D. Bell, 'Empire and International Relations', 282.
[6] Du Bois, *Darkwater*, 25.
[7] E. Green, *Crisis of Conservatism*, 36.
[8] G. Murphy, *Hemispheric Imaginings*.
[9] By the 1880s and the carve-up of Africa, protectorates were colonies in all but name; Baty, 'Protectorates and Mandates', 113.

conservatives and radicals, as well as within both liberal and socialist camps.[10] The historian, Paul Kramer, observes that '[i]n organization, policy making, and legitimation, the architects of colonial rule often turned to rival powers as allies, foils, mirrors, models, and exceptions'.[11] This, then, was a broad and international debate engaging many social forces, including politicians, missionaries, and labour organizations. In general terms, the question of imperialism linked the drive towards colonies with the economic needs of industrial societies. Largely ignoring the consequences for indigenous peoples, commentators in Europe and the United States saw the problem of imperialism ushering in incipient conflict between European powers. What if Europeans ever turned their industrial capacity into a death machine and trained it upon each other?

This chapter explores these early-twentieth century debates by contrasting accounts of the nineteenth-century New Imperialism by Mackinder and the economist John Hobson.[12] Mackinder and Hobson might be taken as paradigmatic ideologists at two ends of the discussion, although in many respects they shared similar concerns. Both gave University Extension lectures to develop marginal academic disciplines; for Mackinder it was Geography, and for Hobson it was a style of Economics that was at once historical, sociological, and institutional. They were in thrall to Evolutionary Biology, framing their analyses consistently with their understanding of the Darwinian revolution. Both began in the Liberal Party but both were led, by the study of imperialism, to question aspects of mid-Victorian Liberalism, particularly its commitment to Free Trade. This was a dramatic ideological shift for each of them although, as I illustrate below, they arrived at very different destinations, for Mackinder wanted tariff protection around the British Empire, and Hobson wanted income redistribution towards the domestic working class and the renunciation of colonial exploitation.

This fundamental difference over the question of Empire meant that they associated themselves with very different social forces, with Mackinder gravitating towards the Tariff Reform crusade and the interests of British entrepreneurs, and Hobson moving towards the Labour Party and many anti-imperialist and peace movements. Whereas Mackinder associated himself very closely with the administrators of the Empire that the historian, Peter Cain, has called the 'ultra-imperialists', Hobson loathed them.[13] Hobson saw the unequal distribution of income as a central problem of modern society and, in 1924, he joined the Labour Party to promote the interests of the proletariat.[14] Mackinder inveighed against the Labour Party as a purely

---

[10] In like manner, today, the significance of 'globalization' is contested both within and between Right and Left; Held, *Debating Globalization*.

[11] Kramer, 'Empires, Exceptions, and Anglo-Saxons', 1316.

[12] For the wider context see: Kearns, 'Fin-de-Siècle Geopolitics'.

[13] Cain, 'Empire and the Languages of Character'.

[14] Townshend, *Hobson*.

sectional interest: 'the one thing essential is to displace class organisation, with its battle cries and purely palliative remedies'.[15] Although Mackinder and Hobson were alike in many respects, then, their political allegiances meant that they drew upon their common organic view of society in distinct ways.

Their central divergence was over the nature of capitalism, which Mackinder treated as the social expression of the natural order and Hobson understood as corrupted by social inequalities. Both saw imperialism as having economic roots, inevitable for Mackinder, reprehensible for Hobson. They also differed in their understanding of the dangers of the present (conjuncture), the nature of the evolutionary processes that had created the current crisis (time), and the geostrategic context that constrained Britain's economic, political, and military options (space). Whereas in 1899, Mackinder declared the world a 'closed circuit', a 'balanced [economic] machine', by 1904 he understood imperialism in terms of political competition. Hobson, in contrast, understood society as an organism and imperialism as a corrupt form of capitalism that took away from the well-being of that organism. For Mackinder, then, force was a constant feature of human society, whereas Hobson saw violence and force as consequences of inequity, injustice, and the concentration of power and wealth in too few hands. Hobson and Mackinder related evolutionary understandings of time to the natural history of humankind and its environmental setting. Considering separate races and nations as biological communities, they understood the social and economic arrangements under which communities interacted with each other as humanity's environment. Finally, Hobson had a very strong sense of the way that some forms of geographical reasoning naturalized the use of force. Although he never referred directly to Mackinder, his criticisms of the spatial metaphors of the world view of military and economic strategists capture perfectly the consequences of Mackinder's spatial thinking.

Conjuncture: New Imperialisms

Towards the end of the nineteenth century, contemporaries of Mackinder detected a greater intensity of international competition, and referred to a New Imperialism in the wake of: the European scramble for Africa (through claim, counterclaim, congress, and treaty) in the 1880s and 1890s; the adoption of protectionist tariffs by much of Europe outside Britain from the early 1880s; and the military involvement of the United States overseas from the late 1890s.[16] Each of these seemed to repudiate the alliance of peace and free trade that the British had preached, practised, and promoted in the 1860s and

---

[15] Mackinder, *Democratic Ideals and Reality*, 250.
[16] Pakenham, *Scramble for Africa*; Marsh, *Bargaining on Europe*; Seelye, *War Games*.

1870s.[17] The ideology of Victorian Liberalism in the 1860s and 1870s stressed the interdependence between laissez-faire (the state should not interfere with the economy), free trade (states should not impose tariffs on imports), and peace (states that traded freely and openly would have a mutual interest in peaceful coexistence). This ideology was qualified and complicated in all sorts of ways so that many free-market ideologists came to accept the regulation of the economy where markets were distorted by natural monopolies (as with some public utilities) or by gross inequality in bargaining strength (as with the employment of women and children). Many liberal commentators committed to world peace insisted that this yet allowed a right to self-defence. Others argued that the respect for the autonomy of other states did not extend to peoples judged too primitive for self-government and in this way justified what the historian, Jennifer Pitts, has called Imperial Liberalism.[18] These qualifications to doctrinaire Liberalism became a more serious challenge when, in the 1880s and 1890s, politicians such as Rosebery and economists such as William Cunningham argued that free trade would no longer serve British prosperity.[19] This new political and intellectual conjuncture challenged the ideology of Liberalism directly, and in their writings and public speaking Mackinder and Hobson both responded to this crisis in distinct ways.

The World as Closed System

Barely three weeks after his return from the climb of Mount Kenya, Mackinder gave to the Institute of Bankers the first of four lectures on 'The Great Trade Routes'.[20] As he had a dozen years earlier in his paper on the 'Scope and Methods of Geography', he noted that 'we have practically come to the end, not of geographical research, but of geographical discovery'.[21] He developed the implications of the end of discovery, not for the discipline of Geography (see Chapter 3), but for the global economy. The inventory of useful places was mostly completed: '[f]or economic purposes, [. . .] the exploration of the world is finished'.[22] These new spaces included 'a number of fertile, relatively vacant insular regions', notably 'North America, South America, South Africa, and Australia'.[23] They drew from Europe people and capital, and would do so for a more or less protracted but certainly finite

---

[17] Kindelberger, 'Rise of Free Trade'.
[18] Pitts, *Turn to Empire*.
[19] Koot, *English Historical Economics*.
[20] The lectures were given in London on four successive Wednesdays from 22 November 1899, and in Cardiff on the following Fridays from 24 November.
[21] Mackinder, 'Great Trade Routes', 266.
[22] Mackinder, ibid., 267.
[23] Mackinder, ibid., 151. They were 'insular' because all, including South Africa, were inaccessible from Europe by overland travel.

period: '[t]he process of suddenly occupying virgin territories, drawing their new resources from them, and fitting them with capital appliances, constitutes, for the organising centres of the old world, a great, though necessarily passing, work'.[24]

This export of capital had consequences, both for production and for imperialism. In terms of the location of production, Mackinder observed that the movement of capital overseas meant that agriculture, then industry, and finally the organization of trade would grow up in the new territories. Europe was developing its new rivals by crafting a fresh global productive system: '[t]he completion of geographical discovery, and the dispersion of economic and commercial activity will tend to give a whole world character to every considerable political problem of the future, and to every considerable economic problem underlying politics'.[25] The world was now one: 'we now have a closed circuit—a machine complete and balanced in all its parts. Touch one and you influence all'.[26] Finance was the one aspect of the world economy that might remain concentrated, for the intricate mechanism of global production and trade could, Mackinder believed, best be oiled from a single 'controlling centre'.[27] While British industry was in relative decline, and, Mackinder predicted, as British commerce soon would be, London could continue as the global banker, as the clearing house for the myriad international exchanges of goods and services. Although Discovery may have been over, this new development project could only be said to have begun; Mackinder dated this new intensification of international trade to the completion of the Erie Canal in 1825, when the North American prairies began exporting grain to European markets.[28] The spread of production might take, thought Mackinder, a century or two, during which time there would be ample scope for the further export of British capital.

The export of capital had immediate consequences for imperialism. While British investors purchased ownership rights in significant sectors of foreign economies, permitting shareholders to earn their living by the sweat of foreign brows, tensions soon emerged within these foreign countries. In some foreign countries, local business elites acted to retain ownership of their economy by keeping profits from new farms and factories local, seeking to 'prevent England from importing to them capital'.[29] For the British, though, their foreign investments were a lien upon the future and they had much at stake in ensuring that those outlays would continue to draw back profits and dividends. This meant 'securing good government for the most various countries', that is, government that respected the rights of investors, foreign or otherwise.[30] Open economies (read 'good government') allowed

[24] Mackinder, 'Great Trade Routes', 151–2.   [25] Mackinder, ibid., 271.
[26] Mackinder, ibid., 271.   [27] Mackinder, ibid., 271.
[28] Earle, 'Beyond the Appalachians', 168.   [29] Mackinder, 'Great Trade Routes', 155.
[30] Mackinder, ibid., 155.

the British to reap the benefits of their early advantage and accumulated capital, and in this regard, protective tariffs were the self-defence of the latecomer: '[i]t is a struggle of nationality against nationality—it is a real struggle for Empire in the world'.[31]

In his lectures to the Institute of Bankers in 1900, Mackinder said more about the way the *location* of economic activity would be affected by the unification of the global economy than he did about how Britain should respond to the increasing protectionism of its rivals. The geostrategic implications discussed in 'The Great Trade Routes' related more to identifying opportunities for continued British capital export (the development of the Tropics) and to sketching the ultimate long-term future for Britain (as global clearing house), than to the struggle between British free-trade and foreign protection. It is for this reason that Bernard Semmel described this discussion as Mackinder's justification for the imperial policies pursued within the Liberal Party by Rosebery and associates.[32]

In January 1899, one of the defenders of the Liberalism of the 1860s and 1870s, John Morley (1838–1923), Member of Parliament and biographer of William Ewart Gladstone, that great ideologist of pacific Liberalism, gave a speech attacking jingoism, militarism, and imperialism. Referring to the legacy of the recently deceased Gladstone, Morley promised to defend 'the lessons Mr. Gladstone taught us', which were that Liberal Party must 'walk steadfastly in the path of these watchwords—peace, economy, and reform'.[33] Morley urged that the British did indeed 'live in critical times' due to 'those larger commotions all over the globe' and he warned of 'the thirst for territorial aggrandisement, and [. . .] the pagan pride of empire'.[34] He identified the dangerous threat he thought imperialism posed to peace, economy, and reform: '[i]mperialism brings with it militarism [. . .]. Militarism means a gigantic expenditure, daily growing. It means an increase in government of the power of aristocratic and privileged classes'.[35] Rosebery responded by asserting that the Liberal Party and Liberalism as an ideology were finished if they did not embrace 'the greater pride in empire which is called Imperialism', a 'larger patriotism' that recognizes 'that British influence, which represents empire, is as potent outside these islands as it is within'.[36]

In October 1899, the Boer War began and the questions of War and Empire became unavoidable. Actually, this was the Second Boer War; there had been an earlier military engagement between the British and the Boers in 1880–1 when the Boers fought to resist the annexation of the Transvaal by the British. The settlement at the end of the earlier brief war had seen Gladstone recognize the autonomy of the Transvaal, but under notional British control. The war

---

[31] Mackinder, 'Great Trade Routes', 155.   [32] Semmel, 'Mackinder'.
[33] *Times*, 18 January 1899, 6b.   [34] *Times*, ibid., 6a, 6d.
[35] *Times*, ibid., 6b.   [36] *Times*, 6 May 1899, 15f.

began as the Boers insisted on full independence and invaded Natal, another of the British provinces in South Africa. In these circumstances, Rosebery turned directly upon Gladstone's legacy, suggesting in a speech that it was Gladstone's generosity as Prime Minister that had allowed the earlier war to end without the complete defeat of the Boers, but '[s]o far from the Boers taking the magnanimity as it was intended, they regarded it as a proof of weakness on which they could encroach'.[37] The British were only safe if they were seen to be strong which meant that they had to prevail against all challenges to the integrity of their Empire. It was in this context that Mackinder presented his four weekly lectures, beginning some six weeks after the Boer War had started.

In 1899, Mackinder seemed willing to accept the switch from industrial to capital exports as an inevitable consequence of global economic development, but when, in 1903, Joseph Chamberlain split from the Liberal Party over his heretical rejection of free trade, Mackinder followed (see Chapter 2).[38] Under the influence of Chamberlain, Mackinder recast his account of the global closed circuit in political terms in what became one of his best-known pieces, 'The Geographical Pivot of History'. In this paper of 1904, he placed imperialism (not development) and war (not trade) at the centre of his spatial vision. He argued that a global crisis had arrived and that there was no time for gradual adjustment over the next two centuries. The end of Discovery presaged not the dispersion of industry and commerce, but rather the competitive establishment of exclusive title: 'there is scarcely a region left for the pegging out of a claim of ownership, unless as the result of a war between civilized or half-civilized powers'.[39] For Mackinder's new vision, the reality was a worldwide 'closed political system', in which '[e]very explosion of social forces, instead of being dissipated in a surrounding circuit of unknown space and barbaric chaos, will be sharply re-echoed from the far side of the globe, and weak elements in the political and economic organism will be shattered in consequence'.[40] He drew attention to the European agreement of 1884, which divided up Africa, as marking the start of the new era and drawing to an end the period when European powers could collect colonies: '[f]rom the time of the Treaty of Berlin the world has entered on a new phase, both politically and economically. [...] Whether we like it or not, we have come to the time of great empires, and of commercial and industrial trusts'.[41] Free-trade imperialism, in other words, was now out of date.

Earlier, when discussing the great trade routes, Mackinder had described ocean-going ships as making the world economically whole: 'the essence of the oceanic stage in the development of the great Trade Routes lies in the fact

---

[37] *Times*, 28 October 1899, 9e.   [38] Blouet, 'Imperial Vision'.
[39] Mackinder, 'Geographical Pivot', 421.   [40] Mackinder, ibid., 422.
[41] Mackinder, 'Geographical Conditions', 474.

that it is possible to reach any shore in the world without breaking bulk'.[42] When, in the 1840s and 1850s, railways were first developed, their purpose, argued Mackinder, had been to connect productive hinterlands to international ports. However, the emerging economic geography of Germany suggested that 'we are now beginning to see what is probably a reversal of some of these conditions'.[43] The trans-Continental railway integrated a land mass drawing all parts closer together and, since 'Germany occupies a central position on the Continent of Europe', the fullest development of the European railways might give Germany an advantage in many European markets because, unlike British goods, its products could move from factory to market without break of bulk at any port.[44] Mackinder developed these contrasts between Britain moving its goods by sea and Germany moving its goods by land in terms of warfare in his 1904 'Pivot' paper.

Studying the rise of Britain and its Empire, the American geostrategist, Alfred Mahan, had drawn the conclusion in 1890 that sea-power would always be triumphant over mere land-power because the unity of the oceans meant that sea-power could apply force in all parts of the globe.[45] But in 1904, Mackinder argued that over much of the globe, space had become integrated by rail rather than by sea, river, and canal, and this must upset the primacy of sea-power that Mahan had asserted so forcefully. Reflecting upon his 'Pivot' paper, Mackinder wrote in 1943 that he was inspired by two events: 'the British war in South Africa and the Russian war in Manchuria'.[46] As he noted in his reflections upon the prospects of peace in 1919, after the First World War: '[i]t was an unprecedented thing in the year 1900 that Britain should maintain a quarter of a million men in her war with the Boers at a distance of 6000 miles over the ocean; but it was as remarkable a feat for Russia to place an army of more than a quarter of a million men against the Japanese in Manchuria in 1904 at a distance of 4000 miles by rail'.[47] In the new closed-space world, land-power bid fair to be as mobile as sea-power: '[t]he Russian army in Manchuria is as significant evidence of mobile land-power as the British army in South Africa was of sea-power'.[48]

Whether considered from the perspective of trade, in 'Great Trade Routes', or in terms of warfare, in 'Pivot', the closed-space world produced a struggle between empires. Both free-trade imperialism and protectionist imperialism approached the same end for Mackinder, writing in 1919: '[i]n my belief, both free trade of the *laissez-faire* type and protection of the predatory type are policies of empire, and both make for war'.[49] Global

---

[42] Mackinder, 'Great Trade Routes', 148.
[43] Mackinder, ibid., 153.
[44] Mackinder, ibid., 153.
[45] Mahan, *Sea Power*.
[46] Mackinder, 'Round World', 596.
[47] Mackinder, *Democratic Ideals and Reality*, 147.
[48] Mackinder, 'Geographical Pivot', 434.
[49] Mackinder, *Democratic Ideals and Reality*, 190.

closure heralded a conflict between empires that Britain must prepare itself
to win.

Only in the dying days of the deadly First World War, did Mackinder
essay an alternative to global struggle. Almost all of his *Democratic Ideals
and Reality* of 1919 is about the geographical realities that threaten to
produce 'in the end [...] a single world-empire'.[50] Because the world was,
for Mackinder, so interconnected, every question was at the same time both
local and international: '[d]o you realise that we have now made the circuit of
the world, and that every system is now a closed system, and that you can
now alter nothing without altering the balance of everything?'.[51] At the very
end of the book, Mackinder turned finally from these realities to his own
version of idealism: he made to refuse the global wager, hinting that he
preferred pacific parochialism over bellicose globalism. Statesmen, he suggested, can direct humanity by appealing to grand ideals. He offered for their
consideration the ideal of 'general economic independence'.[52] Each country
could seek to develop so balanced an economy that no other nation could
capitalize upon its desperate need for any particular range of goods. The
First World War had forced upon nations a degree of economic autarky that
they would do well to continue. Balanced nations would also be based on
balanced regions. Mackinder offered a provincial life as counter to the
internationalism of the closed-space world. People must stay at home more:

It is for neighbourliness that the world to-day calls aloud, and for a refusal to gad ever
about—merely because of modern opportunities for communication. Let us recover
possession of ourselves, lest we become the mere slaves of the world's geography,
exploited by materialistic organizers. Neighbourliness or fraternal duty to those who
are our fellow-dwellers, is the only sure foundation of a happy citizenship.[53]

Although Mackinder termed anarchism 'social suicide' because it smashed
the inertia of what Mackinder called the 'Going Concern', there is much in
this statement that would have gladdened Kropótkin's heart, for Mackinder's provincialism could have been secured only with an equally drastic
alteration in the prevailing social and economic relations.[54]

Did Mackinder seriously entertain this provincial prospect? The implication of *Democratic Ideals and Reality* is that only if the peace treaty at
Versailles had imposed global provincialism could Britons have gone
home to their market towns without being concerned about protectionists
elsewhere who might build up military power to loom maliciously over little
England. The provincial response to closed space may have remained
an ideal for Mackinder, but autarky was not pursued as British national

---

[50] Mackinder, *Democratic Ideals and Reality*, 2.
[51] Mackinder, ibid., 260.
[52] Mackinder, ibid., 230.
[53] Mackinder, ibid., 267.
[54] Mackinder, ibid., 233.

economic policy. Within three years after the end of the First World War, Mackinder quickly returned to warning about the balanced German threat to the unbalanced British nation in a speech before the House of Commons:

[Germany's] whole policy has always been to equip herself as a complete economic unit, and the result will be that she will put out of action a certain amount of your skill and plant in those things which temporarily she was monopolising. Having done that, and having injured you to the extent that you will not be able to restore that skill and that plant, except after that lapse of a certain number of years, she will then return to the position she had before the War, and will attract to herself every trade which will enable her to work upon you a second time.[55]

In other words, Germany would attend to its own economic independence but would undercut, through subsidy, some essential element of British manufacture so that in a future war, the British would not be able to achieve economic autarky but be forced to rely upon German supplies. Free trade, then, exposed Britain to a form of trade that was war by other means, and that prepared the way for war by all means.

More in anger than sorrow, Mackinder took the Second World War as vindication of his understanding of Germany, and yet he relished the contest. In 1942, in the darkest days of conflict with Germany, Mackinder signed off one letter to the secretary of the Royal Geographical Society with the hope that 'all goes well with you in these tremendous days'.[56] Earlier in that war, he had written to Michael Sadler, the friend of his days in the University Extension movement: 'Well, my love to you. It was glorious to hear that you were glad to have lived to see this great hour of our nation'.[57]

The New Imperialism

The Boer War that had set Mackinder thinking about the mobility of force under sea-power caused John Hobson instead to rail at the knavery of British mine-owners in South Africa and of Jewish bankers in London. For Hobson, it was not this war that specified the historical conjuncture of a new global order around 1900; instead it was the transition from colonialism to imperialism. Hobson defined true colonialism as the largely pacific movement of peoples into sparsely settled areas: '[c]olonialism, where it consists in the migration of part of a nation to vacant or sparsely peopled foreign lands, [...] may be considered a genuine expansion of nationality'.[58] This colonialism involved no interaction between new settlers and indigenous peoples.

---

[55] *The Official Report, House of Commons, 5th Series* [*Hansard 5th*], 143 (30 June 1921), 2407.

[56] Mackinder to Arthur Hinks, 30 March 1942, Royal Geographical Society (RGS) Archives, Mackinder Correspondence.

[57] Mackinder to Sadler, 20 October 1940, Bodleian Library, University of Oxford, Sadler Papers, Letters 44191, f. 189.

[58] Hobson, *Imperialism*, 4.

In contrast, he defined modern imperialism, what he called 'New Imperialism', as the movement of European investment into places where it was used to exploit local peoples and local resources. This New Imperialism was likewise different to earlier empire building because modern empires existed in contention with each other. Past empires had expanded in isolation, incorporating into their federation spaces won from the barbarians beyond the pale.

Attributing the New Imperialism to the competition between Germany and Britain, Hobson looked to 1870–1, with 'the unification of Germany and the Franco-Prussian War', as its origin,[59] and to the Berlin (or Congo) Conference of 1884 as its consolidation. He wrote in 1902 that, 'for convenience, the year 1870 has been taken as indicative of the beginning of a conscious policy of Imperialism, it will be evident that the movement did not attain its full impetus until the middle of the eighties'.[60] Hobson both explained and responded to this imperialism very differently than did Mackinder. Critical of the idea that imperialism was somehow a process of biological selection among different races, Hobson rejected the idea that race struggle was some sort of 'divine right of force'.[61] Indeed, he thought that in human affairs, struggle was wasteful because it squandered life. Developing the insights of John Ruskin, Hobson argued that wealth was in essence best understood as vital value, 'the power to sustain life'.[62] Wealth should make people well, and by analogy, he adopted Ruskin's term 'illth' for all spent to opposite effect, such as on armaments. In other words, imperialism diverted wealth to 'illth', but did so by falsely persuading the public, through the pulpit, schoolroom, and press, that imperialism was noble, rational, and unavoidable. For Hobson, then, the problems of imperialism were psychological and ideological, and not just economic.[63]

Chamberlain's tariff reform campaign that had seduced Mackinder away from the Liberal Party was anathema to Hobson: 'when Joseph Chamberlain set out to convert the Empire into a close preserve by his policy of tariffs and preference, and the magnificent projects of Cecil Rhodes began to influence the mind and language of English politicians, the larger significance of our Imperialism became manifest'.[64] Manifest, that is, to Britain's rivals, 'fostering animosities among competing empires'.[65] At first this competition had been directed towards the land and peoples of Africa and Asia, and had resulted in 'the forcible seizure of territory'.[66] The next stage, Hobson explained, was the intensification of exploitation:

---

[59] D. Long, *New Liberal Internationalism*, 63.   [60] Hobson, *Imperialism*, 19.

[61] Hobson, 'Scientific Basis', 463.

[62] Quoted in Long, *New Liberal Internationalism*, 18. Together with Simon Reid-Henry, I have examined ways of placing issues relating to life at the heart of modern human geography in: Kearns and Reid-Henry, 'Vital Geographies'.

[63] Hobson, *Psychology of Jingoism*.   [64] Hobson, *Confessions*, 59–60.

[65] Hobson, *Imperialism*, 11.   [66] Hobson, ibid., 126.

The statement, often made, that the work of imperial expansion is virtually complete is not correct. It is true that most of the 'backward' races have been placed in some sort of dependence upon one or other of the 'civilised' powers as colony, protectorate, hinterland, or sphere of influence. But this in most instances marks rather the beginning of a process of imperialisation rather than a definite attainment of empire. The intensive growth of empire by which interference is increased and governmental control tightened over spheres of influence and protectorates is as important and as perilous an aspect of Imperialism, as the extensive growth which takes shape in assertion of rule over new areas of territory and new populations.[67]

The final stage, fast approaching according to Hobson in 1902, would be 'the cut-throat struggle of competing empires', the apocalypse of global conflict between rival empires.[68]

For Hobson, then, imperialism was an 'insane' form of capitalism that bred illth. It threatened global Armageddon, fed people's baser instincts, and left social and economic life captive to blind, biological necessity. Hobson understood society to be 'a psychical organism, a moral, rational organism with common psychic life, character and purpose'.[69] Societies that surrendered to biological fatalism were like primitive life forms, such as the sponge, showing limited intellectual capacity. A rational response to the British situation would recognize that the Empire 'has been bad business for the nation'.[70] Hobson pointed out that only one-fifth of the British workforce produced goods for exports, and even among them only the smaller proportion was producing for imperial markets. The living standards of most Britons did not depend upon exports to the Empire and, while the costs of imperial defence were met through general taxation, the benefits accrued in the main to the shareholders of mining companies and investment banks.

What were the causes of this dangerous madness? For Hobson, the primary cause was the unequal power of rich and poor, as the rich used their power to move markets away from the ideal of petty producers exchanging goods. Landowners fastened upon the desperate need of workers wishing to live near factories and charged unreasonable rents. Industrialists cornered markets and extracted monopolistic prices. The resulting unfair distribution of income imperilled the reproduction of the capitalist system because workers could not now afford to buy a fraction of the goods they made, and these goods did not tickle the fancies of the rich. Indeed, Hobson saw monopolists as people who did no work, who were more like rentiers than entrepreneurs. Their rents and profits bore no necessary association to any personal needs: '[h]aving no natural relation to effort of production, they impel their recipients to no corresponding satisfaction of consumption: they form a surplus wealth, which, having no proper place in the normal economy of production and consumption, tends to accumulate as excessive savings'.[71] Considered as

---

[67] Hobson, *Imperialism*, 223.   [68] Hobson, ibid., 9.
[69] Hobson, *Crisis of Liberalism*, 74.   [70] Hobson, *Imperialism*, 46.
[71] Hobson, ibid., 86.

a closed system, capitalist industrialism refuted Say's Law, in that supply did not create its own demand, and markets would not clear automatically.[72]

The rich thus looked abroad for more lucrative pickings. According to Hobson, the wealthy attempted to secure quasi-monopolistic conditions abroad—the source of their wealth—by directing Britain's military in their own interest. Over-saving at home drove imperialism abroad. The rich made hostage of their country's foreign policy. Like many others, Hobson was impressed by the Spanish-American war: 'American imperialism was the natural product of the economic pressure of a sudden advance of capitalism which could not find occupation at home and needed foreign markets for goods and for investments'.[73] A 'sinister' class interest was able to pass off as national interest its own selfish needs.

Alongside these national rentiers, Hobson identified two other groups that shaped national policy; both acted conspiratorially. Hobson besmirched Jewish people, 'a single and peculiar race' who directed governments by their close control over the wheels of finance: '[d]oes anyone seriously suppose that a great war could be undertaken by any European State, or a great State loan subscribed, if the house of Rothschild and its connection set their face against it?'[74] In addition, speculative investors who already held exploitative assets abroad drew their home country into foreign adventures to defend or extend their privileges. Like the Jewish bankers, they too did this by stealth. In South Africa, for example, the adventurous investors provoked violence against nominally British interests and then launched retaliations that drew the British army into a colonial war against their rival Dutch settlers.[75] By Hobson's account, they also worked in secret concert with the Jewish bankers to manipulate British foreign policy in favour of war.[76]

Unlike Mackinder, Hobson did not see imperialism as inevitable. A nation might try autarky but here he was even less sanguine than Mackinder for, in praising China, Hobson made clear that its vast extent was crucial to its independence: '[p]ossessing in their enormous area of territory, with its various climatic and other natural conditions, its teeming industrial population, and its ancient well-developed civilisation, a full material basis of self-sufficiency, the Chinese, following a sound instinct of self-defence, have striven to confine their external relations to a casual intercourse'.[77] Few countries could approach China in the range of their resources.

Alternatively, countries might exchange international competition for global governance and Hobson took very seriously the challenge of building

---

[72] Cain, 'Hobson, Cobdenism', 573–4.

[73] Hobson, *Imperialism*, 79.

[74] Hobson, ibid., 57.

[75] Lloyd, 'Africa and Hobson's Imperialism'.

[76] Hobson, *War in South Africa*. Contra Hobson, the strained relations between Cecil Rhodes, the mine-owner, and Nathaniel Rothschild (1840–1915), the banker, are described in Turrell, 'Finance'.

[77] Hobson, *Imperialism*, 305–6.

international institutions after the First World War. He was part of the high-profile Bryce Group, convened by James Bryce, that examined progressive options for international governance after the war.[78] He produced his dissenting opinion in 1915 as *Towards International Government*.[79] Hobson believed that an international government was needed to prevent war. Such an organization should have its own force to counter the perversion of foreign policy by malignant sectional interests in any upstart state that challenged world peace. This produced, for Hobson writing in 1935, the pleasing prospect that a time might come 'when humanity will triumph over nationality—or when the bombing of a city will be accounted a defence of humanity'.[80] Rarely have the implications of humanitarian intervention been stated so baldly.

There were also domestic policies that could address the under-consumptionist causes of imperialism, notably income redistribution (through taxation, welfare, and a minimum wage), providing consumers the means to purchase unsold production. In this way, domestic production could grow further and there would be no 'pressure to export capital, thereby undercutting the drive to imperialism'.[81] By extension, a strong League of Nations might even, Hobson hoped, move eventually from war-prevention to peace-making if it were to address global income redistribution. Finally, an international government could organize economic cooperation between nations, raise the total wealth produced in the world, and, out of this bonus (a 'co-operative surplus'), fund development in places lacking local capital; backward regions could be developed, then, under protectorates or mandates secured by an international government.[82]

The British peace movement of the late-nineteenth and early-twentieth centuries was more extensive than many recognize, and Hobson made a distinguished, if ambivalent, contribution.[83] Faced with the evident intensification of imperialist clamour, the old-fashioned Liberal belief in peace as the political bounty of free-trade policies had received a serious check. Mackinder urged effectively that Britain adopt as its own the protectionist and militaristic policies of Germany to gird itself for the clash of empires sure to come. Hobson challenged this international Darwinism arguing that protectionism was not a practical response to imperialism, but was in fact an accessory. Ultimately, though, Hobson saw the turn to Empire as a change in the nature of capitalism. Capital was coalescing into larger units and using its monopolistic muscle to lever excess profits into banks which,

[78] Robbins, 'Bryce and the First World War'.

[79] Hobson, *Towards International Government*.

[80] Long, *New Liberal Internationalism*, 161.

[81] Long, ibid., 85.

[82] The phrase 'co-operative surplus' comes from David Long's helpful description of Hobson's economic thought: Long, *New Liberal Internationalism*, 1.

[83] Laity, *British Peace Movement*.

faced with poor returns on domestic investments (consequent upon the diminished purchasing power of workers), located investments where returns were highest but risks greater. To control these risks, countries were drawn into imperial adventures that extended formal Empire to places where only informal empire had previously been established. Social reform, for Mackinder, was a way of preparing the imperial people for their great challenge, whereas for Hobson, it was a way of interrupting that climax. Mackinder suggested that imperialism was a response to international pressures, Hobson that its roots were domestic.

Time: The Evolution of the World Organism

New forms of imperialism, the conjuncture I have been describing, was understood by Mackinder and Hobson as a new environment for national and racial development. For both, imperialism gave a new intensity to issues of global economic and political relations. At the same time, their contrasting readings of the causes, consequences, and best responses to imperialism also rested upon distinct ways of situating this new turn in terms of the evolution of the global human community, which both understood as a world organism. As previously mentioned in Chapter 3, for the human sciences that developed under Evolutionary Biology, distinct ways of representing time emerged, including the treatment of geomorphological landscapes as passing through stages equivalent to those of a human life.[84] For both Mackinder and Hobson, three temporal categories were central to understanding the world organism: the progressive growth of a biological community (either in size or strength); the development of environmental changes that may upset balance (particularly with respect to the struggle between biological communities); and the emergence of new biological forms better suited to (new) environmental conditions.

Growth

For Mackinder, human life was best understood as part of the 'liquid envelope' of the world: '[t]he student of the hydrosphere is concerned with water, sap, and blood, moving under sun power and life initiative'.[85] The skin of our planet was of unique interest as shaped by 'fluid envelopes, [...] which by their circulations, their physical and chemical reactions, and their relation

---

[84] In the humanities and social sciences, there are many narrative forms of time. See: Ricoeur, *Time and Narrative 3*, esp. chs. 4 and 5; H. White, *Content of Form*, esp. chs. 2 and 3.

[85] Mackinder, 'Human Habitat', 330–1.

to life, impart to the earth's surface an activity almost akin to life itself'.[86] The global circulation of moisture, then, consisted of interconnected cells, each of which had sustained, historically, a distinct and internally interacting human community, and these natural regions had broken up the 'blood continuity' of the human species allowing distinct local varieties to develop.[87] The success of human communities was determined by their ability to channel water and energy towards building up their own biological force, a product of the number and quality of the people in the community.

The hydrosphere imparted two further aspects to human life. Mackinder said that the hydrosphere 'conveys and stores energy', and, in like manner, '[t]he geographical significance of Life lies in its action in mass'.[88] In addition, 'the hydrosphere is [...] a close system' interconnecting all parts of the world. Geographers, according to Mackinder, study this 'dynamic system' through a framework that represented a 'world conception'.[89] The circulation of water isolated, then built, then interconnected human communities. However, even as the unity of circulating water drew all humanity into a single network there remained, for Mackinder, a fundamental distinction between the rain regimes of the East and of the West.[90] The East (or Asia) was shaped by the monsoon system into 'vast stable peasantries, [...] a tremendous fact of rain, sap, and blood'.[91] The temperate zones of the West (from the eastern coastlands of North America to European Russia) had a very different rainfall regime, with lighter rainfall, more evenly distributed across the year. In the West, while the natural world was less prolific and bountiful, there was little need for centralized systems of water conservation, management, and distribution. Mackinder even saw the emergence of humanity as caused in the main by the hydrosphere since global drought drove the precursors of human beings out of forests onto plains, where they were forced to walk upright: '[t]he inference is obvious that in fighting against drought and frost terrestrial life is stimulated to initiative'.[92] This had clear implications for the relative dynamism of a wet East and drier West: 'in the abundance of moisture humanity appears to lack the incentive to development'.[93]

Chapter 4 documented Mackinder's view that force was the basis of politics and here was the biological grounding of that belief.[94] Mackinder

---

[86] Mackinder, 'Human Habitat', 323.   [87] Mackinder, ibid., 327.
[88] Mackinder, ibid., 328.   [89] Mackinder, ibid., 328.
[90] Karl Wittfogel developed a related contrast between the hydraulic societies of East and West but in terms of the political regimes needed to sustain water management (heavy, centralized, and despotic for the irrigated societies of Asia): Wittfogel, 'Hydraulic Civilizations'. Mackinder's contrast is more elemental and closer to the focus of Fleure upon zones of difficulty: Fleure, 'Régions Humaines'.
[91] Mackinder, 'Human Habitat', 329.
[92] Mackinder, ibid., 331.
[93] Mackinder, ibid., 331.
[94] In earlier times, the centrality of force and of the competition between states had been understood simply in terms of a self-sufficient raison d'État: Foucault, 'Security, Territory, Population'. Mackinder followed Ratzel in biologizing these relations.

argued that the force of a human community rested upon its mass (its manpower), which was its 'life initiative'. Mackinder drew a central distinction between money-power and manpower. He proposed that the misguided worship of money-power rested upon the assumption that money could be converted into goods of any type at any time, yet Mackinder insisted that the 'wealth of this country rests mainly on the country as a going concern'.[95] In other words, the organization of human labour to produce useful goods rested upon investments in human skills and machinery that were not easily replaced once lost; the economy was more than a pile of commodities, it was a set of skills and habits. Mackinder insisted that peace was little more than the successful use of the threat of force, thus he could suggest in all seriousness that the 'problem of problems for British statesmen at the present time concerns the adequacy of the basis of men and wealth upon which in the near future we may maintain peace by preparing adequately for war'.[96] Rather than as purely financial assets, the economy should be seen as composed of 'goods, things' and in terms of 'actual human work, in actual service to the nation'.[97] This service was to be counted in vital terms, literally so, for example, when Mackinder tried to justify the British taking a tribute from the economic development of Nigeria, he said that: '[w]e are entitled to take it because we have fought and spent that which cannot be estimated in cash and that ought to be taken into your economics. It has cost us the lives of our men'.[98]

Hobson had an equally organic understanding of the nature of human communities. Unlike Mackinder, though, he did not think that force, the preparation to use force, nor the threat of force was an effective expression of biological fitness. Indeed, force rested upon what the historian, David Long referred to as the 'unproductive surplus', that Hobson contrasted with the 'co-operative surplus'.[99] For Hobson, public spending upon armaments did not lead to the expansion of social productive forces, nor did it contribute to human welfare. In fact, the preparation for war advanced one thing alone, the likelihood of war. Instead, productive investment would advance the living standards of the needy: investing in people was vital, preparing them to kill others was certainly not. As people worked together they raised both their productivity and their feelings of social solidarity and competence. Hobson believed such a cooperative working experience would itself advance people's own belief in the organic nature of society. The social surplus would sustain community institutions and provide opportunities for individuals to cultivate their own individuality.

[95] *Hansard 5th*, 82 (18 May 1916), 1726.
[96] Mackinder, *Money-Power*, 12.
[97] *Hansard 5th*, 116 (21 May 1919), 456; *Hansard 5th*, 75 (10 November 1915), 1235.
[98] *Hansard 5th*, 85 (3 August 1916), 573.
[99] Long, *New Liberal Internationalism*, 34.

The intellectual historian, Peter Clarke, has commented upon '[t]he persistence and fervour of Hobson's almost mystical adherence to the organic view', whereas his fellow historian, John Townshend, has noted that 'Hobson's organicism reversed the traditional liberal order of priority: the "whole", i.e. society, ultimately took precedence over the "parts", i.e. the individual'.[100] This was evident in Hobson's critique of the doctrine of force. He saw natural selection through the elimination of the weak as a wasteful way of determining the fit and believed that a rational society would substitute for the anarchy of competition, the science of selective breeding. For Hobson, scientific growth could replace natural reproduction, which had clear (but disturbing) implications for international relations. An enthusiastic member of the National Birth Rate Commission (1914), an official inquiry into the dangers posed by the decline in British fertility that was established under the auspices of the National Council of Public Morals, Hobson felt that unless fertility was addressed scientifically, and the fitter British encouraged to breed, the balance of superior British stock in the world might weaken. He was quite explicit about the right of society to prevent reproduction by those the authorities determined to be unfit.[101]

He had an equally eugenic view of international relations. Hobson believed that weaker peoples died with contact with higher civilization, but that such deaths by disease or hunger, were an unscientific way of producing a new balance between the races. The mandate system he proposed for undeveloped places would serve to restrict international interaction with, and hence contact with, indigenous peoples. There could also be immigration controls:

As lower individuals within a society perish by contact with a civilization to which they cannot properly assimilate themselves, so 'lower races' in some instances disappear by similar contact with higher races whose diseases and physical vices prove too strong for them. A rational stirpiculture in the wide social interest might, however, require a repression of the spread of degenerate or unprogressive races, corresponding to the check which a nation might place upon the propagation from bad individual stock.[102]

In other words, higher civilizations were justified in excluding from their living-space, inferior races that would come only to meet an early death.

Hobson claimed that this conclusion was proof even against the remote possibility that racial characteristics were environmentally determined and thus not fixed. The characteristics of inferior stock would not be changed quickly enough in better places. In the face of the suicidal fertility decline in

---

[100] Clarke, 'Introduction', xvii; Townshend, *Hobson*, 138.
[101] Freeden, 'Eugenics and Progressive Thought'; Soloway, *Birth Control*.
[102] Hobson, *Imperialism*, 190–1.

richer countries, planners could not, therefore, hope to replace superior people
with imported inferior stock that would progress upwards in their new home:

Even the minority of thinkers who are persuaded that no inherent differences of racial
values exist and that all the higher qualities of civilised life are due to differences of
environment and education, would have to admit that these differences require a
considerable time for their beneficial operation, and that a rapid decline of the more
civilised peoples could not be compensated immediately by the fuller opportunities
afforded to migrants from the backward countries.[103]

When Hobson considered international relations from the perspective of
economics, his individualism was stronger. He rejected protectionism, in
part, because it assumed that in international trade, nation competed with
nation, but: 'no such collective competition exists at all. So far as trade
involves competition, that competition takes place, not between nations,
but between trading firms'.[104] Here, in considering questions of demography,
his organicism inclined him towards dangerously illiberal views on eugenics.

Disjuncture

Steady population growth, then, was central to the biological views of world
politics in the works of both Mackinder and Hobson. Alongside this treatment of time as linear, there was also repeated reference to historical disjunct-
ures, and a strongly cyclical inflection to their treatment of time. In some
ways, the modern world was a qualified return to an earlier era, for while
Mackinder believed that the world was moving from an open-space system
to a closed one, this was not the first closed-space system (see Table 5.1).[105]

Table 5.1. Mackinder's summary of the evolution of the world organism

Characteristics of the world organism	Historical period		
	Medieval Christendom	Age of Columbus (1500–1900)	Post-Columbian Age
Geopolitical conditions for the West	External barbarism	Unopposed expansion	No lands left to conquer
World political system	Closed	Open	Closed
Scope	Europe	World	World
Dominant form of power	Land	Sea	Land
Result	Nations	Empires	World Empire

---

[103] Hobson, *Confessions*, 149–50.
[104] Hobson, *Work and Wealth*, 273, quoted in Long, *New Liberal Internationalism*, 123.
[105] Based on Mackinder, 'Geographical Pivot'; Parker, *Mackinder*, 242.

The new Post-Columbian Age was a return to closed-space relations that had prevailed earlier during the era of Medieval Christendom but now the closed-space system was global rather than continental in scope.

The geopolitics of Medieval Christendom was set by internal variation and external constraints. The variegated physical environment of medieval Europe, wrinkled by mountain ranges, separated into distinct drainage basins, and scattered with forest and marsh, resolved itself into a bricolage of nations. In physical terms, medieval Europe was hemmed in to the west, north, south, and east. Beyond the continental shelf of the fishermen, the ocean to the west was too dangerous for its boats. To the north, ice was an impassable barrier. To the south, the Sahara blocked movement and, at various times, Muslim Saracens also restricted European congress with the North African coastlands. To the east, the nomadic peoples of the Eurasian steppes made impossible permanent expansion, allowing little more than occasional trading and exploration. Mackinder used various terms to describe the peoples of the steppes; at times he called them Tartars, at others Turks, at others camel-men, at others horse-riding peoples, and more generally Asian hordes. The point was that they were nomadic and that they raided into the agricultural riches of settled societies: '[f]or some recurrent reason— it may have been owing to spells of droughty years—these Tartar mobile hordes have from time to time in the course of history gathered their whole strength together and fallen like a devastating avalanche upon the settled agricultural peoples of China or Europe'.[106] At times nomadic peoples made colonies of China, India, and the so-called Near East of the south-eastern Mediterranean. But from Europe they were repelled, uniting it in a common sense of itself as Christendom: 'European civilization is, in a very real sense, the outcome of the secular struggle against Asiatic invasion'.[107]

The land-power of the Asian nomads, argued Mackinder, set the limits to Europe so that within Europe contention between European nations focused upon territory, or land-power. However, this all changed when Europe broke out of its box and moved onto the oceans to the west. From the beginning of the new open-space phase, Europe used routes to the East around the south of Africa and even around the south of America. The tribute exacted from intercontinental trade by nomadic peoples of the steppes was lifted. New resources from the Americas came into Europe and were, in some part, re-exported to Asia. The new system of global communications was revolutionary. Writing early in the twentieth century, Mackinder claimed that: '[f]our centuries ago the whole outlook of mankind was changed in a single generation by the voyages of the great pioneers, Columbus, Da Gama, and Magellan. The idea of the unity of the ocean, beforehand merely inferred from the likeness of the tides in the Atlantic and Indian waters, suddenly

---

[106] Mackinder, *Democratic Ideals and Reality*, 125.
[107] Mackinder, 'Geographical Pivot', 423.

became a part of the mental equipment of practical men'.[108] For Europeans, this was the 'Columbian epoch [and . . .] its essential characteristic [was] the expansion of Europe against almost negligible resistances'.[109] Europe now moved into what had previously been the internal seas of Asia, notably the Indian Ocean. It took, against weakened indigenous opposition, the vast expanses of North and South America, Southern Africa, and Australia. The expansive European nations converted themselves into contending empires.

Mackinder argued that by the 1890s, the open-spaced era was closing and the constraints of a closed space were returning, but with one essential difference: the economic system was now global rather than European in scope. Recall that Mackinder suggested that tessellated medieval Europe gave little purchase for the consolidation of nations into Empires. Beyond Europe, there was now, Mackinder believed, the possibility of uniting the steppes into a single unit and using this region to establish global sovereignty. Closed space returned at the world scale, with the portent of a world empire as the ultimate land-power.

Although Hobson also had a cyclical understanding of history, he did not identify the same turning points as Mackinder and where they did agree upon the significance of particular events, such as the Berlin Congress of 1884, they invested the moments with different significance. Mackinder saw the expansive phase of imperialism finishing in 1884 as European powers had now to turn on each other in their competition for resources. Yet, as we have seen above, because Hobson thought imperialism had more than a merely territorial form, it might intensify as well as extend. Where Mackinder placed spatial and strategic realities at the heart of his theory, Hobson saw a repeating alternation between militarism and trade but occurring under different political and economic conditions (see Table 5.2).[110]

Table 5.2. Hobson's summary of the evolution of the world organism

Characteristics of the world organism	Historical period			
	Before 1846	1846–84	1885–1919	After 1919
Relation of politics and economics	Separation		Integration	
Primacy	Militarism	Trade	Militarism	Trade
Geopolitical theory	Balance of power	Cobdenism	New Imperialism	New Liberal Internationalism
Shapers of policy	Traditional diplomacy	Commercial interests	Sectional adventurers	Social Democrats

---

[108] Mackinder, *Democratic Ideals and Reality*, 93.
[109] Mackinder, 'Geographical Pivot', 421–2.
[110] Based on Long, *New Liberal Internationalism*, 57–69.

David Long's helpful summary of Hobson's thought identifies the two different ways that Hobson understood surplus as being appropriated, unproductively or cooperatively, and as producing two types of world system: one based on militarism and the other on trade, respectively. In the beggarthy-neighbour world of militarism, the interactions between nations were part of a zero-sum game that, in pre-industrial times, was used to justify mercantilism. In such a world, all that could be achieved was an accumulation of alliances so that some sort of global, or at least European, balance of power might be maintained. These alliances were the very stuff of traditional diplomacy and were frequently secret. It was a world in which international relations had never escaped the forms of feudal dynasties. Economics played little role in these shifting games of nationalist strategy.

With British industrialization, some politicians and economists supported universal trade free trade in order to allow British producers access to foreign markets. Richard Cobden (1804–65), the economist and member of Parliament, was the leading ideologist of a group arguing that free markets benefited most people and countries. If each country pursued its comparative advantage, specializing in what it was best suited to, then each would prosper; a rising tide would raise all boats. The so-called Manchester School of economists and politicians that gathered around Cobden argued that peace and prosperity would follow from free trade.[111] Their first dramatic success was the repeal of the Corn Laws in 1846; for Hobson, this marked a dramatic shift of British policy.[112] Britain would now open its domestic market to foreign corn, and later other goods, on precisely the same terms as for home producers. However, Hobson argued that because war hindered trade, the international arena should be evacuated of nationalist military contention. He proposed that international relations might consist of little more than commercial treaties guaranteeing respect for foreign investments and ensuring open markets for the export and import of raw materials, finished goods, and services.

Hobson argued that the heyday of laissez-faire lasted a mere four decades before sectional interests, including the mine-owners and bankers discussed above, sought to bend foreign policy towards the use of force to support their own private commercial interests. With the Berlin Congress, Hobson saw the melding of military to commercial goals as the end of a phase during which cooperative surplus was pursued. In the new era, society prioritized the search for unproductive surplus, fuelling militarism and preparing for war. Politics and economics were now linked inextricably. Hobson argued that this militaristic version of international relations regarded 'weaker nations as legitimate prey of stronger ones, and considers that the sole moral duty of a statesman is to promote the strength and well-being of his own state,

[111] Sheppard, 'Constructing Free Trade'.
[112] Howe, *Free Trade and Liberal England*; Hobson, *Cobden*.

disregarding utterly the interests and so-called "rights" of others'.[113] It was counterproductive, for Hobson, because it diverted too much surplus towards unproductive ends. The only solution was to enforce peace through an international government that would impose free trade, driving producers towards greater efficiency, and sustaining balanced economic development throughout the world. This, hoped Hobson, would be the agenda for the League of Nations: a new global integration of politics and economics.

New Forms

Alongside the more or less linear treatment of time in their demographic conceptions, Mackinder and Hobson used cyclical frameworks to analyse strategic issues. Their turning points were points of return: from open to closed space again, or from militarism to Free Trade again. Both authors placed international institutions at the heart of their proposed solutions to the new dilemmas: the League of Nations for Hobson, a reformed British Empire for Mackinder. Mackinder believed that this reformed Empire was necessary because a world of independent and aggressively armed states was unstable since a land-based empire might emerge that would threaten the sovereignty of individual states. The reformed British Empire would be a federated structure of the Anglo-Saxon states (Great Britain, the self-governing Dominions within the Empire, and the United States) that would command the resources of the rest of the Empire, those places not fit for self-government, which included India and Ireland. The extended family of the Britains was important for the future of the world because of the exceptional nature of this people with their democratic inheritance, carried in their genes. Given British exceptionalism, Mackinder believed that it was unrealistic to rely upon an international League of Nations since democratic values were not widely accepted outside the lands settled by the British. International relations must, according to Mackinder, take cognisance of the reality of force rather than the idea of democracy.

In direct opposition to Mackinder's account of the world, the central claim of Hobson was that force was primitive, wasteful, and avoidable. The scientific management of life should instead ensure 'that cultivation of the higher inner qualities which for a nation as for an individual constitutes the ascendancy of reason over brute impulse'.[114] This meant that democracy was needed to ensure that the needs of the many took precedence over the greed of the few. For international relations to be characterized by the same pursuit of higher values, there needed to be an international government, or at the very least, as Long notes, 'an international court overseeing

---

[113] Hobson, *Crisis of Liberalism*, 255.
[114] Hobson, *Imperialism*, 368.

arbitration and conciliation and an international executive council'.[115] Contrary to the tendency of much modern theory in international relations (the so-called realist school, in particular), both Mackinder and Hobson were committed to thinking about an international system that included more than just states. They both had reservations about contemporary international institutions but each studied new possibilities, be they imperial federation or global governance.

Mackinder's Spatial Fetish: The Heartland

Space played an important role in theories of imperialism, as illustrated by notions of environmental determinism. If the physical environment produced different types of society in various parts of the globe, for Mackinder this created distinct races, whereas for Hobson it was the basis of different sorts of economy. Clearly another significant understanding of space in the imperialist project was framed by the struggle for territory. While Mackinder saw this scuffle as an almost inevitable consequence of the competitive pursuit of national interest, for Hobson it was the perversion of foreign policy by sectional interests. Hobson believed that imperialism did not require territorial expansion; it could instead be as unpleasantly effective through the intensified exploitation of existing territorial claims. Furthermore, territorial language, argued Hobson, was too frequently used to cloak the exploitation of some people by others:

Paramount power, effective autonomy, emissary of civilisation, rectification of frontier, and a whole sliding scale of terms from 'hinterland' and 'sphere of influence' to 'effective occupation' and 'annexation' will serve as ready illustrations of a phraseology derived for purposes of concealment and encroachment. The Imperialist who sees modern history through these masks never grasps the 'brute' facts, but always sees them at several removes, refracted, interpreted, and glozed by convenient renderings.[116]

Hobson describes here a sort of spatial fetishism whereby geographical terminology makes it appear that spaces are balanced, or arranged, when, in fact, people are being subordinated and pressed into underpaid labour. There was a third sense of space, at least in Mackinder's reading of imperialism, that may be termed strategic, and it is this understanding that I analyse here. There was no comparable geostrategic vision in Hobson's account of imperialism, perhaps because, as remarked above, he was suspicious of accounts of imperialism that rested upon the idea of primal spatial drives.

---

[115] Long, *New Liberal Internationalism*, 151–2.   [116] Hobson, *Imperialism*, 21.

In general terms, Mackinder presented a vision of the world in which the arrangement of different sorts of spaces imposed clear constraints upon the evolution of the world organism.[117] In his discussion of the 'Great Trade Routes', Mackinder drew attention to a belt of deserts that he traced with little interruption from the north-west coast of Africa, through to the east coast of Asia, level with the northern tip of Japan. Some of this land was dry all year round and some, the Steppes, was dry but for a few weeks of rain each year. For much of history, sedentary society was absent from this zone, which effectively isolated what Mackinder described as three major hearths of human settlement: Africa, Asia, and Europe. South of the Sahara, Mackinder named a region as 'the true Africa: Negroland'.[118] There had been little interaction between societies north and south of the African desert, which was 'the great bulwark which had prevented Europe from being overrun by the black races of Africa'.[119] Continuing the desert belt east and north of the Sahara, the Arabian desert was narrowed significantly by the valley of the River Euphrates leading to the Persian Gulf and, even more dramatically, by the Red Sea. South of the Asian deserts and Eurasian Steppes, was the second human hearth, the 'region which is occupied by India and China, with the countries in their immediate neighbourhood'.[120] North of the Sahara, and to the west of the Steppes, was the third hearth: Europe. The steppes and the oases of the Asian deserts were the terrain of a floating population, the Asian nomads identified earlier as camel-men and horse-riders. According to Mackinder, intercourse between Europe and true Africa was limited before the Age of Columbus. But Europe and settled Asia could trade by means of an overland route, the famous Silk Road, that moved from oasis to valley across the Asian deserts to finish up at the eastern end of the Mediterranean.[121] In passing along this way, the traders were subject to interference from the horse-riders and camel-men. Goods were stolen or duties charged. Only those goods most valuable to each party could bear the total costs of such a journey so that silver went east and silk came west.

Mackinder remarked that because luxury goods came to Europe along the Silk Road, overland from Asia to Europe, Europeans became impressed with the idea that Asia was full of such wealth that a search for an alternative route to the Indies became an obsession. For this reason, in Mackinder's account, Christopher Columbus (1451–1506) sailed west, Vasco da Gama (1469–1524) south, and Ferdinand Magellan (1480–1521) south-west from Europe. Their achievements changed the strategic arrangement of the world,

---

[117] Chapter 3 described how he tried to construct a continuous argument from Physical into Human Geography.

[118] Mackinder, 'Great Trade Routes', 2. This area of southern Africa was repeatedly renamed by Mackinder. On occasion he included it within the Insular and Peninsular World and at other times as a second heartland of its own (see Figure 5.1).

[119] Mackinder, ibid., 3.

[120] Mackinder, ibid., 3.

[121] Whitfield, *Life Along the Silk Road*.

for Europe now had access to easily taken, so-called 'empty' lands beyond
the seas. It also tried to make colonies of Asia by moving its navies into the
Indian Ocean and beyond.

In the 'Pivot' paper, Mackinder took up these geographical 'realities' in a
somewhat different manner. Recall that the germ of his new perspective came
to him from the conjunction of two events: the British sending troops to
South Africa in 1899–1902, and the Russians sending troops to Manchuria in
1904. This coincidence underlined for him the near equivalence of land- and
sea-power under modern conditions. It also 'suggested a parallel contrast
between Vasco da Gama rounding the Cape of Good Hope on his voyage to
the Indies, near the end of the fifteenth century, and the ride of Yermak, the
Cossack, at the head of his horsemen, over the Ural range into Siberia early
in the sixteenth century'.[122] In other words, the land-power of the mobile
nomad had repeatedly pressed against the limits of its ecumene. The difference now was organization and manpower. The nomads had not been able to
sustain their pressure on the settled lands around them, although some
groups detached themselves from the grasslands and settled as rulers
among the cultivators of Asia. They could build empires, but only by establishing them in the rain-fed lands beyond their normal range. For Mackinder
the Magyars and Bulgarians were, for this reason, essentially Turks and, as
such, these 'horse-riding peoples of the interior' had ever tried to establish
empires, as with the Habsburg and Balkan Empires respectively, detached
from the core region of nomadic life.[123] But, now, with the Russians extending their land-power to Manchuria while retaining control of their steppe-
lands, the strategic realities of the world had changed.

Land-Power and the Heartland

The Russian troops in Manchuria for Mackinder signalled the return of
land-power, but in a new form: through trains rather than horses and camels.
Indeed, the Russian empire was drawing resources, by railway, out of Siberia
and seeking to develop as a coherent economy its resources from Siberia to
the Black Sea. It had turned the grasslands of the Steppes into wheat fields,
and 'Odessa has here risen to importance with the rapidity of an American
city'.[124] Mackinder speculated that Russia might soon develop the oilfields
around Baku, and the immense coal reserves in the Donets basin of the
Ukraine. Furthermore, most of this region was inaccessible to sea-power.
From the north, the approach by sea was made difficult by the freezing of
estuaries each winter, three of the great river systems (the Obi, Yenisey, and
Lena) drained into the freezing ocean to the north. Three other river systems

---

[122] Mackinder, 'Round World', 596.
[123] Mackinder, 'Geographical Aspects', 7.
[124] Mackinder, 'Geographical Pivot', 434.

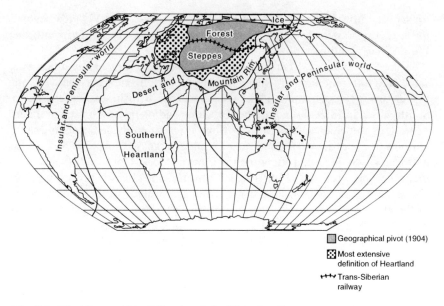

Geographical pivot (1904)

Most extensive
definition of Heartland

⊢⊦⊦⊦ Trans-Siberian
railway

Fig. 5.1. The 'Geographical Pivot' and the 'Heartland'

drained into internal salt lakes (the Volga and the Oxus into the Amu, and the Jaxartes into the Syr). This was the area that Mackinder identified as the 'pivot' (see Figure 5.1), although he did at one stage refer to part of it as an 'arid heart-land'.[125] The main feature of the steppe-land, then, was that 'it is wholly unpenetrated by waterways from the ocean'.[126] An adequate land-power could move from Europe to East Asia and could strike at will along the edges of its living-space without much fear of effective reprisal from opponents along the coastland who must move their main force by sea and river. Should such a power acquire warm-water ports of its own, it could feed its own sea-power from its vast industrial base and strike with impunity wheresoever it wished. Mackinder concluded that the 'great industrial wealth in Siberian and European Russia and a conquest of some of the marginal regions would give the basis for a fleet necessary to found the world em-pire'.[127] However, in 1904, he doubted whether Russia could raise the capital to develop its resource base but hinted that '[t]his might happen if Germany were to ally herself with Russia'.[128] Russian resources under German control was, as I explained in Chapter 1, the dream of the German geopolitician, Karl Haushofer and his master, Adolf Hitler.

In his most extended statement of his strategic theory, in *Democratic Ideals and Reality* of 1919, Mackinder extended the limits of what he conceived as the defensible space of land-power to the east and the west beyond the region

---

[125] Mackinder, 'Geographical Pivot', 430.   [126] Mackinder, ibid., 429.
[127] Mackinder, ibid., 443.   [128] Mackinder, ibid., 436.

of arctic and continental drainage, defining what he now called a Heartland, rather than a Pivot. To the east, a dramatic plateau falls off to the coast down successive mountain ranges presenting little obstacle to horsemen but inaccessible by boat up from the coast. Meanwhile, to the west of his earlier 'Pivot', Mackinder reflecting upon the experience of the First World War concluded that both the Baltic and the Black Seas could be closed with ease by a land-power, as they had been during that conflict by Germany and Russia, respectively. He called this territory the Heartland and said that if it were ever under unified control it would even extend its western limit up to a line from Kiel to Trieste, more or less as Churchill described the limits of the communist bloc in 1946: '[f]rom Stettin in the Baltic to Trieste in the Adriatic, an iron curtain has descended across the Continent'.[129]

This new western limit also marked a central division within Europe itself between the West and the East. Historically, contending European powers had at various times based themselves in one or other of these regions and tried to foment divisions within the other. Germany, however, sat astride this division. Given the political stability of frontiers in Western Europe, Germany was able to look eastwards at the unstable lines between what Mackinder called the Teuton and the Slav. Ethnic Germans were to be found in three extensions from Germany proper: first along the Baltic coast towards St Petersburg; second, along the River Oder through Silesia towards Poland; and, third, along the Danube down into Austria. These three tongues, together with detached outliers, gave Germany ample opportunity to destabilize Slav nations to its east. Mackinder saw the immediate causes of the First World War in the 'extraordinary condition of things in the East'.[130]

In 1674, John Evelyn (1620–1706) had aphorized the sea-power basis of British supremacy: 'Whoever commands the ocean commands the trade of the world, and whoever commands the trade of the world commands the riches of the world, and whoever is master of that commands the world itself'.[131] In 1919, Mackinder put his conclusions about land-power in his own jingle: 'Who rules East Europe commands the Heartland: | Who rules the Heartland commands the World-Island: | Who rules the World-Island commands the World'.[132] The mosaic of Slav and German peoples in Eastern Europe had to be rationalized into a coherent series of defensible nations arranged in a series and filling the isthmus between Baltic, Adriatic, and Black Seas: '[w]e must see to it that East Europe, like West Europe, is divided into self-contained nations. If we do that, we shall not only reduce the German people to its proper position in the world, a great enough position for any single people, but we shall also have created the conditions precedent to a League of Nations'.[133] The relocation of some German

---

[129] Rhodes James, *Churchill*, 7290.   [130] Mackinder, 'Geographical Aspects', 4.
[131] Quoted in: le Billon, 'Resource Wars', 3.
[132] Mackinder, *Democratic Ideals and Reality*, 194.
[133] Mackinder, ibid., 203.

peoples westwards would be necessary in cases where they would not submit to live in the culture and language of the Slav peoples that were to be given exclusive control over territory. In this way, Mackinder argued that coherent spaces could be made for Poland, Bohemia, Hungary, Yugoslavia, Rumania, Bulgaria, and Greece. He urged, further, that several of these states might find their security and prosperity best served by joining some loose federation of Slav peoples. In this way, Mackinder sought to deprive Russia both of the western part of the Heartland and of an outlet through the Black Sea into the Mediterranean. He wanted also to make it difficult for Germany to extend itself eastwards, making a play for sole control of the Heartland itself.

Mackinder returned one more time to his theory of the Heartland during the Second World War, as his work was rediscovered in the United States by report of its fame in Nazi Germany. When a US journalist asked him to reflect again upon his ideas, he thought them only reconfirmed by the strategic questions of the War. In 1904, he had focused upon Russia, and in 1919 upon Germany, and in 1943 at the height of a war with Germany, he turned again to Russia:

All things considered, the conclusion is unavoidable that if the Soviet Union emerges from this war as conqueror of Germany, she must rank as the greatest Land Power on the globe. Moreover, she will be the Power in the strategically strongest defensive position. The Heartland is the greatest natural fortress on earth. For the first time in history it is manned by a garrison sufficient both in number and quality.[134]

The Heartland now had the manpower to try for World Empire.

Sea-Power and Territoriality

As Mackinder's geopolitical writings were primarily about the threat posed by land-power, he cautioned against the belief that sea-power must prevail in all modern contexts. He had much less to say about sea-power itself, which was derived from, and essential to commerce, or about how Britain's rise had been based on sea-power. This last was the principal concern of Alfred Mahan. In his study of sea-power, Mahan had sketched the strategic lessons to be learned from the study of wars involving battles at sea. Mahan was concerned with how states might best fight at sea in conflicts that normally moved across both land and sea. He made, however, a few remarks about the social, economic, and political factors promoting the effective deployment of sea-power, which came down mainly to the traits that promoted merchant adventuring, an 'instinct for commerce, bold enterprise in the pursuit of gain, and a keen scent for the trails that lead to it'.[135] Mahan established the significance of sea-power, but did not try to indicate how its spatial forms related to the global configuration of land and sea masses. He also did not

[134] Mackinder, 'Round World', 601.   [135] Mahan, *Sea Power*, 57–8.

develop any ideas about the effect of sea-power upon the social and political life of countries relying upon its efficacy.

As Chapter 3 explained, Mackinder understood British characteristics primarily in terms of race. Over the very long term, say a thousand years or so, he thought that the physical environment selected social character-istics, which were then passed on in the blood. He believed, for example, that the variegated physical environment of southern England had produced a talent for democracy and self-reliance. He also allowed that more recent developments might affect national character, as with the way that Germany, as a late industrializer, had been forced into aggressive competition with other states. If one took the British era of sea-power as dating from the late seventeenth century, then, according to Mackinder, Britain's conduct in the world was shaped in a profound way by a reliance upon ships rather than infantry. Although Britannia ruled the waves, the liberty of foreign peoples was not thereby endangered, for 'warships cannot navigate mountains', and Mackinder argued that, for this reason, during their period of naval suprem-acy, the British had 'not sought to make permanent European conquests'.[136]

Land-power, then, was territorial, whereas sea-power was not and, in this way, Mackinder drew a parallel between the United States and Great Britain: 'both countries have now passed through the same succession of colonial, continental, and insular stages'.[137] Both nations had been settled by colonists who then consolidated their hold over the land mass before looking across the waters to see continental powers that they had no desire to displace territorially. Both wanted to see a balance of power prevail on the land mass that faced them, and both worried about the emergence of a hegemonic power on any other land mass. Britain's attitude towards Europe in the nineteenth century was to 'be opposed to whatever Power attempt[ed] to organise the resources of East Europe and the Heartland'.[138] Britain was committed to 'preventing the establishment of a united European Empire' for against this 'no power organized merely on the productivity of [the British Isles] could hope to stand'.[139] Mackinder argued that the rise of Germany and Russia meant France could never again aspire to control the Heartland, and so it too must identify with the safety of a balance of powers. France, suggested Mackinder, was a peninsular power and its security rested with the other insular (or sea-) powers.

Mackinder claimed that the First World War became clarified when the United States joined, and Russia abandoned, the allies in 1917. Both the ideals and the geopolitical realities of the war were now evident:

The world-strategy of the contest was entirely altered. We have been fighting since [. . .] to make the world a safe place for democracies. So much as regards idealism. But

---

[136] Mackinder, *Democratic Ideals and Reality*, 74.
[137] Mackinder, ibid., 87.
[138] Mackinder, ibid., 178.
[139] Mackinder, 'Geographical Conditions', 472.

it is equally important that we should bear in mind the new face of reality. We have been fighting lately, in the close of the war, a straight duel between land-power and sea-power [...].[140]

The modalities of land- versus sea-power implied very different attitudes towards the territorial integrity of other states. Land-power was aggressive, whereas sea-power was only ever defensive.

Finally, Mackinder sketched out a few ideas about the geostrategic realities of modern sea-power. In 1902, he proposed that the settler colonies of the Empire might be recruited and sustain a 'navy of the Britains', 'equivalent to those of the United States and Russia'.[141] This new imperial sea-power might, he suggested in 1909, require that 'the economic centre of the British Empire' shift to Canada because 'there will be the greatest seat of natural productivity and of man power'.[142] In this newly reconfigured Empire, 'the British isles will retain much of their old importance, as being the advanced position for the defence of Canada and the other dominions beyond the ocean'.[143] Since the Empire would need to act to maintain a 'balance of power in Europe', it would need a naval base off the European coast. In this way, Britain would come to 'have some of the characteristics of the flying base of naval strategists'.[144]

The experience of the First World War suggested that the British Empire might be an insufficient base from which to resist a consolidated Eurasian heartland under German, Russian, or a combined rule. Resisting the land-power would require the union of the main insular and peninsular powers. In Mackinder's account of 1919, the insular powers would maintain navies and the peninsular powers such as France, Italy, Egypt, India, and Korea would become so many bridgeheads for outside navies to support armies, preventing the land-power from putting to sea.[145] In this new geopolitical arrangement, as Mackinder set it out in his last significant work (1943), sea- (and related air-) power would have three regions: 'a reserve of trained manpower, agriculture and industries in the eastern United States and Canada'; 'a moated aerodrome in Britain'; and 'a bridgehead in France'.[146] For Mackinder, then, North America represented 'depth of defense', Britain was a secure place to assemble an invasion force, and France was the safe place to land troops for 'instant land warfare' against the Eurasian heartland.[147] This strategic use of space was essential because 'sea power must in the final resort

---

[140] Mackinder, *Democratic Ideals and Reality*, 81.
[141] Mackinder, *Britain and the British Seas*, 351.
[142] Mackinder, 'Geographical Conditions', 474.
[143] Mackinder, ibid., 474.
[144] Mackinder, ibid., 474.
[145] Mackinder, *Democratic Ideals and Reality*, 265.
[146] Mackinder, 'Round World', 604.
[147] Mackinder, ibid., 601, 604.

be amphibious if it is to balance land power'.[148] Only these arrangements
would prevent the Heartland from achieving World Empire.

Implications

In many ways, Hobson provided a valuable commentary upon Mackinder's
claims. The most important of Hobson's insights was that imperialism was
an international phenomenon with domestic roots. In contrast, Mackinder
presented imperialism as an international constraint upon domestic policies.
For Mackinder, the causes of imperialism lay in the relations between
nations, whereas for Hobson they lay in the nature of the capitalist economy
itself, and it was the consequences of imperialism that were expressed in the
relations between nations. Further, for Hobson, the articulation of the
domestic and the international occurred not only through national policy
but also through the presentation of sectional economic interests as national
interests. Mackinder, while aware that adventurers would draw nations into
foreign entanglements, thought that, on the whole, such people were the
advanced guard of the national economy. Hobson complicated the notion
of the national interest in a way that Mackinder could not. This meant that,
for Hobson, protectionism was a primary cause of imperialist competition,
whereas for Mackinder it was a response to ever-present imperialist rivalry.

How the domestic, the national, and the international scales are interrelated remains a central issue in explanations of the global geopolitical
economy. Some theories of globalization, for example, present the fundamental causes of economic relations as global. Michael Hardt and Antonio
Negri from the Left, and Kenichi Ohmae from the Right, propose that the
logic of capital at the global level makes irrelevant any national attempts to
impose alternative economic arrangements within states.[149] Other commentators argue that the claim that there is no alternative to a global capitalist
order has been an important spur to the adoption of neo-liberal policies in
many states.[150] In *A Brief History of Neoliberalism*, David Harvey proposes
that national economic policy has been captured by sectional interests, in
precisely the manner suggested by Hobson.[151] To restore profitability, capitalists undermine workers' living standards by claiming that the external
discipline of globalization requires: devaluing the social wage (reducing taxes
on businesses), rescinding restrictions on production and employment practices (lowering business costs), and forcing workers to accept more flexible

---

[148] Mackinder, 'Round World', 601–2.
[149] Hardt and Negri, *Empire*; Ohmae, *Borderless World*.
[150] Munck, 'Neoliberalism'. [151] Harvey, *Neoliberalism*.

working arrangements (reducing wages and benefits). Moreover, in *The New Liberalism*, Harvey locates the short-term solutions to imperialism in precisely the sorts of domestic (Keynesian) redistributive policies that Hobson saw as necessary to address the economic perversions produced by the unfair profits and rents taken out of the economy as 'unproductive' surplus, or 'illth'.[152] We might extend these parallels still further and note that Hobson's argument that imperialism can both deepen as well as widen, shares much with Harvey's notion that successive rounds of 'accumulation by dispossession' can occur within the same territory as new sets of communal resources are first privatized and then sold to foreign interests.[153]

Hobson's and Mackinder's concern with international entities is equally suggestive of parallels between the early-twentieth and early-twenty-first centuries. Anthony Carty, for one, is struck by the way that questions about sustaining the hegemony of American imperialism at the start of the twenty-first century recall very similar debates about international law raised in the context of declining British supremacy during the years before 1914.[154]

Hobson understood individuals to be located within concentric circles of affinity that would follow their interconnectedness from local to global. He thought a civilized society would cede upwards elements of sovereignty so that a global commons could be defined and developed. Mackinder was more suspicious of international, and even national, bodies, which he saw as encouraging class-consciousness, and his version of provincialism was an attempt to cultivate geographical in place of social or economic identities. Yet, both Mackinder and Hobson were committed to an organicism that left them stressing the needs of the group, variously understood, over the rights of the individual. For both, the group was defined biologically, and in broadly racial terms. In other words, their groups were communities of fate, determined at birth, that people could neither join nor leave, and these groups might be arranged in a hierarchy from more to less worthy. This, however, posited radical difference as the basis of community, placing unreasonable strains upon internal homogeneity and justifying an ethnic division of space that in fact ran counter to the many ways that both also recognized people as interconnected economically as well as culturally. Their organic view of community placed a premium on purity that inclined them towards cultural and biological paranoia. This organicism also meant that a collective interest was asserted that, they believed, should prevail over individual rights. In whatever form this utilitarian position be given, it is always dangerously majoritarian. Instead, it is quite possible to argue that there are relevant entities in social life other than the human individual, while also claiming that the individual is uniquely significant from an ethical point of view. Finally, Hobson's and Mackinder's acceptance of a scale of civilization,

---

[152] Harvey, *New Imperialism*.   [153] Harvey, ibid.
[154] A. Carty, 'Marxism and International Law'.

in any form whatsoever, imposes one measure (their own) upon other peoples, without consultation. Allied, as it was in both their cases, to a belief in the justifiable use of force to secure what they saw as the good life, this civilizational scale allowed for dangerous interventions in the affairs of people who claimed not to see the good life in the same terms as they did.

6

Teaching Imperialism

Much of Mackinder's teaching of Imperial Geography is contained in a series of popular school textbooks and in a number of published illustrated lectures. In this chapter some of the main features of these texts are described, starting with the ways that Mackinder trained children to look upon any landscape as would a military leader and how he invited them to extend that strategic gaze to global relations. Markers of visual difference were exoticized by Mackinder within a comparative framework that vaunted British over other values and mores. An imperial gaze was connected to a geopolitical imaginary in these textbooks through stories about and pictures of people in different regions of the world, and maps depicting how these regions were interconnected. Mackinder further taught children that these global dependencies rested upon the threat or use of force, and that in this contest the British needed to prevail because they alone had a uniquely democratic tradition to offer the rest of humanity. Finally, the chapter discusses Mackinder's instruction on the geography of the British Empire itself, including his descriptions of how and why the Empire should be defended, and the particular attention he gave to the jewel in the imperial crown, India.

In 1906, Mackinder published the first of six books to cover the teaching of Geography to children between the ages of eleven and eighteen.[1] *Our Own Islands* took the form of a tourist's journey around Britain and Ireland. The tourist was regularly taken uphill before proceeding further down dale: 'we will advise him to [...] climb, for the sake of the view, the great hill at the northern end of the Pennine Chain which is called Cross Fell'; '[l]et us propose to our traveller that [...] he climb Hart Fell' so that he might 'look

[1] His six books were published, in London by George Philip and Son, and in Liverpool by Philip, Son, and Nephew: *Our Own Islands* (1906), *Our Island History* (1914), *Lands Beyond the Channel* (1908), *Distant Lands* (1910), *The Nations of the Modern World* (1910), and *The Modern British State* (1914). New editions of each appeared most years until the late 1920s. Two of the books (*Our Own Islands* and *Our Island History*) were also published in two parts, and the updating of *Nations of the Modern World* after the First World War was achieved by producing a second volume on the situation 'After 1914' (1921). *Nations of the Modern World* was first promised as *The British Empire*, while its second part was also published for a general audience as *The World War and After: A Concise Narrative and Some Tentative Ideas* (1924). The additions to the planned sequence were extra works on Britain, *Our Island History* and *The Modern British State*. The series was first advertised as 'Mackinder's Geographical Studies' but with these two additions it became 'Elementary Studies in Geography and History'.

southward [...] to the peak of Skiddaw in the Lake District, and [...] north-west [... to] the highland peak of Ben Lomond' so that the pupil 'may realize how large a part of Great Britain is sometimes visible from a single hill'.[2] Using maps and photographs in the text, the pupil is led to act like the tourist and invited: to 'try to picture to ourselves the shape of the whole Pennine Chain', to 'try to make a picture in our minds of the whole district which is known as the North of England', to 'try to print upon our memories the map of the hills which fill northern England and southern Scotland'.[3] Mackinder spoke of geography as building upon 'the eye for the country which characterizes the fox hunter and the soldier'.[4] Geographical education would train young people in the strategic gaze of the fox-hunter and the soldier and, ultimately, they would, through Mackinder's school-books learn to encompass the world with this geographical imagination and thereby develop an imperial vision.

Mackinder believed that education was vital to democracy. Mackinder started upon public life just after the third of the Reform Acts was passed (1884), and universal adult male suffrage was made flesh. 'The extension of the franchise', he suggested, 'made compulsory education inevitable'.[5] British men had important lessons to learn: '[h]is responsibility is great, for he is called upon to vote not only upon local questions, but in regard to imperial issues'.[6] Moreover, a geographical education was to chart and describe the spaces of Empire. Accused by one contemporary reviewer of a 'frankly imperialistic' bias in a book of lectures on India, Mackinder unapologetically avowed 'The Teaching of Geography from an Imperial Point of View'.[7]

The imperialistic tone of Mackinder's geographical teaching was evident to contemporaries and, even though many accepted it, some demurred. For critics, the imperialistic approach was both questionable and pedagogically unnecessary; there were other ways to teach about global environments, cultures, and their interrelations. One of the most impressive alternative presentations of popular geographical education was found in the writings of the anarchist geographer, Élisée Reclus. Like Mackinder, Reclus directed the attention of his public towards the interdependence of peoples in distant parts, but he rejected the world view of imperialistic geographers. Unlike Mackinder, Reclus did not see international relations as resting always and forever upon force. He paid greater attention to ecological history, the dangers of environmental spoliation, and the historical constitution of the economy. In contrast to Mackinder, Reclus analysed the dangerous effects of commercialization upon colonies. However, he was ambivalent about colonialism, which he regarded as in some cases the midwife of social progress,

[2] Mackinder, *Our Own Islands*, 67, 86.
[3] Mackinder, *Our Own Islands*, 45, 66, 87.
[4] Mackinder, 'Teaching of Geography', 80.
[5] Mackinder, *Modern British State*, 248.
[6] Mackinder, *Modern British State*, 251.
[7] R[eynolds], 'Review of Mackinder'; Mackinder, 'Teaching of Geography'.

spreading progressive European values and promoting contact and thus understanding between remote strangers. In this chapter, the discussion of these profoundly different visions of geographical teaching concludes on an aspect common to both Mackinder and Reclus, a belief in a hierarchy of civilizations.

Geographical Visuality

The geographer, James Ryan, analyses Mackinder's geographical pedagogy as a training in visualization, 'derived in part from military training, yet [. . .] applied within a broader framework of civic duty, education and citizenship'.[8] It was in this sense that Mackinder spoke of Geography not only as a science (ordering knowledge), and philosophy (synthesizing knowledge), but also as an art because it relied upon evoking pictures, vistas, and panoramas.[9] The building blocks of geographical study were such 'rudimentary facts' as the 'outlines of continents and oceans' and these 'must be taught by maps: they are purely a question of eye-memory'.[10] Thus, what were called lantern-slides were vital tools of geographical instruction and promotion. In 1893, the Geographical Association was founded, with Mackinder's direct assistance, as a group of schoolteachers promoting Geography through the sharing of educational slides.[11] In 1914, the Liverpool Geographical Society decided that it 'should lend lantern slides to the schools of the city, in order that the study of geography might become more interesting and useful to the scholars'.[12] Photographs and maps peppered the textbooks Mackinder wrote for schoolchildren. Figures 6.1 and 6.2 reproduce images found on facing pages of Mackinder's textbook on the world beyond Europe, *Distant Lands*.[13]

Gearóid Ó Tuathail has brilliantly examined some of the broader political resonances of Mackinder's geographical vision; here I am more narrowly concerned with how vision was trained to cultivate an imperial sensibility in children.[14] Following *Our Own Islands*, with the second of his school-books, *Lands Beyond the Channel*, Mackinder moved from Britain and Ireland to

---

[8] Ryan, *Picturing Empire* 208–9.
[9] Mackinder, 'Development of Geographical Teaching', 192.
[10] 'Mr. Mackinder on Geography-Teaching', 408.
[11] Balchin, *Geographical Association*.
[12] 'How Geography Can be Made Interesting', 7.
[13] Mackinder, *Distant Lands*, 208–9. These images and the accompanying text are discussed in more detail later in the chapter. The myth and exaggeration of the 'Black Hole' is treated in Dalley, *Black Hole*.
[14] Ó Tuathail, *Critical Geopolitics*. More generally, on visual techniques in geographical teaching at this time, see: Ploszajska, 'Representations of Imperial Landscapes'; Walford, *Geography in British Schools*.

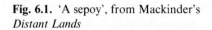

Fig. 6.1. 'A sepoy', from Mackinder's
Distant Lands

describe mainland Europe and, significantly, to northern Africa. At Gibraltar,
Mackinder invited the pupil-reader (the tourist was left in England) to cross
south into Morocco and savour a contrast which is 'one of the most remarkable
in the world. At Gibraltar you are in a civilized and Christian country, under
the British flag, with civilized and Christian Spain close at hand. At Tangier you
are in a barbaric country, the people of which are Mohammedans'.[15] The
contrast was unavoidable for 'everything in Tangier tells us that we have left
civilization behind'.[16] The signs were all visual: from a photograph of a 'street
scene in Tangier', children were asked to 'note the veiled women'.[17] Pupils were
also alerted that in Morocco local men 'wear not coats and trousers but long
white robes', and shop owners 'sit cross-legged on the floor in their white robes
and turbans'.[18] The trained observer was to notice these things and draw
appropriate conclusions. Within Britain, visual differentiation was coded by
the landscape; climate, landscape, flora, and fauna distinguished 'our islands'
from other places, but differences in human appearance were presented as an
exoticism that registered barbarism.

The third book, *Distant Lands*, presented a global perspective of the
physical world before peopling it with a congeries of exotic peoples and
animals. Alongside a photograph of an Arab horse, pupils were asked to

---

[15] Mackinder, *Lands Beyond the Channel*, 103.
[16] Mackinder, ibid., 106.
[17] Mackinder, ibid., 104.
[18] Mackinder, ibid., 103, 104.

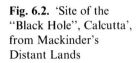

Fig. 6.2. 'Site of the "Black Hole", Calcutta', from Mackinder's Distant Lands

'[n]ote the peculiar setting of the tail', whereas a picture of a fakir indicated '[a] begging monk whose self torture is that he never lowers his arm'. Perhaps not surprisingly, the discussion of India was introduced with a picture of 'Bengal tigers'.[19] The training of the geographical imagination thus instructed pupils to note the peculiarities of foreign persons, animals, and places. While pupils were occasionally enjoined to appreciate that difference was not inferiority, the presentation and explanation of purely visual evidence did little to support Mackinder's warning that '[w]e must beware of thinking of the Indians and Chinese as merely barbarians'.[20] For Mackinder, most foreign people were barbaric, but the 'educated Chinaman' did exist and 'is as much a gentleman in bearing and clothing as any gentleman in the West'.[21] Again, the signs of civilization were visual, 'bearing and clothing'.

Alongside these school-books with their Orientalist accounts of India and China, Mackinder also wrote a series of illustrated lectures intended for use in schools; these examples of Geography as training through visualization were sponsored by the Visual Instruction Committee of the Colonial Office. In 1902, Mackinder's friend Michael Sadler, as Director of Special Inquiries at the Board of Education, persuaded Joseph Chamberlain to commission, as Colonial Secretary, a series of illustrated lectures on the Empire. It was evident to Mackinder that 'the Empire can only be held together by sympathy and understanding' and that for this purpose children in all parts of the

---

[19] Mackinder, *Distant Lands*, 84, 52, 38.
[20] Mackinder, ibid., 70.
[21] Mackinder, ibid., 70.

Fig. 6.3. Hugh Fisher, 'The battleship,
"H.M.S. King Edward VII"'

Source: Used by kind permission of Cambridge
University Library.

Empire must 'understand what the other parts were like', a need best met 'by
some adequate means of visual instruction'.[22] With this intent a photog-
rapher, Hugh Fisher (1867–1945), was sent around the Empire (1907–10) to
capture the scenes Mackinder desired for the lectures. Yet, what Indian
children were shown was not the Empire as a whole, but instead Mackinder
took them on a journey from their home to 'the land in all the world which,
after our own land of India, should be of the greatest interest to us, for it is
the centre of the Empire to which we owe so much'.[23] Following this sea
journey there were five lectures on the United Kingdom before a final lecture
on 'The Defences of the Empire', which included fifty (of fifty-four) slides of
army, navy, guns, or warships. Figure 6.3 is typical of these, showing the
forecastle of the battleship, 'H.M.S. King Edward VII', with, as Fisher
noted, the 'largest guns now carried by any modern ship'.[24] Many of the
slides in other chapters were of British industry and technology, but even
here the military emphasis was evident with the metal industries illustrated by
four slides of the building of a battleship.

It is instructive to compare this set of lectures with another set of Mackinder's lectures written on India for British schoolchildren. The contrast
between the visual representation of Britain to Indian children and that of
India for British schoolchildren was evident, both from the treatment of

---

[22] Mackinder, *Seven Lectures*, v.

[23] Mackinder, *Seven Lectures*, 6.

[24] Cambridge University Library, Fisher Photograph Collection, Album 21, Photograph 5004;
GBR/0115/Fisher/21/5004. Reproduced by kind permission of the Syndics of Cambridge University
Library.

India in the school textbooks and from the illustrated lectures on India. Of the eight lectures on India, four focused on religion (Hinduism, Buddhism, Islam, Sikhism) and the treatment throughout was cultural rather than economic, except where British technology had brought improvements; 'in these mills you will find that the machinery bears the names of Dundee and Leeds makers for the [jute] industry is relatively new to India'.[25] This reflected Mackinder's purpose from the start, for his instructions to Fisher were that he was to photograph colonial scenes that would illustrate either the 'native characteristics of the country', or the 'super-added characteristics due to British rule'.[26] More common, then, were illustrations such as a view of 'the Drug, from the top of which prisoners of war used to be thrown, in the days of the tyranny of [. . .] the Muhummadan sovereigns of Mysore', or the injunction accompanying an image of Fatehpur Sikri that pupils particularly '[n]otice in the quadrangle the stone pierced with a hole which is fixed in the ground. Criminals were put to death by being trampled upon by an elephant, and to that ring the elephant was tied'.[27] One slide, as noted by Ryan, combined these two perspectives (on barbaric Indian culture and progressive British technology). An image of the Landsdowne railway bridge, a symbol of British science, was, as Mackinder pointed out, taken from a location that recalled the barbarism of traditional India, 'an old nunnery founded for women who preferred seclusion rather than the funeral pyre. The Hindu custom was to burn the wife or wives with the husband's body, until the British Government intervened to prevent the practice'.[28]

Geopolitics

Mackinder's understanding of imperialism infused his educational writings through an emphasis upon global interconnectedness, the unavoidability of force, and British exceptionalism. Mackinder insisted upon a global perspective for teaching the youth of one of the world's Great Powers. Reflecting upon the far-flung British Empire, Mackinder observed that '[a]ll these lands, severed by ocean and mountain and desert, would be separate countries were they not tied together by some 9,000 steamers and many thousand miles of submarine electric cable'.[29] The Empire had always been united by the mobility of the British navy across all seven seas but recent interaction had intensified: '[o]f late [. . .], a vast change has come over the affairs of mankind. The means of communication have so increased that the world has

---

[25] Mackinder, *India*, 43.
[26] *Royal Commonwealth Society. Fisher Collection*, n.p.
[27] Mackinder, *India*, 14–15, 116.
[28] Ryan, *Picturing Empire*, 201; Mackinder, *India*, 130.
[29] Mackinder, *Seven Lectures*, 85.

become one'.[30] Given these improvements in travel and communications, 'each of our lives, whether we are conscious of it or not, is now in touch with the whole world', and, as a result, '[a]lmost every great problem of to-day is a whole-world problem, and the comprehensive outlook must be cultivated'.[31] The geographer had this ability to see the world as a whole:

To visualize is the very essence of geographical power, which should be cultivated until it becomes possible to think of the whole World's surface at one in all its complexities, with its girdles of all kinds, telegraphic, railway, steamer, girdles of power, girdles of thought, for every touch of the helm of government, either at Westminster or in the City, produces a ripple which goes right round the World, like the wave in the air emitted from Krakatoa meeting obstacles and producing varied results. Nothing happens without producing results in every part.[32]

In short, concluded Mackinder in 1914, '[t]o-day we have almost annihilated space'.[33]

Mackinder warned against too much optimism regarding economic integration, due to its possible political consequences. He advised pupils that 'whereas critical events were formerly past and over before the majority of the people of the world had heard of them, now every phase of a quarrel between nations is followed by millions, and there is [the] danger of the sudden rise of popular passions'.[34] Indeed, one main purpose of geographical education was to give a 'sense of perspective' that would help pupils become citizens able to 'distinguish the significant from the insignificant even in the halfpenny newspaper'.[35] One contemporary prejudice Mackinder was anxious to scratch from the minds of his readers was the belief that the world was becoming more peaceful:

One fortunate result of the modern unity of the world, and of the fact that the damage done by war is no longer local, is that diplomacy is active for the avoidance of wars, which have become rarer and shorter than they used to be. It must not be forgotten, however, that the diplomats in their negotiations carefully bear in mind the relative strength and preparedness of the contending nations.[36]

This was written on the eve of the First World War, an event that Mackinder later took as proof of the folly of believing in diplomacy without force, and that others took as proof of the folly of believing in force without conflict.

[30] Mackinder, *Nations of the Modern World*, 183.
[31] Mackinder, *Modern British State*, 253; *idem, Nations of the Modern World*, vi.
[32] Mackinder, 'Development of Geographical Teaching', 192–3. Mackinder often used the eruption of Krakatoa, sending dust on a complete circuit around the globe, as a metaphor for the global consequences of local events.
[33] Mackinder, *Modern British State*, 253. The classic modern treatment of this is as 'time-space compression' in: Harvey, *Condition of Postmodernity*. There is a useful discussion of the history of treatments of this theme in: Thrift, 'A Hyperactive World'.
[34] Mackinder, *Nations of the Modern World*, 195.
[35] Mackinder, ibid., vi.
[36] Mackinder, ibid., 197.

Although Mackinder insisted repeatedly that British strength, if unassailed, would guarantee world peace, at other times he thought war to be inevitable, telling Indian pupils with more relish than decency that:

There is a splendid side to war. There are occasionally magnificent scenes in it. There is always room for skill and courage. But it is none the less horrible. Some people have thought that it might be possible to carry on government without wars and to maintain no Navy or Army. Heavy taxation would be avoided and much suffering escaped. As yet, however, no one has shown how this can be accomplished.[37]

In *The Modern British State*, the chapter on the army was subtitled: 'International Relations'. In brief, Mackinder told pupils that force was the invariant basis of global politics, for, when disagreements arose between Great Powers, 'war gives the only decision which an injured people with passions roused is willing to accept'.[38] These conflicts would arise in the normal course of events because the 'growth of trade and of population may render a particular position [or strategic location] essential to both' parties.[39] In this respect, advised Mackinder, 'we have no right to be angry with other nations for their preparedness and success', and must simply 'recognize the changing facts' that 'impose a duty upon us of increased defences and keener activity'.[40] Only within a state, could matters be settled by law and agreement; and yet even there people must remember, argued Mackinder, that the ultimate basis of decision was the balance of force, not argument: '[t]he advantage of the present system is that by counting heads we ascertain which view is in a majority, and which view would therefore probably win were resort had to fighting'.[41]

Mackinder's school-books and lectures noted that not all sorts of peoples used force in the same way although each used it to suit its own geographical circumstances. There were, according to Mackinder, four varieties of peoples: agricultural, nomadic, montane, and marine. Their primary features are shown in Table 6.1.[42] The Germanic peoples began in a series of fertile drainage basins and the basis of their wealth would, in earliest times, have been agricultural. Such a people might have been subject to predatory raids from tribal societies of less hospitable steppe, desert, or mountain. Lands with scant resources breed nomadic or montane people who look with envy upon more fortunate neighbours: '[i]s it surprising [...] that [their] armies should have attacked the rich agricultural districts, sometimes those of Europe in the West, sometimes the great oases of Egypt, and Babylonia, and at other times India or China?'[43] To protect their wealth, argued

[37] Mackinder, *Seven Lectures*, 98.
[38] Mackinder, *Modern British State*, 175.
[39] Mackinder, *Modern British State*, 175.
[40] Mackinder, *Nations of the Modern World*, 250.
[41] Mackinder, *Modern British State*, 143.
[42] Mackinder, *Distant Lands*, 102.
[43] Mackinder, *Distant Lands*, 84.

Table 6.1. Geography, power, and styles of government

People	Setting	Power	Force	Purpose	Government
Agricultural	Fertile river basin	Land	Specialized army	Defensive expansion	Despotic
Nomadic	Steppes/desert	Land	Soldier-subject	Predatory aggression	Tribal
Montane	Mountains	Land	Soldier-subject	Predatory aggression	Tribal
Maritime	Islands	Sea	Specialized navy	Contra tyranny	Free

Mackinder, agricultural people would have been forced to raise a large standing army from among themselves and in this way make 'discipline and organization [...] the first conditions of national existence'.[44] Consider, in contrast, the happy condition of a maritime people such as the British, an amalgam of 'proud and masterful sea races of men'.[45] Mackinder began his first book with a reflection upon the ways 'our island home is fortunate' and the most significant was that, as an island, this ecumene had for some considerable time been free from foreign conquest and thus 'we have had the great blessings of peace and freedom at home'.[46] Whereas the montane and nomadic peoples made soldiers of all adult males, agricultural and maritime peoples had specialized forces. Yet, navies and armies had very different political consequences because while a large standing army served as a temptation to establish overweening central government, '[f]rom its very nature a fleet is of little avail for internal despotism'.[47]

Thus it was that a maritime power such as Britain would enjoy greater freedom than the more disciplined land-powers of continental Europe, or the barbaric societies of the desert, steppe, or mountain. The distinction between Britain on one hand, and Russia or Germany on the other, was, between 'as it were the whale and the elephant, the sea power and the land power'.[48] Land- and sea-power had very different purposes. As Mackinder pointed out, the defence of Britain did not require the acquisition of territory but, rather, depended upon preventing the emergence of a land-power capable of fitting out a navy on a scale to challenge Britain's naval hegemony. Thus 'it has been the traditional policy of Britain to make alliances with minor states in opposition to any great state which threatened to upset the balance of power in Europe', for it had served Britain well to sustain 'smaller peoples who were threatened with foreign tyranny. Thus the strength of Britain on the whole

---

[44] Mackinder, *Nations of the Modern World*, 57.
[45] Mackinder, *Seven Lectures*, 45.
[46] Mackinder, *Our Own Islands*, 1, 5, 3.
[47] Mackinder, *Nations of the Modern World*, 291.
[48] Mackinder, *Nations of the Modern World*, 84.

supported the cause of freedom in the world'.[49] Fortunately, the British were the bravest people on earth: '[t]he rocks and the tempest demand courage and endurance more persistently than the wild beasts and sand storms of the wilderness. So the man who goes down to the seas becomes in the end master of the world'.[50] The British were not only the bravest, they were, Mackinder assured his young readers, also the best: 'the British tradition is [. . .] worth fighting for [. . .] for no other national tradition has equally conduced to the lasting development of what is happiest and highest in mankind'.[51]

Empire

As his textbooks and lectures illustrated, Mackinder's geopolitical lessons for young children were: that the world was now a single organism and that the global order rested upon force and contention. Moreover, Britain's unique historical mission was as a free country challenging the rise of despotism overseas. The threats and the stakes for this world order, and for the Empire, were equally high. Indeed, whereas '[t]hrough the last three centuries [. . .] the recurrent anxiety of our statesmen has been to prevent the rise of a Power in Europe so great in resource that it could outbuild our fleet. Is not this very danger now before us, and not from one quarter only, and not merely from Europe?'[52]

Russia and the Heartland

The land-powers that imperilled Britain included the established powers of Germany and the United States, with whom the British 'should cultivate none but the most friendly feelings of appreciation and respect', since '[w]e and the Germans and the Americans come of the same great Teutonic stock of men'.[53] Mackinder told his pupils that the other rising powers that threatened Britain were Russia, China, and Japan, and that, among these, he was most disturbed by the Russians:

In no European land have the railways made a greater change, for they have been easily and cheaply constructed across the level plain. Russia has a great army, but though there is much wealth in her fertile soils, in her vast forests, in the coalfields which underlie some parts of the country south of Moscow, and in the metals which are found in the Ural Mountains, yet Russia is at present a comparatively poor

[49] Mackinder, *Nations of the Modern World*, 291.
[50] Mackinder, *Distant Lands*, 102.
[51] Mackinder, *Nations of the Modern World*, 288.
[52] Mackinder, ibid., 294.
[53] Mackinder, ibid., 250.

country, for most of her people are not educated like the Germans and the French and the English.[54]

In addition, Russia was 'imprisoned [...] in a geographical sense. She has no access to open warm waters. Except along the Arctic coast her shores are washed only by land-locked seas, [...] and in winter all of these [Arctic] waters are frozen for many miles from the coast'.[55] The prison, though, was also a fortress for, complementing the inaccessible coastlands, the Russian steppe, and forest lands were 'enclosed south-eastward and south-westward by almost continuous upland'.[56] These steppe and forests stretched 'from the Arctic coast to the border of Iran and from the Carpathians to the Altai Mountains, [as] the widest lowland in the world, as large as all Europe'.[57] The meeting of open lowland with frozen or mountainous rim Mackinder described as 'one of the greatest geographical contrasts on the face of the globe'.[58] Here, set out for schoolchildren, was Mackinder's theory of the heartland, a lesson he imprinted early so that British citizens might later have it in mind when contemplating world affairs as reported in their halfpenny newspaper.

Writing on the eve of the First World War, Mackinder's verdict was stark: '[i]f the Russians as a people were as well educated as are the Germans and the Americans they would count as one of the greatest forces of the world. But two generations must probably elapse before this necessary reform can be accomplished'.[59] The Bolshevik Revolution of 1917 and Mackinder's own experiences in Russia in 1919 (see Chapter 7) caused him to revise this prediction later, so that when he wrote the supplementary volume on *The Nations of the Modern World: After 1914*, Mackinder was much less sanguine about the Russian threat and commented upon the tremendous work of organization achieved under communist direction. The land-powered scorpion was now able to act according to its nature; Mackinder warned pupils of the dangers of either Germany or Russia organizing the resources of European Russia and Eastern Europe. He repeated for students the substance of his arguments in favour of the balkanization of Eastern Europe into a tier of buffer states, but by 1924 he also adverted to the possibility that Western Europe and North America might act as 'a single community of nations'.[60]

Inculcating Empire

As I have already suggested, Mackinder's primary response to the dilemma of preserving British power in the face of continental challenges was to

[54] Mackinder, *Lands Beyond the Channel*, 272–3.
[55] Mackinder, *Nations of the Modern World*, 224.
[56] Mackinder, *Distant Lands*, 92.
[57] Mackinder, ibid., 91.
[58] Mackinder, ibid., 91.
[59] Mackinder, *Nations of the Modern World*, 223.
[60] Mackinder, *World War and After*, 251.

emphasize the significance of the British Empire. It is striking that several of the textbooks close on an imperial note. In the first in his series of school-books, *Our Own Islands*, Mackinder bid leave of his young readers with the injunction that:

Those who can find work to-day in Britain should stay among friends, but those who have not work should cross the ocean and make new homes for themselves in Canada, or Australia, or New Zealand, or South Africa. In all these lands they will remain the subjects of our King, Edward VII; the same flag will be theirs and they will not be among foreigners.[61]

Indeed, throughout his textbooks emigration to the Empire was mentioned as a valuable and significant prospect for British adults. Other emigration streams, such as to the United States, were barely mentioned, such as, for example, when the pupils were told that 'a good many Irish men emigrate and become colonists in new countries'.[62] The reference to 'colonists' was not accidental: in introducing for the Coefficients dining club a discussion on 'How far is it practicable and desirable to guide British Emigration rather to British Colonies than to Foreign Countries?', Mackinder bemoaned the fact that too many British emigrants wound up not in 'other parts of the Empire in which additional population was so much required, but in the United States'.[63]

The second work in his series of school-books, *Lands Beyond the Channel*, was about continental Europe. It ended with a discussion of the balance between the Great Powers of the United Kingdom, France, Germany, Russia, Austria-Hungary, and Italy. Again an imperial note was struck:

Small as the British population is, we must remember that so long as our fleet is strong enough, we can sail round all the coasts of Europe, and that we are therefore neighbours to all the other five Great Powers. [...] Our fleet is maintained to keep the ocean free from enemies, so that no one may attack either the lands which belong to us or the ships which trade for us.[64]

The Nations of the Modern World closed in exhortation: '[t]he British Empire, with all its immense power for good among mankind, can endure on one condition only, that the British citizens study to take broad views and are public spirited'.[65] The lectures on the United Kingdom intended for students in India concluded that 'the Empire can only be defended as a whole, and

---

[61] Mackinder, *Our Own Islands, II*, 298. More generally, see: Maddrell, 'Empire, Emigration and School Geography'.

[62] Mackinder, *Our Own Islands, II*, 295.

[63] Coefficients discussion 15 May 1904, [Printed notes on the discussions of the Coefficients 1904–1905], Mackinder Papers, School of Geography, Oxford University, MP/B/200 (1). For a discussion of the place of geographical teaching in promoting emigration to the settler colonies within the British Empire, see: Maddrell, 'Empire, Emigration and School Geography'.

[64] Mackinder, *Lands Beyond the Channel*, 276.

[65] Mackinder, *Nations of the Modern World*, 319.

with the full cooperation of all its citizens? Surely then it is the duty of each of us to uphold the flag and to learn something of the defences of the Empire, and of the way it should be guarded and its rights and honour maintained before the world'.[66] On the other hand, the lectures on India for pupils in the United Kingdom took leave with the observation that 'the administration of such an Empire [as the British] calls for virtues in our race certainly not less than those needed for our own self-government. Above all, we require knowledge of India, and sympathy with the points of view begotten of oriental history'.[67]

This common trajectory of taking leave of his readers with an exhortation to unify and defend the Empire reflects the imperial purpose of Mackinder's geographical teaching. Introducing his account of the historical geography of continental Europe, in *Lands Beyond the Channel*, Mackinder urged the study of France, Netherlands, and northern Africa because 'such historical factors as the French, Dutch, and Mohammedan would be relatively mean-ingless in the more distant continents unless first exhibited in their original environment. It is worth taking some trouble to make these things live in the minds and sympathies of future citizens of the British Empire'.[68] The imper-ial contenders of the British came from Europe and, to prevail in the global struggle, the British must know something of the historical background both of their rivals and of their own imperial subjects: '[e]ducation is essential [. . .] for the rule of an Empire'.[69] Pupils were assured that imperial rule was no selfish enterprise. Mackinder acknowledged that British 'dominion in alien lands began as a commercial venture, and for several generations was con-ducted primarily for a commercial profit', but '[t]o-day it is our proud ideal to exercise that control in the spirit of a trustee, for the benefit of the subordin-ate peoples and of the Empire at large'.[70]

India and Orientalism

Mackinder's geographical teaching was pitched at the justification of Empire and this was nowhere clearer than in his treatments of India and of Ireland. As already noted, Mackinder's writing on India was classically Orientalist. The literary theorist, Edward Said, wrote of the scholar having freedom to imagine the Orient 'with very little resistance on the Orient's part'.[71] Even if Indians were to speak, Mackinder would not be obliged to listen because, while he suggested that 'Western thought instinctively takes for granted the reality of outward things [, . . .] in the East the soul is the only real exist-ence'.[72] For Mackinder, no scientific account of India could be generated by

[66] Mackinder, *Seven Lectures*, 100.
[67] Mackinder, *India*, 133.
[68] Mackinder, *Lands Beyond the Channel*, vi.
[69] Mackinder, *Modern British State*, 252.
[70] Mackinder, *Modern British State*, 225.
[71] Said, *Orientalism*, 7.
[72] Mackinder, *India*, 7.

the people that lived there. When addressing the Indian schoolchildren through his lectures, Mackinder attempted to mimic, and thus direct their responses to the images and facts put before them. Writing in the voice of an Indian child, he suggested that '[i]t is a splendid thought to think of the many separate races, each living their own lives according to their own traditions, which are now held peaceably together within the British Empire'.[73] This mimicry was so satisfying for Mackinder, that when the lectures for Indian schoolchildren were reissued for English children, he described his lectures as 'an account of their own land as seen from the point of view of children in another part of the Empire', and suggesting that the Empire was made more secure 'by sympathy and understanding'.[74] Only in the British sections of his school-books did Mackinder cite any local authorities, literary or historical.

India was an obsession with Mackinder and, although he never travelled there, his accounts were primarily visual. Describing a photograph that featured dancers bearing masks of lions and dragons, Mackinder remarked typically that from such evidence 'we obtain some idea of the stage of barbarism in which the hill tribes remain'.[75] When Mackinder mentioned violence, he almost always noted acts committed by Indian people upon Europeans, or non-European crimes against Indian people. Of Burma, British pupils were advised that '[t]he change which has come over Burma since the British occupation may be appreciated from the fact that twenty years ago it was no uncommon sight on the voyage up from Katha to Bhamo to see along the river banks, and on rafts floating down the river, the dead bodies of Kachins who had been tortured to death under the terrible rule of the kings of Mandalay'.[76] This was, of course, a sight Mackinder himself had never seen, only imagined through his readings. Mackinder likewise branded 'native [Indian] rulers [. . .] guilty of barbarities in the European settlements, as, for instance, at Fort William which has since become Calcutta. There on one occasion more than a hundred British were stifled in a loathsome underground prison, the "Black Hole" of Calcutta'.[77] Mackinder repeatedly mentioned the Indian uprising of 1857 and in his most complete account referred to 'agitators [who] were able to play on the superstitions and prejudices of the ignorant [Indian] soldiers'.[78] The only details of British violence were side notes: two sons of the King of Delhi were shot while they laid siege to the British within the city walls. But 'of the ten thousand British and loyal native troops who took part in [the siege of Delhi] nearly 4,000 were killed [or] wounded'.[79] Mackinder mentioned, but did not detail, the retribution that followed and insisted that '[n]o Briton can visit Lucknow and Cawnpore without being moved. We may well be proud of the heroic deeds of those of our race who in 1857 suffered and fought and died to save the British Raj in

[73] Mackinder, *India*, 3.   [74] Mackinder, *India*, vi, v.   [75] Mackinder, *India*, 48.
[76] Mackinder, *India*, 32.   [77] Mackinder, *Distant Lands*, 209.
[78] Mackinder, *India*, 64.   [79] Mackinder, *India*, 111.

India'.[80] Again, Mackinder assumed the role of the eyewitness, a perspective he had himself never borne.

Fisher, who had taken the photographs for Mackinder, may have been the inspiration for some of this text for in his letters to Mackinder, Fisher wrote of his own responses to the Mutiny sites in Cawnpore, claiming that '[n]o Englishman can go over these places without being moved. Courage, the sap of his nation, stirs in him'.[81] At Cawnpore, Fisher had noted but not photographed the 'neem tree on which rebels were hung', and 'the two larger neem trees, now wealthy with green, where sepoys were blown from the guns'.[82] Mackinder made no mention of the brutal executions. His account of the Indian barbarism at Calcutta used two photographs (see Figures 6.1 and 6.2), one of the notorious cellar itself, and the other of one of the Indian soldiers by whom, Mackinder insisted, India was in reality controlled, as I explain below.

Said noted that 'geography was essentially the material underpinning for knowledge about the Orient. All the latent and unchanging characteristics of the Orient stood upon, were rooted in, its geography'.[83] In like manner, the *Cambridge History of India* published in 1922 began with an essay on 'The Sub-Continent of India'. It was by Mackinder and was a summary of the physical geography contained in his earlier lectures on India. The essay ended with a discussion of the importance of military and economic congress across the North-West Frontier of India: '[t]he one gateway of India which signified [and ...] most [... Indian] history [...] bears, directly or indirectly, some relation to that great geographical fact'.[84] Should the British be expelled from India, then, it would be across this frontier that the next rulers would arrive for, insisted Mackinder, the immediate result of 'the overthrow of the British Raj [...] would not be the freedom of India [...], but an oriental despotism and race domination from the northwest. Such is the teaching of history, and such the obvious fate of the less warlike peoples of India, should the power of Britain be broken either by warfare on the spot, or by the defeat of our navy'.[85]

The vulnerability of India to attack from without was also a central theme in Mackinder's account. For Mackinder, the Indians were a classic agricultural people although, unlike Germany, they were unable to resist domination from locust swarms of nomadic peoples that swept down upon them from time to time, or who settled among them as imperial overlords. Perhaps

---

[80] Mackinder, *India*, 67.
[81] 'A. H. Fisher Letters', Royal Commonwealth Society Collection, Cambridge University Library, RCS10, Item 5, February 1908, 560–1.
[82] 'Fisher Letters', February 1908, 559, 560.
[83] Said, *Orientalism*, 216.
[84] Mackinder, 'Sub-Continent of India', 36.
[85] Mackinder, *India*, 118.

for this reason, the lectures on the United Kingdom for Indian schoolchildren began with a chapter on the benefits to India brought by British rule. Mackinder asserted that 'India owes to the British Raj peace' and justice; 'there is no price at which the judgements of our district magistrates can be bought, a thing almost unknown in an oriental country'.[86] Food security was also a benefit brought by the British-built railways 'which now extend through the whole land [. . . and] help to prevent death from starvation when the harvest fail[s]', and from 'a great investment of British capital' in former desert districts such as the Punjab, '[t]he plain of the Indus has become one of the chief wheat fields of the British Empire'.[87] Mackinder discounted nationalist or separatist sentiment, because 'the peasants know little and care little who is master of India provided that there is peace, and justice and plenty in the land'.[88]

Peace, justice, and plenty: these were the benefits of British rule that replaced the exploitative Mughal rule and bid fair to raise India some way out of the barbarism into which it had fallen. Yet civilizing the Indians would be a slow process and, Mackinder was sure, Indian self-government 'will not be seen be seen in our time, or indeed for long after'.[89] Indeed, it had even taken 'a thousand years to educate the British people to the safe enjoyment of their present rights'.[90] For imperialists such as Mackinder, India was not ready for independence, and did not need it, as Indian people well knew: 'our rule [in India] has continued because it has given what the Indian people have desired—order and justice'.[91] Moreover, Mackinder insisted that because the Indian Army was composed mainly of Indian soldiers, British rule rested upon consent:

It must never be forgotten that India was not conquered by a great army of British blood, nor is it held by such an army to-day. The Army in India always contained and to-day contains a nucleus of white troops, but the majority of the regiments of which it is formed consist of Indians led by British officers. The truth is that under our lead and organisation the Indians have themselves established the British Peace in India'.[92]

This was 'one of the most wonderful things in the world [, . . . t]hat the people of a small and distant island in another ocean should come to rule an empire of three hundred million people of alien race, inhabiting a territory equal to half Europe'.[93]

---

[86] Mackinder, *Seven Lectures*, 2; *idem*, *Nations of the Modern World*, 274.
[87] Mackinder, *Seven Lectures*, 2; *idem*, 'Sub-Continent', 31.
[88] Mackinder, *Nations of the Modern World*, 275.
[89] Mackinder, *Nations of the Modern World*, 285. Mackinder died on 6 March 1947; India gained independence on 15 August 1947.
[90] Mackinder, *Nations of the Modern World*, 285.
[91] Mackinder, *Modern British State*, 232.
[92] Mackinder, *Modern British State*, 232.
[93] Mackinder, *Nations of the Modern World*, 272.

Imperial Unity

While Mackinder promoted the idea of the unity of the Empire through his school-books and published lectures, he did so in part by ignoring evidences within the Empire. There were, indeed, several silences in Mackinder's treatment of Empire in these books, as evident in his account of India. Mackinder said nothing about the negative consequences for Indian manufactures of British policies. He treated the productivity gap between Britain and India as preceding British rule and as thus requiring British technology to correct it. He treated famines as a constant feature of Indian history, mitigated rather than deepened under British rule. He presented British rule as more pacific than it was and as requiring less force than it did. Mackinder himself reported that on the eve of the First World War, the British Army kept 75,000 soldiers in India and in addition, British officers led the various units of an Indian army of 160,000, representing about two-thirds of Britain's soldiers posted overseas.[94]

Ireland, however, was the loudest silence in these texts. In *Our Own Islands*, Mackinder celebrated the integration of Scotland into Great Britain and made much of the suppression of the Scots Jacobite rebellion of 1745, calling it 'the most famous event in Highland history', the moment when 'the Highlanders were reduced to order, and roads were made through the glens', before which the Highlanders had been 'a wild people', 'barbaric Celtic tribes who at times came down the glens in order to rob the peaceful farmers of the Lowlands'.[95] The reduction of the montane Scots to order allowed Mackinder to claim that diversity and amity characterized the British Empire: '[o]nce the English and the Scotch used to fight one another; but now there is peace in Britain as there is in India'.[96] Referring to the 'great Indian Army', Mackinder reminded Indian schoolchildren that '[i]t is composed, as you know, of soldiers of many different races—of Englishmen and Scotchmen, who used formerly to fight with one another in the British Isles'.[97] Yet *Our Own Islands* says very little about Irish history. There is mention of William II and a reference to 'citizens of London' who 'obtained much land in' Derry 'in the time of the Stuart Kings', but nothing further on plantations as a policy or the repeated attempts at complete conquest.[98] Ongoing Irish resistance to British rule is never mentioned. When *The Modern British State* reported in 1922 that 'the new Dominion (Free State) of Southern Ireland [was] in process of separation from the United Kingdom as these words go to Press', pupils who had followed the series of books would have had very little

---

[94] Mackinder, *Modern British State*, 185.
[95] Mackinder, *Our Own Islands I*, 99, 135, 98; *idem, Our Own Islands II*, 189.
[96] Mackinder, *Seven Lectures*, 3.
[97] Mackinder, *Seven Lectures*, 94.
[98] Mackinder, *Our Own Islands II*, 168.

idea why that might have happened; anti-colonial nationalism was neither narrated nor visualized.

Mackinder urged imperial unity instead, announcing to Indian schoolchildren that 'membership of the British Empire is a high privilege'.[99] It was, advised Mackinder, an efficient way of ensuring peace and justice because '[o]ne navy defends one-fifth of all the lands on the globe'.[100] If each member of the Empire were to build a navy that could defend itself against the Great Powers, it would involve tremendous expense. With the rise of Germany and the United States and the future threats from Japan, China, and Russia, the British navy had now to be the navy of 'the Britains—old and new—[. . .] preparing to co-operate to keep the ocean free, and to defend, if need be, the British traditions of government'.[101] The new Britains were the self-governing dominions of Australia, Canada, Newfoundland, South Africa, and New Zealand. This imperial unity required a new way of managing the affairs of the Empire: '[a] truly Imperial Government, in some way representative of all the Britains, must sooner or later come into existence. Until that has been achieved, it is not likely that the overseas dominions will consent to bear their full proportional share of the defences of the Empire'.[102] On the eve of the First World War, just before the constituent parts of the British Empire were to contribute soldiers to the Allied forces (even though none had been consulted on the declaration of war itself), Mackinder declared: '[m]ighty deeds were wrought by the armies of the Dominions and India [, . . . b]ut deep down in their hearts all knew that when peace returned there must be a reconsideration of our relations, and that never again must loyalty be put to the test of a war declared without the express assent of the Empire'.[103]

Élisée Reclus: Questioning Imperialism

Mackinder tried to give schoolchildren not only pride in, but also optimism about, the Empire. In *The Modern British State*, he even referred to the separation of Ireland from Britain as strengthening the Empire because it 'should remove the reason for an anti-British minority both in the Dominions and America'.[104] The British were the bravest and best people on earth and through their Empire they could ensure that their values would continue to shape the world in the future as they had in the past. Mackinder argued that Geography gave pupils an imperial view, trained them to 'think of the

[99] Mackinder, *Seven Lectures*, 98.
[100] Mackinder, *Seven Lectures*, 87.
[101] Mackinder, *Nations of the Modern World*, 296.
[102] Mackinder, *Nations of the Modern World*, 316.
[103] Mackinder, *Modern British State*, 265.
[104] Mackinder, *Modern British State*, 267.

relative condition of the British Empire [...and] compare it with the other great Empires'.[105] Students would look at the world through a British and imperial lens.

The pioneering historical geographer, Percy Roxby, worried about the environmental determinism inherent in Mackinder's approach to Geographical education. There was, thought Roxby, a danger in that 'natural forces' were stressed to the neglect of 'human personality'.[106] Roxby noted that, for example, explaining in geographical terms why the northern states of the United States opposed slavery, while the southern states supported it, 'the ethical issues involved' were left unexamined. Roxby worried that '[i]f we are always dwelling on how the stage shapes the acting, we may lose sight of the inner meaning of the acting itself'.[107] Roxby was exercised by Mackinder's imperialism and commented on another occasion that '[t]he political ideals of Victorian and Edwardian times favoured political history rather than geography, the record of power changes rather than the evolution of human life'.[108]

Certainly, Mackinder emphasized spatial and environmental controls upon human choices, discussing slavery with nary a comment upon its immorality, but his educational books did not eschew all ethical and political commentary. As I have shown, Mackinder justified the British Empire, anticipating and even countering many common attacks upon it. In his own way, Mackinder was certainly a geographer militant. He told schoolchildren that they should serve the Empire because it brought freedom, justice, and prosperity to peoples across the fifth of the globe it claimed as its own. There were, however, other geographers who refused to celebrate Geography Militant, who challenged Mackinder's ethical stance and preached empathy not force. Many of these geographers were anarchists, and the most famous among them was Élisée Reclus.

Reclus was born in 1830 in a small village in south-west France, where his father was pastor. In some respects, Reclus practised anarchism as a secular religion, based upon science, particularly upon Geography. When Reclus abandoned his theological studies, it was to study Political Economy, the History of Diseases, and Geography at the University of Berlin. He was drawn particularly to the lectures of Carl Ritter (1779–1859), where he learned that the study of Geography revealed the divine design on earth. Reclus soon dropped the deism, but retained much from Ritter's geographical writings: namely, that the earth should be studied as the common possession of all humanity, that society and environment influenced each other, and that these mutual relations had to be studied historically. Reclus returned to France at the end of 1851, and following the coup by Louis

[105] Mackinder, 'Development of Geographical Teaching', 196.
[106] Roxby, 'Mackinder's Books', 407.
[107] Roxby, 'Mackinder's Books', 407.
[108] Roxby, 'Sixty Years of Geography and Education', 264.

Napoléon in December of that year and fearing that his pronounced republican views would mark him out for arrest, left France for Britain. After short stays in Britain and Ireland, he went to the United States where a stint as tutor for a Louisiana plantation-owning family left him with an intense hatred of racism and slavery. In 1856, he helped found a utopian colony in what is now Colombia. After a bout of yellow fever in 1857, Reclus returned to France.

Following the publication of an account of his journey from the United States to Colombia, *Voyage to the Sierra Nevada* (1861), Reclus began to earn his living as geographer, publishing in the 1860s his famous *Story of a Stream* (1869) and a two-volume history of *The Earth* (1868–9). He also involved himself more directly in socialist politics, joining the First International (the International Workingmen's Association) in 1865, and accepting, at this time, the direction of Karl Marx that socialists should work within the institutions of the liberal state with the ultimate goal of revolutionizing bourgeois society from within. In 1870, he was present in Paris during the famous siege by the Prussian army, and then again when the Commune was declared on 18 March 1871. While fighting alongside fellow communards, he was arrested by French government forces on 4 April 1871 and imprisoned. His reputation among earth scientists called forth several international petitions and the initial sentence of transportation to New Caledonia was commuted and Reclus was exiled for ten years to Switzerland in March 1872.

The failure of the French Republic to defend the Commune destroyed his faith in democratic institutions and the parliamentary route to socialism. He also rejected the idea of an authoritarian vanguard party that he feared would turn despotic once it made a revolution based on ideas that were not already widely accepted among the working class. In the summary of his biographer, Marie Fleming, '[t]he anarchist way to socialism, according to Reclus, had to avoid the hazards of the parliamentary arena and the tragedy of despotism'.[109] Reclus believed that socialists would fail if they did not prepare the workers by raising their consciousness about their own oppressed condition, and helping them realize what freedoms would be theirs once the bourgeoisie was dispossessed of the means of production. He stressed the importance of individual initiative and differed from many anarchists in believing that robbery could be a valid act of redistribution. Even more controversially, he refused to condemn violence against the bourgeoisie, by dynamite or dagger, believing this propaganda by deed could be a principled act, educating workers by inviting them to reflect upon such summary acts of justice. Yet his tacit approval of anarchist bombings and assassinations caused his home to be raided in 1894 and also resulted in the peremptory withdrawal of an invitation to lecture at Brussels. This insult called forth a student and faculty movement that resulted in the creation of the Free

[109] Fleming, *Geography of Freedom*, 173.

University of Brussels outside the control of the existing university. Reclus went there, and, in his mid-sixties, took up his first faculty position, lecturing there in Geography until his death, in 1905.

In 1872, while still in prison, Reclus signed a contract with Hachette to publish a world regional geography in monthly instalments. Thus began a colossal enterprise that issued in 1,061 monthly booklets, which were collected into 19 volumes of the *Nouvelle Géographie universelle* published between 1876 and 1894.[110] Reclus employed many colleagues to help him gather materials, to write, and to edit. Significantly, the sections on Siberia were subcontracted to Kropótkin and featured both map and discussion of the carceral archipelago to which Kropótkin and his brother had once been consigned. His fellow anarchist was also involved in some of the editing of the European volumes. At one point Reclus pleaded with Kropótkin to complete the editing to 'feed the presses'.[111] As noted in Chapter 3, John Scott Keltie sent Kropótkin issues of *Nature* as well as other scientific journals. Kropótkin in his turn must have passed some of this precious reading material to Reclus, for in 1884, the French geographer sent thanks to the imprisoned Russian for the 'parcel of *Nature* that you sent to me, as well as the clippings from English journals'.[112] In prison, Kropótkin received many books on loan from Reclus, but at one stage Reclus asked that he return any books not being used because 'there are big gaps in my library that often make research very difficult or even impossible'.[113] Kropótkin and Reclus were also involved in one of Mackinder's projects, a series of world regional geography books in which Mackinder advertised both Kropótkin and Reclus as contributing. Writing to Kropótkin, Reclus complained that Mackinder's letters were 'so rare that I wonder if the project is a serious one'.[114] Two years later, Reclus was none the wiser. In response to numerous letters, all he received from Mackinder was the dry question 'Are you ready?'[115]

---

[110] B. Giblin, 'Un Géographe d'Exception', 24.

[111] '[I]l est urgent d'alimenter les presses'; Reclus to Kropótkin, 24 January 1884; Reclus, *Correspondance II*, 312.

[112] 'Je viens de recevoir le pacquet de *Nature* que vous m'envoyez, ainsi que diverses coupillures prises dans des journaux anglais'; Reclus to Kropótkin, 20 June 1884; Reclus, *Correspondance II*, 320.

[113] '[I]l ya dans ma bibliothèque de grands vides qui me rendent parfois les recherches bien difficiles ou meme impossibles'; Reclus to Kropótkin, 2 January 1883; Reclus, *Correspondance II*, 270.

[114] Reclus to Kropótkin, 7 May 1900; Reclus, *Correspondance III*, 222.

[115] Reclus to Kropótkin, 11 February 1902; Reclus, *Correspondance III*, 244. There clearly was a problem with this series and with Mackinder's management of it. This was also the period of Mackinder's marital break up. In 1902, appeared with Heinemann: Mackinder's own *British and the British Seas*, and David Hogarth's *The Nearer East*. In the following year was published with Heinemann, a work on Central Europe abridged and translated from the German, Joseph Partsch's *Central Europe*. In 1904, when a second edition of *Britain and the British Seas* appeared it was not with the initial publisher, Heinemann, but with the Clarendon Press at Oxford. In 1904, the series added, published with Oxford University Press in London, Thomas Holdich's *India*, and Israel Russell's *North America*. In 1905, Archibald Little's *Far East* was published by the Clarendon Press at Oxford. Later editions of the books of Hogarth (1905) and Partsch (1905) were also published by the Clarendon Press in Oxford.

After their initial disagreements over anarchist tactics in the 1870s (Kropótkin, but not Reclus, was committed to the development of an organized anarchist party), the two supported each other politically and academically ever after. In 1880, Reclus sponsored Kropótkin's membership of the Geographical Society of Switzerland.[116] Their radical politics did not exclude them from broader educational arenas; moreover, both were welcomed into geographical societies and their work received favourable review in established geographical journals. They shared many intellectual and even educational goals with people who disagreed fundamentally with their politics. The French geographer, Béatrice Giblin, has remarked that Élisée Reclus put his geographical knowledge at the service not only of science but also of his political ideals.[117] I have already suggested that the same could be said of Mackinder. Giblin proposed that Reclus's life and work were dedicated to the struggle for a society based on justice and freedom, again similar to the basis upon which Mackinder justified Empire.[118] Thus, while Reclus and Mackinder avowed similar goals, they taught very different geographies. The question of imperialism, in particular, was a controversial matter within the teaching of Geography and there is no more striking way of exploring this than by examining a little more closely the main themes of Reclus's monumental geographical scholarship.

The Earth

Reclus's principal contribution to popularizing geographical knowledge was his awesome nineteen-volume *Nouvelle Géographie universelle*, which Dunbar has justly claimed as 'probably the greatest individual writing feat in the history of geography'.[119] When its final volume appeared, the Royal Geographical Society honoured Reclus with a medal and in its journal Mackinder praised the series as 'the most complete geographical survey of the world of this or any other age'.[120] Reclus wrote beginning in the 1860s and died in 1905, before Mackinder published his own geographical textbooks. Whereas Mackinder wanted to teach young people to look upon nature with the strategic eye of the hunter or the general, Reclus urged people to imagine how to harmonize their own lives with the pulse of the planet.

Mackinder followed the model of Reclus's story of a river in his own work on the Rhine but it is notable, however, that Mackinder treated the Rhine in very large part as a setting for political history, 'the gage of European battle',

---

[116] Fleming, *Geography of Freedom*, 137.
[117] '[S]on travail de géographe n'est pas seulement au service de la "science", mais aussi au service de son idéal politique'; Giblin, 'Un Géographe d'Exception', 13.
[118] Reclus was 'totalement engage dans ce combat pour une société juste et libre'; Giblin, 'Un Géographe d'Exception', 13.
[119] Dunbar, *Reclus*, 95.
[120] Mackinder, 'Reclus', 158.

whereas Reclus's emphasis was more cultural, reminding readers, for example, that many peoples imagined the sources of streams as eyes through which beings trapped in rocks gaze out at the world around.[121] Reclus, like Mackinder, understood the development of human values as shaped through engagement with the natural world, but within similar spaces, he found different virtues to praise. While Mackinder treated montane people as branches of the marauding groups that preyed upon civilized and productive lowland farmers, Reclus stressed the place of grand vistas in framing an aspiration towards radical liberty.[122] With Kropótkin, Reclus cherished the communitarian societies of the watchmakers of the Jura. Reclus was also particularly sensitive to environmental degradation, and, unlike Mackinder, feared that in modern society children were educated to be indifferent to the integrity and dignity of physical and biological nature.

Reclus believed that a child's alienation from nature began with food and butchery; teachers, parents, 'not to speak of the powerful individual whom we call "everybody", all work together to harden the character of the child with respect to this "four-footed food", which, nevertheless, loves as we do, feels as we do'.[123] Early inured to this brutality, the child, argued Reclus, would later accept the attitudes of engineers who want everywhere 'to put their own work in evidence, and to mask Nature under their heaps of broken stones and coal', or become soldiers who follow 'the word of the crowned master, "Be pitiless"'.[124] He feared that as adults, the savagery first accepted as part of their daily diet, would be practiced upon other people.

Reclus stressed the role of humans in diversifying the earth's surface; on one hand, through destruction and, on the other, through amelioration and embellishment. While the barbarian moved over the land ravaging its resources, civilized people repaired their use of nature and, beyond their work as farmers or industrialists, acted as artists to adorn the majesty of the natural world. Civilized people thus became the 'conscience of the earth'.[125] Reclus fixed the charge of pillage upon the nomadic predations described also by Mackinder, yet, he went further and pinned it also upon various acts of colonialism. Reclus included in his work the poignant remark of a Maori person: 'the white man's rat drives away our rat, his fly drives away our fly, his clover kills our ferns, and the white man will end by destroying the Maori'.[126] Reclus was highly critical of colonialists suggesting that they had no goal

---

[121] Mackinder, *Rhine*, 2. '[H]ommes de toute race et de tout climat ont vu dans les fontaines des "yeux" par lesquels les êtres enfermés dans les roches ténébreuses viennent un moment contempler l'espace et la verdure'; Reclus, *Histoire d'un Ruisseau*, 4.

[122] 'Sans aucun doute, la vue des grands horizons contribue pour une forte part aux qualités des populations des montagnes, et ce n'est point par une vaine formule de langage que l'on a désigné les Alpes comme le boulevard de la liberté'; Reclus, 'Du Sentiment de la Nature', 381.

[123] Reclus, 'On Vegetarianism', 2.

[124] Reclus, 'On Vegetarianism', 2, 3.

[125] '[L]a conscience de la terre'; Reclus, 'L'Homme et la Nature', 763.

[126] Quoted in Clark, 'Dialectical Social Geography', 130.

other than to turn local wealth, resources, people, and authority to their benefit, all in the name of progress.[127]

One World

Reclus approached 'anarchism as a theory capable of being supported scientifically' and he saw Geography as central to the 'scientific argument for the idea of universal brotherhood'.[128] Taking a global perspective, Reclus stressed, as did Mackinder, that there was no alternative to recognizing the interdependence of peoples living in all corners of the world: '[t]here is no longer any possibility of progress, other than for the world as a whole'.[129] For Reclus, universal fraternity was incompatible with the unequal relations that characterized most forms of colonialism, since he felt that injustice always called forth balancing acts of vengeance.[130] Geographers, according to Reclus, would have to set aside national chauvinism if they were to understand the world; they must give up 'those feelings of contempt, hatred, and passion which still set nation against nation'.[131] Thus, for example, the English bemoaned 'the extreme bad faith of the Afghans. But it should be remembered', he continued, that 'the Europeans enter the land generally as conquerors, so that their very presence is regarded as an insult. Hence it is not surprising that in their weakness [the Afghans] have recourse to every sort of ruse and stratagem against the hated invader'.[132] Subjugation abused the subject people, leaving it 'in a state of shameful thraldom' and thus too easily 'consumed by vice as by a moral leprosy'.[133] Signs taken by Orientalists as marks of decadence, were for Reclus evidences of misrule. He rejected force as fiercely as Mackinder embraced it, because, for Reclus, it demeaned the perpetrator and degraded its victims, producing further violence in its turn.

Whereas Mackinder presented a vision of the world divided between civilized and barbaric people and argued that the British were exceptional, Reclus emphasized instead the intermingling of peoples so that there was no 'longer to be found completely homogeneous races, except perhaps in the Andaman Islands and Yesso'.[134] For Reclus, cultural diversity rather than racial purity drove human creativity. Cultural exchange—not racial identity—defined civilization, as Reclus noted: 'Western civilisation would never

---

[127] 'Le "colonial" n'a d'autre objectif que de prendre, soit des trésors, soit des terres et les hommes qui les peuplent, soit le pouvoir et des titres à l'avancement'; Reclus, 'Preface'; quoted in Creagh, 'Critique: Badouin'.

[128] Fleming, *Geography of Freedom*, 128.

[129] 'Il n'y a plus question de progrès que pour la Terre entière'; Reclus, *L'Homme et la Terre, I*, 37.

[130] '[L]e viol de la justice crie toujours vengeance'; Reclus, *L'Homme et la Terre, I*, ii.

[131] Reclus, *Earth and its Inhabitants, I. Europe, Greece*, 2.

[132] Reclus, ibid., *VIII. Asia, India*, 35.

[133] Reclus, ibid., *VIII. Asia, India*, 9.

[134] Reclus, ibid., *VI. Asia, Asiatic Russia*, 19.

have seen the light had not the waters of the Mediterranean washed the
shores of Egypt, Phoenicia, Asia Minor, Hellas, Italy, Spain, and Car-
thage'.[135] The hierarchy of peoples was inconstant: 'the great drama of
universal history resolves itself into endless struggles, with varying issues,
between Europe and Asia'.[136] Reclus reminded his readers that the Ancients
often described Europe as the 'daughter of Asia' to challenge directly views
such as Mackinder's on the nature of the Eastern mind.[137] Indeed, Reclus
dismissed the view of an 'irreducible racial difference' by which 'the Eastern
and Western races were created different, the Eastern mind cloudy and
chimerical, [...]; while the Western was gifted with the very genius of
observation', as no more than a conclusion drawn by the victors in a struggle
that took place between an Eastern civilization in decline and a Western in
first flush of growth.[138] The relative standing of East and West had switched
back and forward over the *longue durée*. In contrast, Mackinder led his
young readers towards a view of the East as damaged by Mongol and Islamic
tyranny but as having been rescued by enlightened British rule. Reclus
instead presented a continuity between British and earlier overlords.

The six volumes of Reclus's *L'Homme et La Terre* were illustrated
with maps, photographs and with over 100 Chinese ink paintings by František Kupka (1871–1957). Kupka depicted the grand march of civilization, the
battle between enlightenment and obscurantism, between freedom and oppression. Kupka (like Picasso) was part of a group of artists, associated with
political radicalism, who were particularly animated by anti-colonialism.[139]
Having read the final volume of Reclus's work, Kupka chose to illustrate its
first chapter ('L'Angleterre et son Cortège') by depicting England as a
bewhiskered gentleman in plus-fours and a pith helmet, with battleships
blazing away behind him, and beneath his feet, the emaciated bodies of
famine victims (see Figure 6.4).[140] This image captures very well Reclus's
critique of British colonialism.

Reclus noted that among 1,250,000 civil servants in India, there were but
'928 officials, of whom seven only are natives'.[141] Far from governing by
consent, Reclus claimed that 'England rules at present by force and prestige
alone'.[142] Although Reclus, like Mackinder, saw a titanic struggle afoot
between Britain and Russia for control of the overland route between Europe
and Asia, for 'water highways are insufficient, and [Britain] will also have to
hold the overland routes beyond Europe', Reclus, unlike Mackinder, believed
that '[t]he English cannot, of course, rely on the sympathy of their [Indian]

[135] Reclus, *Earth and its Inhabitants, I. Europe, Greece*, 23.
[136] Reclus, ibid., *VI. Asia, Asiatic Russia*, 23.
[137] Reclus, ibid., *I. Europe, Greece*, 5.
[138] Reclus, 'East and West', 482.
[139] Leighton, 'White Peril'.
[140] Reclus, *L'Homme et La Terre, VI*, 77.
[141] Reclus, *Earth and its Inhabitants, VIII. Asia, India*, 415.
[142] Reclus, ibid., *VIII. Asia, India*, 416.

Fig. 6.4. František Kupka, 'England and its cortège'

subjects, whom they probably despise too much to expect it of them', and that British rule would end with the inevitable evolution of a distinct 'national spirit' among Indian Hindus.[143] For Reclus, British domination would produce the equal and opposite reaction of an Indian independence struggle.

Reclus thought that civilizations declined through internal dismemberment. Complex societies lacked unity of purpose, pursuing contradictory goals.[144] He believed that he lived in a happy time when several ethnic groups had arrived at the glorious truth that humanity was one and indivisible and in this way they might even have become 'immunised against decadence and death'.[145] His belief in Western humanism led him to discount horrors that he yet described in detail: '[w]herever the European explorers first settled they doubtless began their civilising work by massacring, enslaving, or otherwise debasing the natives. But the beneficial influences of superior races have ever commenced by mutual hatred, mistrust, and antagonism. The conflicting elements everywhere contend for the mastery before they awaken to the conviction that all alike are members of the same family'.[146] Yet even war could be an agent of progress despite its horrors, for wars brought peoples into contact with each other and frequently concluded with treaties that heralded 'busy relations of trade and friendship'.[147]

For Reclus, the interaction between Europe and the rest of the world should be seen in both economic and cultural terms. Mackinder had very little to say about economic systems beyond a broad vision of modernization driven by the diffusion of technology. Reclus offered, as Mackinder did not,

---

[143] Reclus, *Earth and its Inhabitants, VI. Asia, Asiatic Russia,* 31, 30.

[144] '[S]ans unité, poursuivant à la fois des objectifs opposés'; Reclus, *L'Homme et la Terre VI,* 515.

[145] 'Des nos jours, les divers groupes ethniques civilisés sont déja tellement pénétrés de cette idée de l'unité humaine qu'ils sont, pour ainsi dire, immunisés contre la decadence et contre la mort'; Reclus, *L'Homme et la Terre VI,* 519.

[146] Reclus, *Earth and its Inhabitants, VI. Asia, Asiatic Russia,* 25.

[147] '[Les guerres] eut pour conclusion des traits d'alliance et des relations fréquentes de commerce et d'amité'; Reclus, 'Pages de Sociologie préhistorique', 141.

an analysis of the effect of market relations upon subsistence agriculture and artisanal manufacturing. Of the Indian famine of 1877, with its mortality of 4 million, for example, Reclus remarked that 'while such multitudes were perishing for want of food, the port of Calcutta continued to export large quantities of corn to foreign countries, the famished districts being too poor to pay its market price'.[148] Reclus was angry that in famine districts, starving people bagged rice for export, while local prices reflected a capitalist specu-lation that exploited poverty and pressed down local wages.[149] He was sure that, in Giblin's terms, '[f]amines and shortages cannot be systematically explained as natural disasters, but result also from the development of a market economy'.[150] There was no comparable appreciation of the relations between economic systems and food security in the writings of Mackinder; schoolchildren would learn there only of the positive contribution made by European technology to mitigating famines produced by cruel nature.

Colonialism

As noted above, Reclus remained ambivalent about the European impact upon the rest of the world. In one of his earliest writings he described the indigenous peoples of the San Blas islands, off what is now the coast of Panama: '[t]hese people are happy: in exchange for their peace, would modern commerce give them anything but the masked slavery, poverty and abandon of alcohol?'[151] The geographer, Axel Baudouin, is right to note that it is capitalism rather than colonialism itself that drew Reclus's ire.[152] Giblin has good reason to stress that for Reclus, property relations were one of the main expressions of the equilibrium or disequilibrium of any given agricul-tural system, and that Reclus railed against great landlords, comparing them to feudal lords dominating peasants through debts that could never be repaid.[153] His criticisms of colonialism were generally economic, noting that in good times or bad, colonial authorities claimed administrative

---

[148] Reclus, *Earth and its Inhabitants, VIII, Asia, India*, 392.

[149] 'Le riz qui pourrait servir à sa nourriture est ensaché par lui-même et empilé dans les trains de merchandises pour les brasseries de bière et les menneries d'Europe, on spécule meme sur sa misère pour diminuer chaque année son maigre salaire'; Reclus, *L'Homme et la Terre VI*, 306.

[150] 'Famines et disettes ne sont donc pas systématiquement à mettre sur le compte des catastrophes naturelles, mais résultent aussi du développement d'une économie du marché'; Giblin, 'Reclus et les Colonisations', 149.

[151] 'Ces peuplades sont heureuses: le commerce tel qu'il est compris aujourd'hui, saura-t-il, en échange de leur paix, leur donner autre chose qu'une servitude déguisée, la misère et les joies sauvages puisées dan l'eau-de-vie'; Reclus, *Voyage à la Sierra Nevada*, 35.

[152] Baudouin, 'Reclus colonialiste?', 14.

[153] 'Pour ce géographe anarchist, le regime de la propriété est l'un des principaux révélateurs de l'équilibre ou du déséquilibre d'une situation agricole donnée. [...] Régulièrement, Reclus attaque violemment le régime des grandes propriétés [...]. Il compare les propriétaires à des grands feodaux tenant leurs paysans à leur merci par les dettes que ceux-ci ont contractées auprès de leurs maîtres en étant bien trop pauvres pour pouvoir les rembourser un jour', Giblin, 'Reclus et les Colonisations', 147.

expenses and yet did not maintain necessary reserves to help peasants through hungry times.[154] Colonialism produced local nationalisms in reaction: '[i]n truth, one could say that the collective identity of Arab nationalism was due entirely to the presence of the French in Algeria'.[155] Reclus was a passionate opponent of coercion and he identified violence and exploitation as the dark heart of the colonial enterprise, evident wherever colonialism served modern commerce. Yet this was not all he saw in colonialism.

Reclus made a distinction between, as Giblin points out, settlement and exploitative colonialism. Where Europeans settled, they might improve both local culture and local economies in the longer term, since Reclus believed, in Giblin's summary, that settler colonialism was one of the chief 'ways that people achieved mastery of the earth'.[156] He believed that colonialism could have progressive consequences and remarked upon the 'rapid internal dissolution of the native religions [of India ...] largely under the influence of European ideas'.[157] Reclus saw this as part of 'the onward movement of thought' and as evidence pointed to 'the utter extinction of suttee [....,] the rapid suppression of female infanticide, the cessation of human sacrifices'.[158] He also commented upon environmental improvements made by the British colonial authorities, for once 'the woodland districts have been placed under State control; the barbarous system of culture by firing the jungle is now forbidden, and here and there [in southern India] the work of plantation has been seriously taken in hand'.[159]

Reclus, then, was ambivalent about colonialism, and remained in thrall to a Saint-Simonian belief in technology.[160] Michael Heffernan, the historical geographer, has noted a similar attitude in the work of Reclus's friend, Henry Duveyrier (1840–92).[161] As Giblin describes, these men supported Western forms of freedom, humanism, and progress, which meant that for Reclus:

A friend of liberty could not but support the resistance of indigenous people to the French conquest of Algeria; but as a friend of progress and of the development of new lands, he had to support the colonists who struggled to break the soil, especially as, at

---

[154] '[L]ibertaire, il ne peut pas soutenir la résistance de la population indigène à la conquête française, mais, partisan du progress et de la mise en valeur de terres nouvelles, il ne peut que soutenir l'actions des colons qui luttent et travaillent durement pour conquérir le sol, dautant plus qu'au moment où il écrit bon nombre de nouveaux colons sont, comme lui, d'anciens communards!'; Giblin, 'Reclus et les Colonisations', 149. A very similar argument is made in: Watts, *Silent Violence*.

[155] 'En réalité, on peut dire que la conscience collective de la nationalité arabe est due surtout à la présence des Français en Algérie'; Reclus, *L'Homme et la Terre V*, 423.

[156] '[C]olonialisation de peuplement [...] représente pour lui une des modalités de la maîtrise de l'homme sur la terre'; Giblin, 'Reclus et les Colonisations', 142.

[157] Reclus, *Earth and its Inhabitants, VIII. Asia, India*, 412.

[158] Reclus, ibid., *VIII. Asia, India*, 412–3.

[159] Reclus, ibid., *VIII. Asia, India*, 397.

[160] Bataillon, 'La Vision coloniale'.

[161] Heffernan, 'Limits of Utopia'. Duveyrier was the principal responsible for embarrassing Reclus with the award of a medal from the French Geographical Society; Fleming, *Geography of Freedom*, 167.

the time he was writing, a good number of the new colonists were ex-communards like himself.[162]

Giblin argues that the problem of colonialism for Reclus was due to his belief that the settlement of people overseas was a distinct type of colonialism by which the colonists developed economic resources for local, not distant, benefit. The French scholar of Geopolitics, Yves Lacoste, suggests that this distinction was developed by Reclus solely to address the case of French Algeria.[163] Mackinder also criticized Reclus's nineteen-volume Universal Geography for this reason: '[o]ccasionally a sentence seems flavoured with a spice of *la perfide Albion*; once in a way a paragraph apologizes too vehemently for the author's fatherland, and excusing, accuses'.[164] Yet the basis of Reclus's optimism allowed that colonialism more generally could have a civilizing mission: 'Élisée Reclus, who did not approve of the violence of conquest nor of expropriations, thought nevertheless [...] that with colonisation, civilisation progressed'.[165]

The grounds on which Reclus excused colonialism were not confined to Algeria, nor even to his account of French colonialism. Rather, Reclus saw settlement in the colonies as striking a new and better balance between overpopulation in Europe and underused resources in Africa, Asia, and Latin America: '[p]opulation tends increasingly to redistribute itself around the planet in accordance with the natural advantages of each country, in terms of climate, raw materials, subsistence, and even the beauty of the landscape'.[166] In many cases, he suggested, colonial settlement created inter-bred populations in which the enmity and incomprehension of the initial encounter were superseded, 'bringing the final union of diverse peoples, and the birth for humanity of an age of peace and happiness'.[167] Finally, Reclus believed that the latest phase in the endlessly repeating struggle between Mutual Aid and Mutual War was being born in Europe. Cooper-ation, according to Reclus, while basic to the development of the earliest agricultural societies and 'all the elements of mental and moral improvement, very often gave way to mutual war, to the wild abandon of hatred and vengeance'.[168] According to Reclus, the revolutionaries of 1848 launched,

---

[162] Giblin, 'Reclus et les Colonisations', 137.

[163] 'Il faut se demander pourquoi Élisée Reclus si souvent anticolonialiste (bien que le terme n'existait pas encore) tient sur l'Algérie, et uniquement sur l'Algérie, un tel discours, celui que tiendront les colonialists de l'Algérie française'; Lacoste, 'Reclus', 49.

[164] Mackinder, 'Reclus', 159.

[165] 'Élisée Reclus, qui n'adhere pas aux violences des conquêtes ni aux expropriations, considère cependant [...] qu'avec la colonisation, c'est la civilisation qui progresse'; Liauzu, 'Les sociétés musulmanes', 128.

[166] 'La population tend de plus en plus à se répartir sur la planete suivant les avantages de toute nature que présentent les diverse contrées, au point de vue du climat, des resources pour le travail, des facilités de la vie, meme de la beauté des paysages'; Reclus, *L'Homme et la Terre V*, 327.

[167] '[E]ntraîne la réconciliation finale des tous les peuples d'origine diverse, et la naissance de l'humanité à une ère de paix et de bonheur'; Reclus, *Voyage à la Sierra Nevada*, v.

[168] 'L'entr'aide, qui a tant fait pour développer [...] tous les éléments d'amélioration mentale et morale, fait très souvent place à l'entre-lutte, au féroce déchaînement des haines et des vengeances'; Reclus, 'Pages de Sociologie préhistorique', 141.

in the name of humanity, a new era of cooperation where mutuality recognized no national boundaries.[169]

Mutual War, on the other hand, was rooted in class struggle: '[i]n each country, capital tries to dominate workers; likewise on the world market, capital accrues beyond measure, contemptuous of old borders, seeking to profit from all the world's producers, and to assure itself the custom of all the world's consumers'.[170] In one of his very first political works, Reclus made these connections clear: 'in every nation our political goal is the abolition of aristocratic privilege, and throughout the world it is the fusion of all peoples'.[171] In his last works he equated civilization with solidarity: '[i]n its essence, human progress consists in common cause being found among all peoples'.[172] In this respect, the struggle of labour against capital was the start of the current round of civilizing works of solidarity: 'it is among [. . .] labouring men, combined, free, equal, independent of patronage, that one finds the cause of progress'.[173] This solidarity was, believed Reclus, moving beyond the realm of labour and there was a 'growing sentiment of equality between the representatives of [. . .] different castes, until recently hostile one to the other'.[174]

Geographical Education and Colonialism

Reclus's geographical vision was more resolutely historical than Mackinder's. Reclus's three geographical syntheses moved from a primary focus upon the history of the physical earth in *La Terre* (two volumes 1868–9), through a balance between physical and human historical geography in *Nouvelle Géographie universelle* (nineteen volumes 1876–94), to an emphasis upon human and social development in *L'Homme et la Terre* (six volumes 1905–8). For Mackinder, the environment was broadly constant and it produced distinct racial identities, which then interacted. The West's current upper hand, for Reclus, was due to the accident that the morphology of Asia did not focus its great civilizations upon a common zone of interaction, and the further acci-

---

[169] 'Les révolutionnaires de 1848 lancèrent avec un éclat particulier le mot d'humanité'; Reclus, *L'Homme et la Terre VI*, 520.

[170] 'En chaque pays, le capital cherche à maîtriser les travailleurs; de même sur le grand marché du monde, le capital accru démesurément, insoucieux de toutes les anciennes frontiers, tente de fair oeuvre à son profit la mass des producteurs et à s'assurer tous les consommateurs du globe'; Reclus, *L'Homme et la Terre V*, 287.

[171] 'Notre but politique dans chaque nation particulière c'est l'abolition des privilèges aristocratiques, et dans la Terre entière c'est la fusion de tous les peuples'; Reclus, 'Développement de la liberté dans le monde' [1851], quoted in Giblin, 'Un Géographe d'Exception', 15.

[172] 'Dans son essence, le progress humain consiste à trouver l'ensemble des intérêts et des volontés commun à tous peuples'; Reclus, *L'Homme et la Terre VI*, 531.

[173] 'C'est aux [. . .] hommes de labour, associés, libres, égaux, dégagés du patronage, que se trouve remise la cause du progrès'; Reclus, *L'Homme et la Terre VI*, 530.

[174] Reclus, 'Progress of Mankind', 783.

dent of the gradual dessication of Asia as glaciers retreated. Beyond this, Reclus made the argument, repeated later by the geographer, James Blaut, that Europe was simply in the better place to wander into the Americas, a matter of geographical luck; to 'the happy conditions of soil, climate, configuration, and geographical position, the inhabitants of Europe owe[d] the honour of having been the first to obtain a knowledge of the earth in its entirety, and to have remained for so long a period at the head of mankind'.[175]

For Reclus, from contact would come knowledge, from knowledge empathy, from empathy equality, and from equality rights. Science might teach that the world could produce sufficient for all but it took empathy, equality, and rights to insist upon the correct use of these techniques. In this sense, progress in nutrition came not with greater production nor even with better distribution but only with an indefeasible right to food: '[t]he conquest of bread [...] does not consist only in eating, but in eating bread that is one's human right'.[176] Much like other advances in science, geographical research need pay no heed to national borders. Some scientific advances, such as in public health, could only be applied to the whole of humanity as if it were simply one immense individual.[177] In disease, humanity was one and indivisible ('solidaire').[178] The teaching of Geography was part of this broadening circle for it might educate people to see the world as the common possession of all humanity.

Reclus taught that Geography showed the solidarity of humanity and its embedding in the rhythms of physical and biological nature. This was very different to Mackinder's vision of British persistence through maintaining an advantage of forcefulness. Although both saw colonialism as diffusing civilization, the idea that there was a hierarchy of civilizations had a fierce grip upon Mackinder and his contemporaries. Neither Reclus's materialism nor his trenchant criticisms of capitalism, however, challenged the belief in Western democratic ideals as universal, and worth broadcasting, even if the only way to do so were at the point of a gun. For very many commentators, military intervention served the liberal purpose of spreading democratic values that could find purchase in non-Western societies only through violence. The silence of Reclus about the justice of Algerian resistance to French occupation is matched by the silence of Mackinder about the reality of Irish resistance to British occupation. In the next chapter, I explore more fully the question of intervention by telling the story of Mackinder's most significant imperialist project outside education; his adventure in South Russia fighting Bolshevism.

[175] Reclus, *Earth and its Inhabitants. I Europe, Greece*, 6; Blaut, *Colonizer's Model of the World*.

[176] 'La conquête du Pain [...] ne s'agit pas simplement de manger, mais de manger le pain dû a son droit d'homme'; Reclus, *L'Homme et la Terre VI*, 528.

[177] 'Les changements [...] s'appliquent directement à l'ensemble de l'humanité comme si elle constituait un immense individu'; Reclus, *L'Homme et la Terre VI*, 468–9.

[178] Reclus, *L'Homme et la Terre, VI*, 470.

7

Practising Imperialism

Mackinder insisted that his work in politics and in education were of a piece, both dedicated to defending and promoting the British Empire. In the early years of the twentieth century, he encouraged the British state in its arms race with Germany, seeing Germany as the main threat to the British Empire, and he viewed the First World War as vindication of his warnings. The conduct of the war, however, raised further questions about the sustainability of the British Empire. For Mackinder, the main issue was the problem of imperial governance. In fighting the war, the British had called upon and been supported by soldiers from the dominions and dependencies within the Empire despite the fact that the war had been declared without consulting them. From 1917, the Defence Minister of the Union of South Africa, Jan Smuts (1870–1950), was added to the British War Cabinet in order to facilitate, and further legitimate, the coordination of troops from different parts of the British Empire. In this way, for Mackinder, the conduct of the war prefigured a new and more perfect form of imperial federation, at least among the self-governing dominions of the British Empire.

The First World War raised other questions about Empire that sat less easily with the arguments of Mackinder's theoretical and pedagogical works. The phenomenal cost of the World War raised serious doubts about the capacity of the British state to live up to its imperial ambitions, with or without the aid of its friends and vassals within its Empire. The Fourteen Points that Woodrow Wilson (1856–1924), as US President (1913–21), set out as the basis for the peace settlement after the war, encouraged anti-colonial nationalism in recognizing national self-determination, a flagrant rebuke to the ambitions of European colonial powers, such as Britain. Finally, the Russian Revolution of 1917 brought a new political principle into international relations, the possibility of a non-capitalist future for colonies, ex-colonies, and other poor states.

These material and ideological developments, which cast a shadow over Mackinder's schemes and designs, were crystallized for Mackinder by his personal involvement in the British campaign of 1919–20 to prise Russia from the Bolshevik grip. Conservatives, like Mackinder, were horrified by the Bolshevik rejection of monarchy and private property. Britain's interest in Russia was initially expressed solely in terms of what the revolution meant for British interests. In other words, it was seen in terms of what I have described as Colonial Imperialism. The main aspects of this British self-interest concerned: denying the resources of South Russia to an adversary (during the war, Germany, and after, Soviet Russia); preventing Russian control of the strategically important lands between the east Mediterranean and north-west India; and reversing the fillip to British socialism that the victory of the labour movement in Russia represented. These were powerful arguments within the British government but they met powerful checks: the British people were fed up with war and its associated costs, material and human; the British exchequer was seriously embarrassed by the costs of the war and this further war could only be fought to a successful conclusion by raising taxes; and the Bolshevik army proved better able to hold or regain territory than Britain's allies were at acquiring or consolidating it.

In this context, the attempt to displace the Bolsheviks failed and, in a gesture more characteristic of what I have called Liberal Imperialism, the British government set out the terms under which it would accept (what it could no longer deny) Soviet Russia as a member of an international system of mutually recognized states. These conditions hinted at the right of military intervention at some future date if the Soviet state failed in what it was told were its duties to its people, the responsibilities and practices of a liberal state in terms of freedom, efficacy, and respect for its neighbours. In reserving this right of intervention, the British set out an argument for military interference not in its own national interest but in the cause of the people of Russia and abutting states. The First World War and its coda in South Russia illustrated imperialism in practice and highlight material as well as ideological challenges to Mackinder's geopolitical imagination. Ironically, Mackinder met these checks through being sent to enact a colonial policy within the very region he insisted was vital to the prospects of any land-based imperial rival to Britain; his Heartland.

Disintegrating Empires

The First World War was precipitated by the question of Empire. The failure of the Ottoman Empire to hold its European territories produced new nation states and complicated alliances in the Balkans. In 1908, Austria-Hungary had taken unto itself the Ottoman provinces of Bosnia and Herzegovina. In 1912–13, in alliance with Greece, the further provinces of Serbia, Montenegro, and Bulgaria managed to expel the Turkish army from Europe and claim independence. To prevent Greece and Serbia dividing Albania between them, the Great Powers of Europe (Britain, France, Germany, and Russia) created it as another independent state. Within the remnant Ottoman Empire, a movement of so-called Young Turks sought internal reforms that would produce a modern, Islamic state.[1] Sensing that the European Great Powers would love dearly to wipe their empire off the map, they sought, in vain, a powerful ally to help secure their borders while they turned attention to a belated modernization.

On 28 June 1914, in an example of the anarchist ideal of propaganda by deed, a Serbian nationalist, Gavrilo Princip (1894–1918), wishing to eject Austria-Hungary from its new provinces (which he saw as rightly part of Greater Serbia) killed the heir to Austrian throne. Austria-Hungary took this as cause of war and threatened Serbia, bringing in Germany and Russia respectively as their allies, and the web of secret diplomacy pulled in France and Britain behind Russia. The Turks now got their wish and lonely Germany (facing Russia, Serbia, France, and Britain) entered into alliance with them. By 1915, in another secret deal, the French, British, and Russians agreed in broad terms how they would carve up the Ottoman Empire after the war, with Russia getting territory in the north, in modern Iran and Turkey, including Constantinople with its access to the Mediterranean; Britain taking lands in the south from the Mediterranean to the Caspian through modern Israel/Palestine, Jordan, Iraq, and Iran; and France getting a wedge in between, a Greater Syria comprising modern Syria and Lebanon.

In 1917, the Russian Empire collapsed in revolution and 'Milner, and perhaps Lloyd George, flirted with the idea of coming to an understanding with Germany, in which the Russian empire rather than the Ottoman Empire could be partitioned as the spoils of victory'.[2] War was now the agent of imperialism, not its result. The historian, David Fromkin, concluded that, for Lloyd George (British prime minister from December 1916), 'the enormity of the war required indemnities and annexations on an enormous scale'.[3] The deal between the three powers was annulled and Britain sought, in the last year of the war, to create new facts on the ground by occupying as much as it could manage of Arab territories wrenched away from Turkey. The British, promising to liberate Arab peoples from Ottoman domination, sought to establish dependencies under British control, arguing that Arab people were as yet too uncivilized to rule themselves.

Bolshevik Russia withdrew itself from the war by making peace with Germany in March 1918, ceding, in humiliation and with evident hope of later retaking them, vast territories in Poland, the Baltics, Ukraine, Georgia, and Armenia. Germany moved fifty-one of its eighty-nine divisions on the Eastern front in Russia to the Western front, in France.[4] Prisoners of war in Russia were asked to go back to Europe. A Czech force wanted to return to fight for independence from Austria-Hungary. A Hungarian force wanted to return home to fight for Bolshevik revolution. The Soviets would not let the Czechs retain their weapons so, to avoid disarmament, they headed east along the trans-Siberian railway towards Vladivostok, whence they planned sailing

---

[1] Fromkin, *Peace*, ch. 4.   [2] Fromkin, *Peace*, 248.
[3] Fromkin, *Peace*, 263.   [4] Kinvig, *Churchill's Crusade*, 8.

to France. Along the way they clashed with the Bolshevik Hungarians moving west. The Czechs prevailed and, by the end of the First World War, they were ensconced in Siberia controlling the railway.

The Russian Imperial Army had split, with some officers and soldiers joining the Bolsheviks and others making civil war against the new regime. There were two main counter-revolutionary groups that formed around remnants of the Tsar's army. In Siberia, Admiral Aleksandr Kolchak (1874–1920) had a force that displaced a local Directorate of socialists and in November 1918 declared itself a Russian government from Omsk.[5] When the Bolsheviks declared a truce with the Germans in December 1917, another section of the Russian Imperial Army, based at the time in the Don region, refused allegiance and, promising eventually to continue the war against Germany, this Volunteer Army began receiving aid from the Allies for their struggle.

Under the Brest–Litovsk treaty of March 1918, Germany took Poland, Lithuania, Finland, Estonia, Livonia, Ukraine, and parts of the Caucasus including Batum from Russia (see Figure 7.1).[6] In Churchill's lively account, Germany had at its disposal '[t]he granaries of the Ukraine and Siberia, the oil of the Caspian, all the resources of a vast continent [. . .] to nourish and maintain the German armies now increasing so formidably in the West'.[7] The Allies followed Germany into Russia, with the French establishing themselves north of the Black Sea, and the British moving east in the Cossack territories and the Caucasus. In this way, they displaced Turkish forces and moving onto Russian territory denied Germany the oil it sought. In particular, the six-week occupation of Baku 'was long enough to deny the Germans access to much-needed oil at a critical moment in the war'.[8] In the north, the British likewise moved onto Russian land, occupying Murmansk and Archangel to limit German gains in the Baltic states. The Allies also called Canadian and Japanese troops into Siberia, again to support the anti-Bolshevik forces who claimed fealty to the anti-German struggle.

The armistice with Germany on 11 November 1918 embarrassed the Allied presence in Russia. Two days later, Britain's senior soldier, Henry Wilson (1864–1922), the Chief of the Imperial General Staff, told fellow members of the War Cabinet that Britain could not raise an army sufficient to eject the Bolshevik government.[9] Later that month, another senior soldier, Albemarle Blackwood (1881–1921) visited the British zone in South Russia and reported that the anti-Bolshevik forces were hopelessly disunited and needed

---

[5] Ullman, *Anglo-Soviet Relations*, 27.

[6] Figure 7.1 is based upon 'A map showing Russia as it was partitioned by the treaty between the Germans and the Bolsheviks signed at Litovsk, March 14, 1918', in: Morris, *Winston's Cumulative Encyclopaedia*, 2; downloaded from 'Maps ETC'.

[7] W. S. Churchill, *World Crisis*, 88.

[8] O'Hara, 'Grubby Game', 141.

[9] Kinvig, *Churchill's Crusade*, 78.

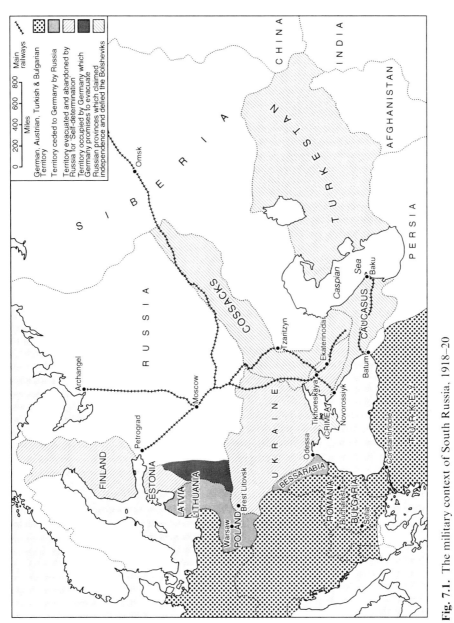

Fig. 7.1. The military context of South Russia, 1918–20

British political assistance to find harmony and effectiveness.[10] The end of the month saw the British Foreign Secretary, Arthur Balfour (1848–1930), redefine the British aims in Russia as protecting Russians who had refused to accept the peace with Germany. In mid-December 1918, Lloyd George called his 'khaki' election during the first flush of national rejoicing at the victory over Germany. The result was that he returned to power, but only on the basis of a pact between his wartime 'coalition' and the Conservative (Unionist) party. The anti-Bolshevik crusade now took greater prominence since the Tories loathed Bolshevism and feared the threat of international communism. Churchill was probably right to remind Lloyd George that he would lose support 'if it is believed in the Conservative party that we are not the enemies of Bolshevism in every form and in every land'.[11]

The Cabinet decided to arm local anti-Bolshevik forces, but to remove from Russia all British troops as part of general demobilization. Once again, the British were advised, this time in January 1919 by their spy, Sidney Reilly (1874–1925), that the anti-Bolshevik movement needed more than military aid: '[t]he usefulness of a High Commissioner with wide powers and [...] assisted by a Staff of experts on military, political and economic affairs, would be very considerable'.[12] To give a stronger impression of unity, in June 1919 General Anton Denikin (1872–1947) placed his forces under the political control of the government established by Kolchak.[13] However, because the central anti-Bolshevik forces were led by reactionaries, many were dedicated to the restoration of Tsar, most to the undoing of the land reforms of 1917, and all committed to the reconstitution of Greater Russia within the boundaries established by 1914. Poland, the Baltic States, the Ukraine, and the Transcaucasian territories were also up in arms against Bolshevism precisely to resist incorporation into a centralized Russian state. In July 1919, the diplomat, Oliver Wardrop (1864–1948) was sent to Denikin and to the Caucasus to see if he could broker an anti-Bolshevik deal.[14] This was recognized as a political rather than military dilemma, requiring diplomacy and agreements, rather than main force.

During 1919, Kolchak advanced from Siberia towards the heart of Russia, taking Tsaritsyn (Volgograd), and then was beaten back; Denikin then led the Volunteer Army from the Don region towards Moscow before this force too was beaten back. The British reporter for the *Daily Chronicle*, Harold Williams (1876–1928), who functioned, effectively, as a British intelligence officer reported that Denikin's difficulties were due, in part, to his failure

---

[10] Kinvig, *Churchill's Crusade*, 94.
[11] Churchill to Lloyd George, 20 September 1919, Churchill Archives, Churchill College, Cambridge University, CHAR 16/11, f. 115.
[12] Ainsworth, 'Reilly's Reports from South Russia', 1453.
[13] Kenez, *Civil War*, 53.
[14] Brinkley, *Volunteer Army*, 175.

to organize the territories he had taken.[15] Williams argued that this was something the British should be able to:

We are not as popular as we ought to be. Somehow we don't seem to be able to display ourselves, and our lack of commercial enterprise and our inability to organise such things as a decent postal and telegraphic service and a regular and abundant supply of papers hampers us terrible. I simply cannot understand why we are so impotent. The Germans had all this running two days after they go in. We are dependent for news on the Soviet wireless.[16]

In mid-October 1919, when passing this letter to the British War Secretary, Winston Churchill, his private secretary commented on the situation as 'disappointing. Why don't the Foreign Office send out a High Commissioner? They told me the other day that this question was postponed for another month'.[17] Henry Wilson had written to Churchill in the same terms:

I have [never] been able to understand why the Foreign Office do not send out a really high-class man to Denikin and attach to this ambassadorial person financiers and trade experts. Everything that the Foreign Office does throws the responsibility on the soldiers with the consequence and no doubt pleasing feeling of being able to damn the soldiers' efforts. [. . .] I am quite sure that this is not Lord Curzon's fault. I am told by the house sparrow that he has been unable to find good men to go because he has been unable to obtain any policy wherewith to guide their footsteps.[18]

Churchill himself considered going to Russia, but only when Denikin was successful, and even then 'as a sort of Ambassador to help Denikin mould the new Russian Constitution'.[19] At the Foreign Office, Curzon had similar reservations, thinking that the recognition implied by sending a high-level Commissioner would misfire if Denikin and Kolchak were defeated.[20]

In the context of global war, then, the British and French had expected the Ottoman Empire to collapse and they were ready with their claims to its lands. Before that *denouément*, the Russian Empire collapsed instead and a new sort of state emerged promising to export workers' revolution across Europe. More immediately, this new state made peace with Germany and the Allies decided to support an anti-Bolshevik movement in Russia in an attempt to reopen the Eastern front and deny the Germans the resource dividend expected from their peace with Russia. The consolidation of that anti-Bolshevik effort required more than military skills, and the Russian principals involved seemed incapable both of organizing the commerce of the territory they held and finding a common basis for border-nationalities and

[15] Borman, 'Williams'.
[16] Williams (with British Mission, South Russia) to Rex Leeper (Political Intelligence Department, Foreign Office), 18 September 1919, CHAR 16/12, f. 113.
[17] Sinclair to Churchill, 10 October 1919, CHAR 16/12, f. 105.
[18] Wilson to Churchill, 18 September 1919, CHAR 16/11, ff. 107, 108.
[19] Ullman, *Anglo-Soviet Relations*, 247; quoting an entry in Henry Wilson's diary.
[20] Ullman, *Anglo-Soviet Relations*, 249.

Greater Russian reactionaries to capitalize upon their common anti-Bolshevism. British military advisers were likewise unsuited to supply the deficiency. Someone was needed who could take a broader view of the imperial project and in late October 1919, the Foreign Office took up the matter once again. Mackinder got the chance to swap imperial propaganda for imperial practice and travel to his Heartland.

Mackinder's Mission

Mackinder later recalled the invitation:

In the year after the War, I went down to the House [of Commons] one day and found a note from Lord Curzon awaiting me. He asked me to go to the bar [entrance] of the House of Lords and said that he would see me and come out. We went to his room. [...] He now asked me to go to South Russia as British High Commissioner. He advised me to accept the position because I should probably enter Moscow beside General Denikin.[21]

Curzon told Mackinder, as the latter noted, that 'he had to be ready to advise General Denikin on every subject except military matters'.[22] The next day, 24 October 1919, Mackinder wrote that he was disposed to accept 'the great charge which you have offered me'.[23] Mackinder's mission did not end with glory in Moscow, and both its ambition and its frustration reveal much about the relations between Geopolitics and Empire. Before turning to these broader concerns, I provide a brief account of his activities.

Preparations

Curzon told Mackinder that both Lloyd George and Churchill had approved of his appointment, and, indeed, Mackinder met separately with each of them. Lloyd George, said Mackinder, had 'asked me to speak without fear of any man when I came to express my opinions formed during the Mission'.[24] Lloyd George also spoke in the House of Commons (13 November) about Mackinder's mission saying that a central purpose was to re-establish commerce within the area under Denikin's control:

---

[21] Mackinder, 'Autobiographical Fragments', Mackinder Papers, School of Geography, Oxford University, MP/C/100 [b, i], f. 12.

[22] Mackinder to Curzon, 20 November 1919, National Archives, Kew, Sir Halford John Mackinder Papers, FO 800/251, f. 30.

[23] Mackinder to Curzon, 24 October 1919, FO 800/251, f. 3.

[24] 'Report on the Situation in South Russia by Sir H. Mackinder M.P.', 21 January 1920, National Archives, Cabinet Papers CAB 24/97, C.P. 516, f. 91–103, 94(r).

It is the policy of the Government to open up trade and commerce as much as possible with South Russia in the interest not only of Russia, but of the world. We have made special efforts in that direction during the last few months, and the hon. member for the Camlachie Division of Glasgow—a well-known and able member of this House—has been appointed to go on a special mission to South Russia with the object of, among other things, investigating what can be done in these respects, and of generally advising the Government on the position.[25]

Curzon, Churchill, and Lloyd George each had distinct priorities and expectations. The Prime Minister was anxious to make peace with Soviet Russia while respecting the rights of the newly independent border states in the Baltic and in the Caucasus, but he was willing to let the anti-Bolshevik forces have some of Britain's surplus military material so that they might try to consolidate hold over the southern part of Russia. The true focus of Lloyd George's imperial interests was the so-called Middle East. Curzon, by contrast, was obsessed with Persia, the Caucasus, Afghanistan, and the integrity of British India. Churchill was a monomaniacal anti-Bolshevik and saw a great arc of territories from Latvia, Lithuania, and Poland through Galicia, Moldavia, and Bessarabia, and on to Georgia, Azerbaijan, Armenia, and Persia, as little more than potential allies for a grand crusade against Bolshevik tyranny. Each briefed Mackinder, in his own way. Mackinder asked that he be forewarned should the British government change its policy towards Russia for fear that his own 'influence with General Denikin should be injured because I had apparently been in ignorance of my Government's policy. I venture to say this because I understand that communication with me may at times be difficult, and because two separate Government Departments are involved'.[26] The two branches of government were, of course, the Foreign Office (Curzon) and the War Office (Churchill), although in effect Lloyd George conjured his own policies and the Cabinet developed ideas independently of all three. In fact, within a few days of Mackinder's letter, Lloyd George hoisted the kite of just such a change in policy when at the annual dinner of the Lord Mayor of London (8 November), he announced to cheers: '[W]e cannot [. . .] afford to continue so costly an intervention in an interminable civil war. Our troops are out of Russia—frankly, I am glad. Russia is a quicksand'.[27]

The reorganization of government in October 1919, that brought Curzon promotion to Foreign Secretary, also involved Lloyd George abandoning the small War Cabinet, of half a dozen, and reverting to a full Cabinet, of twenty-two Ministers. Milner was unimpressed, bemoaning its first two-hour discussion of Russia (4 November) as '[l]ong [and] very rambling, [and] wh[ich] left us as much at sea as ever. This lasted till nearly 2, [and]

[25] *Times*, 14 November 1919, 18b.
[26] Mackinder to Curzon, 29 October 1919, FO 800/251, f. 14.
[27] *Times*, 10 November 1919, 9c.

no other business was done'.[28] In fact, the Cabinet had reviewed their commitments in Russia and recorded that their support for the anti-Bolshevik forces had been continued after the war because 'we had not, up till now, been justified in abandoning a movement that had come into existence at our instance, but the Government recognised that their assistance could not be continued much longer'.[29] The Cabinet concluded that Mackinder should tell Denikin that 'if General Denikin had designs on the independence of the newly-formed states in the Caucasus, the despatch of supplies to him should be stopped'.[30] The next week, Milner noted with evident sarcasm: '[a]t 12 the "Conference of Ministers" [full Cabinet] resumed the discussion of Russia. We came to no conclusion, though the question was examined with unusual thoroughness'.[31] Once again, Mackinder's responsibilities were discussed: '[i]t was pointed out that South Russia could not be completely pacified by military means alone, and that its economic development was of vital importance, and with this object in view Mr. Mackinder had been appointed'.[32] News was also reaching Britain of pogroms against Jewish people in South Russia. The Red Cross was blaming Denikin's soldiers, and Curzon assured a Joint Foreign Committee of the Jewish Board of Deputies and the Anglo-Jewish Association that Mackinder would 'make a thorough investigation of the Jewish situation in the Ukraine, and [. . .] do all possible for the population who have suffered under the pogroms'.[33] According to the military historian, Clifford Kinvig, it is likely that the majority of the 100,000 Jewish people slaughtered in South Russia during the Civil War were killed by Denikin's soldiers.[34]

Mackinder began assembling his team. He wanted a clerical staff of four, plus four personal servants. He expected to be gone for 'six months or more'.[35] He next began to add to the team an economic competence, a Mr. Young who had been 'President of the Caisse at Archangel' and who might help in establishing a currency in South Russia, and 'Food control and Railway experts', so that he might quickly establish an agricultural export trade 'out of the unexampled harvests of the present year'.[36] Nearly a month after agreeing to go to South Russia, Mackinder was still in preparation. Curzon urged 'greater rapidity' and was 'rather startled at the dimensions to which your Mission is expanding in respect more particularly to staff estab-

[28] 'Milner Diary', 4 November 1919, Milner Papers, Bodleian Library, Oxford University, MSS Milner, dep. 90, X. Films 9/36, f. 308.

[29] 'Conclusions of Meeting of Cabinet', 4 November 1919; CAB 23/19, f. 4.

[30] 'Conclusions of Meeting of Cabinet', 4 November 1919, f. 4.

[31] 'Milner Diary', 12 November 1919, f. 316.

[32] 'Conclusions of Meeting of Cabinet', 12 November 1919, CAB 23/19, f. 78.

[33] *Times*, 16 December 1919, 13b.

[34] Kinvig, *Churchill's Crusade*, 233.

[35] Mackinder to Charles Sargeant, 5 November 1919, FO 800/251, f. 21.

[36] Mackinder to Charles Hardinge, 13 November 1919, FO 800/251, f. 27.

lishment'.[37] Mackinder pleaded that the commercial aspects of his mission had been mentioned specifically by Lloyd George and that far from the four to five persons now mentioned by Curzon, Churchill had said that he would need about a dozen: 'I am quite sure that my staff is the minimum with which I could hope to form an independent judgement of the situation, or to render any real help to General Denikin. Of course, I have had no written instructions [and] have therefore tried to piece together the various utterances, public [and] private of yourself, the Prime Minister, [and] Mr. Churchill'.[38] He promised to leave on 28 November. The next day Mackinder returned to the question of his written instructions: 'I have repeatedly asked for them, and I now appeal for your personal intervention'.[39] Mackinder wanted his superiority to other British officials in South Russia guaranteed. In a subsequent meeting with Curzon, Mackinder claimed that his staff had been chosen so that he could liaise with local political and economic functionaries, but Curzon had, it would appear, been sharp and 'rightly reminded me that the responsibility is yours [Curzon's]'.[40] Curzon reined Mackinder in more tightly still when he finally sent him a written set of instructions, approved by Cabinet on 2 December, and told him that 'the Cabinet particularly desired that [the instructions] should be supplemented in one respect' and Mackinder was told not to act on his own initiative and 'that before embarking upon any fresh policy for the future, H[is] M[ajesty's] G[overnment] would like to receive a report from you on the entire situation in its various aspects'.[41]

In planning his mission, then, Mackinder had to attend to three masters. Curzon wanted him to ensure that Denikin did not undermine the new Caucasian states, for Curzon did not want Russia to re-establish its sovereignty over territories abutting the passage from Egypt to India. The Cabinet conclusions of 4 November also noted that Mackinder was to act as envoy for the wishes of the British government and impress upon Denikin that failure to respect these new states would lose him his military supplies. Lloyd George wanted markets for British goods and to see trade flowing again. He was willing to negotiate with the Soviets on this, but he was also keen to give the White Russians a chance to produce the same from the territories they currently held. This was reflected in the Cabinet conclusions of 12 November and to achieve these goals Mackinder would indeed need a currency expert to move the local economy beyond its present state of mere barter, a food expert to assess and market the harvest, and a railway expert to get communications effective again so that goods might travel. Given the cauldron of refugees in the region, moreover, Mackinder wanted a medical advisor to manage the

[37] Curzon to Mackinder, 20 November 1919, FO 800/251, ff. 37, 33.
[38] Mackinder to Curzon, 20 November 1919, FO 800/251, ff. 30–1.
[39] ibid., 21 November 1919, FO 800/251, f. 39.
[40] ibid., 23 November 1919, FO 800/251, f. 42.
[41] Curzon to Mackinder, 2 December 1919, FO 800/251, ff. 44–5, 46–7.

threat of disease. Curzon, however, refused to let Mackinder have a mission on this scale.

Churchill had no Cabinet decisions to back him up, but probably had most success in shaping Mackinder's own view of his responsibilities. Churchill's War Office shared with Mackinder the reports of the senior British military officer in South Russia, Hubert Holman (1869–1949), including his confidential telegrams to Cabinet.[42] Lloyd George had the measure both of Churchill and of public opinion:

The reconquest of Russia would cost hundreds of millions. It would cost hundreds of millions more to maintain the new Government until it had established itself. You are prepared to spend all that money, and I know perfectly well that is what you really desire. But as you know [...] you won't find another responsible person in the whole land who will take your view.[43]

Certainly Churchill was isolated in the Cabinet and, when he tried to get his colleagues to recognize the newly asserted Baltic republics, none supported him; even the ultra-imperialist Milner apologized afterwards, pleading that Churchill not thereby 'regard me as weakening in my anti-Bolshevism'.[44] Mackinder's mission gave Churchill one more throw of the dice, but to do this, Mackinder had to bring the Polish and the Volunteer army into alliance, and they had to espouse anti-Bolshevism in a form that could appeal to a purely defensive rather than offensive set of military objectives.

Implementation

Mackinder left England on 4 December and went to Paris where he met members of the All-Russian Council. This group represented Denikin and Kolchak, as the anti-Bolshevik Russian interest at the Paris Peace Conference.[45] He then went to Warsaw, at the 'instigation' of Churchill.[46] There, in company with the British ambassador to Poland, Horace Rumbold (1869–1941), Mackinder spent time with Josef Piłsudski (1867–1935), the military and political leader of the new state. They gained two concessions that were important if Churchill's strategy were to have a chance. Piłsudski agreed that he would meet Denikin at some halfway place, such as Czernowitz, so that they might discuss military cooperation. He also denied any imperialistic aims saying that he would submit all districts 'as far back as the [...] line through Brest Litovsk [...] to a plebiscite'.[47] This was more accommodating

[42] Sinclair to Mackinder, 27 November 1919, CHAR 16/13, f. 97.
[43] Lloyd George to Churchill, 22 September 1919, CHAR 16/11, f. 128(v).
[44] Milner to Churchill, 24 September 1919, CHAR 16/11, f 144(r).
[45] Alston, 'Suggested Basis'.
[46] Davies, 'Lloyd George and Poland', 137.
[47] Rumbold to Foreign Office, 16 December 1919, Telegram No. 487, 'Report on South Russia by Mackinder', f. 98(v).

than the Polish delegates had been at the Paris Peace Conference and when, ultimately at the end of January 1920, the British refused to give military assistance for a Polish advance on Moscow, no more was heard of plebiscites.[48]

After four days in Warsaw, Mackinder left on 17 December and after brief stays in Bucharest and Sofia, arrived at Constantinople (Istanbul) on 28 December, having spent Christmas day stranded in a railway siding as the result of a strike. He left Constantinople after two days and then spent a week aboard H.M.S. Marlborough awaiting suitable quarters onshore at Novorossiysk (see Figure 7.1). He arrived in South Russia on 7 January, about ten weeks after his appointment, and left for the Front the next day. On 10 January, he met Denikin for five hours in the General's railway carriage at Tikhoretskaya Junction, but by this time Denikin's strategic position was desperate.

Back in London, the Foreign Office had already trimmed Mackinder's mission deciding not to send the food experts on to him. This brought a rebuke from Churchill's office and a letter to Curzon begging reconsideration of the refusal to send food and railway experts since '[a]t the present time the railways are congested with train loads of passengers carrying sacks of flour from the country to the towns for themselves and their families, because no adequate organisation exists to take the grain into the towns in goods trains'.[49] The War Department itself had by now decided not to send the railway assistants Mackinder had requested. As a result, Mackinder lost the commercial mission altogether. Apologizing for resigning from the mission on 22 December, his railway officer wrote: '[a]fter you left England the Government failed to give me any support: the War Office stated that they could not transfer my staff from the military mission: the food organisation staff was cancelled: and finally the Vickers–Beardmore–Docker group retired owing to lack of Government help and policy. It was a sorrow to me to sever my connection with Russia but under the circumstances I could do nothing else'.[50]

With the new year, the British Government learned that Denikin was likely soon to lose control of the Caspian Sea and that 'at least two divisions' would be needed if Britain were to retain control of the Batum–Baku railway line.[51] Henry Wilson drew up a plan for 'several alternative lines of defence against possible Bolshevik aggression, but, in view of our inability to find the necessary troops, the [Eastern] Committee had advised against attempting to hold any of the lines indicated'.[52] However, Mackinder knew none of this;

[48] Elcock, 'Britain and the Russo-Polish Frontier'.

[49] Unknown to Curzon, 17 December 1919, Churchill Archives, CHAR 16/14, f. 75.

[50] Colonel Hull to Mackinder, 9 January 1920, FO 800/251, ff. 58–9.

[51] 'Conclusions of Meeting of Cabinet', 7 January 1920, CAB 23/20, f. 32.

[52] 'Conclusions of Meeting of Cabinet', 14 January 1920, CAB 23/20, f. 49. The Eastern Committee was a strategic review of British policy in Asia and the Middle East. It was chaired, and directed, by Curzon.

the telegraph wires between Ekatarinodar and Tikhoretskaya had been cut.[53] He told Denikin that the White Russian advance of the previous summer had collapsed because '[t]he ground gained was not properly organised and administered in the rear'.[54] Armies had to sustain themselves without antagonizing people in the lands they occupied and to do this, Mackinder told him, they had to organize commerce and taxes: '[i]n other words, a state, and not merely an army, must be set going. The riches of South Russia are such that this could be done in a few months with Western help'.[55] Mackinder promised that this assistance would be forthcoming only if the anti-Bolshevik forces showed that they 'had learned [. . .] from the events of the last few years'.[56] The era of centralized despotism was over and Russia needed 'not [. . .] necessarily a fully democratic government in the western sense, but a modern government'.[57] Denikin too must have local allies, 'the Finns, the Estonians, the Letts, the Poles, the Georgians, and perhaps the Roumanians'.[58] Although Mackinder argued that France and Britain would provide 'economic methods and organizing brain' Denikin would have to gain the support of these neighbours by promising those new states that he would submit border questions to a commission of the Great Powers.[59] Denikin gave, at first, little reassurance on the border states: '[h]e said that his principle was to restore the All-Russia, great and indivisible'.[60] Yet, when Mackinder said that the survival of Russia could not be secured without alliances, Denikin then said that he needed to think further. Mackinder made no record of having raised the question of Jewish pogroms with Denikin.

In a few days, Denikin, having consulted the immediate members of his administration, sent Mackinder a telegram stating he would recognize 'the *de facto* independence of the border governments' and agreeing that their future borders and status would be settled through negotiations in which the Allies would mediate.[61] He also promised that the border with Poland would be settled 'on ethnographical principles'.[62] In return, he anticipated that Poland would continue the fight against Bolshevism, that the Allies would protect his own Government in its Black Sea base, and that the supply of arms would continue. Mackinder replied immediately that no further military aid would be available after 31 March 1920, but that if South Russia were properly

[53] Times, 9 March 1922, 8a.
[54] 'Memorandum by Mr. Mackinder of interview between General Denikin and himself at Tikhoretskaya on January 10, 1920', 'Report on South Russia by Mackinder', f. 99(v).
[55] 'Memorandum of interview', f. 99(v).
[56] ibid., f. 99(v).
[57] ibid., f. 99(v).
[58] ibid., f. 99(v)–100(r).
[59] ibid., f. 100(r).
[60] ibid., f. 100(r).
[61] 'Telegram from Lieutenant-General Denikin to Lieutenant-General Lumosky, January 1/14, 1920', 'Report on South Russia by Mackinder', f. 100(v).
[62] 'Telegram from Denikin', f. 100(v).

organized, the Volunteer Army would be self-sufficient by then. In a letter of the following day, Denikin also accepted Mackinder's commercial proposals recognizing the 'extreme desirability' of the British government helping restore the 'economic life of the country' under his control.[63] These were significant concessions, but came too late.

The British military commander in South Russia, Holman, wrote to Churchill on 8 January that Mackinder had arrived eight months too late to be useful.[64] When Mackinder arrived to talk with Denikin, Holman told him of the serious problems with the morale of the Volunteer Army officers. Their wives and children were living in railway carriages back at Ekaterinodar, and, as rumours of a British withdrawal spread, Russian officers feared for these dependents. Many abandoned the front line to go back to Ekaterinodar and arrange passage for their families away from the fighting. Rumour and terror chased each other as tactics and consequences on both sides of the front line.[65] Mackinder was told, by Holman, that '[b]lack looks had taken the place of the former friendship, and at any moment a mad cry of British treachery might endanger the lives of our men'.[66] Mackinder gave Denikin the following promise:

The British High Commissioner for South Russia on behalf of His Majesty's Government guarantees that all available ships, naval and commercial, will be used to evacuate the wives and families of Russian Officers if and when the necessity arises, and that the British Military Mission will form the rearguard for the protection of these wives and families, but both the High Commissioner and General Holman are convinced that the necessity will not arise if all Russian Officers will rise to the great occasion which confronts them.[67]

In his report, Mackinder said that:

This was done to arrest the panic, for most certainly all these women would be murdered if they fell into the hands of the Bolsheviks. I felt it was unthinkable that we should abandon them after having encouraged their husbands to fight. I need hardly add that the private soldiers ran no similar risk, since they and their families could disappear into the general population.[68]

The effect was immediate: '[the n]ext day General Wrangel came to me on behalf of General Denikin to tell me that my message had gone through the army and the desertion of the officers had been arrested'.[69]

---

[63] Denikin to Mackinder, 15 January 1920, 'Report on South Russia by Mackinder', f. 101(v).

[64] Kinvig, *Churchill's Crusade*, 309.

[65] Bortnevski, 'White Administration'; O. Figes, 'Red Army and Mass Mobilization'; Smith, 'Anatomy of a Rumour'.

[66] *Times*, 9 March 1922, 8a.

[67] 'Guarantee given by Mr. Mackinder to General Denikin at Ti[k]horetskaya on the 10th January, 1920', 'Report on South Russia by Mackinder', f. 103(r).

[68] 'Report on South Russia by Mackinder', ff. 92(v)–93(r).

[69] *Times*, 9 March 1922, 8a.

By then, Mackinder had left the front line and was back among the refugees at Ekaterinodar. On 12 January, he had established himself at Novorossiysk again and there, on the 14th, he convened a meeting of Denikin's civil administration. He also spoke with British traders in the region. However, by this time the news from elsewhere in the Caucasus was grave: Georgia seemed about to throw its lot in with the Bolsheviks. Mackinder reported that '[i]n view of the urgency of the whole situation and the need of formulating an all-round policy, I now determined to run home for a few days'.[70] He left Novorossiysk on 16 January and arrived in Marseilles four days later, whence he sent his report to Curzon.

Mackinder was back in London in time to explain and defend both his actions and his recommendations to a Cabinet meeting of 29 January. He had been ashore in South Russia a mere week, yet he might have been pleased with his achievements. He could assure Lloyd George that he had Denikin's agreement to British cooperation in creating a viable commercial state. Curzon could be told of the recognition of the Caucasian republics. Churchill might agree that Mackinder had brought Piłsudski and Denikin closer together. However, Mackinder's meeting with the Cabinet was preceded by an anxious note from the First Sea Lord (Head of the Admiralty), Walter Long (1854–1924) that:

The Admiralty view with great concern the grave and farreaching commitment of His Majesty's Government by Mr. Mackinder. The numbers to be evacuated in the event of further withdrawal of Denikin's army will be very large and may run into hundreds of thousands. [... T]he Board of Admiralty have arrived at the conclusion with regret that the responsibilities involved in Mr. Mackinder's guarantees are too heavy, to be met in their entirety. Half measures have invariably proved to do more harm than good and [...] the Board consider that the time has come to reconsider whether [...] any attempt as regards evacuation is justified.[71]

Aftermath

Long was at the Cabinet of 29 January to present in person the case for withdrawing the promise of support to the families of the White Russian officers. The Cabinet decided that it was 'impossible to evacuate refugees from [...] any [...] Russian port, for on sanitary grounds no country will receive them', and the Cabinet confined itself to meeting the letter of Mackinder's guarantee by promising to move the officers' dependents from Ekaterinador down to the Crimea on the Black Sea.[72] The refuguees accumulated at Odessa before Denikin's successor, Pyotr Wrangel (1878–1928),

---

[70] 'Report on South Russia by Mackinder', f. 93(r).
[71] 'Evacuation of Refugees from South Russia and Russian Prisoners of War from Germany. Memorandum for the Cabinet by the First Sea Lord. 28 January 1920', CAB 24/97 Cabinet Papers, C.P. 519, ff. 107–8.
[72] 'Conclusions of Meeting of Cabinet', 29 January 1920, CAB 23/20, f. 69.

evacuated almost 150,000 soldiers and dependents to islands off the coast of Turkey in November 1920. Eventually Bulgaria, Czechoslovakia, and Yugoslavia were persuaded each to take a share of the refugees.[73]

Mackinder's report was distributed to the Cabinet, it recorded his movements and meetings and contained an analysis of the causes of Denikin's current dilemma, making proposals for future policy. His account of the failure of Denikin's summer advance on Moscow was unexceptional except in one point. He laid particular stress upon the depressive effect of Lloyd George's speeches in favour of a trade treaty with the Bolsheviks, which gave 'the impression that England intended to change her policy and abandon the anti-Bolshevik cause'.[74] Mackinder, like other ultra-imperialists, was anxious about the German influence upon the Bolsheviks and still believed in a German–Jewish conspiracy even with little or no evidence: '[i]t may well be that there are subterranean German agencies, probably through Jewish channels'.[75] Mackinder's view was bleak: 'Bolshevism is for the moment triumphant. The wheat and coal areas of South Russia are now accessible from Moscow, and Bolshevik tyranny has a new lease of life'.[76]

Mackinder argued that the primary vehicle of Bolshevik influence, equivalent to the British navy or the Germany army, was communist propaganda: '[u]nless destroyed at the root the Bolshevik propaganda may be a danger to all civilisation before long. Its centre is a great office at Moscow, in the Kremlin I believe, and it has a trained personnel at its disposal which is as efficient as the general staff of one of the great armies'.[77] Mackinder never believed that workers could reach socialist conclusions from daily experience, they had to be brainwashed into them. A couple of years after his return from Russia, when the Glasgow proletariat voted him out of Parliament, he wrote to the *Times* that the cause lay with 'Proletarian Sunday Schools', for '[t]he children of the "Proletarian" upbringing have now grown to be young men and young women. The Marxian catchwords have, for them, taken the place of Biblical texts. Only experience of life will win them to saner views; no argument will penetrate their ingrained doctrines'.[78]

Mackinder's solution to the Bolshevik threat was to accept Denikin's promise of treating with the border regions as independent states and, on these terms, forming an alliance from the Crimea around to Poland. To preserve this long front against Soviet Russia, Denikin had to be sustained, and Mackinder argued that Denikin's regime should be recognized as the legal government of Russia. The British would have to set up a company of merchant adventurers to restore a commercial economy to South Russia. In

---

[73] Kenez, *Civil War*, 307.
[74] 'Report on South Russia by Mackinder', f. 94(r).
[75] ibid., f. 94(v).
[76] ibid., f. 95(r).
[77] ibid., f. 95(r).
[78] *Times*, 23 November 1922, 15a.

answer to questions at the Cabinet, Mackinder admitted that this would place leading responsibility upon Britain but, he added, 'we should obtain what we required in the form of wheat, sugar, oil, etc'.[79] Most importantly for Mackinder, Britain should announce 'that it will not make peace with Bolshevism'.[80] This would, he assured the Cabinet, 'send a thrill though all the east of Europe, which in a month would wholly alter the *morale* of the people'.[81] In the discussion after Mackinder left the room, his proposals 'did not meet with any support'.[82] Herbert Fisher (1865–1940), Minister of Education, considered the report 'absurd', and recorded that Andrew Bonar Law (1858–1923), leader of the Unionist Party, agreed, whereas Walter Long, head of the Admiralty, had considered it 'an able effort!'.[83] The Cabinet decided that there was no point in sending Mackinder back to South Russia. In a few days, Mackinder sent Lloyd George an offer to resign, which was accepted. Curzon said that the collapse in South Russia was 'tragic but[,] as you will remember from our communication before you started[, ...] not altogether unforeseen'.[84]

Mackinder continued to urge that Britain act to contain what he saw as Bolshevik aggression. In May 1920, in the House of Commons, he argued that Britain should interfere in eastern Europe because 'we preserve a detached', indeed a 'world point of view'.[85] Yet, in taking that view, the British needed to realize that the Polish people had great experience of what it meant to be ruled by Russia, so that their belief that 'you are going to see a new despotism' in Russia, justified giving them military assistance and enlisting them to fight the Bolshevik reconquest of the border states.[86] The detached (British) world point of view, according to Mackinder, required arming Polish people to push their borders as far east as made them feel safe, and in this way, sue for peace. In July 1920, he was writing once more to the principal advocate of intervention, Churchill, with the news that the South Russian army was again growing and that he would be 'quite willing to run out to them', should the British government contemplate reviving the strategy of supporting a broad coalition of anti-Bolshevik forces.[87] Churchill sent a non-committal reply pointing out that 'the course of events in Poland will be the decisive factor'.[88]

[79] 'Notes of points [...] made by Sir H. J. Mackinder in reply to questions put to him at the Cabinet meeting held on Thursday, January 29, 1920, at 11–30 a.m.', FO 800/251, f. 65.

[80] 'Conclusions of Meeting of Cabinet', 29 January 1920, CAB 23/20, f. 66.

[81] ibid., 29 January 1920, CAB 23/20, f. 66.

[82] ibid., 29 January 1920, CAB 23/20, f. 61.

[83] Quoted in Blouet, 'Mackinder as High Commissioner', 234.

[84] Curzon to Mackinder, 7 February 1920, FO 800/251, ff. 68–9.

[85] *The Official Report, House of Commons, 5th Series* [*Hansard 5th*], 129 (20 May 1920), 1712.

[86] *Hansard 5th*, 129 (20 May 1920), 1717.

[87] Mackinder to Churchill, 22 July 1920, CHAR 16/48A, f. 75(r).

[88] Churchill to Mackinder, 23 July 1920, CHAR 16/48A, f. 80.

Mackinder had been to South Russia, had made diplomatic progress, but his return to consult on how strategy should capitalize upon these gains secured only the termination of his mission altogether. He had expected to be away in South Russia for months, he was there a matter of days. Despite this failure, Mackinder's aborted mission was very suggestive about the contexts of imperial practice.

Implications

Empires and Nations

The first significant lesson of Mackinder's mission concerns the way that war and peace challenged the future of empires. As Chapter 5 described, Mackinder believed that international relations would be shaped increasingly by empires, yet, the war's vortex had taken up and broken three of them: the Ottoman, the Russian, and the Habsburg (Austria-Hungary). In shaping the peace, Woodrow Wilson, as president of the United States, was 'opposed to [the] imperialist ambitions [of England and France] and intended to thwart them'.[89] When the Russian Bolsheviks published the details of the secret treaties by which France, Russia, and Britain had planned to profit from the collapse of the Ottoman Empire, Wilson took the advice of Walter Lippmann to publish a more elevated set of war aims. Principal among his Fourteen Points was the idea that new territorial arrangements would be based on national self-determination rather than imperial expansion.[90] His principal adviser, Edward House (1858–1938), 'took [a] longer-term view: separate representation for the [British] dominions and India in the Peace Conference and on new international bodies such as the League of Nations and the International Labour Organization could only hurry along "the eventual disintegration of the British Empire"'.[91] On its more idealistic reading, Wilson's proposals signalled the end of what, in Chapter 1, I identified as Colonial Imperialism. In other words, Wilson argued that it was no longer justified for powerful states to appeal to their own self-interest as justification for interfering in the internal affairs of weaker states.

In practice, as Margaret Macmillan shows in her excellent history of the Paris Peace Conference, this apparently simple idea of the right to self-determination was subverted at every turn of the peace negotiations.[92] Self-determination assumed that groups were easily defined and neatly separated in space. States, such as Poland, claimed territories up to the limit where a dominant group could absorb foreign lands yet retain a majority

---

[89] Fromkin, *Peace*, 253. [90] Fromkin, *Peace*, 258.
[91] Macmillan, *Peacemakers*, 53. [92] Macmillan, *Peacemakers*.

position overall. Other states wanted to push their borders beyond even the claims of ethnicity; in order to render their country viable, economically, as with German claims on Silesia, or militarily, as with Rumanian claims to Transylvania. On the grounds of religion or race, some minority groups, such as the Croats, appealed that they should not be placed under the suzerainty of other groups, such as the Serbs, that they argued were less civilized than themselves. Some states posed as bulwarks against Bolshevism and claimed territory to save their state from communist clutches, as with Rumanian claims to save Bessarabia from Bolshevik Russia and Bukovina from Bolshevik Hungary.

Wilson's call for national self-determination and the equality of peoples, however, bent the knee to geopolitics and racial chauvinism at Versailles. When Japan proposed that the charter of the new League of Nations include a commitment to racial equality, it challenged the racist division between civilized and less-civilized peoples that was explicit in the Orientalism of Mackinder and that compromised the more liberal world views of Hobson and Reclus. The Japanese were concerned at the prejudiced treatment they received when it came to migration, and their clause was rejected by the United States and Australia precisely for fear it would prevent them from excluding Japanese people from their countries. One of the Australian delegation at Paris, wrote to his Prime Minister that '[n]o Gov[ernmen]t could live for a day in Australia if it tampered with a White Australia'.[93] In pleading their right to imperial control, the Great Powers appealed: to their pre-existing treaty commitments (France had been promised Syria), to the sovereign interest implicit in the share they held of the national debt of foreign states (French interests in both Russian and Ottoman territories), to less-civilized peoples' unfitness for self-government (British claims to the Arab territories of the Ottoman Empire), or to the strategic integrity of existing imperial possessions (British claims to former German colonies in East Africa which could link its own Arabian and South African interests).

In Paris, the rearrangement of territories incorporated the strategic priorities of Empire. The dissolution of German, Ottoman, Habsburg, and Russian Empires need not in each case have to mean creating new independent states. Some of the European peoples could be directed towards statehood, but in the Middle East, Asia, and Africa, lived people whom Jan Smuts, in his prospectus for the League of Nations, described as people 'to whom it would be impracticable to apply any ideas of political self-determination in the European sense'.[94] Under cover of League of Nations' mandates, the dominant imperial powers helped themselves: France claimed African regions from which it could recruit native soldiers to quiet worries about its manpower imbalance with Germany; and Britain added pieces to the imperial arc it saw running from South Africa through to Egypt, on to

---

[93] Macmillan, *Peacemakers*, 328.   [94] Macmillan, *Peacemakers*, 108.

India, and down to Australia and New Zealand. Yet, while serving their own imperial interests, the Great Powers sought also to contain rivals, most notably Bolshevik Russia. The fear of provoking socialist revolutions in Europe was the main reason behind many of the concessions made to conservative nationalism; national shame was understood as a direct cause of proletarian revolution in Russia, Hungary, and Germany. At the close of the war, when defeated Germany pulled out of the Ukraine, the Bolsheviks moved in. To prevent the same happening in the Baltics, the president of newly independent Latvia, with the agreement of the British, invited the Germans to reoccupy his country, which they did with ill-disciplined alacrity.[95] The Allies were quick to recognize the bites that the putative Baltic states took out of European Russia. Their failure to be as accommodating in the Caucasus was because they hoped South Russia might be the springboard for the counter-revolutionary re-conquest of Russia as a whole.

Colonial Imperialism

These colonial strategies of Empire, anti-Bolshevism, and resource conflict, as promoted by Curzon and Churchill, were central to Mackinder's mission. The integrity of the Empire mattered mightily to Curzon, who adopted a singularly geopolitical perspective, with the southern borderlands of Russia as his bailiwick: 'Turkestan, Afghanistan, Transcaspia, Persia—to many these names breathe only a sense of utter remoteness. [. . .] To me, I confess they are the pieces on a chessboard upon which is being played out a game for dominion of the world'.[96] Curzon urged that 'the integrity of Persia must be regarded as a cardinal precept of our Imperial creed'.[97] In 1919, he claimed that the unacceptable alternatives to British control were to let Persia 'rot in picturesque decay' or 'be over-run by Bolshevik influences from the north'.[98] Curzon was especially struck by the significance of communications, offering the claim that easier travel would make it possible to begin exploiting the minerals of South-West Persia, particularly the oil evidenced by the 'naphtha springs'.[99] In addition, by laying railway lines, Russians had been able to pacify lands on its borders and push 'the Russian frontier by rapid stages in the direction of Afghanistan'.[100] Curzon's writings on Persia and on Russian ambitions in Central Asia were an important part of the intellectual context for Mackinder's own geopolitical ideas.[101] Curzon returned the

---

[95] Macmillan, *Peacemakers*, 233.
[96] Curzon, *Persia 1*, 3–4.
[97] Curzon, *Persia 2*, 605.
[98] Wright, 'Curzon and Persia', 350.
[99] Curzon, 'Karun River', 526. In the year of this paper, Curzon himself became a shareholder in an oil company that was ultimately unsuccessful in finding Persian oil; Gilmour, *Curzon*, 76.
[100] Curzon, 'Transcaspian Railway', 275.
[101] Curzon, *Russia in Central Asia*; O'Hara, Heffernan, and Endfield, 'Mackinder and British Perceptions of Central Asia'.

favour, asking the secretary of the Royal Geographical Society for a copy of Mackinder's 'excellent' paper on the 'Geographical Pivot of History' when preparing his own work on frontiers.[102]

Mackinder's report on South Russia drew upon his own earlier writings to paint a picture of the reversion of Russia to the predatory state of earlier times with 'bands of marauders roaming the country. Out of such a welter history might produce again, as so often before from these very plains, some great leader of nomads who would gather the bands together and fall now on this border region and now on that. Asia and Europe alike would have to maintain military borders'.[103] Alternatively, Bolshevik Russia might organize itself for industrial warfare, a threatening prospect which necessitated immediate pre-emptive action so that 'the advance of Bolshevism, sweeping forward like a prairie fire, can be limited and kept away from India and Lower Asia'.[104] In emphasizing the pressure of Russia upon its southern borderlands, Mackinder was in tune with Curzon's own obsessions. In a briefing paper for the Cabinet, Curzon referred to Georgia and Azerbaijan as 'one of the most important gateways to the East' and that the railways there were so important that [i]t would seem essential that [these] countries [. . .] should be prosperous and well-disposed to Great Britain and British policy'.[105] This geopolitical perspective connected Russia to India through a sort of domino theory. Arthur Balfour, at a meeting of Curzon's Eastern Committee of the War Cabinet, highlighted the fallacy of the geographical reasoning: '[e]very time I come to a discussion[, . . .] I find there is a new sphere which we have got to guard, which is supposed to protect the gateways of India. Those gateways are getting further and further from India, and I do not know how far west they are going to be brought'.[106]

Anti-Communism was a novel element of Colonial Imperialism in the early twentieth century. Conservatives considered the success of communism abroad as a threat to respect for authority and property at home, and both Conservatives and Liberals worried that it was a development threatening British export markets. In 1919, Curzon described the Bolsheviks as 'a horde of savages who know no restraint and are resolved to destroy all law'.[107] In April 1919, Churchill said that Bolshevik tyranny was 'far worse than German militarism', and Lloyd George's personal secretary described Churchill as 'simply *raving*', and 'almost like a madman', when the Allies decided in January 1920 to explore opening trade with Bolshevik Russia.[108] In his public speeches, Churchill tried to rouse Britain to renewing war in Russia, calling Bolsheviks 'troops of ferocious baboons', a 'foul combination of

---

[102] Goudie, 'Curzon', 207; Mackinder, 'Geographical Pivot'; Curzon, *Frontiers*.

[103] 'Report on South Russia by Mackinder', f. 97(v).

[104] 'Report on South Russia by Mackinder', f. 97(r).

[105] 'Transcaucasian republics and situation. Memorandum by Lord Curzon, 24 December 1919', CAB 24/95, C.P. 336, ff. 159–163, f. 162(v).

[106] Macmillan, *Peacemakers*, 396.

[107] Macmillan, *Peacemakers*, 454.

[108] Carlton, 'Churchill', 333, 334.

criminality and animalism': 'Bolshevism is not a policy; it is a disease. It is not a creed; it is a pestilence'.[109] Churchill also played on anti-Semitism referring to 'the international Soviet of the Russian and Polish Jew'.[110] In allowing Lenin to return in the midst of the 1917 revolution, Churchill argued that the Germans had unleashed 'the most grisly of all weapons. They transported Lenin in a sealed truck like a plague bacillus from Switzerland to Russia'.[111] Churchill also claimed that the Bolsheviks were using gas against the White Russians although, as he knew, it was the British who were using knock-out gas in North Russia against the Bolsheviks.[112] Echoing Curzon's account of Bolsheviks as lawless, Churchill characterized Lenin as 'the Grand Repudiator. He repudiated everything. He repudiated God, King, Country, morals, treaties, debts, rents, interest, the laws and customs of centuries, all contracts written or implied, the whole structure—such as it is—of human society'.[113]

Churchill fed stories of Bolshevik atrocities to William Aitken (Lord Beaverbrook, 1879–1964) asking that he publish them in his *Daily Express*, a popular newspaper.[114] In April 1919, he produced an official dossier of claims about the horrors of the regime, a one-sided amalgam of the credible and the absurd, including the claims that the Bolsheviks had nationalized women, and were torturing priests.[115] Thousands of these circulated as a tuppenny pamphlet and, so informed, 200 Members of Parliament signed a letter to Lloyd George urging that the Bolshevik regime be shunned.[116]

For Churchill, there could be no compromise with Bolshevik revolution. Mackinder, likewise, made much of the breakdown in Russia of society, arguing that society was a set of habitual disciplines that allowed rule to be exercised without detailed force; 'social discipline [...] becomes innate'.[117] Mackinder stressed the importance of the inertia of established expectations and the momentum of convention. He called society a 'Going Concern', and represented the Bolshevik revolution as a form of 'social suicide' because it degraded discipline and habits.[118] The revolutions of 1917 dissolved order and rule and now 'the whole mechanism of its society must be reconstituted, and that quickly, if the men and women who survive its impoverishment are not to forget the habits and lose the aptitudes on which their civilization depends. History shows no remedy but force upon which to found a fresh nucleus of discipline in such circumstances'.[119] The civilized world, argued Mackinder, could not recognize Bolshevism because the Bolsheviks did not recognize society. Bolshevik Russia was simply not like other nations, being organized by Jewish people who, 'homeless' and 'brainful', 'lent [themselves] to such internationalist work' as socialism.[120]

[109] Carlton, 'Churchill', 334–5.   [110] Ullman, *Anglo-Soviet Relations*, 328.
[111] Churchill, *World Crisis*, 73.   [112] Ullman, *Anglo-Soviet Relations*, 181.
[113] Churchill, *World Crisis*, 75.   [114] Kinvig, *Churchill's Crusade*, 155.
[115] *Collection of Reports on Bolshevism in Russia*.
[116] Kinvig, *Churchill's Crusade*, 160–2.
[117] Mackinder, *Democratic Ideals and Reality*, 16.
[118] Mackinder, ibid. 233. See Chapter 5 above.
[119] Mackinder, ibid. 17.
[120] Mackinder, ibid. 226.

The influence of Churchill was clear in the language Mackinder later used when writing about Soviet Russia in his popular textbook. He referred not only to the threat to Europe from 'Bolshevik extremists', and to Lenin as 'a poison which fermented', but also told his young readers that 'Russia has for the present ceased to be part of the civilized world'.[121] The dissolution of society under communism returned the Heartland to the rule of predatory hordes, although now they had locomotives instead of horses. They had to be contained at least and replaced at best: 'the only final remedy is to kill Bolshevism at the source'.[122]

The very same territories that mattered so much to Curzon for the British strategic position within the imperial arc from the Middle East through the Caucasus were likewise significant for their mineral resources, particularly oil. This had an independent influence upon British policy in the Arab regions of Ottoman Empire.[123] The historian, Arnold Toynbee (1889–1975), who was attached to the British peace team in Paris, overheard Lloyd George rehearsing his views on the Middle East: 'Mesopotamia... yes... oil... irrigation... we must have Mesopotamia; Palestine... yes... the Holy Land... Zionism... we must have Palestine; Syria... h'm... what is there in Syria? Let the French have that'.[124] At the same time, the resource basket that Mackinder had described in 1904 as the prize falling to whomever controlled the Heartland was an explicit concern of British military strategy during the War. Recall that in 1918, intervention against non-belligerent Russia began as an attempt to deny Germany the oil, coal, and wheat the latter might expect from its peace-treaty with the Bolsheviks. As First Lord of the Admiralty before the First World War, Churchill had overseen the conversion of the navy from coal to oil and in this context there sat, in 1912–13, a significant Royal Commission on securing Britain's oil supplies.[125] By the start of the war, the British were responsible for three-fifths of the foreign investment in the Russian oil industry.[126]

Curzon was sure that Britain's access to oil and Germany's difficulties of supply had been crucial in the war and barely a week after the end of the war, he told a victory dinner of the Inter-Allied Petroleum Conference that the allies had 'floated to victory on a wave of oil'.[127] The major Caspian oilfield was at Baku and this port was also convenient for the export of oil up the Volga into the rest of Russia. Baku was in the province of Azerbaijan, which claimed its independence from Russia with the revolution of 1917. The Bolsheviks were anxious to reclaim this resource. Curzon had another plan. To the west of Baku ran a railway line through Georgia to the Black Sea port of Batum (see Figure 7.1). The tiny province around this city was ceded from

[121] Mackinder, *World War and After*, 154, 138, 226.
[122] 'Report on South Russia by Mackinder', f. 97(r).
[123] Yergin, *Prize*.
[124] Macmillan, *Peacemakers*, 392.
[125] Jenkins, *Churchill*, 218.
[126] O'Hara, 'Grubby Game', 140.
[127] O'Hara, 'Grubby Game', 142.

Russia to Turkey under the Brest-Litovsk treaty of 1918. It, together with the railway to Baku, was occupied by the British at the end of the War. Curzon wanted Batum to become a free port, despite the competing claims of the nationalists in Georgia and the Bolsheviks in Russia. Britain would control the railway, while the Baku oilfields would be held for the international community under a British protectorate. For Curzon, the 'idea that the [Azerbaijanis], the Armenians, or the Bolsheviks, or any other party could permanently hold Baku and control the vast resources there is one that cannot be entertained for a moment'.[128]

There were, then, a series of reasons why colonial imperialism could be urged for the region to which Mackinder went on mission: the region was integral to the defence of India, it was at danger of annexation to the evil empire of Bolshevism, and it was the repository of resources vital to British economic development and military security. With varying emphases, these were the main points in the imperialist views of Curzon, Churchill, and Mackinder. Yet, British troops were withdrawn, military assistance stopped, and Britain saw the anti-Bolshevik forces collapse. Within two years, commercial relations with the Soviet regime had been re-established and Russia turned its attention to consolidating its new economic system.

Liberal Imperialism

Although the British withdrew their military support for the anti-Bolshevik forces, the Cabinet did not do so out of unqualified respect for the principle of non-interference. Instead, it set out rather different grounds for military intervention than were still being urged by Curzon and Churchill. I believe that this alternative, framed in terms of the needs of the Russian people themselves rather than for more selfish British purposes, anticipates and illustrates some of the dangers of the current strategy of humanitarian interventionism. As I described in the Introduction, Liberal Imperialism outlined a set of principles of good governance which if practised would earn a state the right to be left alone, but where violated would invite the intervention of more liberal states justified in replacing a government that was failing its subjects. Countries were invited to join an international system of states by meeting certain minimum standards: providing physical security (including food and shelter) to the people they claimed as subjects or citizens; respecting the autonomy of other states; and upholding democracy within their borders.

The transition between Colonial Imperialism and Liberal Imperialism needs to be understood in terms of the economic arguments against Colonial Imperialism and the political arguments in favour of Liberal Imperialism. The naval historian, Paul Kennedy, has suggested that empires overreach themselves; in other words, that there are economic limits to Colonial

---

[128] Ullman, *Anglo-Soviet Relations*, 68.

Imperialism.[129] Imperial space must ever incorporate more to protect what it has. In doing so, empires sink under the weight of their military spending, while rivals develop leaner, fitter economies based on new technologies that the behemoth has neither the incentive nor the resources to adopt. The ways that empires can be made profitable, and to which sectors of society, is a complex story. Certainly, Hobson (see Chapter 5) understood the dangers of assuming that imperialism expressed a single national interest rather than being a policy with divergent costs and benefits for different classes and interest groups. Asserting that there was a clear and unified national interest was all too often a way of presenting a purely sectional interest as incontrovertibly of universal benefit. The concept of imperial overreach implies that the balance of private benefit over public cost becomes so evident as to affect foreign policy directly, and this I think becomes apparent in both economic and ideological terms.

The debate over Mackinder's mission illustrated three central features of the political economy of British imperialism that indicated imperial overreach. In the first place, the dialectic between militarized-free-trade and militarized-protection was never resolved decisively in favour of either pole so that both retained advocates, more or less vocal at various times. Secondly, anti-colonial nationalism challenged the British hold on what they had already claimed as their Empire. Some of the American colonies had rebelled successfully in 1776. Ireland had tried and failed in 1798. At the time of Mackinder's mission there were active nationalist rebellions in Ireland and in Egypt, and there was a nationalist mass movement in India. The settler colonies of the Empire were gradually claiming greater autonomy as dominions, after, in the case of South Africa, armed rebellion.

Finally, the First World War was an exceptional moment of colonial imperialism: troops were conscripted, territories were occupied, and domestic criticism of foreign policy silenced as treason. Chapter 4 showed the ways that the Empire gave scope for a masculinized exercise of force and I noted the pleasures that this afforded. The Great War was a heightened moment of force-politics for ultra-imperialists such as Churchill. At the depths of the disaster at Gallipoli, for which many (unfairly) held him personally and solely responsible, Churchill confided to an intimate: 'I think a curse should rest on me because I am so happy. I know this war is smashing and shattering the lives of thousands every moment—and yet—I cannot help it—I enjoy every second I live'.[130] However, this force-politics could not long survive the rebirth of domestic politics, the end of conscription, the process of demobilization, and the consequent vacation of foreign bases. The British public were weary of war and there were mutinies and ill-discipline in both the army and navy. Many British sympathized with the socialists in Russia, with some

---

[129] Kennedy, *Rise and Fall.*
[130] Fromkin, *Peace,* 135.

dockers refusing to load armaments onto ships bringing them to the anti-Bolshevik forces in Russia.

Lloyd George, with devious skill, put Churchill in charge of demobilization and held him to the task. Of course, the abandonment of force-politics frustrated Churchill and, after the carnage of the War, he could still address Lloyd George about the folly of not throwing more troops into Russia:

Half hearted war is being followed by half hearted peace. We are going I fear to lose both! [and] be left quite alone. There is much to be said for a comprehensive arrangement providing for all interests, viz. Poles, Wrangel, Russians, our eastern interests simultaneously. But we are just crumbling our power away. Before long we shall not have a single card in our hands.[131]

At the end of the war in November 1918, the daily rate of British military expenditure was over £4 million and a year later it was down to £1 million per day.[132] Within a year of the end of the war, Churchill had overseen the demobilization of almost all the 4 million conscripted soldiers and had recruited a new, smaller, 'volunteer Regular Army to guard our Empire'.[133] The military aid to the anti-Bolshevik forces had probably cost over £100 million by this point.[134] From the date of the Armistice until the final defeat of the Volunteer Army in mid-July 1920, the Russian adventure cost the British perhaps £63 million.[135] In comparison, between the end of the War and mid-July 1921, the British spent £150 million on armed forces in the Middle East.[136] An Afghan incursion into India in May 1919 cost the British Government of India about £15 million to eject.[137] The First World War had drawn the British into many more places than they could afford to hold, particularly in the face of nationalist challenges that spread on evidence of British demobilization and war-weariness.

In one sense, the practise of imperialism now had to be selective; this was the economic argument for Liberal Imperialism. By April 1919, the Chief of the Imperial General Staff, Henry Wilson, had been already anxious to withdraw British troops from all theatres of war in order that they might be concentrated in India, Ireland, Egypt, and Britain.[138] Resource wars, anti-Bolshevism, and the grand imperial arc, were less important to him than defeating anti-colonial nationalism abroad and fighting the class-warfare of a General Strike at home. He wanted to pick his fights and not engage at every point where British economic or ideological interests were in question. This was imposed upon by him by the need to cut his military suit to the cloth

---

[131] Churchill to Lloyd George, Bonar Law, and Balfour, 1 July 1920, CHAR 16/48A, f. 2.

[132] Memorandum of 15 October 1919, CHAR 16/12, f. 136.

[133] Churchill to Lloyd George, 15 October 1919, CHAR 16/12, f. 142.

[134] Kinvig, *Churchill's Crusade*, 316. Perhaps three-quarters of this total refers to expenditure before the Armistice.

[135] Ullman, *Anglo-Soviet Relations*, Appendix.

[136] Fromkin, *Peace*, 470. This excludes secret bribes.

[137] Fromkin, *Peace*, 422.

[138] Macmillan, *Peacemakers*, 415.

bought at acceptable levels of taxation. The anti-Bolshevik crusade was abandoned because, as the Cabinet concluded, 'we have neither the men, the money, nor the credit, and public opinion is altogether opposed to such a course'.[139]

An alternative policy, the political case for Liberal Imperialism, was then set out:

There can be no question of entering into Peace negotiations with the Bolsheviks until they have demonstrated their capacity to conduct an orderly, decent administration in their own country and their intention not to interfere, by propaganda or otherwise, in the affairs of their neighbours, nor until they can show that they represent the governing authority of the areas for which they claim to speak. A hint might be given to the Bolsheviks in a public speech that when they have accomplished this, and only then, should we be prepared to treat with them.[140]

This was an important formulation of a style and justification for intervening in the affairs of other nations that I described in the Introduction as Liberal Imperialism. By being asked to show 'orderly, decent administration', the Bolsheviks were being asked to feed, house, and keep safe the Russian people. I infer these requirements from the terms in which politicians spoke about the breakdown of civilization in Russia although, of course, the list could be extended. The Bolsheviks were also enjoined to respect the auton-omy of other states by giving up their project of exporting or supporting revolutions abroad. Already, in 1920, the Bolsheviks were sending military aid to Turkey in what they claimed as an anti-colonial (because anti-British) struggle. Finally, Bolsheviks were asked to submit their legitimacy to some sort of test to justify a claim to representativeness, that is, they were required to accept the discipline of democracy.

Meeting the three principles of adequate governance, non-interference, and democracy would justify diplomatic recognition from the British gov-ernment and thus implicitly from the community of mutually acceptable liberal states. While imperial overreach was central to the reluctance to act on Mackinder's report and the earlier associated injunctions of both Curzon and Churchill, we can understand Lloyd George directing Mackinder's mission as one to reshape South Russia in this liberal image of good govern-ance, the better perhaps to present Denikin as controlling a region deserving of separate recognition. Certainly, these three principles evaluated how a regime served its people and respected its neighbours, rather than asking how it fitted into a colonial scheme of British imperial interests. As much as they may have represented a threat to others, on this reading, outlaw states were those that failed their own people. Of course, Russia did not submit to these tests and was treated as an international pariah for three-quarters of a century.

[139] 'Conclusions of Meeting of Cabinet', 29 November 1919, f. 68.
[140] 'Conclusions of Meeting of Cabinet', 29 November 1919, f. 68.

The Dialectic of Colonial and Liberal Imperialism

As outlined in the Introduction, Colonial and Liberal Imperialism are two contrasting moments within imperialism. In schematic terms, we might say that colonial imperialism justifies intervention on the basis of the interests of the metropole, whereas liberal imperialism rests upon assertions about the domestic needs of the periphery. The first can be very expensive and the interventions range from rich states pressuring poorer states (withdrawing embassy staff, suspending grants, refusing entry visas to citizens and even government officials, expelling states from international fora) on behalf of citizens and companies from the rich countries, to military intervention displacing regimes considered unfriendly to the national interests of the rich country.

Liberal Imperialism can be equally as brutal as Colonial Imperialism, but it disavows self-interest, seeking to install well-managed states and presenting its primary constituency as the people held captive by rogue regimes. It can appeal to international standards, and even cooperation. After 1919, faced with the costs of direct rule and regime change, the British pursued a range of options to meet the economic dangers of imperial overreach. They failed in Russia but in much of the Middle East they managed to shape regimes of indirect rule whereby the property arrangements suited British business interests and the political arrangements were sufficiently local to meet a minimal standard of representativeness. Alongside this, Churchill installed air force bases in the region and hoped to rely upon aerial bombing to provide a cheap and mobile response to local insurgency. Having gassed the Bolsheviks, the British also bombed Afghan and Iraqi villages, delighted with the panic produced by a weapon that could eliminate two-fifths of the population in under half-an-hour and at no appreciable risk to the aggressor.[141] Why govern when you can rule? Why invade if you can bomb?

The echoes today of Colonial and Liberal Imperialism are very strong indeed.[142] There are evident similarities between the three colonial–imperialist policies (strategic integrity of empire, anti-Communism, and resource wars) and debates today about foreign influence in the very same region to which Mackinder was sent. There are estimated to be 540,076 troops maintained outside the countries to which they owe allegiance, and the United States accounts for about three of every four such foreign-based troops.[143] While many US troops remain 'where they happened to be when the last war stopped', explaining the high presence in Europe and Korea, from 2002 the Pentagon began a Global Force Posture Review that planned the redeploy-

---

[141] On using gas in Iraq in 1920, see: Simons, *Iraq*, 179–81. On the cheap terror tactic of bombing villages in Iraq in 1917 and in the 1920s, see: Lindqvist, 'Bombing the Savages'.

[142] See the discussion of the similarities between the policies of the British in Iraq in the 1920s and of the United States in Iraq today, in: Dodge, *Inventing Iraq*.

[143] 'World Wide Military Deployments'.

ment of US commitments in line with the perceived strategic demands of the so-called Global War on Terror.[144] The first stage of the new global conflict, the war in Afghanistan had:

[S]ubstantially altered the importance in US military planning of the southern regions of the former Soviet Union. [. . .] The former Central Asian republics, in particular Uzbekistan, became crucial for the basing of troops, for intelligence and for humanitarian cooperation. The South Caucasus states, chiefly Georgia and Azerbaijan, were equally vital for logistical reasons: their airspace was the only realistic route through which military aircraft could be deployed from NATO territory to Afghanistan.[145]

The United States now pursues, with mixed success, a strategy of maintaining bare-bones bases, or 'lily pads' in the ironic innocence of military-speak, in as many of the countries of the Caspian Basin as it is able to arrange these facilities; it was, for example, ejected from Uzbekistan in 2005 and had to pay a dramatically increased price to remain in Kyrgystan in the same year.[146]

Similarly, the same region is at the forefront of US efforts to prevent the spread of terrorist networks associated with the Taliban or with Muslim insurgency more generally; anti-Islamism being the modern parallel to the earlier anti-Communism. In this respect, the United States wants secure and friendly regimes throughout the region and it sees oil and gas revenues as the basis for such domestic stability.[147]

In similar fashion, the case made today for humanitarian intervention recalls in striking manner the policy prescriptions that I have described as Liberal Imperialism. The aim appears to be to make universal a broadly liberal form of statehood and it is very easy to see how this liberal template might be cut to stamp out copies of the ideal-typical bourgeois-capitalist political and economic order. Reviewing the current vogue for humanitarian intervention, the Marxist historian, Ellen Meiksins Wood, claims that 'subordinate economies must be made and kept vulnerable to economic manipulation by capital and the capitalist market'.[148] The international community can take upon itself the responsibility to determine that a state provides good, decent administration. In economic terms, though, this means that its internal arrangements are compared to an ideal type that would allow wealth, happiness, and the pursuit of liberty. These issues remain salient and the next chapter explores some of the pertinent echoes of this dialectic between Colonial and Liberal Imperialism as they have shaped debates over international relations since the end of the Cold War.

---

[144] Campbell and Johnson Ward, 'New Battle Stations?', 96.
[145] Cornell, 'US and Central Asia', 239.
[146] Cooley, 'US Bases and Democratization'.
[147] Myers Jaffe and Soligo, 'Re-evaluating US Strategic Priorities'.
[148] Meiksins Wood, *Empire of Capital*, 21. This is discussed further in Chapter 8.

8

Conservative Geopolitics

In July 2007, Senator Barack Obama (b. 1961), then candidate for the Democratic presidential nomination, set out his thoughts on foreign policy. Like other candidates, he urged the United States to show diplomatic leadership by pressing for political solutions in Iraq and elsewhere in the Middle East. He also argued for committing troops to end genocide in Darfur, and cooperating with Russia to prevent nuclear weapons from falling into terrorist hands.[1] Obama's team of advisers initially included younger staff, some of whom had worked previously with President Bill Clinton or with Senator Hillary Clinton (b. 1947) (as she prepared her own bid for the Democratic presidential nomination), but would later include more established figures, perhaps in response to criticisms of his team's relative lack of experience.[2] In August 2007, Obama received the endorsement of Zbigniew Brzezinski (b. 1928), former national security adviser to President Jimmy Carter (1977–81), 'a paragon of foreign policy eminence', at least to the *Washington Post*.[3] In turning to Brzezinski, Obama called upon one of the foremost among the modern thinkers who echo Mackinder's geopolitical imagination.

In his articles and books, Brzezinski occasionally cites Mackinder directly and more often refers to similar themes indirectly.[4] In particular, Brzezinski emphasizes the dangers of an interconnected world, the threat of any single power controlling the Eurasian land mass, the strategic control of resources in locations in the South Caucasus and Caspian Basin, and the risks posed by an expansionist Russia—the most likely candidate for imperial status in Eurasia. Brzezinski's has long been a closed-space perspective. In 1971, he wrote that 'time and space have become so compressed' that 'proximity, instead of promoting unity, gives rise to tensions prompted by a new sense of global congestion'.[5] In this context, there needed to be a 'community of the developed nations' under the leadership of the United States to prevent poorer countries from exploiting nationalistic divisions and thereby gaining

---

[1] Obama, 'Renewing American Leadership'.

[2] King, 'Obama Tones Foreign-Policy Muscle'; J. Newton-Small, 'Obama's Foreign-Policy Problem'.

[3] MacGillis, 'Brzezinski Backs Obama'.

[4] In June 2001, Brzezinski gave a talk on 'Geopolitical Thinking and the Modern World' to the US-based Mackinder Forum (see Chapter 9); 'Mackinder Forum. Earlier Meetings'.

[5] Brzezinski, *Between Two Ages*, 3.

protectionist benefits, or communist states from insinuating ideological divisions within the cadre of modern states.[6] This coalition of developed nations from North America, Western Europe, and Japan would offer modern, or US, leadership and inspiration to the rest of the world. As Brzezinski reflected: 'John Kennedy caught the essence of America's novel position in the world when he saw himself as "the first American president for whom the whole world was, in a sense, domestic politics" '.[7] In 1973, a Trilateral Commission along the lines Brzezinski suggested was established by the international financier, and Chair of Chase-Manhattan Bank, David Rockefeller, who installed Brzezinski as Director.[8] Jimmy Carter was invited to join the 300-strong Commission of the rich, influential, and powerful, which worked to their mutual benefit when Carter was elected US President. As the socialist scholar of international relations, Noam Chomsky, observed in 1981:

All of the top positions in the government—the office of President [Carter], Vice-President [Walter Mondale], Secretary of State [Cyrus Vance], Defense [Harold Brown] and Treasury [Michael Blumenthal]—are held by members of the Trilateral Commission, and the National Security Advisor [Brzezinski] was its director. Many lesser officials also came from this group. It is rare for such an easily identified private group to play such a prominent role in an American Administration.[9]

Brzezinski was almost obsessive in his goal of preventing Soviet control of critical resources in Eurasia. In July 1979, Carter, advised by Brzezinski, began secret aid to the anti-Soviet forces in Afghanistan, the Mujahideen.[10] This drew the Soviet army into Afghanistan, which Brzezinski defended as 'the chance to give the Soviet Union its own Vietnam War'.[11] In January 1980, one month after the Soviets entered Afghanistan, and six months after the United States had intervened covertly, Jimmy Carter claimed that the Soviet involvement in Afghanistan was a threat to American security:

The region which is now threatened by Soviet troops in Afghanistan is of great strategic importance: It contains more than two-thirds of the world's exportable oil. The Soviet effort to dominate Afghanistan has brought Soviet military forces to within 300 miles of the Indian Ocean and close to the Straits of Hormuz, a waterway through which most of the world's oil must flow. The Soviet Union is now attempting to consolidate a strategic position, therefore, that poses a grave threat to the free movement of Middle East oil.[12]

[6] Brzezinski, *Between Two Ages*, 296.
[7] Brzezinski, ibid., 307.
[8] Sklar, *Trilateralism*.
[9] Chomsky, *Radical Priorities*, 158.
[10] Blum, *Killing Hope*.
[11] '[L]'occasion de donner à l'URSS sa guerre du Vietnam'; Jauvert, 'Les révélations'. The English language edition of *Le Nouvel Observateur* did not include this interview.
[12] Carter, 'State of the Union'.

This recalls the discussion in Chapter 7 of the territorial imagination of Curzon who described a set of geographical connections that extended the defence of India back to the Eastern Mediterranean. For Brzezinski, the continuity was explicit. In a memorandum to Carter that followed immediately on the heels of the Soviet invasion he warned:

If the Soviets succeed in Afghanistan, and [text censored] the age-long dream of Moscow to have direct access to the Indian Ocean will have been fulfilled.

Historically, the British provided the barrier to that drive, and Afghanistan was their buffer state. We assumed the role in 1945, but the Iranian crisis has led to the collapse of the balance of power in Southwest Asia, and it could produce Soviet presence right down on the edge of the Arabian and Oman gulfs.[13]

In fact, Brzezinski and Carter hoped that, mired in Afghanistan in the medium term, the Soviets would be kept out of the so-called Middle East, allowing the United States to deal alone with the Islamic Revolution in Iran (February 1979). Ultimately, the Soviet Union was contained but the Islamic Revolution was not. In 1998, with hindsight, Brzezinski was still happy with the result: 'the collapse of the Soviet Empire', albeit at the price of creating a few 'stirred up Muslims', the Taliban, which he thought an overrated threat because 'there is no global Islamism'.[14]

The political scientist, Stephen Walt, has noted that '[t]he goal of preventing Soviet expansion reflects the traditional US interest in preventing any single power from controlling the combined resources of the Eurasia landmass'.[15] Indeed, Brzezinski explicitly evoked Mackinder in describing this goal in his 1986 book, *Game Plan: The Geostrategic Framework for the Conduct of the US–Soviet Contest*: 'Whoever controls Eurasia dominates the globe. If the Soviet Union captures the peripheries of this landmass [...] it would not only win control of vast human, economic and military resources, but also gain access to the geostrategic approaches to the Western Hemisphere—the Atlantic and the Pacific'.[16] He described the Cold War as, '[g]eopolitically, [a] struggle [...] for control over the Eurasian landmass'.[17] Reviewing the state of the world towards the end of the Cold War, Brzezinski was sure that '[i]t is most improbable that a grand American-Soviet accommodation can take place. The interests of the two sides are simply too conflicting. The notion of a global US-Soviet partnership for peace and development is even more illusory'.[18] With the end of the Cold War, when Brzezinski's containment strategy appeared less necessary, he nevertheless did not waver, arguing in 1997 that, '[i]n a volatile Eurasia, the immediate

[13] Brzezinski, 'Memo to President'.

[14] '[L]'éclatement de l'empire soviétique'; '[q]uelques excités islamistes'; 'il n'y a pas d'islamisme global'; Jauvert, 'Les révélations'.

[15] Walt, 'Case for Finite Containment', 9.

[16] Brzezinski, *Game Plan*, 22–3.

[17] Brzezinski, 'Cold War', 31.

[18] Brzezinski, 'America's New Geostrategy', 695.

task is to ensure that no state or combination of states gains the ability to expel the United States or even diminish its decisive role'.[19] In terms that again recalled Mackinder, he asserted that 'Europe is America's essential geopolitical bridgehead in Eurasia'.[20] While he suggested that geopoliticians such as Mackinder had been concerned with two questions that were no longer relevant—whether land- or sea-power was the most powerful, and which part of the Eurasian land mass was the most effective springboard for global domination—the geostrategic issue of the modern world was whether the United States could resist the rise of a consolidated power controlling the Eurasian landmass, 'for it is on the globe's most important playing field—Eurasia—that a potential rival to America might at some point arise. Thus, focusing on the key players and properly assessing the terrain has to be the point of departure for the formulation of American geostrategy for the long-term management of America's geopolitical interests'.[21]

Both Mackinder and Curzon would have recognized many features of Brzezinski's analysis of the flashpoints of the Eurasian geopolitical theatre. Even the title of one of Brzezinski's books, *The Grand Chessboard: American Primacy and its Geostrategic Imperatives* (1997), is an explicit echo of Curzon. Brzezinski's aim has been to prolong American global dominance by accepting the 'three grand imperatives of imperial geostrategy', which he glosses as the need 'to prevent collusion and maintain security dependence among the vassals, to keep tributaries pliant and protected, and to keep the barbarians from coming together'.[22] It is not clear if Azerbaijan is a vassal, a tributary, or a barbarian, but Brzezinski describes its significance in terms that could have been taken directly from Mackinder:

Azerbaijan's vulnerability has wider regional implications because the country's location makes it a geopolitical pivot. It can be described as the vitally important 'cork' controlling access to the 'bottle' that contains the riches of the Caspian Sea basin and Central Asia. An independent, Turkic-speaking Azerbaijan, with pipelines running from it to the ethnically related and politically supportive Turkey, would prevent Russia from exercising a monopoly on access to the region and would thus also deprive Russia of decisive political leverage over the policies of the new Central Asian states.[23]

I consider perspectives such as Brzezinski's 'Conservative Geopolitics', and in this chapter analyse modern conservative geopolitical thinkers, who cite directly, or indirectly echo, Mackinder's geopolitical imagination. Conservative Geopolitics frames the global order in terms of the territorial arrangement of friendly and hostile states; defines international relations as the use of power (asserted, deployed, or devalued) between competing states; and seeks to perpetuate existing global inequalities. These perspectives not only

---

[19] Brzezinski, 'Geostrategy for Eurasia', 52.   [20] Brzezinski, 'Geostrategy for Eurasia', 53.
[21] Brzezinski, *Grand Chessboard*, 39.   [22] Brzezinski, *Grand Chessboard*, 40.
[23] Brzezinski, ibid., 129.

influenced global political and economic strategies during the Cold War, they continue to mark the current so-called Global War on Terror (Chapter 1) and even the younger generation's calls for changes in foreign policy. Indeed, this is the context in which to read Obama's promise to preserve 'American leadership' in the world, a phrase that recalls both in his language and in argument Brzezinski's own *The Choice: Global Domination or Global Leadership* (2004).[24] During the last days of his campaign to secure the Democratic nomination, Obama stressed his continuity with earlier US policy. He identified himself with the general US strategy of rolling back Communism, for example, by meeting the Cuban American National Foundation in Miami (23 May 2008), when, despite having argued in 2004 that the US embargo against Cuba was not working and talking ever since of ways to lift it selectively, he reassured his audience: 'Don't be confused about this. I will maintain the embargo. It provides us with the leverage to present the regime with a clear choice: If you take significant steps toward democracy, beginning with the freeing of all political prisoners, we will take steps to begin normalizing relations'.[25] He then went to Chicago to the American Israel Public Affairs Committee (4 June 2008), promising a significantly conservative stance in supporting Israel: 'Israel's security is sacrosanct. It is non-negotiable. The Palestinians need a state that is contiguous and cohesive, and that allows them to prosper—but any agreement with the Palestinian people must preserve Israel's identity as a Jewish state, with secure, recognized and defensible borders. Jerusalem will remain the capital of Israel, and it must remain undivided'.[26]

Within US foreign policy circles, there remain, of course, virile debates about the geostrategic status of Russia, the Caspian Basin, the Persian Gulf, Cuba, and Israel, but the echoes of Mackinder that I have noted in Brzezinski extend to a wide swathe of current opinion. I call this common ground Conservative Geopolitics because it seeks to preserve existing global inequalities. The collapse of the Soviet Union left the United States alone as a global superpower, and the Neo-conservatives want to prolong that '"unipolar moment" into a unipolar era'.[27] This project requires abridging the sovereignty of other states (US leadership is an offer they cannot refuse) and is thus imperialist. In this and the following chapter, I argue that insofar as Geopolitics serves this cause of imperialism it is conservative; where it serves instead to question or redress these inequalities it is progressive.[28]

---

[24] Brzezinski, *Choice*.

[25] Zeleny, 'Obama, in Miami'.

[26] Obama, 'Remarks at AIPAC'.

[27] Kristol and Kagan, 'National Interest', 57; quoting Krauthammer, 'Unipolar Moment'.

[28] My use of the terms 'conservative' and 'progressive' parallels Edmund Carr's distinction between 'status quo' and 'revisionist' powers in international relations: Carr, *Twenty Years' Crisis*, 191.

This chapter draws together those aspects of Mackinder's geopolitics echoed in modern debates. Although there is little evidence that all of the authors cited here have read Mackinder's work, there remains the indirect influence through earlier thinkers such as Spykman who did. There is also the striking fact that when strategists use territorial logic to promote or maintain global hegemony many of Mackinder's motifs surface, because, I would suggest, these spatial metaphors provide a very effective way to make imperialism seem unavoidable, even natural. As I demonstrate, present-day parallels with Mackinder extend not only to geostrategies focused upon the Eurasian Heartland and the need to contain Russia, but modern Conservative Geopolitics comprehends also more fundamental elements of the geopolitical imaginary, including a view of the world as containing incompatible civilizations, hostile states, intense spatial integration, political anarchy, and relentless conflict (see Chapter 3). In other words, modern writers conceive the world as containing more or less the same sorts of forces, threats, and opportunities that Mackinder outlined in his writings and enacted through his deeds.

This chapter enumerates five central themes of Conservative Geopolitics by briefly recapitulating the main themes of Mackinder's work, and then documenting the fealty of modern politicians, think tanks, and public intellectuals to these basic premises. The main themes framing Mackinder's geopolitical imaginary that recur in the Conservative Geopolitics of today include: the novelty of intense global interconnectedness; the incompatibility of the aspirations of people in different parts of the world; the idea that the international political and economic system is essentially a competitive zero-sum game; the distinctiveness of land- and sea-power; and, finally, the tension between colonial and liberal versions of imperialism. I end this chapter by relating Conservative Geopolitics to the cause of Empire.[29] Yet throughout this book, I have also identified contemporaries of Mackinder who saw the world very differently, highlighting the contested nature of geopolitical discourses. From a critical engagement with these alternative historical visions and considering possible lessons from their work for the present day, I will sketch in the next chapter a prospectus for a Progressive Geopolitics.

Themes and Echoes: Mackinder's Geopolitical Discourse

Mackinder argued that the world system had essentially been closed by the conclusion of the territorial acquisitions of the European and North American powers (Chapter 5). This novel circumstance meant that competition

---

[29] I set out some of these arguments in an earlier article: Kearns, 'Naturalising Empire'.

between Great Powers could no longer be dispersed into empty spaces beyond Europe and now would have to take place in already existing imperial territories. This was a closed-space world, in which events in any one part of the world would have global ramifications. The interconnectedness of this new world gave each state a national self-interest in the affairs of every other part of the world; national strategy was now perforce global. Changes in the alignment of polities or economies in any place, howsoever remote, had direct consequences for the balance of power and prosperity. Although the novelty of the situation might hide its urgency for a time, Mackinder argued that national statecraft would have to assume international responsibilities in a more intensive way than before. As described in Chapter 6, Mackinder thought that these new truths also had to be taught to the whole nation, from schoolchild to premier. His Geography was an Imperial Education.

Not everyone else in the world shared British values, however. Other peoples might even threaten what the British held dear—not only their prosperity, but more vitally, their freedom. There was, in Mackinder's view, a fundamental incompatibility of peoples and, as explained in Chapter 3, Mackinder understood these differences primarily in racial terms. Mackinder believed that races were immutable in the short term and that they determined culture and attitudes; people could no more choose their race, and thus their values, than they could their parents. Mackinder saw the races as ordered hierarchically, there was no relativism of difference. Moreover, he worried that racial contact weakened the superior race. He understood the races to be naturally and continually in struggle.

In terms of the Great Powers, he identified a conflict between what he variously described as the British or the Anglo-Saxon on one side, and its main rivals on the other, namely, the races that could conceivably control the heartland, the Teuton (Germany) and the Slav (Russian). Races were, for Mackinder, relatively stable identities that grew out of the long-term shaping of personality by environment. The Slavs, for example, were products of the vast open steppes, and, as a people, followed strong leaders and tended towards authoritarianism. The Teutons, although stemming from similar racial stock to the British, never enjoyed the environmental advantage of insularity and retained an expansionary drive that set at nought the democratic rights of rivals. The British, in contrast, gave up expansionary ambitions once they had colonized their own island, whereupon they developed self-governance and non-interference in the affairs of powerful continental neighbours. Beyond this, Mackinder saw also a range of peoples with little chance of challenging the Teuton or Slav for control of the Heartland (see Chapter 5), and thus no chance of controlling the World Island or threatening the prosperity and liberty of the British. As Chapter 6 described, these other peoples were seen by Mackinder as arranged in a hierarchy of civilizations, and thus of human worth, from the lowliest savages of jungle or desert, to the atrophied civilizations of Asia. None of these peoples, he argued, had a capacity for self-government in the short term, and it was the duty of the British to introduce among them democratic, rather than authoritarian Teuton or Slav, rule.

Mackinder believed that only the British race, its offshoots in the British Dominions, and its former colonies of the United States embraced the values of democracy and non-interference. The challengers to British and American hegemony would have to be resisted. Their every attempt to extend their own territory, and thus resources, must be countered. Mackinder envisioned a geopolitical world maintained by force; international relations were a zero-sum competition. Chapter 3 described the Evolutionary Biology that Mackinder invoked in defence of this view of the world, one structured by a struggle for survival between races, or between their state-proxies. Chapter 4 described how this inter-imperial competition drew upon contemporary notions of masculinity, and suggested that the racial difference between metropole and colony allowed the latter to serve as a sphere of hyper-masculinity. The colony was a stage for manly endeavours. In the metropole, both women's resistance to patriarchy and the impossibility of the demands that ideals of masculinity placed upon subjects created a crisis of masculinity. For some, this crisis could be addressed by projecting masculine force into colonial spaces as both test and expression of manliness. Thus, Mackinder understood Empire as a spectacle of geopolitical force and manliness, qualities essential for avoiding feminized thraldom.

In this international force-field, the struggle between democracy and authoritarianism mapped also onto a distinction between the modalities of sea-power and those of land-power (Chapter 5). Mackinder proposed that, in territorial terms, and in competition with land-power, sea-power was essentially defensive; it could not take and hold any significant territory on a distant continent. In contrast, land-power was territorially aggressive and operated by expansion, taking in new countries at its margins. Land-powers competed with each other to establish territorial hegemony. In the case of the Eurasian land mass, a struggle for the control of the Heartland was sure to ensue, for this region was a basket of resources immune to naval attack and capable of sustaining control over the World Island.

In his efforts as British High Commissioner, Mackinder drew not only upon his own geopolitical world view, he also engaged with different sets of justifications for imperialism. Yet his actions in the political realm demonstrated the tension between colonial and liberal forms of imperialism. Chapter 7 described the agendas of Churchill, Curzon, and Lloyd George to which Mackinder was servant during his brief career as the British High Commissioner to South Russia. As colonial imperialists, Churchill and Curzon justified military interventions as building British influence to serve the needs of the British people and their Empire. In broad terms, Colonial

Imperialism abrogated the sovereignty of foreign peoples to serve the needs of the people of the metropole. Mackinder, working with Curzon, stressed both the importance of wars over foreign resources vital to British prosperity, and the necessity of strategic military interventions to safeguard the integrity of the British Empire. Like Churchill, Mackinder was a fierce opponent of Bolshevism, stressing that Bolshevik Communism was a threat well beyond Russian borders. To suppress working-class politics at home, communism in Russia had also to be put down. The three dimensions of Colonial Imperialism found in Curzon and Churchill, then, were: a plea for establishing control over foreign territories holding valuable resources; an emphasis upon the geostrategic dimensions of national defence as including influence in foreign parts; and an argument that certain ideologies represent such clear and present danger that regimes espousing them should be deposed. These justifications in terms of resources, influence, and ideology made up the Colonial Imperialist dimensions of Mackinder's Geopolitics.

However, Mackinder was made very aware of a rather different set of arguments about the cause of Empire; supporters of this alternative, Liberal Imperialism, argued that Colonial Imperialism might overreach itself and that Britain might not be able to afford the selfish agendas of Curzon and Churchill. Lloyd George tried to justify interference in foreign parts as serving the best interests of local people suffering under oppressive, ineffective, or aggressive rule. While liberal imperialists, such as Lloyd George, restated many of the interests expressed by colonial imperialists, they used the rather different language of fair governance. Rather than justify resource wars, for example, liberal imperialists argued that a decently run economy would serve its people best by allowing foreign capital to assist in the development of national resources. Moreover, for a state to become a recognized sovereign member of the international society of states, it must show that it harboured no aggressive intentions towards other states. In other words, the well-managed state would pose no threat to its neighbours and thus not endanger the set of alliances upon which the existing global order was based. Rather than seeking to unseat regimes that practised the unfreedoms of collective ownership, liberal imperialists asked only that each regime subject itself to popular legitimation through fair elections conducted by debate through a free, privately owned, press. Liberal imperialists retained a right of intervention where these three tests were not met. In practice, therefore, Liberal Imperialism could justify interventions in a very wide range of contexts but, by shifting the stated purpose from the needs of the metropole to those of putative colony; it appealed to a higher purpose than grubby self-interest. In cutting their colonial suit to the national-economic cloth available, liberal imperialists made Empire more sustainable than under the adventurous Colonial Imperialist agenda.

One World

Modern echoes of these five themes—one world, hostile peoples, enduring conflict, land- and sea-power, and tensions between colonialisms—exist in the writings of a number of influential politicians, think-tank spokespersons, and academics. Today, interconnectedness is called globalization and the journalist, Thomas Friedman's, claim that *The World is Flat* (2005) is one notorious variant. Friedman suggests that since 2000, the Internet has given individuals an opportunity to engage with the rest of the world from any-where on the earth, thereby lifting the latch of national borders.[30] Other authors similarly argue that the political consequences of interconnectedness promote the breakdown of state autonomy, and hence, the collapse of a world order based on sovereign nation states.[31] The assumption that states should respect each other's right to order their internal affairs in whatever way they saw fit was at the heart of what many call the Westphalian world order. In the wake of the deadly Thirty Years War, the Peace of Westphalia (1648) included an agreement on the part of their Emperor that the princi-palities of the Holy Roman Empire would each be allowed to choose their own state religion; Catholicism would not be imposed. This arrangement incorporated, tacitly at least, the majority of European states in the following centuries. Religious difference was too dangerous and absolute to be allowed military expression within Europe.

The Marxist philosophers, Michael Hardt and Antonio Negri, in their acclaimed book *Empire* (2000), adopt this perspective, insisting that 'the notion of international order that European modernity continually proposed and re-proposed, at least since the Peace of Westphalia, is now in crisis' as a result of economic globalization.[32] In turn, they suggest that globalization is a consequence of two political developments: the end both of formal coloni-alism and of the Cold War. Hardt and Negri propose that the waning of the system of nation states has brought a new form of sovereignty that, unlike the United Nations, does not rest upon states for its implementation. We have now, they suggest, a global order that anticipates its own supranational government through collective policing practices—invoking ' "just wars" at the borders against the barbarians and internally against the rebellious'— rather than an international system reaching towards a supranational gov-ernment.[33] Hardt and Negri call this new global sovereignty, Empire.

Although Hardt and Negri call out to forces (their 'Multitude') resisting this new Empire, others argue that these policing actions work in the name of the very world order of nation states that Hardt and Negri claim is passing away. Robert Cooper, for example, welcomes 'a new kind of imperialism,

---

[30] Friedman, *The World is Flat*.   [31] Rosecrance and Stein, *No More States?*.
[32] Hardt and Negri, *Empire*, 4.   [33] Hardt and Negri, *Empire*, 10.

one acceptable to a world of human rights and cosmopolitan values'.[34] Cooper has been at times a foreign policy advisor (1999–2001) to Britain's prime minister, Tony Blair, and was earlier head of the Policy Planning Staff at the British Foreign Office (1989–93). He subsequently was appointed as the UK's Special Representative in Afghanistan (2001–2) before taking up the post of Director General for External and Politico-Military Affairs at the General Secretariat of the Council of the European Union. Blair's biographer, Anthony Seldon, suggests that Cooper's views on the terrorist threat from failed states had some influence upon Tony Blair's view of the world. Indeed, Cooper told Seldon that his first account of the distinction between failed, modern, and postmodern states began as 'a memo to Blair'.[35]

Cooper's view of an interconnected world, as articulated in his 2003 book, *The Breaking of Nations: Order and Chaos in the Twenty-First Century*, and his writings in the popular press, shares much with Mackinder's geopolitical imagination. His description of the Ancient World is very similar to the picture Mackinder painted of the pre-Columbian global system: '[i]n the ancient world, order meant empire. Those within the empire had order, culture and civilisation. Outside it lay barbarians, chaos and disorder'.[36] Again like Mackinder, Cooper emphasizes a new shift to a closed-space world; this time described as globalization. There is, he argues, a new interconnectedness: '[i]n an age of globalisation no country is an island. Crises in Kashmir, the Middle East or the Korean Peninsula affect security in every continent and are the concern of everybody'.[37] This interconnectedness is not only new, it is, Cooper argues, dangerous. The security of the West is threatened by the 'chaotic' spaces created when states beyond the Western imperium 'collapse'.[38] For Cooper, these wild spaces harbour fanatical terrorists and unfriendly powers with weapons of mass destruction. Blair said much the same in his most extensive statement of the case for what has come to be called humanitarian interventionism. In Chicago, in April 1999, Blair stated that 'the world has changed in a [. . .] fundamental way' because, due to globalization, national security was now an international matter: '[w]e live in a world where isolationism has ceased to have a reason to exist. [. . .] We cannot turn our backs on conflicts and the violation of human rights in other countries if we want still to be secure'.[39]

Echoing Mackinder's claim that liberal policies suited an historical era that had passed and that a more interventionist national stance suited the new times, Cooper proposes that Western societies now stand at the end of their 'Westphalian Age' (1648–1989) and must adopt a more assertive stance towards the dangers lurking beyond their borders.[40] During the Westphalian Age, suggests Cooper, Europe was organized as a series of nation states that

[34] Cooper, 'Empires'.
[36] Cooper, 'Empires', 27.
[38] Cooper, *Breaking*, 68, 66.
[40] Cooper, ibid., 4.

[35] Seldon, *Blair*, 570; Cooper, *Postmodern State*.
[37] Cooper, ibid., 83.
[39] Blair, 'Economic Club, Chicago'.

ordered the rest of the world as a series of colonies. Now, Western Europe is moving towards a 'post-modern state' wherein several states agree to share sovereignty. At the other extreme, in Africa people struggle to create something resembling strong nation states out of the chaotic soup of post-colonialism, since the end of colonialism left fragmented states, regional war-lords, and endemic civil conflict in an ironic echo of pre-Westphalian Europe.

Implicit in Cooper's account of order and chaos in the twenty-first century, then, is a particular understanding of historical geography, as represented schematically in Figure 8.1. In Antiquity, numerous empires tried to extend their reign to newer places (shown in 8.1a as ovals with expansionary arrows); within empires, order and regularity were the norm and outside there was barbaric chaos. At some point, a modern system of nation states developed in Europe (shown in 8.1b as the grid of squares), and on this basis, the Europeans gradually colonized virtually all the world (the separate European and American empires are shown schematically in 8.1c as distinct territories). In this way, Europeans, by Cooper's account, brought order where once there had been only pre-modern anarchy. After the Second World War, the European powers gradually abandoned their empires; the Cold War structured two rival systems of nation states, one capitalist and one socialist (shown in 8.1d as a divided world). According to Cooper, the Cold War 'froze Europe for forty years'.[41] A postmodern system of states, how-ever, developed in Europe through the European Union (represented in 8.1e as a grid of diamonds), an experiment in pooled sovereignty. While modern states still exist outside of the EU, a dangerous mix of pre-modern (failed), post-colonial, and post-socialist states has emerged beyond these national territories. Cooper would like the modern and post-modern states to adopt sections of these 'wild lands' and offer them the protection of Liberal Im-perialism, or some extension of pooled post-modern sovereignty. In this spirit, 8.1f shows an expanded area of postmodern-pooled-sovereignty states (hatched) and then a series of empires in the rest of the world.

As Figure 8.1 demonstrates, the notion of a radical historical break—Columbian to post-Columbian for Mackinder, Westphalian to post-West-phalian for Cooper—is an important rhetorical device when arguing for a new direction in foreign policy. Cooper argues for a new wave of imperial-ism, like Mackinder, based upon his narration of history. Rather than contest the accuracy of the analyses upon which current practice rests, the positing of a radical historical break implies instead that previous analyses are no longer relevant to the new situation. The end of the Cold War, with the demolition of the Berlin Wall in 1989 and the collapse of the Soviet Union in 1991, was clearly a dramatic and unexpected turn in world events. The Cold War against the Soviet Union had been the main justification for defence budgets in Western Europe and North America; indeed, the end of the

---

[41] Cooper, *Breaking*, 4.

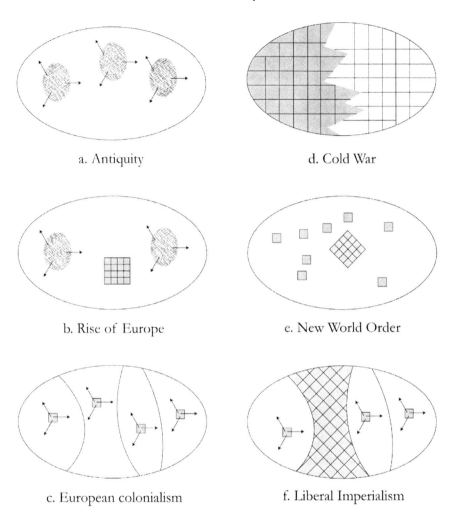

Fig. 8.1. The evolution of the world political order, after Cooper

conflict brought a strong expectation of reduced military spending as a peace dividend both east and west of the Iron Curtain. But as I outlined in Chapter 1, this did not transpire in the United States. Instead, a new era was announced, the Global War on Terror, wherein barbaric pre-modern, post-colonial, and post-socialist states were said to pose newly intensified threats to US national security. Like Mackinder once did, Cooper advocates a transatlantic solidarity against these hostile peoples.

Yet, underlying the closed-space perspective are two assumptions. First, economic growth is understood in terms of external expansion. Territory must be acquired for resources; at the very least, rivals must be prevented from acquiring new land and assets. This extensive model of growth ignores the possibility of intensive development, as through technological change.[42] Technological change produces benefits without the addition of further territory. Furthermore, welfare, as well as wealth creation, can be addressed through internal redistribution, following Hobson's underconsumptionist theory of crisis (see Chapter 5) and the later arguments of John Maynard Keynes (1883–1946).

The second problem with the closed-space view of the world is its reliance upon a trickle-down theory of economic development. The incorporation of peripheral areas into metropolitan economies is assumed to be of mutual benefit, with technology trickling into these underdeveloped spaces and raw materials flowing back to the metropole. Of course, the raw materials cannot be used in both places at the same time and where the poorer country exports agricultural products, land is taken away from domestic food production. As discussed in Chapter 6, Reclus questioned whether capitalist colonialism was generally favourable to local peoples or whether, indeed, food security was not better served by a subsistence economy. Many peoples would be better served by what the historian, Edward Thompson, has called a moral economy than by the introduction, or imposition, of a political economy.[43]

Hostile Peoples

Not only have Mackinder's views of closed space reappeared in recent discussions, so too has his conception of a world divided between different and mutually hostile peoples. The historian of the Ottoman Empire, Bernard Lewis, introduced the idea of a 'clash of civilisations' in his 1990 essay, 'The Roots of Muslim Rage'. Lewis claimed that in parts of the Muslim world there was a loathing of the United States that could be explained neither as racism, nor as a reaction to Western imperialism, but rather, as civilizational jealousy: 'a feeling of humiliation—a growing awareness, among the heirs of an old, proud, and long dominant civilization, of having been overtaken, overborne, and overwhelmed by those whom they regarded as their inferiors'.[44] Lewis is representative of a strand of scholarship that explains Arab identities solely in terms of religion, and understands as the principal context for the expression of those identities the relations between those countries and the West.[45]

---

[42] In many ways, Mackinder echoes Malthus in his understanding of the agrarian limits to development. The alternative emphasis on the intensification of resource use that results from technological change has come to be associated with the work of Boserup, *Conditions of Agricultural Growth*.

[43] E. Thompson, *Customs in Common*.

[44] Lewis, 'Roots of Muslim Rage', 59.

[45] Halliday, *Islam*; Trumpbour, 'Clash of Civilizations'.

In May 2006, under the auspices of the World Affairs Council, Vice President Dick Cheney led a tribute conference for Bernard Lewis's 90th birthday.[46] Cheney praised Lewis, declaring that '[y]ou simply cannot find a greater authority on Middle Eastern history', and revealing not only that Lewis was among a group of experts consulted by Cheney when, as Secretary for Defense, he was formulating a response to the Iraqi invasion of Kuwait (August 1990), but that '[s]ince then we have met often, particularly during the last four-and-a-half years [in other words, since 9/11], and Bernard has always had some very good meetings with President Bush'.[47] A year later, when he gave a public lecture on 'Europe and Islam', Lewis 'surprised everyone by expressing "cautious optimism" regarding Iraq. Lewis credited President Bush for being "tough and consistent" in Iraq and ridiculed the attitudes of congressional Democrats who oppose the Iraq war'.[48] Lewis's proposal that Islamic societies are inherently hostile towards the West has found ready recognition in the Bush administration, as the scholar of Japan and China, Ian Buruma, remarked in a review essay in the *New Yorker*, 'if anyone can be said to have provided the intellectual muscle for recent United States policy towards the Middle East it would have to be [Lewis]'.[49]

In like fashion to Lewis, Samuel Huntington, former Director of Security Planning for the National Security Council under the Carter administration (1976–80), understood civilizations as shaped by history and anchored by religion. Like Brzezinski, Huntington had been a member of the Trilateral Commission, and considered many accounts of the dramatic changes of 1989 to be too optimistic. For example, Francis Fukuyama, part of the Trilateral Commission and member of the Policy Planning Staff of the US Department of State, reflected on the new world order in an influential essay, 'The End of History?'.[50] Fukuyama pronounced that, with the fall of communism, all alternatives to democratic capitalism had been rejected: '[t]oday, we who live in stable, long-standing liberal democracies [...] have trouble imagining a world that is radically better than our own, or a future that is not essentially democratic and capitalist'.[51] The long historical debate was over; democracy was the system of governance peoples wanted, and capitalism was the way to deliver them prosperity. In this Panglossian world, economic grievance faded in the face of 'the smallness of actual remaining inequalities', leaving people to address residual injustices attaching to gender or physical incapacity.[52] Arguing that capitalism had made poverty history, Fukuyama opined that

---

[46] Henry Kissinger and Francis Fukuyama were among the others present; 'World Affairs Council'.

[47] Cheney, 'Vice President's Remarks'.

[48] Puder, 'Lewis Credits Bush on Iraq'. On this advisory group on terrorism and the Middle East set up by Paul Wolfowitz, see: R. Woodward, *State of Denial*, 83.

[49] Buruma, 'Lost in Translation'.

[50] Fukuyama, 'End of History?'.

[51] Fukuyama, ibid., 46.

[52] Fukuyama, ibid., 295.

class would cease to matter, and people would seek self-recognition through identity politics, an essentially harmless pursuit.

Huntington, by contrast, offered a very different and much less benign view of identity politics. Echoing Mackinder's closed-space perspective, Huntington declared in 1993 that: '[t]he world is becoming a smaller place'.[53] Intensified contact for Huntington, produced a heightened awareness of difference, leading to anxiety about threats to one's own identity. The end of the ideological conflict of the Cold War promised not a peace dividend but a new round of global conflict. With Fukuyama, Huntington argued that settling matters of economic contention with the global acceptance of capitalism gave greater prominence to identity politics. Yet he went further by asserting that warfare between ideological camps would be supplanted by a struggle to the finish between cultures: '[t]he fault lines between civilizations will be the battle lines of the future'.[54]

Huntington divided the world into nine religiously based civilizations (he was not really sure if Africa had any distinct civilization) and he offered a map of these divisions based upon groups of countries.[55] Huntington's civilizations function very much like Mackinder's races: individuals neither choose nor change their civilization. For Huntington, there was a clear hierarchy of civilizations, with only one, the 'Christian bloc', demonstrating pacific tendencies.[56] In its commitment to peace and arms reduction, the Christian civilization is superior and stands in contrast to all the other peoples that believe in expansionism whenever possible. Islam, in particular, claimed Huntington, 'has bloody borders'.[57]

In addition to this anticipation of global conflict, Huntington considered Western spaces to be threatened also from within. Mackinder believed that both democracy and miscegenation hindered British effectiveness (Chapter 3). Mackinder was both authoritarian and elitist, as he stated in one parliamentary debate on Irish Home Rule: 'For my part I do not worship King Demos; I am of a more rationalistic turn of mind'.[58] The efficient use of force, he believed, relied upon clear lines of command and rule by experts. Huntington shared Mackinder's suspicion of democracy. In 1975, he wrote an essay on US democracy for the Trilateral Commission, in which he presented a conflict between democracy on one side, and the efficiency and authority of government on the other: '[t]he impulse of democracy is to make government less powerful and more active, to increase its functions and to decrease its authority'.[59] Voters, he

---

[53] Huntington, 'Clash of Civilizations?', 25.

[54] Huntington, ibid., 22.

[55] Huntington, *Clash of Civilizations*, 21.

[56] On Huntington's sense of cultural superiority, see: Shapiro, 'Huntington's Moral Geography'; Buckley, 'Remaking the World Order'; Connolly, 'Civilizational Superiority'.

[57] Huntington, 'Clash of Civilizations?', 33.

[58] *The Official Report, House of Commons, 5th Series*, 34 (19 February 1912), 368.

[59] Huntington, 'United States', 64.

argued, were inclined to demand increased welfare spending while a powerful national media undermined presidential discretion, leaving the United States ill-prepared to exercise the power it possessed: 'a government which lacks authority, and which is committed to substantial domestic programs will have little ability, short of a cataclysmic crisis, to impose on its people the sacrifices which may be necessary to deal with foreign policy problems and defense'.[60] Huntington wanted the 'excess of democracy' trimmed by greater respect for 'expertise, seniority, experience, and special talents'.[61]

In a fashion that echoed Mackinder's anxieties about dilution, Huntington also warned that the fundamental values of the United States were threatened by Asian-Americans, Spanish-Americans, and African-Americans. The Catholicization of American culture by Latinos was dangerous, according to Huntington, for this group lacked the work ethic of WASPs.[62] Huntington's ideal of Western civilization thus was clearly not only Christian but Protestant, not only Protestant but White, not only White but Anglo-Saxon. His vision of the world is indeed a racist one.[63]

The promotion of a paranoid understanding of geopolitical relations based upon a religious fundamentalist understanding of the necessity of protecting Western civilization, while not new, appears to have had a strong resonance among Republican voters and US conservative politicians, which has only grown in intensity since the atrocities of 11 September 2001. With the Republican victories in 2000 and 2004, for example, journalist and former strategist for the Republic Party, Kevin Phillips identified the development of an 'American Theocracy' in which, for the 'first time', a religious party had won the Presidential elections in the United States.[64] Similarly, Stephen Zunes, a political scientist, noted the 'calculated strategy by leading conservatives in the Republican party [. . .] to enlist the support' of the substantial 'religious right' in order to win power.[65] For Phillips the use of Christian fundamentalist rhetoric to win office and then to justify policies was new insofar as it embraced a sense of radical difference allied to the conviction of supremacy. In other words, religious belief functioned as a dangerous form of racism through an Othering that justified the use of violence. George W. Bush's division of the world into good and evil, freedom and insecurity, prosperity and poverty was not only inaccurate, it was (and remains) dangerous.[66]

Fundamentalism emphasizes doctrinal purity; it loathes syncretism and calls a society back to unquestionable core values, which perhaps explains why Bush was so comfortable in proclaiming the renewal of America in his

[60] Huntington, 'United States', 105.
[61] Huntington, ibid., 113.
[62] Huntington, *Who are We?*.
[63] Mazrui, 'Racial Conflict'; Halim, 'Clash of Civilizations Revisited'.
[64] K. Phillips, *American Theocracy*, vii.
[65] Zunes, 'Influence of the Christian Right', 73.
[66] Kellner, *From 9/11 to the Terror War*.

declaration of the War on Terror: 'we have found our mission and our moment'.[67] Bush's claim that the United States had a global mission 'defending liberty and justice because they are right and true and unchanging for all people everywhere' appears specious when these terms are operationalized in ways that reflect, as the anthropologist Richard Schweder notes, their meaning among a much smaller community than the world for which they are asserted.[68] It is one thing to invoke, as Bush did, the freedom of the press but it is quite another to imply that this is served only by a press in private hands, subject to all sorts of monopolistic temptations, and eager to use its influence to create an effective political oligopoly.[69] For example, Bush has asserted that: 'Freedom of the press and the free flow of ideas are vital foundations of liberty. To cut through the hateful propaganda that fills the airwaves in the Muslim world and to promote open debate, we're broadcasting the message of tolerance and truth in Arabic and Persian to tens of millions'.[70] Yet, faced with local reports of the unbridled violence of its assault on Fallujah in April 2004, Donald Rumsfeld, Secretary of Defense, attacked the Al Jazeera news channel as 'vicious, inaccurate and inexcusable', and George Bush proposed to Tony Blair that the headquarters of Al Jazeera in Qatar be taken out by bombing.[71]

One study of the rhetoric of Bush's announcement of the Global War on Terror noted that Bush invoked God to unify his nation against, in his words, 'a new kind of evil', which would require a 'crusade'.[72] This was, however, an explicitly Christian unity and thus satisfied a domestic political constituency that wanted to impose its values as trenchantly against an internal as any external enemy. Fundamentalism can all too easily figure alternative religions as rivals to be suppressed, at home or abroad. According to Bush, the Global War on Terror, '[t]his crusade, this war on terrorism is going to take a while'.[73] Bush's Manichean vision, pronouncing the world divided into two camps—'you're either with us or with the terrorists'—was wedded to an apocalyptic rhetoric that, as Phillips demonstrated, derived from the millennial vision of the Rapture.[74] The apocalyptic imagery encouraged an arrogant and aggressive foreign policy: 'the preemptive righteousness of a biblical nation become a high-technology, gospel-spreading superpower'.[75] When a state identifies itself with a religion, and becomes a theocracy, then, it may

---

[67] Bush, 'Address to Congress'.

[68] Schweder, 'Bush and the Missionary Position', 26.

[69] There is also, in the case of George W. Bush, the simple hypocrisy of insisting on the freedom of press in theory while simultaneously suppressing it in practice, see: Wolf, *End of America*.

[70] Bush, 'Winston Churchill and the War on Terror'.

[71] Scahill, 'Did Bush Really Want to Bomb Al Jazeera?'; Maguire and Lines, 'Bush Plot to Bomb his Arab Ally'.

[72] Graham, Keenan, and Dowd, 'Call to Arms', 209.

[73] Bush, 'Remarks by the President'.

[74] Phillips, *American Theocracy*, 239.

[75] Phillips, ibid., 103.

treat other states as heretics unleashing against them absolutist violence. Global politics thus becomes always animated by an existential crisis of true faith versus damnation and oblivion.[76]

Religious fundamentalism is the modern American manifestation of a view of the world as made up of peoples not only different but also essentially hostile. In Mackinder's day this hostility was expressed as White racial supremacism, during the Cold War it took the ideological form of anti-Communism, and today it takes the shape of Islamophobia. The co-authored book by David Frum, former speech writer for George Bush, and Richard Perle, member of the Pentagon's Defense Advisory Board, described how to put *An End to Evil: How to Win the War on Terror* (2004). The environmental racism of Mackinder pales beside their account of the Middle East: '[t]his fetid environment nourishes the most venomous vermin in the Middle Eastern swamp'.[77] Frum and Perle tell fellow Americans that militant Islam must be put to the knife, that this is war to the death, 'victory or holocaust'.[78]

The two central problems with this view of the world as divided into mutually hostile camps are at once ethical and methodological. There is a failure of empathy, allowing protagonists to objectify the Other as embodying the bestial instincts that they imagine themselves as keeping under civilized check. And there is a related failure to recognize complexity either in distant societies or in one's own. In his accounts of exotic societies, Mackinder never tried to see matters through local eyes, never discussed the many disqualifications placed upon indigenous peoples by colonial administration. Yet, for all his casual racism, Mackinder avoided anti-Semitism, an all too common contemporary prejudice.

Kingsley showed the virtues of trying to understand exotic behaviour as if it made sense to the people who practised it. Given the prevailing chauvinism of her society, Kingsley's effort to appreciate the adequacy of native understandings of disease and the suitability of local arrangements regarding marriage and women's work, was admirable. While Kingsley most likely did not capture every nuance of local customs and beliefs, she reached empathy sufficient to retire the prejudices of racial hierarchy with which she claims to have set out. In other words, the effort to understand was perhaps itself enough to puncture the pretensions of radical mutual incomprehension that paraded along the colour line. Kingsley's example shows that if people tried to appreciate a common humanity, they might give up the notion of incompatible difference and suspend their own sense of racial superiority.

Reclus, for all the benefits he allowed to colonialism, gave heed to local voices, citing, for example, the reckoning by the Pandit intellectual, Sivanath

[76] Maddox, 'Crusade Against Evil'.
[77] Frum and Perle, *End to Evil*, 138.
[78] Frum and Perle, ibid., 7.

Sastri (1847–1919), of the benefits and irritations of English education in Bengal.[79] Like Hobson, however, who discussed the perfidy of Jewish bankers, Reclus distinguished rather weakly between a Jewish ethnic identity and a Jewish social position, referring to one group, the Osses, 'resembl[ing] Jewish dealers in their black or brown eyes, and even in their wheedling voice'.[80] Not only did Reclus resort to anti-Semitic 'caricature' in his great encyclopaedic work, but, when, asked about anti-Semitism at the height of the Dreyfus Affair, he belittled it: '[i]n fact, in France this deafening anti-Semitism is a very superficial movement without deep roots or reach, and is due almost entirely to the envy of less successful examinees and officials'.[81]

Kropótkin offered a different model of how peoples developed as distinctive groups, challenging the claim that the basis of identity was biological. History, for him, showed not the evolution of distinct races but rather the elaboration of different styles of civilization rooted in particular ecologies of work. He proposed that the great bond was social; it was cooperation in making a living. The test of society, then, was based not on inherited identities, but rather on how one might contribute to the well-being of one's neighbours, the common weal, by working alongside them. It was by working together that people shaped a collective identity. This was how migrants joined new communities. Even were one to focus upon the biology of human communities, Reclus, for one, was sure that the extent of migration undermined all claims to racial purity—outside some very few small and remote tribes. Beyond this, communication was the basis of cultural and economic energy, and Reclus saw the interactions facilitated by the Mediterranean Sea as vital to the dynamism of Europe. Most religions, and thus ethical principles, were transnational and passing to and fro were inflected by local conditions and innovation.

The view of civilizations, cultures, or races as bounded and as posing existential threats to each other is a tragic rejection of the evident benefits of sharing. Historian, Richard Bulliet, for example, criticizes Bernard Lewis's failure to see the long-standing interaction, rather than hostility, between Christianity and Islam.[82] Historically, many of the critics of the conduct of

---

[79] 'Un savant *pandit*, Sivanath Sastri, énumère en six arguments principaux les bienfaits de l'éducation anglaise au Bengale, qu'il oppose cinq consequences fâcheuses'; Reclus, *L'Homme et La Terre VI*, 50.

[80] Reclus, *The Earth and Its Inhabitants. VI. Asia, Asiatic Russia*, 72. The insinuation is in the original French, speaking of 'ceux qui ressemblent aux broanteurs juifs et parle comme eux d'une voix caressante, ont les yeux brun ou noirs'; Reclus, *Nouvelle Géographie universelle: L'Asie Russe*, 131.

[81] 'Il ne s'agit absolument pas de nier le caractère dépassé de certaines de ses approches, et même choquant, comme à propos des juifs que Reclus présente toujours comme des usuriers accapareurs. Lui, [...], tombe dans l'antisémitisme le plus primaire voire caricatural [...]'; Giblin, 'Un Géographe d'Exception', 25. 'Actuellement, en France, l'Antisémitisme qui nous assourdit est un movement très superficiel, sans cause profondes et sans portée, dû presque en entire à la basse envie de candidats distancés dans les concours, de fonctionnaires écartés dans la distribution des places'; quoted in Dagan, *Enquête sur l'Antisémitisme*, 39.

[82] Bulliet, *Islamo-Christian Civilization*.

Empire avowed the unity of the human race. When, in 1837, the Aborigines' Protection Society developed from the anti-slavery movement, its motto was *ab uno sanguine* (of one blood) and its target was the abuse of native peoples within the British Empire by 'the enterprising, avaricious and powerful'.[83] These ethical conflicts reverberated through academia, dividing, for example, Ethnology, the study of the connections between the branches of humanity, from Anthropology, concerned at the time with documenting the diversity of human societies.[84] There were, and are, alternatives to the tragic view of humanity as divided and antagonistic. One was the ethical standpoint that one should begin from the presumption of a common humanity and the other was that all people have rights and that respect for these should be the basis for reviewing Empire.

Enduring Conflict

The economist and philosopher, Amartya Sen, has identified serious problems with singularistic understandings of group identity, such as Huntington's, including how a 'solitarist' approach to civilizational belonging may lead to violence:

Underlying this line of thinking is the odd presumption that the people of the world can be uniquely categorized according to some *singular and overarching* system of partitioning. Civilizational or religious partitioning of the world population yields a 'solitarist' approach to human identity, which sees human beings as members of exactly one group (in this case defined by civilization or religion, in contrast with earlier reliance on nationalities and classes). [. . .] Central to leading a human life [. . .] are the responsibilities of choice and reasoning. In contrast, violence is promoted by the cultivation of a sense of inevitability about some allegedly unique—often belligerent—identity that we are supposed to have and which apparently makes extensive demands on us (sometimes of a most disagreeable kind).[85]

For conservative political analysts, global conflict is a challenge requiring the United States to set aside its natural desire to be a law-abiding global citizen.[86] Such is the view of Robert Kagan, a political commentator popular with the Pentagon, who, as adviser (1985–8) on Central American affairs to the Reagan administration, was associated with the covert US campaign in support of the Nicaraguan Contras in the mid-1980s, pleading guilty to two charges of withholding information from Congress in the subsequent

---

[83] Swaisland, 'Aborigines Protection Society'; report of the Society (1838) quoted in Pels, 'Prehistory of Ethical Codes', 104.
[84] Reining, 'Applied Anthropology'; Stocking, 'What's in a Name?'.
[85] Sen, *Identity and Violence*, xii–xiii.
[86] Kaplan, *Warrior Politics*.

Iran-Contra trials. With William Kristol, he was co-founder of the influential Project for a New American Century, the group that did so much to shape the foreign agenda of the administrations of George W. Bush since 2000. Kagan offers faint praise for Europe, as a 'self-contained world of laws and rules and transnational negotiation and cooperation', a 'post-historical paradise of peace and relative prosperity'.[87] Kagan is contemptuous of this idealism, precisely because it requires Europe to be 'self-contained' and 'post-historical', for in adopting this stance Europe has turned its back upon the realism of remaining 'mired in history [...] where true security and the defense and promotion of a liberal order still depend on the possession and use of military might'.[88] Kagan also points out that before the First World War, when they had the military capacity to participate in imperialism, Europeans too 'believed in *Machtpolitik*'.[89] Such an understanding of geopolitics, that power is its own justification, is clearly reflected in the US National Security Strategy of September 2002, proposing that the United States should have the force to prevail in all world regions, across all forms of warfare; 'full-spectrum dominance'.[90]

The idea that might makes right is also explicit in Philip Bobbitt's 2003 book, *The Shield of Achilles*.[91] Bobbitt, nephew of Lyndon Johnson and Law professor at the University of Texas, has 'served successively as Associate Counsel to the President under Carter, Counsel to the Senate Iran-Contra Committee under Reagan, Counsellor on International Law at the State Department under Bush senior, and Director of Intelligence on the National Security Council under Clinton'.[92] Bobbitt argues that historically, there are relations between military technology and strategy on one hand, and systems of international law on the other. Bobbitt's historical lesson is that: '[t]he State is born in violence: only when it has achieved a legitimate monopoly on violence can it promulgate law: only when it is free of the coercive violence of other states can it pursue strategy'.[93] As depicted in Figure 8.2, the column on the left lists the successive military revolutions that Bobbitt claims drove the earliest revolutions in government, shown in the right-hand column. So, for example, the transition from warfare based on pikemen and sieges, to warfare based on archers and battles, allowed and required an increase in the scale of polities from smaller princely states to the larger kingly states. New modalities of warfare each grew from innovations in the military strategies of certain key leaders, shown in the central column. Thus, for example, Napoléon Bonaparte was the pioneer of the associated techniques of con- scription and the use of massed concentrations of soldiers to terrify opposing armies. The result of these new techniques produced panic, disarray, and

---

[87] Kagan, *Paradise and Power*, 3.   [88] Kagan, ibid., 3.
[89] Kagan, ibid., 8.   [90] *National Security Strategy 2002*.
[91] Bobbitt, *Shield of Achilles*.   [92] Balakrishnan, 'Algorithms of War', 7.
[93] P. Bobbitt, *Shield of Achilles*, 336.

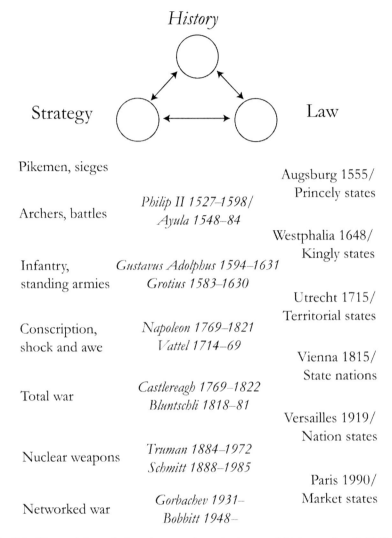

Fig. 8.2. The evolving relations between law, strategy, and history, after Bobbitt

flight among the opposing forces. The new realities of military conflict also required reorderings of the legal basis of international relations.

In Bobbitt's historical schema, state strategists have historically realized the potential of new arrangements, and intellectuals have reflected upon what these arrangements mean for systems of international law; both are listed in the central column. In each historical moment, a key theorist reflected upon these revolutions in government to produce a new understanding of the appropriate framework for international law (emblematic versions of such treaties are given in the third column). Thus, while US President Harry Truman (in office, 1945–53) is presented by Bobbitt as a pioneer of the military revolution created by the availability of nuclear weapons, the theorist of the new world of mutually assured destruction was, according to Bobbitt, the German political scientist and Nazi, Carl Schmitt (1888–1985).

I have taken the liberty of adding Bobbitt to his own analysis as the theorist of the international system under conditions of networked war between market states, or between market states and not-yet market states.[94] Bobbitt, the constitutional lawyer, holds out much less hope for law than for force. He presents the Cold War as a noble and generous act by the United States, through which nuclear deterrence held the ring against communist expansion following the failure of Wilsonian ideals of global democracy. Changes in the technology of force require adjustments in political arrangements; law follows arms. However, there is a puzzling interruption in Bobbitt's argument. He might have argued that nuclear weapons created a crisis for the system of nation states, ushering the new state form he identifies as the market state. However, he does not. Instead, he argues that the rise of the market state is essentially an ideological victory.

In a market state, public opinion is influenced by commercially owned media and by political candidates who are funded by special interests. Ronald Reagan (US President, 1981–9) and Margaret Thatcher (UK Prime Minister, 1979–90) are credited with creating the market state by persuading their electorates that the state could no longer deliver welfare, only opportunity. For Bobbitt and the so-called neo-Conservatives, this was a welcome departure from earlier majoritarian forms of democracy.[95] This is because, according to Bobbitt, politicians, together with the media, can ensure that those who have the largest stake in society, defined as those who own most of it, maintain the most influence over government. He proposes that, until the United States is honest about the sort of society it has actually become, it will not be able to evolve an appropriate strategic posture. Because the United States has a practical monopoly on the capacity to wage global conflict, it cannot agree to be bound by restrictions, such as the International Court of Justice, which was proposed by states with little capacity, and hence responsibility, to maintain a global order. Following this logic, Bobbitt believes that the United States must prevent Russia and China from destroying the environment and that it must restrain Germany and Japan in their ambition to acquire nuclear weapons.[96] The rest of the world, Bobbitt is confident, will accept American leadership, so long as environmental protection and nuclear non-proliferation are assured.[97]

---

[94] On the novelty of networked war, see: Duffield, 'War as a Network Enterprise'.
[95] Norton, *Strauss*, 239.
[96] Bobbitt, *Shield of Achilles*, 293.   [97] Bobbitt, ibid., 309.

The United States, argues Bobbitt, should act as the global leader of shifting coalitions of the willing, both in war-making and peace-making. By controlling access to strategic intelligence, the United States can prevent any nation from defying American interests, even in regional wars. For Bobbitt, this information umbrella replaces the nuclear protection offered by the United States during the Cold War; the United States assumes thereby the cost of making the world safe by policing terrorists, tyrants, and other miscreants. Following the ideology of the market state, Bobbitt further argues that the United States must intervene in places where the inhabitants do not yet have the right to explore (commercial) opportunities, policing a world in which borders are about markets and not territory.[98] It will fund its own armed forces so that all peoples of the world get the opportunity to choose prosperity instead of being constrained by, what Thomas Barnett, a commentator close to strategists in the Pentagon, has described as the 'civilisational apartheid' of autocratic orders such as Islamic theocracies, or what the journalist Christopher Hitchens has called 'fascism with an Islamic face', 'violent Islamic theocratism'.[99] Barnett, indeed, proposes that the rest of the world should accept the large trade deficit of the United States as minimal recompense due to its role as international sheriff.[100]

Condoleeza Rice, National Security Adviser during the Bush presidency of 2000–4, and Secretary of State from 2004–8, argued that the United States should pursue a foreign policy in its own national interest, not in 'the interests of an illusory international community'.[101] Humanitarian consequences are, for Rice, at best a 'second-order effect' of pursuing America's self-interest because 'American values are universal'.[102] Exercising power should be at the centre of American policy and, given its 'special role in the world', the United States 'should not adhere to every international convention and agreement that someone thinks to propose'.[103] In the main, power means fighting wars: 'America's military power must be secure because the United Sates is the only guarantor of global peace and stability'.[104]

As with Mackinder, this warrior politics not only draws upon intellectual arguments, it also interpellates the national subject as masculine. Europe is figured as old and the United States as virile. Not surprisingly, George W. Bush, as US President, has been shown variously wearing his Texan cowboy attire, attacking trees with a chainsaw, decked out in the combat gear of a fighter pilot, and jogging ahead of aides. In a psychological study of Bush's sadism and irresponsibility, the psychoanalyst, Justin Frank, claims

---

[98] Bobbitt, *Shield of Achilles*, 354.
[99] Barnett, *Pentagon's New Map*, 32; Hitchens, 'Against Rationalization', 8; *idem*, 'Holy Writ', 93.
[100] Barnett, ibid., 308.
[101] Rice, 'National Interest', 62.
[102] Rice, ibid., 47, 49.
[103] Rice, ibid., 49.
[104] Rice, ibid., 50.

that '[h]is strutting, swaggering behavior is infectious; it gives us license to feel as puffed up and powerful as he does. Bush also shows us, by example, that we can assuage our narcissistic feelings of injury through fantasies of revenge'.[105] Through Bush's public performances, the unilateral turn of the United States is enacted as a masculine, and forceful, response to a world of savages. As with Mackinder, global democratic ideals are shown as based on a misplaced faith in the power of compromise and rationality. Instead, global realities dictate relying upon force. There is even a chivalric veneer available for this (defending weak people against their local tyrant), although the sadism of inflicting violence also feminizes the enemy as weak and submissive, as in the abuse of prisoners at Abu Ghraib.[106] Imperialism continues to provide a spectacle of aggressive, heterosexual masculinity, as the sociologist, Joane Nagel, remarks:

[S]exualised military discourse is very much from a heterosexual standpoint, as is clear when we consider the imagery of rape during the 1991 Gulf War; attacks that needed to be defended or retaliated against were cast as heterosexual rapes of women ('the rape of Kuwait'); attacks that were offensive against the Iraqi enemy were phrased as homosexual rapes of men ('bend over, Saddam').[107]

Theorists such as Kaplan, Kagan, Bobbitt, and Barnett, and a host of fellow travellers, encourage the United States to view force as essential and primary in international relations. Attempts to constrain force by law are, as in Mackinder's analysis, presented as naïve and idealistic. From their perspective, only force is adequate to face the realities of a world where states must prevail or die. International relations cannot be idealistic in the new world order, in which good must prevail over evil, and in which one state's gain must be another state's loss. Just as Mackinder did, these new theorists of global conflict hail the citizens of the imperial power to their imperial duty. They enjoin their fellow citizens to act like the real men of the world system and prevail by force abroad.

   The competition between nations, advocated and even celebrated by Mackinder, was heavily criticized by some of his contemporaries. Reclus and Hobson anathemized colonialism. Reclus condemned non-settler colonies as mere spaces of exploitation. Hobson railed against the human cost of the alliance of state power and transnational corporations involved in the extractive industries. The crucial matter was labour relations and here the case of the Belgian Congo was the most notorious exemplar, although it was never mentioned in any of Mackinder's textbooks. The profits from colonies came from coerced labour. In the Congo, soldiers of the government and the security personnel of the rubber companies, each forced local people to

---

[105] J. Frank, *Bush on the Couch*, 173.
[106] Tétreault, 'Sexual Politics of Abu Ghraib'.
[107] Nagel, 'Masculinity and Nationalism', 258. Of course, the sexuality at play in such attitudes is equally capable expressing the homoerotics of the closet; Boone, 'Vacation Cruises'.

provide food and rubber. In a brilliant report of 1903, Roger Casement (1864–1916) noted imposts upon villages taxed to such a degree that people ran away if they could evade the armed thugs of state or company. Casement estimated that the companies given regional monopoly rights over the rubber trade 'direct an armed force of not less than 10,000 men'.[108] This was serfdom: local people were kidnapped as hostage against the delivery of rubber or food; they were murdered, beaten, imprisoned, or conscripted into the army for shortcomings; and their children were subject to kidnap, murder, or mutilation. Yet, the Congo Free State was at first presented to the world as a humanitarian enterprise devoted to eliminating slavery and taxing but lightly to raise the funds for its anti-slavery crusade. Casement held the official Belgian account in contempt. He explained to one American journalist that '[t]here are two ways of seeing the interior of the Congo state—either blindfolded or looking for the facts affecting the social condition of the natives underlying the veneer of European officialdom which had imposed itself upon them'.[109] Competition between the capitalist countries certainly resulted in more rubber from Congo entering world trade but it resulted also in depopulation in the country itself and from the standpoint advised by the Aborigines Protection Society, the competition destroyed many lives, perhaps producing a million deaths in the 1890s alone.[110] The extent to which a richness of natural resources draws to less powerful countries such interference from more powerful countries and their semi-militarized commercial enterprises has given rise to the idea of a 'resource curse'.[111] Casement brought together two elements that remain important in the critique of imperialism: an insistence upon the equal dignity of all people and empirical work on how force is used to degrade human beings in pursuit of profit.[112]

Land- and Sea-Power

In some ways, the most startling echo of Mackinder's vision is found in the international relations theorist, John Mearsheimer's *The Tragedy of Great Power Politics* (2001). Mearsheimer describes his theory as offensive realism: states pursue the accumulation of power to survive against unknown threats from rivals they can neither fully predict nor trust. Through war or blackmail, states may acquire power, and any state may indirectly influence the distribution of power among its rivals through balancing (threatening to

---

[108] Casement, 'Main Report', 113.
[109] Ó Siocháin and O'Sullivan, 'Introduction', 13.
[110] Nworah, 'Aborigines' Protection Society'.
[111] Auty, 'Resource-Driven Growth'; Dalby, 'Ecological Politics'.
[112] Porter, 'Casement'.

intervene if a rival seeks advantage through subjugation of a third party), or buck-passing (persuading another state to make such a threat against a common rival). For Mearsheimer, the 'stopping power of water' places spatial constraints on consolidating global power.[113] It is, he suggests, very difficult to project power across water, or to place and consolidate armed forces on the shores of a hostile land, because the separation between domestic reserves and foreign exertion imposes strains upon supply lines. Because states cannot project force across the seas onto distant shores, there has never been a 'global hegemon', according to Mearsheimer, even though one power could dominate its own land mass and become a 'regional hegemon'.[114] Like Mackinder, Mearsheimer noted that continental powers, with land-power or large armies, 'have initiated most of the past wars of conquest between great powers'.[115] They do this by attacking other continental powers because insular powers 'are protected by the water surrounding them'.[116] On the other hand, 'insular powers are unlikely to initiate wars of conquest against other great powers, because they have to traverse a large body of water to reach their target'.[117]

According to Mearsheimer, the United States is currently the only regional hegemon in the world, dominating its own land mass, the Americas. It has interests in all other parts of the world and thus does not want to see rival states achieve hegemonic status within their own region. It is for this reason, he argues, that the United States maintains troops in Europe (to deter Germany or Russia) and in North East Asia (to deter Japan or China). Having pacified the Americas and established its own unassailable position, Mearsheimer implies that the United States no longer has any need to act as a land-power. Rather, it should project its force across the seas into other regions, and there it can act most effectively when it pursues the role of 'offshore balancer'.[118] In Mearsheimer's account, an offshore balancer is a power that influences rivals from the detached position of a reserve force threatening to intervene only if one or other state threatens to become a regional hegemon. Where there are rivals on the land mass, the offshore balancer need only play them off against each other or develop alliances that can produce a deadlock. Where there is no possibility of local opposition to a rising threat, then, the offshore balancer must itself become a resident power and stand against the potential hegemon. For example, Mearsheimer proposes that the United States had to act as an offshore balancer for Europe after the Second World War. In 1948, the United Kingdom had only a total of 847,000 troops, whereas the Soviet Union had 2,870,000. With its 1,360,000 troops, the United States was, reflects Mearsheimer, the only

---

[113] Mearsheimer, *Tragedy*, 41.
[114] Mearsheimer, ibid., 42, 41.
[115] Mearsheimer, ibid., 135.
[116] Mearsheimer, ibid., 136.
[117] Mearsheimer, ibid., 136.
[118] Mearsheimer, ibid., 237.

power that could defy Soviet expansionism in Europe.[119] Building up its troop numbers in Europe from 80,000 in 1950 to 427,000 in 1953, the United States set up a tripwire to resist Soviet advances, putting itself at the heart of any future territorial conflict in Europe.[120]

Mearsheimer's view of the United States as the world's most powerful yet peaceful state is widely shared. By presenting aggression as the taking and holding of territory (Colonial Imperialism), all other forms of intervention slip under the radar. Thus, Condoleeza Rice is sure that the United States 'has had no territorial ambitions for nearly a century. Its national interest has been defined instead by a desire to foster the spread of freedom, prosperity, and peace'.[121] In 1999, commenting on American foreign policy in the twentieth century, President Bill Clinton said that 'no one suggests that we ever sought territorial advantage'.[122]

Many of Mackinder's British contemporaries likewise believed that they were fortunate to live in the most powerful nation on earth, they recognized that it spent more on arms than any other nation and perhaps more than all other nations combined, they were proud that their nation controlled one-fifth of the earth's land surface, and yet they argued that there was no real connection between military force and the acquisition of an empire; indeed the historian, John Seeley, wrote that the British 'seemed to have conquered and peopled half the world in a fit of absence of mind', while Mackinder himself wrote that the 'British fight only in defence'.[123] They might accept that British force was useful against imperial rivals but not that it was routinely used against peoples native to the colonies and dependencies. This is, of course, the myth of empty space, so important to ideologies of imperial expansion, both British and American.[124]

However, Reclus and Hobson saw nothing inadvertent about British colonialism. At the start of the last volume of *L'Homme et La Terre*, Reclus discussed the British belief in the innocence of their colonialism. When Reclus turned to India, his conclusion was clear: '[t]he English who live in India [...] are not equivalent even to one thousandth part of the native population, and there can be no doubt that the immense Indian empire is made subject by violence, and continues to be held by physical force and the complementary attractions of canons, rifles, tribunes, and prisons'.[125] Both

---

[119] Mearsheimer, *Tragedy*, 327.
[120] Mearsheimer, ibid., 256.
[121] Rice, 'National Interest', 62.
[122] Quoted in Mearsheimer, *Tragedy*, 527.
[123] Seeley, *Expansion of England*, 8; Mackinder, *Nations of the Modern World*, 287.
[124] Harris, 'How did Colonialism Dispossess?'.
[125] 'Le personnel des Anglais [...] qui séjourne dans l'Inde, ne représente pas même la millième partie de la population indigène, et cependant il n'est pas douteux que l'immense empire de l'Inde fut assujetti par la violence, qu'il est encore contenu par la force matérielle et l'attirait complémentaire des canons et des fusils, des tribunaux et des prisons'; Reclus, *L'Homme et la Terre VI*, 50.

Reclus and Hobson stressed the place of aggression within the Empire. In the name of national autonomy, Hobson dismissed the utilitarian argument that imperialism was good for the dependent nations. He argued that '[t]he notions that the arts of government are portable commodities, that there is one best brand, the Anglo-Saxon, and that forcibly to fasten this upon as large a portion of the globe as possible makes for the civilization of the world, imply an utter misunderstanding of the very rudiments of social psychology'.[126] Any attempt to impose democracy would surely 'steriliz[e] the most promising seeds of the wider, saner nationalism which will seek to realize itself by cherishing the friendship of other nations, and cooperating with them for the attainment of the widest human ends'.[127] Imposing democracy, then, was a contradiction in terms.

Colonial and Liberal Imperialisms

Resource wars have at various times been evoked explicitly in debates over American foreign policy. Recent discussions about the oil crisis and national security have many precedents. In the context of the Soviet invasion of Afghanistan in December 1979, for example, President Carter marked out a line in the sand: '[a]n attempt by any outside force to gain control of the Persian Gulf region will be regarded as an assault on the vital interests of the United States of America, and such an assault will be repelled by any means necessary, including military force'.[128] This account of the US strategic and geopolitical dilemma echoes the positions of both Curzon and Mackinder. The resources of the Persian Gulf and the Caspian Basin were seen as vital to the national interest of the United Sates and, for this reason, military intervention was necessary. In this case, the Soviet threat to the established relations between oil producers and American companies and consumers would justify overturning any alternative arrangements, such as agreements entered into by Arab nations and the Soviet Union.

A very broad reading of the nature of threats to national security (going far beyond the risk of foreign military aggression) can encourage colonial imperialist policies as pre-emptive defensive measures. When, in the mid-1970s, several Arab countries nationalized their oilfields and raised the price of oil to pressure Western governments to force an Israeli withdrawal from the territory occupied in the war of October 1973, Henry Kissinger, the US Secretary of State, responded by promoting 'just short of openly, a plan for

---

[126] Hobson, 'Socialistic Imperialism', 58.
[127] Hobson, ibid., 50.
[128] Carter, 'State of the Union'.

using US airborne forces to seize the oil fields of Saudi Arabia, Kuwait, and Abu Dhabi'.[129] The plan was proposed to the British government, which rejected it.[130] Kissinger set out the explicit colonial case in an article, 'Seizing Arab Oil', written for *Harper's Magazine* (1975) under the pen name of Miles Ignotus (Latin for the Unknown Soldier). He argued against what he termed the 'appeasement' of the oil cartel by the West.[131] For Kissinger, there was but a single way out: '[t]he only feasible countervailing power to OPEC's control of oil is power itself—military power'.[132] Although impossible to justify invasion on the basis of the price of oil, '[f]ortunately for us, while all members of OPEC are extortionists, some (the Arabs) are also black-mailers'.[133] Sketching out a likely scenario, Kissinger predicted that the Arab countries would use the price of oil to blackmail Western powers into demanding concessions of Israel that the latter would refuse and ultimately would go to war to defend. At that point, the Arab countries might impose an oil embargo on the West, that would in turn produce 'an atmosphere of crisis [. . .]. Then we go in'.[134] His proposal was that the United States would occupy the oilfields of Saudi Arabia and then blackmail OPEC into reducing prices, '[f]aced with armed consumers occupying vast oil fields whose full output can eventually bring the price down to 50 cents per barrel, most of the producers would see virtue in agreeing to a price four or five times as high, but still six times lower than present prices'.[135] To develop sufficiently the underdeveloped Saudi oilfields, 'an occupation of ten years and probably much less would suffice'.[136] A British intelligence memorandum of December 1973 'cites a warning from Defense Secretary James R. Schlesinger to the British ambassador in Washington, Lord Cromer, that the United States would not tolerate threats from "under-developed, under-populated" countries and that "it was no longer obvious to him that the United States could not use force" '.[137]

The Saudi oilfields have perhaps since passed their peak yet secure access to cheap foreign oil remains a priority of US foreign policy. Under the Bush administration, Vice President Dick Cheney (2001–9) was responsible for devising an energy policy for the United States. According to the journalist, Paul Roberts, Cheney convened a team that focused on the oil potential of Iraq, as the country with the cheapest and largest untapped reserves in the world: 'Iraq had been producing 3.5 million barrels a day, and many in the industry and the administration believed that the volume could easily

---

[129] K. Phillips, *American Theocracy*, 41.   [130] Frankel, 'US Mulled Seizing Oil'.
[131] Ignotus, 'Seizing Arab Oil', 45. The attribution of authorship is testified by James Akins who, although US Ambassador to Saudi Arabia at the time, was not aware this was Kissinger's work and, having dismissed the plan as madness, was promptly sacked; 'Ambassador James Akins'. The same is claimed by a former CIA analyst, Ray McGovern; McGovern, 'Bush, Oil, and Moral Bankruptcy'.
[132] Ignotus, 'Seizing Arab Oil', 48.   [133] Ignotus, ibid., 48–50.
[134] Ignotus, ibid., 50.   [135] Ignotus, ibid., 50.
[136] Ignotus, ibid., 62.   [137] Frankel, 'US Mulled Seizing Oil'.

be increased to seven million by 2010. If so—and if Iraq could be convinced to ignore its OPEC quota and start producing at maximum capacity—the flood of oil would effectively end OPEC's ability to control prices'.[138] One industry expert suggested that with 'fifty years of production and 40% royalties, Iraq could yield annual profits of \$80–90 billion per year, more than the total annual profits of the top five companies'.[139] To ensure that this energy resource would go to the United States, the American government would have to pressure the Iraqi regime to stop developing concessions to non-American companies. The UN sanctions against Iraq from 1990 limited both oil exports and foreign investment thus 'Saddam could not implement his own plan to extend large-scale oil concessions (estimated to be worth \$1.1 trillion) to French, Russian, Chinese and other oil companies'.[140] As David Frum, Bush's speechwriter, wryly noted, the Global War on Terror would bring 'new prosperity to us all, by securing the world's largest pool of oil'.[141] The cost is significant. Milton Copulus, an economist with the National Defense Council Foundation estimated for 2003 that the military cost of defending oil supplies from the Persian Gulf was \$49.1 billion, at a time when the total cost of oil imports was \$99 billion.[142] In later testimony to the Senate Foreign Relations Committee, he updated the estimate of military costs for Middle East oil to \$320 billion for 2006.[143] The current cost of imported oil is about \$350 billion.[144] In other words, for every dollar the United States spends importing oil, it spends another defending this supply.

The Global War on Terror serves as a new round of Colonial Imperialism through which the United States attempts to secure its access to cheap oil for the next few decades. The war has sent American troops, secured new bases, and created a continuing military presence in those parts of Central Asia and the so-called Middle East that sit on oilfields or athwart oil pipelines.[145] The Pakistani journalist, Ahmed Rashid, has called this strategic positioning 'the New Great Game', an explicit reference to Rudyard Kipling's description of the imperial projects of Russia and Britain in the lands between India and the Arab lands at the eastern end of the Mediterranean.[146] This new imperial

[138] Roberts, *End of Oil*, 111.

[139] James Paul of the Global Policy Forum, quoted in Phillips, *American Theocracy*, 91.

[140] Phillips, *American Theocracy*, 76.

[141] Quoted in Phillips, *American Theocracy*, 83.

[142] Copulus, *America's Achilles Heel*.

[143] Copulus, 'Testimony before the Senate Foreign Relations Committee March 30, 2006'. No longer on the Senate web page (http://www.senate.gov/~foreign/testimony/2006/Copulos Testimony060330.pdf), but still at http://www.evworld.com/article.cfm?storyid=1003, accessed 20 July 2008.

[144] Energy Information Administration, 'Official Energy Statistics'. Based on oil imports for 2006 and a barrel price in 2008 of \$100.

[145] Kleveman, *New Great Game*.

[146] Rashid, *Taliban*.

project is, however, subject to many of the objections that Mackinder encountered when beating the drum for intervention in Russia in 1919–20. There is a very real concern that the whole venture might be too expensive. Joseph Stiglitz, Chief Economist to the World Bank 1997–2000, and his colleague Linda Bilmes have estimated the cost of the war in Iraq as likely to be $2 trillion by the end of 2015, a significant figure given that the current, and to many observers unsustainable, national debt held by the US government is between $10 trillion and $15 trillion.[147] Moreover, as this massive expenditure seems far from providing a secure environment in which American companies and American consumers can exploit the oil of Iraq, many worry about the costs and risk of imperial overreach, including Brzezinski, who warns that: 'America is acting like a colonial power in Iraq. But the age of colonialism is over. Waging a colonial war in the post-colonial age is self-defeating'.[148] Mearsheimer, likewise, criticizes the war in Iraq as a mistaken venture, for it demonstrates that the United States has abandoned its effective role as an offshore balancer and now acts instead as a land-power attacking other regimes, and holding territory that it must then administer.[149]

In other words, individuals who believe very firmly in the right of the United States to use force are criticizing the occupation of Iraq as the wrong sort of application of military might. They justify extensive infringements upon the sovereignty of others as acts of Liberal Imperialism. Foregoing the claim that intervention abroad is in the national interest, imperialists can yet claim that it is in the interest of the foreign people themselves. Robert Cooper, for example, bemoans the fact that '[t]he imperial instinct is dead, at least among the Western powers'.[150] To his mind, there are precious few alternative ways to bring order and stability to the 'failed states' of the world system. Michael Ignatieff is one of many commentators to see a new, and justified, strain of imperialism in American foreign policy; one based on democracy, human rights, and free markets.[151] The former UK Prime Minister, Tony Blair, differed from these commentators only in seeing a role for Europe alongside the United States in this new imperialism. He defended NATO's intervention in Kosovo, for example, as a new kind of war, 'based not on any territorial ambitions but on values'.[152]

Liberal Imperialism is understood as addressing the incompleteness of the Western triumph of globalization that Fukuyama saw ending history. According to the historian of Empire, Niall Ferguson:

[A]lthough Anglophone economic and political liberalism remains the most alluring of the world's cultures, it continues to face, as it has since the Iranian revolution, a

---

[147] Bilmes and Stiglitz, 'Economic Costs of the Iraq War'; Phillips, *American Theocracy*, 338.
[148] Brzezinski, 'Five Flaws'.
[149] Mearsheimer, 'Morgenthau and the Iraq War'.
[150] Cooper, *Breaking*, 32.
[151] Ignatieff, *Empire Lite*.
[152] Blair, 'Economic Club, Chicago'.

serious threat from Islamic fundamentalism. In the absence of formal empire, it must be open to question how far the dissemination of Western 'civilization'—meaning the Protestant–Deist–Catholic–Jewish mix that emanates from modern America—can safely be entrusted to Messrs Disney and McDonald.[153]

The United States, in Ferguson's view, needs to recognize that along with global economic and military hegemony comes imperial responsibilities—'to export its capital, its people and its culture to those backward regions which need them most urgently and which, if they are neglected, will breed the greatest threats to its security'.[154] The US military strategist, Thomas Barnett, argues in similar fashion that the United States must enforce 'connectedness' upon other countries because only in this fashion will they become good neighbours in the world system.[155] Similarly, Bobbitt does not see that states should be given the option of autarky. The United States as a market state might justifiably eliminate the 'leadership cadres' of states that refuse to let their people engage with the benefits of globalization.[156]

Very clear connections exist between calls for military intervention to install democracy in the post-Cold War world and the style of Liberal Imperialism pursued by Lloyd George and Mackinder (Chapter 7). It is, in short, to use the words of the legal theorist, Anne Orford, 'a new form of imperial domination'.[157] Refusing the invitation of globalization is, for Bobbitt and Barnett, anti-democratic; liberal economies benefit all people. Autarkic states and economies are, they believe, corrupt and inefficient and will thus fail. On this view, the pre-emptive imposition of liberal social, political, and economic arrangements might well save blood and expense later on. This imposition can be done by military means but it can also be achieved by attaching liberal, or governance, conditions to grants or loans. Imposing democracy, human rights, and free markets in effect abridges the sovereignty of other countries, albeit for reasons that the imperial power insists are selfless.

This Liberal Imperialism is in one important respect a continuation of Cold War policies towards ex-colonies. Imposing free markets prevents states holding natural resources as national assets, or remitting profits to national development. During the Cold War, in place after place, such projects of nationalist economic autarky were presented as communist; to defend the free world many such regimes were deposed.[158] However, the recognition that there are dangers of imperial overreach now, as in the 1920s, can mean that intervention becomes more selective. As such, invasion or occupation is legitimated in terms of saving those suffering subjects repressed

---

[153] Ferguson, *Empire: How Britain Made the Modern World*, 373.
[154] Ferguson, ibid., 381.
[155] Barnett, *Pentagon's New Map*, 169.
[156] Bobbitt, *Shield of Achilles*, 303.
[157] Orford, *Reading Humanitarian Intervention*, 20.
[158] Curtis, *Web of Deceit*.

by tryrants who deny them access to the global market. Today, much like the 1920s, the use of the term 'liberal' is a claim to include not only the opening of national markets and national resources to foreign capital, but also to introduce human rights and democracy, thereby conflating capitalist opportunity with the protection of political liberty.

Naturalizing Empire

Gearóid Ó Tuathail is convinced that Geopolitics 'appeals to right wing countermoderns because it imposes a constructed certitude upon the unruly complexity of world politics, uncovering transcendent struggles between seemingly permanent opposites ("land power" versus "sea power, "oceanic" versus "continental", "East" versus "West") and folding geographical difference into depluralized geopolitical categories like "heartland", "rimland", "shatterbelt", and the like'.[159] Conceptualizing the world as the interrelations between states all too frequently means that state interests appear in theory with a coherence that hides many of the most important aspects of international relations; indeed states get presented as if they were individuals with, consequently, a naïve psychologism.[160] International relations comprise also the relations between people in different places, connections that the philosopher Anthony Appiah insists can be cosmopolitan and not nationalist in character.[161] The incompatibility principle, invoked by Mackinder to explain the urgency of defending Anglo-Saxon dominance, downplays the internal variations within states and the diversity of types of connection between people in different places. We might, for example, invoke a moral economy of migration that recognizes some of the ways that global interrelations tie us in diverse ways as consumers, citizens, and producers to people in distant places and to whom we should extend the opportunity of sharing in our wealth through relocating among us.[162] Today, the incompatibility principle seems to be invoked primarily to prevent such sharing, and any other benefits that may come from in-migration. In this, there is a clear continuity with the substance if not the precise terms of Mackinder's own racism.

---

[159] Ó Tuathail, 'Understanding Critical Geopolitics'.
[160] Fettweis, 'Revisiting Mackinder and Angell', 116.
[161] Appiah, *Cosmopolitanism*.
[162] Kearns, 'Moral Economy of Migration'. There is, for example, a marked distinction between the United States and Sweden in their attitude towards Iraqi refugees yet, while the responsibility for this massive displacement of Iraqis lies more with the United States, far more refugees have been taken in by Sweden. Since the start of the conflict in 2003, 3,775 Iraqis been allowed to move to the United States whereas 'more than 115,000 Iraqis have made their way to Sweden since 2003, and the great majority have been granted asylum': D. Campbell, 'Exodus', 56.

Modern echoes of Mackinder's geopolitical imagination are far from accidental. In this manner, politicians, scholars, and conservative thinkers persuasively make imperialism seem inevitable. This is a new world in which: statecraft must abandon isolationism in recognition of the global interconnectedness of peoples; and, with hostile and incompatible civilizations, national survival relies upon force. By light of our own pacific and defensive use of power, the brazen aggression of others is shown as all the more reprehensible. Should public opinion turn against the selfishness or the expense of imperial ventures, there is always the possibility of recasting them in liberal rather than colonial terms, and offering them as a war for values, not territory or resources.

To find Mackinder echoed so clearly, among a range of current-day thinkers, however, raises preliminary questions about both the novelty and urgency claimed for modern dilemmas. The end of the Cold War caused problems for the exercise of military power by the world's remaining superpower—a peace dividend seemed unavoidable. One alternative was to find danger in the very thing that removed the earlier threat. Thus the apparent triumph of capitalism, signalled by the collapse of the command economies of Eastern Europe and the Soviet Union, was re-imagined as globalization, dissolving state borders and sustaining a new paranoia. When cultural (and religious) triumphalism nourishes fundamentalist arrogance, the unilateral position of the United States can be justified as an exceptionalism that identifies threats behind every difference. Power is seen as an essential resource renewed only through conflict. The United States represents itself as the exemplar of the triumphant liberal paradigm; its own exercise of power defends freedom while keeping the world safe from others who threaten liberty.

Conservative Geopolitics is an unstable compound of *realpolitik* and mission. As *realpolitik*, it treats other states as possessing more or less power and as having interests more or less consonant with one's own. As mission, it treats these interests as mappable onto ideological conflicts of universal and thus supra-state significance. Realist theorists of international relations worry about national supremacy, but missionary Neo-conservatives, are obsessed also with US exceptionalism.[163] Hence domestic social policy is very important to Neo-conservatives; the United States has to embody the values it seeks to impose overseas, and these values are not just the political forms of representative democracy, but include also a series of norms governing the fields of sexuality, the family, religion, and the economy.[164] While both Neo-conservatives and Realists share many of the assumptions of

---

[163] Thus, on a realist reading, Henry Kissinger could ask if better relations with China might have helped US interests despite the ideological antipathy between the two states; Warner, 'Nixon, Kissinger and China'. Similarly, the realists John Mearsheimer and Stephen Walt can ask whether uncritical support for Israel is always the way to serve US interests despite the evident support that they feel Israel deserves: Mearsheimer and Walt, *Israel Lobby*.

[164] Guelke, 'Political Morality of the Neo-conservatives'.

Conservative Geopolitics, Mackinder's legacy is more fully expressed among the former.

In the next chapter of this book, I build upon the alternative perspectives I set out in earlier chapters to offer a brief prospectus for a Progressive Geopolitics that can challenge both the ideals and the account of reality offered by Conservative Geopolitics.

9

Progressive Geopolitics

In 2000, British and US disciples of Mackinder created a think tank, the Mackinder Forum. This Anglo-American group is self-described as 'monitoring political risks to the US, its allies, and multinational corporations' through Geopolitics, defined by the group as the study of 'how states: enhance their national security at the expense of adversaries; take advantage of economic globalization; and regulate the impact of other cultures on national values'.[1] The Mackinder Forum exemplifies the geostrategic perspective of Conservative Geopolitics, that is, a global system of states resolving their conflicts by force. Moreover, the international economy, understood as interconnected markets, is viewed as embedded within this set of conflicts such that war is economics by other means, and vice versa.

Basing statecraft on this perspective is to act in the world as, what the Marxist historian Edward Carr (1892–1982) termed, a status quo power.[2] Such an approach to Geopolitics seeks to preserve power and privilege—then, as a British Empire, and now as a unipolar world under US hegemony—and is depicted in very broad terms in the upper diagram of Figure 9.1. In this book, I have argued that Conservative Geopolitics described and explained global inequalities of wealth and power in ways that made them appear inevitable, even desirable. Yet, I have also noted some of the ways that Mackinder's world view was challenged by contemporaries, and some of the possible lessons we can learn from these historical thinkers. Kingsley, for example, reflected upon the felt injuries of class and gender to energize both her empathy with indigenous peoples in West Africa, and her sense of the injustice of the force used against them. Hobson joined socialist and anti-imperialist causes, and, in this context, articulated his theory of the instability of the capitalist system to demonstrate that the violence of imperialism created benefits for only a few. Kropótkin's illusions about the possibility of enlightened imperialism were shattered by his early experiences as a soldier

---

[1] 'Mackinder Forum, Mission Statement, The Geopolitical Challenge'; 'Mackinder Forum, Mission, What We Do'.

[2] Johnston, 'Carr's Theory of International Relations'. Carr's distinction between status quo and revisionist powers is more helpful than his related distinctions between politics and ethics and between reality and utopia. Ethics is, as Robert Jackson insists, a real element of international relations: Jackson, *Global Covenant*, 8.

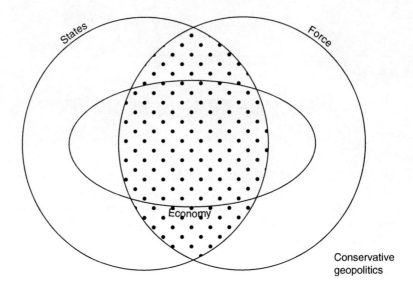

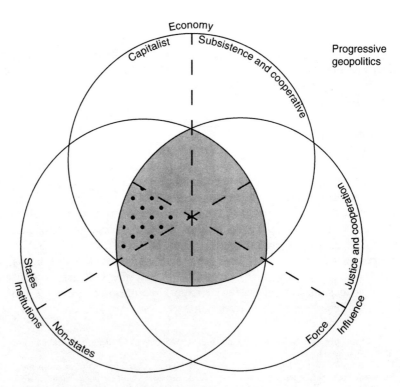

Fig. 9.1. Conservative and progressive geopolitics

and then as a civil servant in Siberia. His suspicion of both state and capitalism was reinforced by the example of the cooperatives of watchmakers in Jura, from whom he learned alternative ways of living. Kropótkin also remained active and prominent in socialist and anarchist politics throughout his life, and spoke on behalf of the Russian socialists at the funeral of Friedrich Engels in London in 1895.[3] Reclus, too, sympathized from an early age with socialism, fighting with and for the Paris Commune of 1871. His experiences in Louisiana produced an intense hatred of slavery and his travels in South America showed him that colonialism often diminished the life chances of indigenous peoples, producing food insecurity and undermining economic and cultural resilience.

Kingsley, Hobson, Kropótkin, and Reclus offered distinct criticisms of international institutions, international relations, and capitalism. Their works were normative and based upon their experience;[4] their ideals were grounded by their observations of imperialism, of relations between states based purely on force, and of the consequences of the restructuring of indigenous societies around free-market capitalism. These critics articulated elements of an alternative world view, a geopolitical imaginary that paid attention to questions of social justice. Based upon their insights, and drawing from empirical examples and social theoretical insights from the present day, I explore the possibilities of such an alternative, or Progressive Geopolitics. In this chapter, I attempt to counter the related conservative geopolitical claims that the global system has to be understood as an anarchy of competing states, that force is ubiquitous and unavoidable in international relations, and that the capitalist system is so dominant that it does not need to be theorized as a distinct element within imperialism. Below I argue that there is more to the reality of international relations than Mackinder accepted in his opposition of 'democratic ideals' to 'reality'. Of course, states, force, and markets do matter, and in some circumstances have the potential to make some people's lives much better. In many cases, however, each of these has been used to make many people's lives much worse, to further advantage for the rich. A broader perspective of international relations is necessary if we are to take full account of the progressive potential of our age.

My three central claims are illustrated in the lower diagram of Figure 9.1. There is more to international relations than either states or force, and I begin by underlining the progressive potential of non-state entities, such as transnational corporations (TNCs), non-governmental organizations (NGOs), and multilateral agencies. Secondly, the significance of cooperation and conflict resolution in world affairs is highlighted to indicate the value of peacemaking and international law. Finally, I treat the economy as an important and independent dimension of international relations rather than

---

[3] J. Green, *Engels*, 288.

[4] I have discussed in more general terms these relations between science and norms in: Kearns, 'Virtuous Circle'.

as completely embedded within the relations of force between states. I divide the economy further into capitalist and non-capitalist elements, and, in recalling the close relations between contemporary imperialism and modern capitalism, I indicate the toughness and potential of non-commodified labour.

This chapter treats Conservative Geopolitics as comprising only one of the six segments included in Progressive Geopolitics, while acknowledging that the dualism depicted in the lower diagram of Figure 9.1 is a preliminary, if inadequate, way to question the 'naturalness' of the former. Yet if force, states, and a capitalist economy define a geopolitical imaginary, then, what counts as the reality of the world, as well as the potential prospects for change, are seriously limited. The feminist geographical author J. K. Gibson-Graham put this very clearly:

> When theorists depict patriarchy, or racism, or compulsory heterosexuality, or capitalist hegemony they are not only delineating a formation they hope to see destabilized or replaced. They are also generating a representation of the social world and endowing it with performative force. To the extent that this representation becomes influential it may contribute to the hegemony of a 'hegemonic formation'; and it will undoubtedly influence people's ideas about the possibilities of difference and change, including the potential for successful political interventions.[5]

Progressive Geopolitics supplements the vision of the world that counts as reality within Conservative Geopolitics by: adding a recognition of the scope of non-force alongside the study of the role of force in the world; including a review of other institutions that operate internationally beside states; and acknowledging that there are more ways that goods and services are produced and supplied than as commodities and through unregulated competition. A Progressive Geopolitics recognizes that the most effective ways to resolve global issues without resorting to force often involve multilateral institutions, and that without coercion, capitalism would not spread nearly so 'naturally'. Indeed, force has often been used to break down the resistance of the non-capitalist sector to the commodification of land, labour, and resources; the mutual dependence of states and economic agents of various kinds make evident the political choices at the heart of economic regulation.

Claiming the term Progressive for this alternative perspective indicates the normative intent. While questioning the naturalness of inequalities is not new, it remains, to some extent, a marginalized perspective, particularly when expressed by those excluded from the privileges of power. This chapter draws heavily from such perspectives and theories. As social theorist, Robert Young, helpfully explains, post-structuralist theory built upon the insights and challenges articulated first as part of anti-colonial struggles.[6]

---

[5] Gibson-Graham, *End of Capitalism*, x.

[6] Young, *White Mythologies*. Richard Kearney has made related arguments about the creative engagement of Irish thinkers historically in critiquing British 'enlightened' discourses; Kearney, 'Irish Mind'.

Geographer David Slater has also outlined some of what we can learn about North–South relations from theory produced in the Global South.[7] In addition, environmentalist Paul Hawken describes the wisdom and imagination articulated by social justice and environmentalist activists arising from indigenous-peoples' movements.[8] Solidarity and empathy can help us hear these lessons.

International Institutions

Many states and non-state actors deepen global inequalities of wealth and opportunity. The World Trade Organization, for example, enforces the Trade Related Aspects of Intellectual Property agreements (known as TRIPs) to permit companies based in wealthier countries to act as rentiers collecting tribute from producers in poorer countries. Many countries in the Global South are thus judged to have used technologies or plants upon which companies based in wealthier countries claim a patent, even where these plants, for example, have long been used in indigenous agriculture.[9] Transnational corporations (TNCs), likewise, are notorious for undermining the sovereignty of states, blackmailing them with threat of relocation if favourable terms are not offered with regard to taxation, environmental regulation, or labour discipline—actions celebrated by some as 'lean production'.[10] Beyond this, some TNCs have directly aided repressive regimes to secure access to local resources and labour. Legal scholar Erin Borg, for example, writes of the 'American corporations acting in violation of human rights standards through their activities in foreign countries', noting in particular that:

Throughout the early- to mid-1990s [the] Firestone [Tire and Rubber Company] financially supported a violent warlord [Charles Taylor] in Liberia so the company could continue to extract rubber from the African nation without incident. Its support of the warlord directly paid for military training and communications that were necessary to stage violent uprisings against the Liberian people and the internationally-recognized Liberian government.[11]

While these powerful criticisms are valid and necessary, and scholars and activists need to continue documenting such matters, the meta-narrative of an all-powerful globalization that operates through non-state actors is a

---

[7] Slater, *Geopolitics and the Post-colonial*. In related terms, on urban theory, see: Robinson, *Ordinary Cities*.

[8] Hawken, *Blessed Unrest*.

[9] Wallach and Woodall, Public Citizen, *Whose Trade Organization?*; Shiva, *Stolen Harvest*.

[10] Womack, Jones, and Roos, *Machine that Changed the World*.

[11] Borg, 'Sharing the Blame', 610–11.

rather limited way of theorizing both state and non-state actors. States retain greater powers than neoliberal ideologists wish to admit, and the labour practices of any non-state actor, such as a TNC, continue to be influenced strongly by the regulatory regime that prevails in its home country.[12] Furthermore, there does not, in fact, appear to be a general dilution of national policies on labour or environmental regulation in many countries: there is no general race to the bottom.[13] The economist William Tabb argues that first 'we must address the defeatist acceptance of inexorable capital hegemony' and that second we must 'look more carefully at what *is* new in the present conjuncture'.[14] While Tabb focuses on the first task, here I take up the second by outlining ways to regulate TNCs, acknowledging the agency of NGOs, and exploring the covenance and treaty powers of multilateral agencies.

The Regulation of Transnational Corporations

The regulation of the rights of capital in the interests of labour is nothing new. Karl Marx, for example, endorsed the British legislation (1847) that aimed to restrict the working day to no more than ten hours. He called it 'the victory of a principle; it was the first time in broad daylight the political economy of the middle class succumbed to the political economy of the working class'.[15] The international nature of non-state actors such as TNCs creates further challenges but also new opportunities for regulating capital in the interests in labour. George Tsogas, an economist, suggests that trade regulations provide a useful framework within which to police labour practices.[16] The legal theorist, Beth Stephens argues that international law can be an effective arena for imposing on TNCs minimum standards in employment practices (according to a human rights framework).[17] There are three main ways to regulate TNCs and increase international labour standards: through international law, voluntary compacts, and international solidarity.

International law prohibits inhumane and unethical practices, such as slavery. In some countries, local courts can be used to prosecute abuses of human rights, even if the crime occurred abroad. For example, Burmese plaintiffs used the US 1789 Alien Tort Claims Act to prosecute a US oil company, Unocal, for its use of the Burmese military to coerce workers Unocal employed to build a pipeline.[18] This rare success, which ran from 1996 to 2004, was finally decided in the US Supreme Court. Unocal settled

[12] Hirst and Thompson, *Globalization in Question*; Christopherson and Lillie, 'Neither Global nor Standard'.
[13] Drezner, 'Globalization and Policy Convergence'.
[14] Tabb, 'Globalization is *an* Issue', 21.
[15] K. Marx, 'Inaugural Address of the IWMA', 79.   [16] Tsogas, *Labor Regulation*.
[17] Stephens, 'Amorality of Profit'.   [18] Collingsworth, *Alien Torts Act*.

out of court.[19] Borg concluded that because 'the statute's lack of clarity, conflicting court interpretations, and other flaws have almost swallowed the statute whole', new statutes are needed to prevent companies from the United States abusing human rights abroad.[20] Reform is needed to fulfil the promise of the Alien Tort Claims Act.

The second way that TNCs may be subjected to regulation is through voluntary compacts and international pressure. Some of these arrangements were developed by TNCs themselves as a result of building 'trans-territorial production' spaces within which to establish legal and technological norms for conducting business.[21] In 2000, the United Nations tried to promote corporate social responsibility through a Global Compact that set out ten principles.[22] Companies were invited to affirm these principles and report annually on the progress they had made. Although the UN lists those companies that make no report, there is no clear mechanism that enforces inspection, independent reporting, or punishes violation of the compact.[23] Some commentators have argued that where the public standards acceptable in the home country of the corporation reinforce the commitment to the Global Compact, then domestic public opinion forces corporations to be seen to comply with the Compact's labour and environmental standards abroad.[24]

The third mechanism for regulating TNCs is international solidarity. This operates in a number of ways. Consumers in one country can boycott or patronize companies on the basis of their record on labour or the environment in another country.[25] Campaigns by trades unions may promote the right to labour organization within particular TNCs across borders.[26] In addition, some international fora build international solidarity in giving standing to a diverse range of organizations, including pressure groups, NGOs, states, and even TNCs themselves, throwing light upon TNC activities and drawing them into making commitments on labour and environmental standards.[27] Finally, indigenous groups may appeal to the liberalism of both human rights and international law to recruit international support for a local campaign, as did the people living in the Niger Delta who mobilized around an Ogoni Bill of Rights in 1990.[28] The legal scholar, Bradley Karkkainen, argues that the evolving forms of environmental law

[19] Rosencranz and Louk, 'Doe v. Unocal'.
[20] Borg, 'Sharing the Blame', 643.
[21] A. Amin, 'European Union', 671; Barry, 'Technological Zones'.
[22] McIntosh, Waddock, and Kell, *Learning to Talk*.
[23] Monshipouri, Welch, and Kennedy, 'Multinational Corporations'.
[24] Bennie, Bernhagen, and Mitchell, 'Logic of Transnational Action'.
[25] Stolle, Hooghe, and Micheletti, 'Politics in the Supermarket'.
[26] Herod, 'International Labor Solidarity'; Rodriguez-Garavito, 'Global Governance and Labor Rights'; Wills, 'Taking on the CosmoCorps?'.
[27] Freeman, 'Collaborative Governance'.
[28] Osaghae, 'Ogoni Uprising'; Watts, 'Righteous Oil?'.

suspend elements both of the sovereignty and the territoriality of the nation state.[29]

In each of these cases, states extend the agency of TNCs and vice versa; there is not a contradiction but a clear interdependence between state action and the agency of the TNC.[30] Nevertheless, because TNCs operate across borders, an opportunity to regulate international labour and environmental practices exists through each of the three mechanisms described above. A Progressive Geopolitics, in considering the role of non-state actors in global affairs, should pay attention to the shaping of TNC practices as one of the campaigns around which international solidarity can prove effective.

The Agency of Non-governmental Organizations

In the 1950s, there were roughly 1,000 NGOs; today there are around 30,000.[31] As with the TNCs, NGOs are significant non-state actors that have complex relations with states; any theory of geopolitics must account for their role in the creation and maintenance of global social relations.

NGOs operate as networks connecting people in different parts of the world, often by sliding under the wire of national frontiers.[32] Although they still mostly recruit staff in the Global North, the focus of their activity is mainly in the Global South, where they are, claims political geographer, Peter Taylor, 'providing a legitimising platform for dissent and diverse voices'.[33] These connections are not always as effective as they could be since, according to one comprehensive study, there are limited flows of information between NGO branches, and donors in richer countries, for example, are often unaware of the local evaluations and interventions in poorer countries.[34] Geographer Richa Nagar, moreover, with the Sangtin Writers, has described how the excellent work and successes of many communal, village, and/or feminist activist groups sometimes get claimed as their own by NGO workers.[35] Nevertheless, NGOs have a potential, sometimes realized, for shaping new and more egalitarian networks whereby understandings of development issues flow from residents in poorer places to concerned parties in richer ones.[36]

Clearly, NGOs operate in a different manner to states. They have no coercive powers but enable the soft power of networks to collect information, formulate campaigns, and lobby.[37] In a very helpful review, the environmen-

---

[29] Karkkainen, 'Post-Sovereign Environmental Governance'.
[30] Hirst, *Space and Power*.
[31] Beyer, 'Non-Governmental Organizations'.
[32] Bebbington, 'NGOs and Uneven Development'.
[33] Taylor, 'New Geography of Global Civil Society', 270.
[34] Riddell et al., *Searching for Impact and Methods*.
[35] Sangtin Writers Collective and Nagar, *Playing with Fire*.
[36] McFarlane, 'Crossing Borders'.
[37] Wapner, *Environmental Activism*.

tal lawyer, Farhana Yamin, identified six aspects of NGO agency: setting agendas; representing the conscience of people's best hopes; working in partnership with governmental and intergovernmental bodies to deliver services; developing topical expertise; lobbying policy makers; and holding states, corporations, and multilateral agencies to account.[38] Each of these activities is problematic, however, as some of the most intelligent criticism, stemming from within the NGO community itself, documents. Still, many of the most productive suggestions for ameliorating these problems also are offered by NGO experts or participants. For example, NGOs may meet basic needs in ways that result in their actually replacing local political and social capacities, what geographer, Juanita Sundberg, refers to as 'NGO landscapes' and others, even more despondently, as 'white jeep states'.[39] The French sociologist, Alain Joxe, describes humanitarian interventions and the management of the aftermath of conflict by NGOs in terms of a new logic of chaotic empire; the United States, he argues, wishes to manage not the political life of other places but merely their 'demographics and the economy'.[40] This is to understand NGOs as maintaining within the spaces they are given to control, nothing beyond what Agamben has termed 'bare life'.[41]

Yet, there is more to NGO actions than this. The medical sociologist, Paul Farmer, has made a very good case that some medical charities not only dispense medicine, but they also train local medical expertise and raise expectations among people about what they have a right to expect from their own government.[42] Nonetheless, as geographer Jennifer Hyndman's excellent account testifies, the management of refugee people by humanitarian agencies often disconnects refugees from camp administrators in ways that compromise the NGOs' 'best intentions towards achieving participatory structures'.[43] The United Nations High Commission on Refugees is aware of these problems, but pressures from the host countries have usually restricted political life within camps to little more than introducing a representative principle into local administration.[44] NGOs that try to develop rights for refugees may at present only have paper arguments, but it is clear that countries that do accept refugees, and more particularly those that do not, do not always grant individuals cultural, economic, and political rights. These governments have reneged upon commitments they made in signing international conventions.[45] NGOs, as well as multilateral agencies, have an important role to play in making this charge stick.

---

[38] Yamin, 'NGOs and International Environmental Law'.
[39] Sundberg, 'NGO Landscapes'; Sampson, 'Trouble Spots', 332.
[40] Joxe, *Empire of Disorder*, 12.
[41] Redfield, 'Doctors, Borders, and Life in Crisis'; Agamben, *Homo Sacer*.
[42] Farmer, 'Never Again?'; Farmer and Gastineau Campos, 'Rethinking Medical Ethics'.
[43] Hyndman, *Managing Displacement*, 115.
[44] Turner, 'Suspended Spaces'.
[45] Hathaway, 'Why Refugee Law Still Matters'.

Covenanting through Multilateral Agencies

States enter by treaty all manner of multilateral agencies, including the UN, NATO, and the EU, and find these a helpful way of cooperating with other states to manage matters of mutual interest, be they economic, educational, cultural, environmental, or military. Although on occasion multilateral agencies may give standing, or at least a hearing, to other bodies, their primary members are states.[46]

The political scientist, Robert Jackson, has described the United Nations as the embodiment of a 'Global Covenant'. He observes that '[i]f people from the different quarters of the planet are going to deal with each other politically on a regular basis they are going to have to find some mutually intelligible and mutually acceptable, or adequate terms upon which they can conduct their relations. Those terms must go beyond existing cultures and civilizations'.[47] Jackson suggests that a system of states has evolved based upon the respect for the sovereignty of individual states—and thus upon the principle of non-interference by states in the affairs of other states, unless their own security or the stability of the international system of states is under threat.

This is more than just a stand-off between powerful rivals, it expresses a normative principle that the United Nations both enshrines and enacts. The UN began with 51 states in 1945 and now has 190 members due in large part to the extension of the states system to replace European colonies:

The construction of a fully global society of locally sovereign states was only completed in the period after 1945. Many states became independent with the active encouragement of the UN and with a view to joining that organization immediately afterward. The UN General Assembly became a vocal site of anticolonial opposition which undermined the international legitimacy of colonies and culminated in the Assembly's celebrated 1960 Declaration on the Granting of Independence to Colonial Countries and Peoples (Resolution 1514). That broke the back of moral and legal resistance to decolonization, after 1960 it was no longer possible to justify the possession of colonies if their inhabitants wanted to be independent.[48]

The UN, and the principles it embodied, was instrumental in the process of decolonization.

Through the representation of the so-called Great Powers on its Security Council, the United Nations was also charged with keeping world peace after the maelstrom of the Second World War. The Security Council performed indifferently during the Cold War. While open warfare did not break out between the United States and the Soviet Union, the Council was in other

---

[46] The political scientist and peace scholar, Jackie Smith, believes that social justice movements may contribute to the development of global citizenship through being given standing by multilateral agencies: J. Smith, 'Response to Wallerstein'; *idem*, 'Social Movements and Multilateralism'.

[47] Jackson, *Global Covenant*, 14–15.

[48] Jackson, *Global Covenant*, 13.

respects crippled by the competitive ideological crusade that the two powers waged throughout the unaligned world. One or other would use their veto to block the Security Council taking too much interest in conflicts as they arose since the two powers were usually anxious to sponsor rival sides in any war between or within states.[49] This adoption of client states fuelled these conflicts with weapons, money, and other covert military assistance, producing, as political scientist, Ken Booth, reminds readers, 'millions of deaths in proxy wars or wars legitimised or excused by supposed bipolar strategic necessities'.[50]

The end of the Cold War gave the United Nations and the Security Council a much wider scope in peacekeeping and resolving conflicts, as discussed in the next section. It also raised the prospect of military intervention in support of a wide range of human rights and civil liberties. This may easily become a variety of Liberal Imperialism where the intervention is in support of a broader range of principles than the states have committed themselves to by the explicit terms of the Charter of the United Nations. A broader agenda for the United Nations than the general principles of non-interference and state sovereignty runs the risk of bringing the institution into discredit with those who would see, for example, the requirement for representative democracy as an imposition of Western values, what Jackson castigates as a 'crusade'.[51]

Other multilateral agencies, of more limited geographical range, do indeed express and require allegiance to a fuller and more specific set of values, as for example with NATO or the European Union. The reluctance of wealthier countries to provide funds and soldiers for peacekeeping in distant places, and anxiety about the Western, even colonial, nature of such interventions, however, may mean that conflict resolution and peacekeeping relies increasingly upon regional multilateral agencies, such as the Southern African Development Community or the Association of South East Asian Nations.[52] Western countries should consider funding these developments in order to remove the suspicion of colonialism from interventions. Writing of the frustrating attempts to bring aid to Burmese people whose physical security was destroyed by Cyclone Nargis in May 2008, Alex de Waal, Programme Director at the Social Science Research Council in the United States, and Ohnmar Khin, an aid worker in Burma, observed that: 'Burma's generals will simply fight an international aid invasion. A glimmer of hope exists in Asian countries using diplomacy to gain access'.[53]

---

[49] The significant exception proving the rule, was when the Security Council passed a motion censuring North Korea for incursions into the South, precisely because the Soviet delegate was boycotting the Council at the time; Pak, *Korea*, 109.
[50] Booth, 'Cold Wars of the Mind', 38.
[51] Jackson, *Global Covenant*, 343.
[52] McCoubrey and Morris, *Regional Peacekeeping*.
[53] de Waal and Khin, 'Against Gunboat Diplomacy', 19.

International Relations

States and their forceful relations with each other are at the heart of Conservative Geopolitics. Mackinder conflated a productive economy with a forceful foreign policy; both expressed manliness. The costs of competition between nations include the military expenditure that Mackinder promoted so vigorously, yet as Figures 9.2–9.4 demonstrate, force does not necessarily translate directly into better living standards. Figure 9.2 is a scatter-plot that shows the relationship between absolute levels of military spending and GDP per capita in 1900.[54] Historically, there was a broad association but with significant dispersion.[55] Russia spent as much (£43.1 million at 1900 values) as the United States (£41.5 million) but enjoyed a GDP per capita ($1,237 at 2000 values) that was less than a third of the US value ($4,091). The United Kingdom was ahead of the field spending £119.6 million and enjoyed a GDP per capita equivalent to $4,492 at 2000 values. However, it is worth noting that the Netherlands spent only £3.1 million and had a higher GDP per capita ($3,424) than Germany ($2,985) or France ($2,876) who spent much more (£39.7 million and £40.6 million, respectively). It was the failure of the Netherlands to sustain its force in the world, after its Golden Age in the seventeenth century that justified Mackinder's dismissal of the nation as fat, bourgeois, and living on past capital.[56]

Longer-term comparisons between GDP and military spending demonstrate far from straightforward relations. In 2001, the United Kingdom was fifth among the world's military spenders, behind the US, Russia, China and Japan, as illustrated in Figure 9.3,[57] whereas in 1900, from its GDP of £1,885 million, the UK spent £119.6 million (6.3%) on its military.[58] By comparison, the US government budget of $2,407 billion proposed spending the equivalent of 20.3 per cent of the national GDP in 2008, and, of this, 'Security Funding' makes up $553.9 billion and the 'Global War on Terror' a further $145.2 billion.[59] In other words, from every $20 made by the US economy, one (4.8%) is spent on international conflict. The Netherlands is twentieth in the military spending lists but its GDP per capita is better than that of sixteen

[54] The data are from Angus Maddison's historical series for national economic statistics and the National Material Capabilities data set. Both are discussed above in the Introduction.

[55] The rank correlation (Spearman's; r_s) between the two series is 0.324, the associated t-value is 1.713 which is but slightly above the value for a confidence level of .05 for a sample with 27 individuals ($n = 27$; $v = 26$; $t = 1.706$) and in fact corresponds to a confidence level (p) of .0493. If we said that this association occurred by chance we would be right on 4.93 per cent of occasions.

[56] *The Official Report, House of Commons, 5th Series*, 114 (25 March 1919), 333–4; see the discussion in Chapter 4.

[57] The association between military strength and the size of the economy is now much closer than in 1900; $r_s = 0.595$; $t = 9.047$; $n = 150$; $p = 0.000$.

[58] The GDP figure in contemporary pounds sterling is from Officer, 'What Was the UK GDP Then?'.

[59] Office of Management and Budget, *Budget 2008*, 151–2.

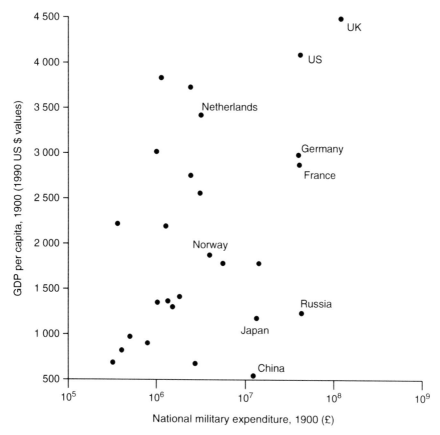

Fig. 9.2. Military spending and GDP per capita, 1900

states that spend more on their military, demonstrating that states don't die, or even go into terminal economic decline, when they cease being Great Powers. Again, some of Mackinder's contemporaries seemed to understand this logic; Hobson argued that competition was inherently wasteful, and Kropótkin emphasized the value of cooperation.

The United States may have the largest military budget in the world and it may also have the largest relative share of the world's wealth with the globe's highest GDP per capita, but a whole series of measures relating to quality of life, such as on education, health, and longevity, indicate that its people gain little from the muscular stance of their country. For all its wealth and power, the United States was only twelfth on the rankings produced by the United Nations Human Development Index, 2005.[60] Figure 9.4 shows that many

[60] United Nations Development Programme, *Human Development Report 2007/2008*, 229–32.

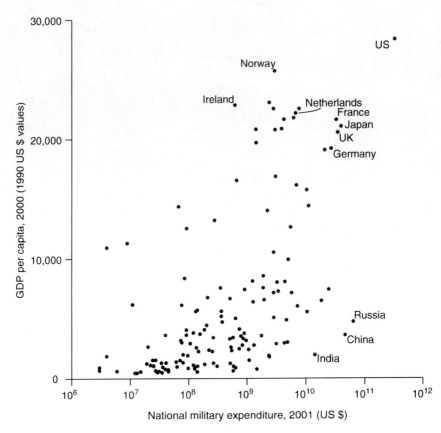

Fig. 9.3. Military spending and GDP per capita, 2001

countries, including Ireland, Norway, and the Netherlands, serve their citizens well without heavy military spending.[61] Many countries might serve their populations much better by cutting their military spending. Moreover, countries that sell arms to states that prioritize military spending, while failing to meet the basic needs of food security, primary education, family planning, water and sanitation, and primary health care are complicit in the resulting tragedy. The economist, Partha Dasgupta, calculated that it would require 5.5 per cent of Gross National Product for the countries of Sub-Saharan Africa to meet their citizens' basic needs, yet they spend only 2.65 per cent on these matters compared to 4.2 per cent on their military.[62] Several European states pay lip-service (quite loudly in the case of the UK) to the idea

---

[61] The overall association although weaker than between military spending and per capita GDP is still strong: $r_s = 0.189$; $t = 2.351$; $n = 143$; $p = .010$.

[62] Dasgupta, *An Inquiry*, 275.

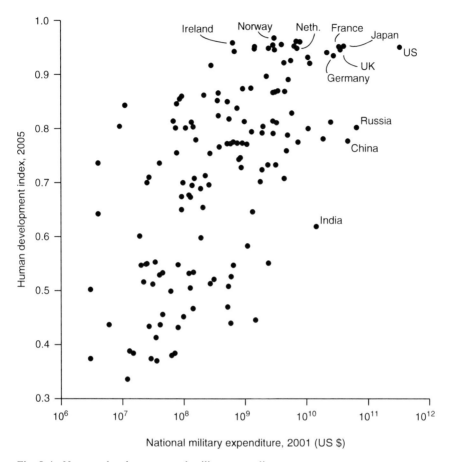

Fig. 9.4. Human development and military spending

that arms should not be sold to countries that are pursuing military strength while ignoring basic needs.[63] The supposed economic benefits of exports often win out, but even here selling expensive goods, on long loans, to poor countries who may default is poor business, and a rather sick sort of aid.[64]

Certainly military strength is now imposed very differently than in the past, and in ways that have changed the relations between states and force more generally. Christopher Fettweis, Associate Professor at the US Naval War College, believes that the world of military strategy has changed dramatically since Mackinder's day.[65] Fettweis argues that, with modern airpower, military force is essentially amphibious and Mackinder's concerns

[63] Stavrianakis, '(Big) Business as Usual', 45–67.
[64] Brittan, 'Weapons Exports'.
[65] Fettweis, 'Mackinder, Geopolitics, and Policymaking'.

about land-power are now largely irrelevant. The British General Rupert Smith argues that the sort of force understood by Mackinder may be termed industrial war.[66] This type of war involves a conscript army using industrial technology to hurl shells and explosives in large quantities at an opposing conscript army. Such war tested which side possessed the larger combination of population and industry. This model of war was later undermined technologically and strategically. Technologically, the atomic bomb represented a weapon that could not be traded with impunity, once the genie had sprung the American box. Strategically, the elaboration of guerrilla war reduced the value of large armies in serried ranks. Today, war is fought, as Smith puts it, 'among the people'.[67] The result is that civilians are used as shield by one side and very often as target by another.

Despite these data by military theorists and experts, the realist model of international relations assumes a world still structured by the prospect of violent struggle between Great Power states. According to Smith, nothing is less likely. Using the Stockholm Peace Research Institute data, Figure 9.5 shows the chronology of types of armed conflict since the Second World War.[68] Not only do these data support Smith's analysis, it demonstrates that the very type of conflict, i.e. between states, upon which International Relations builds its account of the world system, rarely happens. After a flurry of independence struggles after the Second World War, coded as colonial/imperial wars, civil wars dominated the post-war record.[69] Some are shown as involving outside military, although Figure 9.5 significantly underestimates the number that might in some sense have involved external assistance, even provocation. The second striking feature of this graph is the steady fall in armed conflict between states since the end of the Cold War.

An exclusive focus upon force makes peace difficult to imagine, and yet the striking feature of recent history has been the decline in armed conflict. This recession has been widely commented upon.[70] The Human Security Centre reports that '[b]etween 1991 [...] and 2004, 28 armed struggles for self-determination started or restarted, while 43 were contained or ended. There were just 25 armed secessionist conflicts under way in 2004, the lowest number since 1976'.[71] Two reasons explain this decline, both of which are related in some way to the end of the Cold War: the greater salience of the

---

[66] R. Smith, *Utility of Force*.

[67] R. Smith, *Utility of Force*, 17.

[68] Gleditsch et al., 'Armed Conflict'. My diagram uses their latest data to update Figure 1 in Harbom and Wallensteen, 'Armed Conflict', 625; 'Armed Conflicts Version 4-2007'. I am grateful to these researchers for sharing their data so freely.

[69] These civil wars are also the main reason for the steady growth in the number of internally displaced persons over the past two decades, so that now, at about 25 million, they outstrip the number of international refugees, two to one; Office of the United Nations High Commissioner for Refugees, *State of the World's Refugees*.

[70] Goodhand, *Aiding Peace?*; Gurr, 'Ethnic Warfare on the Wane'; Harbom and Wallensteen, 'Armed Conflict'; Marshall and Goldstone, 'Global Report on Conflict'.

[71] Human Security Centre [HSC], *Human Security Report 2005*, 1.

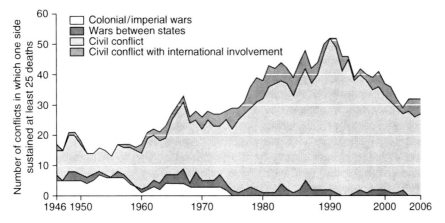

Fig. 9.5. Global patterns of conflict, 1946–2006

United Nations, and an increased attention to international law.[72] During the Cold War, the stand-off between the United States and the Soviet Union paralysed the United Nations, since in almost every case of civil conflict, the two superpowers adopted opposite sides and were able each in turn to veto UN intervention while their side was winning.[73] The Human Security Centre concludes that '[w]ith the Security Council no longer paralysed by Cold War politics, the UN spearheaded a veritable explosion of conflict prevention, peacemaking and post-conflict peace-building activities in the early 1990s'.[74] In addition, the UN promoted humanitarian intervention where human rights abuses within states came to be seen as 'morally entitling other states to use force to stop the oppression'.[75]

The decline in global violence can also be attributed to the greater prestige enjoyed by international law. International war tribunals, originally set up in Tokyo and Nuremberg following the Second World War, are now successfully charging a number of former heads of state and politicians in office with crimes against humanity. When, in 2006, Charles Taylor, former president of Liberia, was surrendered by Nigeria to a Special Court in Sierra Leone, 'Libya's president, Muammar Qaddafi, noted nervously that a precedent had been set. "This means that every head of state could meet a similar fate", he said. Quite so'.[76] Moreover, human rights have developed from being understood as in the possession of individuals, to now include groups, such that both individual and group claims can now be made against the

[72] Since 1988 the United Nations has accepted thirty-three new members; Hobsbawm, *Globalisation, Democracy and Terrorism*, 84.
[73] Traub, *Best Intentions*, 22; Urquhart, 'Limits on the Use of Force'.
[74] HSC, *Human Security Report 2005*, 8.
[75] Wheeler, *Saving Strangers*, 12–13.
[76] 'Bringing Bigwigs to Justice', 52.

arrogance of majoritarian democracies.[77] Within European states, the rights
of minorities, rather than fuelling continual secessionist struggles, have instead been recognized through territorial or non-territorial devolution within
states.[78] The Spanish state, for example, accorded significant regional autonomy to the Basque and Catalan peoples, thereby reducing significantly the
political pressure for complete independence, since, as political scientist,
Robert Agranoff remarks in a study of Spanish devolution, 'autonomy
through federal arrangements provides a channel for resolving center and
periphery differences'.[79] These models for preserving the rights of minorities
were articulated very clearly by the Organisation for Security and Cooperation in Europe and by the Council of Europe. They were adopted by many
Eastern European states when they exchanged state communism for liberal
democracy. The prestige and economic benefits of these models made them
acceptable as alternatives to conflict in very many other places so that '[b]y
the late 1990s, the most common strategy among ethnic groups was not
armed conflict but prosaic politics'.[80] For many groups, of course, there
are real advantages in moving beyond states, by pooling sovereignty in
order to reduce regional tensions.[81] This is what Germany and France
achieved after the Second World War through institutions such as the
European Coal and Steel Community and (later) the European Union.[82] In
other cases, such as the Philippines, regional autonomy allows all parties
to benefit from economic growth; there is both a peace dividend and an
opportunity to embed economic growth at a sub-national scale.[83]

Violence is, at base, a refusal to listen, but justice, rather than force, is the
salve for many conflicts.[84] Legality and negotiation, as alternatives to force,
are available in more cases than often acknowledged. Peace studies scholar
David Cortright, for example, argues that the spirit of the non-violence
movement is a love of honesty and integrity.[85] Vaclav Havel, campaigning
for civil liberties in communist Czechoslovakia, described the need for parallel civic institutions as a hunger for living in truth.[86] Distinguishing the
power of people acting in concert, from the use of violence by states, the
philosopher, Hannah Arendt, insisted that it was a sense of justice that
allowed people to exploit the opportunities for cooperation rather than
conflict.[87] There are obvious links, then, between non-violence, respect for

---

[77] Elster, 'Majoritarianism and Rights'.
[78] Rudolph, 'Ethnic Sub-states'; Coakley, 'Resolution of Ethnic Conflict'.
[79] Agranoff, 'Federal Evolution in Spain', 496.
[80] Gurr, 'Ethnic Warfare', 53.
[81] Deudney, 'Geopolitics as Theory'.
[82] Jesse and Williams, *Identities and Institutions*.
[83] Schiavo-Campo and Judd, *Mindanao Conflict*; Jones, 'Rise of the Regional State'; Rodríguez-Pose, 'Growth and Institutional Change'.
[84] Dower, 'Against War'.
[85] Cortright, *Gandhi and Beyond*.
[86] Schell, *Unconquerable World*.
[87] Arendt, *On Violence*.

other people, negotiation, and cooperation, as the historical example of Kingsley demonstrated. Yet this circle is difficult to break into if one starts from the premise that all that has ever prevailed is force and rumours of war.

As comparative anthropology demonstrates, war is a recent development in human history, only as old as agriculture and the emergence of states, according to Douglas Fry.[88] Although demeaned by masculinist expressions of state power, techniques for managing aggression and avoiding conflict are everywhere in society. Cooperation has chalked up some impressive successes, as documented by the historian and journalist, Mark Kurlanksy, who has researched numerous examples of the effectiveness of non-violence in a wide range of religious and independence struggles.[89] From her experience of anti-globalization activism, Susan George has also insisted that the discipline of non-violence has been essential to its authority and effectiveness.[90] Coercion offers the misleading promise of a quicker resolution but the alternatives are well established: law, justice, negotiation. Winston Churchill was a late learner but he spoke well in popularizing the aphorism: 'to jaw jaw is always better than to war war'.[91]

Realist theorists of international relations consider international law to be an oxymoron in the absence of a global state. Yet, there are three ways that international law achieves salience. In the first place, states sometimes choose to bring international regulations into national law. On occasion, this is because the international body has such status that it can lead national opinion. Some states agree to accept the guidance of the European Court of Human Rights, for example, out of a recognition that it is a calmer place than tabloid pages for considering what is fair.[92] The transnational, moreover, incorporates more than just states. Some international bodies now allow representation by NGOs and voluntary associations, such that they have become 'the focus of a transnational politics of movements and organizations, and not only an intergovernmental politics between states'.[93]

International law can also become effective if the community of states acts as if it has force. Even in that most bellicose of documents, *The National Defense Strategy of the United States of America 2005*, so-called problem states are described as those which 'often disregard international law and violate international agreements'; 'those who employ a strategy of the weak using international fora, judicial processes, and terrorism', so the strategy continues, contribute to US vulnerability.[94] Conflating law with terror is disingenuous, but the recognition that law can serve as a weapon of the

---

[88] Fry, *Beyond War*.
[89] Kurlansky, *Nonviolence*.
[90] George, *Another World*.
[91] Weidhorn, 'Contrarian's Approach', 47.
[92] Moravcsik, 'Reassessing Legitimacy'.
[93] Cohen and Sabel, 'Extra Rempublicam', 165.
[94] *National Defense Strategy 2005*, 4, 5.

weak is a welcome insight. Yet, more generally, the Neo-conservatives tend to see the recourse to law as in fact a sign of weakness, even of derelict femininity. Writing of the so-called Global War on Terror that followed the international crimes of 11 September 2001, the communications theorist, Usha Zacharias, noted that '[r]efusal by the US to pursue a lengthy process of justice, to avoid dialog, negotiation, and peaceful alternatives come from a culture of hypermasculinity that fears feminine tactics as expressions of weakness'.[95] This rejection of complexity goes also with a moral panic that identifies 'suitable villains', while suppressing dissent in the cause of an 'exaggerated response' to a broadly acknowledged danger.[96] Not only does a militaristic view of the world both draw upon and reinforce a certain version of masculinity but it reinforces also an account of an external threat that translates easily into a politics of domestic racial and cultural purity.[97] To withdraw from this maelstrom of prejudice and violence, states must respect negotiation, international law, and justice as effective alternatives.

The Queen's Counsel, Geoffrey Robertson, has done much to explain, and indeed to advance, the progressive use of international law.[98] He describes three stages in the establishment of international human rights and, on the other side of the coin, crimes against humanity. Some rights have such repute that governments claim to respect them (*opinio juris*). At some point the community of states accepts these rights as universal, acknowledging no option of derogation (*jus cogens*). Finally, each state may come to believe that it is responsible to the community of states and choose to bring to justice anyone who violates these rights, wherever the crime against humanity has been committed (*erga omnes*). Once it has been accepted that certain actions are crimes against humanity, then international law becomes manifest, either through a national court that may agree to hear a case against the accused or through the UN which may establish an ad hoc court for prosecuting individuals for state-sanctioned policies of genocide, torture, or war crimes. In the former instance, the British House of Lords helped establish an important principle when, in 1998, it agreed that the former dictator Pinochet could be extradited to Spain to answer the warrant of a Spanish court accusing him of directing a systematic campaign of torture in Chile. On the other hand, Rwanda and the former Yugoslavia—two egregious failures of UN peacekeeping—resulted in the establishment of international courts. Robertson concludes that since 1993 the International Criminal Tribunal for the Former Yugoslavia has achieved a lot 'in processing and punishing most of the persons responsible for commanding atrocities in the Balkans'

---

[95] Zacharias, 'Legitimizing Empire', 128.
[96] Welch, *Scapegoats of September 11th*, 13.
[97] Sivanandan, 'Race, Terror and Civil Society'.
[98] Robertson, *Crimes Against Humanity*.

and that since 1994 the International Criminal Tribunal for Rwanda has served notice upon the self-claimed 'impunity of genocidal heavyweights'.[99]

The third way that international law is effective is where it provides models that are followed by national jurisprudence. Recently, international law has led the way in formulating group rights and some states have followed suit, thereby placing limits on the so-called tyranny of the majority.[100] The treatment of Quebec and French-speaking Canadians is a very good example.[101] The availability of forms of democracy that respect minority rights has helped some post-communist states, for example, to accommodate regional ethnic claims without secession.

The links between non-violence and justice place a significant premium upon international law and multilateral institutions. The above examples demonstrate that states are necessary, but not sufficient, institutions for moving beyond force. They remain necessary because they are important vehicles for ensuring local consent and accountability, and, as the literary critic, Timothy Brennan insists, will be essential to any strategy for disciplining capital in the interests of labour, of promoting proletarian over bourgeois political economy.[102] Critics of non-state institutions are also right to warn that NGOs can become the tools of Western imperialism, installing external expertise where local capacity and democracy are needed.[103] Justice and legitimacy, therefore, require democratic accountability and a transparent legal framework for both states and non-state institutions.[104] Transparency and accountability are achieved in different ways by states and companies, NGOs and multilateral agencies. While the balance between democracy and law in each case may vary, none of these state and non-state entities should be beyond the reach of either democratic account or legal answer.

Economics and Imperialism

The conflation of national strategic interest with national economic interest is characteristic of the broadly mercantilist perspective of Conservative Geopolitics. Charles Wilson (1890–1961) is only one of many people who have seen no gap between business interests and the national interest. In 1953, while yet CEO of General Motors, he was nominated by President Dwight Eisenhower to the position of Secretary of Defense. Reluctant to give up his holdings in General Motors while in public office, he explained during

---

[99] Robertson, *Crimes Against Humanity*, 405, 409.
[100] Elster, 'Majoritarianism and Rights'.
[101] Brett, 'Language Laws'.
[102] Brennan, 'Subtlety of Caesar'.
[103] de Waal, *Famine Crimes*; Kamat, 'NGOs and the New Democracy'.
[104] Biermann and Dingwerth, *Global Environmental Change*.

his confirmation hearings that while he would put country before firm if necessary, he could not conceive the conflict ever arising, 'because for years I thought what was good for the country was good for General Motors and vice versa'.[105] In 1997, Jeffrey Garten, the former Under Secretary of Commerce for International Trade (1993–5) could straightforwardly report that:

> For most of America's history, foreign policy has reflected an obsession with open markets for American business. The United States has sought outlets for surplus wheat, new markets for autos and airplanes, and access to raw materials like oil or copper. Business expansion abroad was often seen as an extension of the American frontier, part of the nation's manifest destiny. History even records numerous instances when foreign policy seems to have been made or executed by individual companies; protecting the interests of United Fruit, for example, was once synonymous with Washington's policy toward Latin America. More recently, the Big Three auto companies pushed the first Clinton administration to the brink of a trade war with Japan.[106]

Economic interests across class and national boundaries are often contradictory. Moreover, if some business interests have been able to define the national interest as coincident with their own, then others have not. Within discussions of geopolitics, however, the distributional effects of foreign policy, i.e. the way it affects global, national, and regional patterns of wealth and poverty, have not been conspicuous. A Progressive Geopolitics must not only pay attention to such patterns, it must examine how legal and economic forms of imperialism link Neoliberalism to the use of military force. In addition, it must attend to the ways that commodification is itself a global strategy of imperialism that seeks to displace other economic systems, in particular, those associated with the communal use of resources and environments.

Accumulation by Occupation

The political philosophers, Hardt and Negri, raise an important question when they suggest that the 'problematic of Empire' is '[w]ho will decide on the definitions of justice and order [...]? Who will be able to define the concept of peace?'[107] For legal philosopher Susan Marks this is equivalent to asking 'what sovereignty is'.[108] My suggestion is that the sovereignty under construction in the Global War on Terror is a Global State of America. I am not persuaded by Hardt and Negri's claim that the United States has an important but not constitutive role in these developments. Bilateral agreements are part of a specifically US imperialism and do not shape a dispersed Empire.

---

[105] Pelfrey, *Billy, Alfred, and General Motors*, 277.
[106] Garten, 'Business and Foreign Policy', 68.
[107] Hardt and Negri, *Empire*, 3, 19.
[108] Marks, 'Empire's Law', 466.

Imperialism—actions by one state that pursues its own self-interest by compromising the sovereign autonomy of another state—may take legal forms, including what Harvey Rishikof, a US military strategist, has called juridical warfare.[109] Restricting the use that the subordinate state can make of its territory allows the dominant state to secure military bases. These bases and the persons resident thereon are usually not subject to the integrity of local law, but are covered by an assertion of extraterritorial rights by the foreign military power under what are now termed 'Status of Forces Agreements'.[110]

Extraterritorial agreements are rarely reciprocal and have now been supplemented by further unequal arrangements concerning extradition of people identified by the United States as suspected terrorists. Drawing upon Giorgio Agamben's analysis of the state of exception, the Belgian sociologist, Jean-Claude Paye, remarks that the War on Terror 'abolishes the distinction between enemy and criminal'.[111] The United States now claims police powers without allowing for reciprocity; not only are military bases part of the territorial claim but through the status of Forced Agreements, the entire territories, and hence sovereign powers, of states are now subject to the extraterritorial claims of the United States. This one-sided pursuit of freedom of manoeuvre within the territory of formally sovereign states may be subject to serious checks at some point, but the political scientist, John Ikenberry, is rather optimistic in expecting the United States to abandon unilateralism in the near future.[112]

Imperialism takes economic as well as political forms. Activist Naomi Klein has described a 'shock doctrine', or the use of economic blackmail by corporations from rich countries to create opportunities to buy resources cheaply within poor countries, or to create longer-term dependencies in areas vital to national survival, such as water supply or pharmaceuticals.[113] States may be pressured to allow food imports at prices that damage domestic food markets, putting local farmers out of business. For example, the United States and the European Union subsidize some of their local agribusiness to a very large extent. Yet, the United States is currently attempting to negotiate bilateral agreements with poorer countries to deny them access to the US market unless they open their domestic markets to subsidized American produce.[114] States may also be forced to accept seeds that tie farmers to expensive fertilizer purchases or to annual purchases of seeds from the same company.[115] Furthermore, the measures imposed as structural adjustment

---

[109] Rishikof, 'Juridical Warfare'. See the discussion of this in Morrissey, 'Basing and Biopolitics'.

[110] Raustiala, 'Geography of Justice', 2511. The local social and economic consequences of bases are outlined in: R. Woodward, 'Military Geography'.

[111] Paye, *Global War on Terror*, 3.

[112] Ikenberry, 'American Multilateralism'.

[113] Klein, *Shock Doctrine*.

[114] Evenett and Meier, 'Interim Assessment'.

[115] Lehmann, 'Patent on Seed Sterility'.

can destabilize regimes.[116] If, for example, a country does not respond to a balance of payments problem by slashing social spending, or by letting commodity-speculation price food beyond the means of the poor, its currency may be threatened by bankruptcy.

One of the most important challenges for a Progressive Geopolitics, therefore, is to understand how these two dimensions of imperialism are related; to understand, in short, how the War on Terror is related to Neoliberalism.[117] The sociologist, Jan Nederveen Pieterse, has described 'the emerging features of a hybrid formation of neoliberal empire, a mélange of political-military and economic unilateralism, an attempt to merge geopolitics with the aims and techniques of neoliberalism'.[118] To some extent, Pieterse sees militaristic geopolitics as succeeding the period of neoliberalism and he documents a number of tensions between the two while suggesting that both are attempts to maintain US supremacy. If he is right in asserting that the Neoliberal Empire is 'an attempt to merge the America whose business is business with the America whose business is war, at a time when business is not doing so well', then the failure of the United States to raise international revenue to pay for its occupation of Iraq and Afghanistan will only deepen the deficit, making recovery through economic competitiveness less likely.[119] The America whose business is business may become even more reliant on its bellicose partner for its global standing.

Alongside the juridical warfare that tried to make occupation of Iraq immune to local or international law, there was, as the economist Paul Krugman reported, a systematic privatization of many economic sectors, particularly following the appointment of Paul Bremer as Director of Reconstruction and Humanitarian Assistance in May 2003:

A number of people, including Jay Garner, the first US administrator of Iraq, think that the Bush administration shunned early elections, which might have given legitimacy to a transitional government, so it could impose economic policies that no elected Iraqi government would have approved. Indeed, over the past year the Coalition Provisional Authority has slashed tariffs, flattened taxes and thrown Iraqi industry wide open to foreign investors—reinforcing the sense of many Iraqis that we came as occupiers, not liberators.[120]

In Iraq, Bremer both imposed a neoliberal reorganization of the Iraqi economy and, at the same time, purged Iraqi public employment of over 400,000 former members of the ruling Baathist party. Naomi Klein detected a link between the two:

[116] Bradshaw and Huang, 'Intensifying Global Dependency'.
[117] Kearns, 'Geography of Terror'.
[118] Pieterse, 'Neoliberal Empire', 119.
[119] Pieterse, 'Neoliberal Empire', 123.
[120] Krugman, 'Battlefield of Dreams'.

As the Bush Administration becomes increasingly open about its plans to privatize Iraq's state industries and parts of the government, Bremer's de-Baathification takes on new meaning. Is he working only to get rid of Baath Party members, or is he also working to shrink the public sector as a whole so that hospitals, schools and even the army are primed for privatization by US firms?[121]

In 2001, writing in the journal of the insurance company he then worked for, Paul Bremer noted that: '[r]apid economic change often means that large parts of the older controlled economy exist alongside a developing market economy. This creates huge opportunities for arbitrage between the two economies. Anyone who can get control of assets or services in the state part of the economy and dispose of them in the liberalized part can become very rich very fast'.[122] Privatization, then, is a significant business opportunity, for those who organize it.

The War on Terror has multiple causes, or it may be called overdetermined, but among the complex of relevant factors are these associations between imposing democracy and privatizing economies, what I am suggesting here as accumulation by occupation. The political geographer, John Morrissey, has noted the dramatic increase in the military presence of the United States throughout the energy-rich states of the Gulf Cooperation Council: '[f]or the first time, there now appears the contours of a continuous US "ground presence", which has been facilitated by the ongoing Iraq War and broader war on terror'.[123] Morrissey also shows that this was a conscious strategy and cites one advisor to the US Army, Sami Hajjar, who, before the invasion and occupation of the oilfields, described the goals of the United States in terms that recall both Kissinger and Mackinder: 'land power is, in the final analysis, what will secure the world's most precious and coveted real estate'.[124] In June 2008, Patrick Cockburn, a journalist with the British *Independent*, wrote that President Bush was pushing for Iraq to agree to a 'strategic alliance' with the United States under which 'the Americans would retain the long-term use of more than 50 bases in Iraq. American negotiators are also demanding immunity from Iraqi law for US troops and contractors'. Cockburn further reported that 'Ali Akbar Hashemi Rafsanjani, the powerful and usually moderate Iranian leader, said [...] that such a deal would create "a permanent occupation"'.[125]

The Geopolitics of Economic Systems

In political democracy, there is a formal equality (one person, one vote), even though this is compromised in all sorts of ways by the class-selection of representatives, the private ownership of significant parts of the opinion-

---

[121] Klein, 'Downsizing in Disguise'.
[122] P. Bremer, 'New Risks'.
[123] Morrissey, 'Basing and Biopolitics'.
[124] Hajjar, *US Military Presence in the Gulf*, 58–9.
[125] Cockburn, 'Revealed'.

forming media, and the corruption of legislative, executive, and judicial institutions by private wealth. There is neither formal nor substantive equality in the economy. Conservative Geopolitics treats these inequalities as unavoidable, deserved, or ameliorable through general economic growth. Its central claim is that it is not the function of government to address these inequalities as a primary obligation. Indeed, doing so would get in the way of free markets and hamper initiative.

Conservative Geopolitics assimilates economic to military power, seeing this amalgam as the force that secures national survival. In related terms, political and economic freedoms are likewise conflated so that democracy and private property are treated as complementary. In 1990, the economist, John Williamson, coined the term 'Washington Consensus' to refer to the advice he thought most US administrations would offer Latin American countries trying to deal with a debt crisis.[126] The intention was to create conditions under which a capitalist system could work efficiently, but it was broadly about disciplining states so that they did not interfere while market forces rebalanced their economies. The policy advice included privatization of state assets, removing constraints on foreign direct investment, removing import tariffs, deregulating the economy, and creating more secure property titles in the so-called informal sector. The phrase 'Washington Consensus' was taken up with alacrity by people promoting a more extreme neoliberal agenda. They rejected Williamson's suggestion that the policy consensus included state investments enhancing labour and capital productivity (health care, education, and infrastructure), arguing instead for drastic cuts in almost all forms of government spending—except the military. The state should get out of the way while international capitalism did its work. Consider, for example, this economics lesson delivered to the British Labour Party in 2005 by its leader, Prime Minister Tony Blair: 'I hear people say we have to stop and debate globalisation. You might as well debate whether autumn should follow summer. [. . .] In the era of globalisation, there is no mystery about what works—an open liberal economy, prepared constantly to change to remain competitive. The new world rewards those who are open to it.'[127] Markets were treated as both natural and beneficent, unless meddled with by states.

The neoliberal ideology of globalization treats the commodification of everything as both necessary and desirable, and it proposes open markets and deregulation as the way to get there. The neoliberal version of the Washington Consensus was always an international movement, producing a regressive redistribution of income both within countries and between them: the local rich got richer and the foreign investors picked up state assets at fire-sale prices. The geographer, David Harvey, has shown that neoliberal policies have significant '[r]edistributive effects' in favour of the rich, such

---

[126] Williamson, 'What Washington Means.'   [127] Blair, 'Keynote Speech Brighton'.

that they might best be seen as 'from the very beginning a project to restore class power'.[128] In contrast to this neoliberal Washington Consensus form of Conservative Geopolitcs, a Progressive Geopolitics might draw insights from the historical lessons of Reclus, Hobson, and Kropótkin, each of whom, in distinctive ways, were conscious of the ways that inequalities were produced and reproduced (both within and between states) through the practices of imperialism. Their insights point to the need to separate those arguments that delineate when and under what conditions markets are useful, on the one hand, from those arguments that set out whether and what sorts of property are justifiable. In addition, arguments pleading the institution of property in the abstract must be further separated from apologias for any particular distribution of property (between the have-nots, the haves, and the have-mores). Reclus's emphasis upon food security raises another methodological point: an analysis of an economy based purely on exchange values is literally useless. In some contexts money simply can't buy food, and in all contexts the consequences of starvation today cannot be rescued by the next feast.

A Progressive Geopolitics must identify and criticize these mutually reinforcing political and economic dimensions of globalization. Whereas neoliberal policies were applied most stringently in Latin America and in Sub-Saharan Africa, advocates of neoliberalism promote these policies with reference to the success of East Asian economies. Yet this is historically and geographically inaccurate; the Asian tiger economies developed behind pro-tectionist walls.[129] Richard Kozul-Wright and Paul Rayment, two econo-mists who worked formerly with some of the institutions of the United Nations, conclude that '[m]arket fundamentalists insist on putting the liber-alising cart before the domestic-development horse, a mistake that none of the present advanced market economies made when they were starting to industrialise'.[130] Rather than opening their markets, new industrializers must be allowed to offer some protection to nascent industries. Moreover, not all forms of foreign investment help build the capacity of economies or create new production. In many cases, the ownership of existing enterprises simply changes; foreign investors are also often volatile, withdrawing their funds as easily as they brought them in. Finally, the segmentation of many production processes means that while industrial employment may move to poorer countries, the wages remain so low in those parts of the labour process that little of the final sales price returns to the country where most of the work gets done. For example, whereas manufacturing exports from Latin American and the Caribbean moved from being responsible for 1.4 per cent of global manufacturing exports in 1980 to 4.1 per cent in 2001, their share of the global value-added in manufacturing only rose from 4.7 to 5.3 per cent in the

[128] Harvey, *Neoliberalism*, 16.
[129] For an analysis of Japanese economic development along these lines, see: Lee, *The Japanese Challenge*.
[130] Kozul-Wright and Rayment, *Resistible Rise*, 124.

same period. Similarly, the manufacturing export share of the second tier of newly industrializing countries in East Asia (Indonesia, Malaysia, Philippines, and Thailand) went from 0.4 to 3.8 per cent over the same period, while its share of global value added in manufacturing went from 1.1 to 2.2 per cent.[131]

Trade liberalization, therefore, does not redistribute wealth globally, even if work is redistributed. In poorer countries, structural adjustment policies reduce public spending on food distribution, the stocks in public granaries (which mitigate harvest fluctuations), subsidies for fertilizer, and land reform. In general terms, land is transferred from local food production to export cash crop harvests, while more food is imported to meet local demands. European and North American producers maintain global dominance in grain markets, bolstered by subsidies. One 1994 estimate for the subsidy on US wheat was equivalent to 46 per cent of the world price, while for the European Union it was 114 per cent.[132] The consequences for food security in the Global South have been disastrous. Moreover, as production in rural areas moves from food for domestic markets to cash crops for export, resources often move from the women responsible for food to the men who control interactions with commodity markets. One result of this shift in gender labour roles is often that the nutritional status of dependent members of the household drops, since caring for them in many countries is the job of the female heads of house—the wife who now commands fewer resources.[133]

Governments should intervene to redistribute land to poorer people to avoid food insecurity and in this way to extend life to their citizens.[134] Land reform may also directly increase the productivity of land and labour, and create more efficient capital markets. The economist Partha Dasgupta notes that small farms that grow crops more intensively and with greater local knowledge produce more food per unit of land than larger farms; these farmers, while poorer, often feed themselves better (and thus work more effectively) from their own land than they are able to from waged labour. In addition, small farmers with land collateral can get better credit terms than otherwise.[135] Liberalization policies of the past thirty years, in contrast, have undermined food security and deepened rural poverty. The Indian economist, Utsa Patnaik, documented the consequences for the Indian poor. In 1973–4, 56.4 per cent of India's rural population earned too little to afford a daily diet with 2,400 calories and were thus judged to be in poverty. In 1999–2000, the share of the rural population who were poor on this measure,

---

[131] Kozul-Wright and Rayment, *Resistible Rise*, 87.
[132] Patnaik, *Republic of Hunger*, 77; quoting from an OECD report of 1995.
[133] Dasgupta, *An Inquiry*, 275.
[134] Together with Simon Reid-Henry, I have set out some of the arguments why preserving life should be central to modern politics: Kearns and Reid-Henry, 'Vital Geographies'.
[135] Dasgupta, *An Inquiry*, 525.

increased to 74.5 per cent.[136] Yet the Government of India claimed that the poverty figure had *dropped* to 27.4 per cent in this period between the mid-1970s and the end of the century, and the explanation for this disparity sheds further light upon food insecurity.[137] The official figure takes the salary from 1973–4 that was associated with an adequate diet and then adjusts it for price inflation between 1973–4 and 1999–2000. Using inflation adjusted figures, they count as poor only those who fall below that income. However, rural societies are now more commoditized than in 1973–4 when farmers and labourers did not buy all the food they ate; some wages were paid in kind, while both other food and some resources, such as fuelwood, were obtained from the local commons that are now privatized. Finally, more income must now be used for such basics as utilities and health care, before any food is bought. In short, the rural poor must buy more of their food from less of their wages. As the real wage falls, effective demand for food falls; people go hungry and work less effectively. Once again, an analysis of the economy purely in terms of exchange values proves misleading.

The neoliberal imaginary includes only markets and commodities and yet these examples demonstrate that the reality of people's lives in both rich and poor countries includes other significant types of economic relations. Neoliberal policies at best ignore, but more generally undermine the resilience of non-commodified economic relations. The Management Studies theorist, Colin Williams, suggests that non-commodified work, defined as subsistence/household (not done to produce something for sale), voluntary (not done for money), or public (done for money but not-for-profit), is both common and desirable, and should be reinforced and facilitated.[138] In rich countries, there are various ways this might be promoted by the state, such as through collective provision of social goods (education, health), through rewarding new forms of volunteering and communal service, and perhaps the development of a broader form of national service. Grass roots movements include garden allotments, slow cities, farm cooperatives, various non-commercial systems of sale and re-sale (such as eBay, garage sales, or car boot sales), and local systems of work-swaps (such as in Local Employment Trading Systems).[139] In the Global South, non-commodified systems may structure many people's livelihoods to an even greater extent. One indirect indicator is the so-called informal sector. In developing countries, for example, about two in every three women working outside agriculture are in the informal sector.[140] Throughout the world, about 250 million indigenous peoples who make up 4 per cent of the global population have very different

---

[136] Patnaik, *Republic of Hunger*, 180.
[137] Much of this account is taken from the excellent: Patnaik, *Republic of Hunger*.
[138] C. Williams, *Commodified World*, 14–15.
[139] Crouch and Ward, *Allotment*; Mayer and Knox, 'Slow Cities'; Gibson-Graham, 'Enabling Ethical Economies'; Leyshon, Lee, and Williams, *Alternative Economic Spaces*; Lee, 'Moral Money?'.
[140] Chen et al., *Women, Work and Poverty*, 6.

relationships to land, place, history, resources, work, and non-human na-
tures from which a Progressive Geopolitics could do well to learn.[141]

The demographic historian, Stephen Kunitz, has suggested that global
media may offer some support for indigenous movements to develop a
'politics of embarrassment, embarrassment of national governments in the
eyes of the world', whereas international institutions and treaties can encourage states to respect indigenous rights.[142] Some native peoples are gaining
confidence that their folkways have something to teach others about how to
live respectfully with non-human animals and the natural world more generally.[143] The United Nations highlighted 1993 as the Year of the World's
Indigenous Peoples and passed in that year a 'Declaration on the Rights of
Persons belonging to National, Ethnic, Religious or Linguistic Minorities'.
Of course, many indigenous groups for good reason baulk at the notion of
being labelled a minority since in many countries they are sovereign peoples,
and in some places they are majority populations. In all cases, they define
themselves autonomously and not with reference to the other peoples who
claim suzerainty over them. A 1991 resolution of the Home Rule Parliament
of Greenland put the matter very clearly:

It is important that the world's indigenous peoples have fundamental human rights of
a collective and individual nature. Indigenous peoples are not, and do not consider
themselves, minorities. The rights of indigenous peoples are derived from their own
history, culture, traditions, laws, and special relationship to their lands, resources
and environment. Their basic rights must be addressed within their values and perspectives.[144]

The political leadership of these sovereign groups resulted in an UN General
Assembly Declaration on the Rights of Indigenous Peoples in September
2007.[145]

The treatment of indigenous peoples by peoples derived from Europe is
shameful; globalization is only the latest term for the ongoing violent processes associated with European contact that have more than decimated
aboriginal populations through disease, murder, theft of resources, and
disruption of indigenous social, cultural, and economic systems. The historian, Russell Thornton, gives the most judicious estimates for America north
of Mexico, for example, with a decline from 7 million at contact to one-tenth
of this by 1800.[146] For the Americas as a whole, the population in 1492 may
have been 100 million and the indigenous peoples probably declined by

---

[141] Davis, 'Executive Summary', ix. See also: Tuhuwai Smith, *Decolonizing Methodologies*.
[142] Kunitz, 'Health of Indigenous Peoples', 1537.
[143] See, for example, the The Ded Unkunpi (We are Here) Projects, promoted by Mona Smith and
the Dakota, which try, through immersive media art (whether stationary or mobile) to enhance
learning from Native people'; 'Ded Unkunpi Projects'.
[144] Stamatopoulou, 'Indigenous Peoples and the UN', 73.
[145] Godden, 'Invention of Tradition', 396.
[146] R. Thornton, *American Indian Holocaust*, 32.

90 per cent during the following two centuries.[147] These processes continue and, in the first half of the twentieth century, the remaining 1 million indigenous population of Brazil declined by a further 80 per cent. In one part of Amazonia, a gold rush in the 1980s introduced malaria into a new area and within three years, the level of malaria infection among the local Yanomami people had reached two-thirds; while one-third of their population were malnourished, three-quarters were anaemic, and one child in eight had lost one or both parents.[148]

The dispossession of indigenous peoples was central to the accumulation of advantages by Europeans and their descendants abroad. This theft was also the source of the poverty and marginalization of native peoples. As these matters continue to structure life-chances for rich Westerner and much poorer native, there is a clear basis for some form of redress. However, this is simply unimaginable within the framework of universal commodification. One dimension of Colonial Imperialism was, as the legal scholar, Lee Godden, puts it, the imposition of 'the legal space of title and property law [...] over the collective and communal spaces of the [global] South'.[149] For all sorts of reasons, including redress for the current consequences of past injury and out of respect for civilizations older and in many ways wiser than the Western, indigenous rights cannot be framed within the dominant ideologies of capitalist society. Indigenous peoples require communal, individual, and other forms of rights if their cultural norms are to have content and purpose. The right to collective deliberation over resources, for example, is a cultural norm that gives meaning to individual lives.[150] Furthermore, maximalist views of resource-use to foster short-term development must be changed.[151] In managing the use values of the environment, indigenous peoples have and currently conserve a very large part of global species diversity and, as the legal scholar, Matthew Jaska, proposes, there is much to be said for 'entrusting stewardship of particular ecosystems to the finely tuned cultural expertise that indigenous peoples have developed through millennial relationships with their ancestral lands'.[152] Of course, this veritable 'ark' of diversity is a sore temptation to prospectors.[153] Their imperialism needs to be checked.

Any effective respect for the lives of indigenous peoples, as well as the lands upon which they are stewards, requires recognizing that human survival is not well served by the commodification of environment.

---

[147] Churchill, *Genocide*, 97.
[148] Kunitz, 'Health of Indigenous Peoples', 1536.
[149] Godden, 'Invention of Tradition', 388.
[150] Newman, 'Collective Indigenous Rights', 283.
[151] Jaska, 'Putting the "Sustainable" Back'.
[152] Jaska, 'Putting the "Sustainable" Back', 162.
[153] Hawken, *Blessed Unrest*, 30.

A Progressive Geopolitics must include use- as well as exchange-values, and highlight the achievements and further potential of the idea of a Global Commons. The anthropologist, Donald Nonini, asserts that:

What is now at stake at this point in world history is control over 'the commons'—the great variety of natural, physical, social, intellectual, and cultural resources that make human survival possible. By 'the commons' I mean those assemblages and ensembles of resources that human beings hold in common or in trust to use on behalf of themselves, other living human beings, and past and future generations of human beings, and which are essential to their biological, cultural, and social reproduction.[154]

Of course, all societies have a rich heritage of common-use agreements and although these arrangements were marginalized by capitalist enclosure, they were not all eliminated. In many ways, they are being reasserted as communities attempt to control the externalities of modern farming, manufacturing, and residential developments.[155]

These traditions and legal instruments are available to be adapted for international use, as demonstrated by the example of the Law of the Sea. Treating the sea and the seabed as if it were an open resource is less responsible and efficient than treating it as a common resource. This recognition was at the heart of the international process (1989–94) by which the Law of the Sea was revised so that the industrialized nations were willing to accept its constraints on seabed mining:

The motivation for the start of negotiations was the common view that open access does not provide adequate incentives to use the mineral resources in a responsible way: investors were interested in legally secure rights, consumers in stable metal markets, and developing countries in restricting an intense and asymmetric exploitation of the ocean resources by those industrialized states with the necessary technology.[156]

Some commentators suggest that the Law of the Sea could provide a model for other agreements about the global commons.[157] The failure of the collective management of fish-stocks shows the necessity of basing these agreements on scientifically defensible estimates of sustainable levels of use, not merely putting the veneer of common resource over the door to open access.[158] Nevertheless, the study of the geopolitics of the recognition and management of commons provides a necessary corrective to Conservative Geopolitics, which, by contrast, assumes universal commodification.

---

[154] Nonini, 'Introduction', 1.
[155] See, for example, the discussion of the problems of determining boundaries and giving status to relevant stakeholders in: Michel, 'Defining Hydrocommons'.
[156] Bräuniger and König, 'Making Rules', 610–11.
[157] Scheiber, *Law of the Sea*.
[158] Roberts, *Unnatural History*.

Geopolitics: Beyond and Against Empire

I began this book by establishing the close links between the principal questions of Geopolitics and the dominant practices of imperialism. In large
measure, the founders took Geopolitics to be largely about imperialism: the
expansion of states beyond their borders and how this was to be achieved by
their own exceptional home-country. However, I also noted a series of contemporaries of Mackinder who resisted the force of Empire. I have tried to
systematize this set of criticisms, not as a rejection of Geopolitics outright but
rather as laying the basis for a rather different investigation, of the sorts of
international relations that sustain a realistic hope that there is more to
human relations than the tragedy of Empire. A realistic basis for Progressive
Geopolitics must include analysis of the material and political forces of
imperialism, but it must do more and shine light upon the actually existing
alternatives to imperialism, so that these might be built upon rather than
dismissed with indecent haste as both ineffective and impossible.

Progressive Geopolitics must recognize that global political relations can
only be understood as part of a global political economy. It must take
account not only of states but of various non-state agents. It must build
upon and articulate the values of non-violence if it is to serve the cause of
making a better world. Geopolitics in the service of Empire will deny each of
these principles. It will insist that international relations can be understood as
a contest between national wills, based on the relative force of states. When
Mackinder set out this sort of vision for the British people he was challenged
by some contemporaries who questioned British exceptionalism, the inevitability of conflict, and the incompatibility of peoples. It is now our turn to do
the same, to challenge the inevitability of globalization and the emergence of
a Global State of America.

While the parties, economies, and military technologies have changed over
time, this book has pointed to the ways that the central question of imperialism recurs: should the powerful enrich themselves by abridging the sovereignty of others? Now, more than ever before, the peoples of the world
cannot afford to allow the rich and privileged to strip-mine global resources
to serve the Moloch of Empire:

> And a few there are who have the steel
> And it does not suit them to build a plough
> And for those few the whole earth is no big deal
> And nothing for them is eno'.
> They count the men, they count the gold
> And war is the final balance-sheet
> And these few are too much for the world to hold.[159]

---

[159] Brecht, 'War has been Created by Men', ll. 9–15.

BIBLIOGRAPHY

Agamben, G., *Homo Sacer: Sovereign Power and Bare Life* (Stanford CA: Stanford University Press, 1998 [1995]).

Agnew, J., *Geopolitics: Re-Visioning World Politics*, second edition (New York: Routledge, 2003 [1998]).

Agranoff, R., 'Federal Evolution in Spain', *International Political Science Review*, 17 (1996), 385–401.

Ainsworth, J., 'Sidney Reilly's Reports from South Russia, December 1918–March 1919', *Europe-Asia Studies*, 50 (1998), 1447–70.

Alavi, H., 'Imperialism Old and New', in R. Milliband and J. Saville (eds.), *Socialist Register* (London: Merlin, 1964), 104–26.

Allen, J., 'Men Interminably in Crisis? Historians on Masculinity, Sexual Boundaries, and Manhood', *Radical History Review*, 82 (2002), 192–207.

Alston, C., ' "The Suggested Basis for a Russian Federal Republic": Britain, Anti-Bolshevik Russia and the Border States at the Paris Peace Conference', *History*, 91 (2006), 24–44.

Alvaro, G., 'Kropotkin between Lamarck and Darwin: The Impossible Synthesis', *Asclepio*, 55:1 (2003), 189–213.

'Ambassador James Akins Discusses American Middle East Policy at Al-Hewar Center [29 January 2003]', at <http://www.alhewar.org/james_akins.htm>, accessed 14 July 2008.

Amery, L. S., *The Fundamental Fallacies of Free Trade: Four Addresses on the Logical Groundwork of the Free Trade Theory* (London: Compatriots Club, 1908).

—— *My Political Life. Volume One. England Before the Storm, 1896–1914* (London: Hutchinson, 1953).

—— *My Political Life. Volume Two. War and Peace, 1914–1929* (London: Hutchinson, 1953).

Amin, A. 'The European Union as More than a Triad Market for National Economic Spaces', in G. L. Clark, M. P. Feldman, and M. S. Gertler (eds.), *The Oxford Handbook of Economic Geography* (Oxford UK: Oxford University Press, 2000), 671–85.

Amin, S., *Eurocentrism* (London: Zed Books, 1989).

Anderson, W., 'The Trespass Speaks: White Masculinity and Colonial Breakdown', *American Historical Review*, 102 (1997), 1343–70.

Appiah, K. A., *Cosmopolitanism: Ethics in a World of Strangers* (New York: W. W. Norton and Co., 2006).

Arendt, H., 'The Imperialist Character', *Review of Politics*, 12 (1950), 303–20.

—— *On Violence* (New York: Harcourt Brace, 1969).

'Armed Conflicts Version 4–2007' at <http://www.prio.no/CSCW/Datasets/Armed-Conflict/UCDP-PRIO/Old-Versions/4–2007/>, accessed 1 June 2008.

Arshi, S., C. Kirstein, R. Naqvi, and F. Pankow, 'Why Travel? Tropics, En-Tropics and Apo-Tropaics', in G. Robertson, M. Mash, L. Tickner, J. Bird, B. Curtis, and T. Putnam (eds.), *Travellers' Tales: Narratives of Home Displacement* (London: Routledge, 1994), 225–41.

Atkinson, D., 'Geopolitical Imaginations in Modern Italy', in K. Dodds and D. Atkinson (eds.), *Geopolitical Traditions: A Century of Geopolitical Thought* (London: Routledge, 2000), 93–117.

Auty, R. M., 'The Political Economy of Resource-Driven Growth', *European Economic Review*, 45 (2001), 839–946.

Balakrishnan, G., 'Algorithms of War', *New Left Review*, 23 (2003), 5–33.

Balchin, W. G. V., (ed.), *The Geographical Association: The First Hundred Years, 1893–1993* (Sheffield UK: Geographical Association, 1993).

Barbour, K. M., 'Introduction', in *idem* (ed.), *H. J. Mackinder: The First Ascent of Mount Kenya* (London: Hurst, 1991), 1–25.

Barnes, T. J., and M. Farish, 'Between Regions: Science, Militarism, and American Geography from World War to Cold War', *Annals of the Association of American Geographers*, 96 (2006), 807–26.

Barnett, T. M. P., *The Pentagon's New Map: War and Peace in the Twenty-First Century* (New York: G. P. Putnam, 2004).

Barry, A., 'Technological Zones', *European Journal of Social Theory*, 9 (2006), 239–53.

Bassin, M., and A. Konstantin, 'Mackinder and the Heartland Theory in Post-Soviet Geopolitical Discourse', *Geopolitics*, 11 (2006), 99–118.

Bataillon, C., 'La Vision coloniale de l'Amerique latine dans Elisée Reclus', in M. Bruneau and D. Daniel (eds.), *Geographie des Colonisations, XVe–XXe siècles* (Paris: L'Harmattan, 1994), 123–8.

Baty, T., 'Protectorates and Mandates', *British Yearbook of International Law*, 2 (1921), 109–21.

Baudouin, A., 'Réclus colonialiste? Réclus a Colonialist?', *Cybergeo*, (26 May 2003), 1–22.

Bebbington, A., 'NGOs and Uneven Development: Geographies of Development Intervention', *Progress in Human Geography*, 28 (2004), 725–45.

Beddoe, J., 'Colour and Race', *Journal of the Anthropological Institute of Britain and Ireland*, 35 (1905), 219–50.

Bell, D. S. A., 'Empire and International Relations in Victorian Political Thought', *Historical Journal*, 49 (2006), 281–98.

—— 'Victorian Visions of Global Order: An Introduction', in *idem* (ed.), *Victorian Visions of Global Order: Empire and International Relations in Nineteenth-Century Political Thought* (Cambridge UK: Cambridge University Press, 2007), 1–25.

—— and C. Sylvest, 'International Society in Victorian Political Thought: T. H. Green, Herbert Spencer, and Henry Sidgwick', *Modern Intellectual History*, 3 (2006), 207–38.

Bell, M., and C. McEwan, 'The Admission of Women Fellows to the Royal Geographical Society, 1892–1914; the Controversy and the Outcome', *Geographical Journal*, 162 (1996), 295–312.

Bennie, L., P. Bernhagen, and N. J. Mitchell, 'The Logic of Transnational Action: The Good Corporation and the Global Compact', *Political Studies*, 55 (2007), 733–53.

Berghahn, V. R., *Germany and the Approach of War in 1914* (London: Macmillan, 1973).

Berman, I., 'Slouching Toward Eurasia?', *Perspective*, 12:1 (2001) at <http://www.bu. edu/iscip/vol12/berman.html>, accessed 1 April 2008.

Berry, N., *Articles of Faith: The Story of British Intellectual Journalism* (London: Waywiser Press, 2000).

Beyer, C., 'Non-Governmental Organizations as Motors of Change', *Government and Opposition*, 42 (2007), 513–35.

Biermann, F., and K. Dingwerth (eds.), *Global Environmental Change and the Nation State* (Cambridge MA: MIT Press, 2004).

Bilmes, L., and J. Stiglitz, 'The Economic Costs of the Iraq War: An Appraisal Three Years after the Beginning of the Conflict', *National Bureau of Economic Research, Working Paper 12054* (2006).

Birkett, D., *Mary Kingsley: Imperial Adventuress* (London: Macmillan, 1992).

Blair, A., 'Prime Minister's Speech: Doctrine of the International Community; at the Economic Club, Chicago, 24 April 1999' at <http://www.number-10.gov.uk/output/Page1297.asp>, accessed 18 September 2007.

—— 'Prime Minister Tony Blair's Keynote Speech to the Labour Party's 2005 Conference in Brighton', *BBC News Online*, 27 September 2005, at <http://news. bbc.co.uk/1/hi/uk_politics/4287370.stm>, accessed 20 June 2008.

Blaut, J., *The Colonizer's Model of the World: Geographical Diffusionism and Eurocentric History* (London: Guilford, 1993).

Blouet, B. W., 'Sir Halford Mackinder 1861–1947: Some New Perspectives', *Oxford School of Geography, Research Paper*, 13 (1975).

—— 'Sir Halford Mackinder as British High Commissioner to South Russia', *Geographical Journal*, 142 (1976), 228–36.

—— *Halford Mackinder: A Biography* (College Station TX: Texas A&M University Press, 1987).

—— 'The Imperial Vision of Halford Mackinder', *Geographical Journal*, 170 (2004), 322–9.

Blum, W., *Killing Hope: U.S. Military and CIA Interventions Since World War II* (Monroe ME: Common Courage Press, 1995).

Blunt, A., 'Mapping Authorship and Authority: Reading Mary Kingsley's Landscape Descriptions', in A. Blunt and G. Rose (eds.), *Writing Women and Space: Colonial and Postcolonial Geographies* (London: Guilford Press, 1994), 51–72.

—— *Travel, Gender and Imperialism: Mary Kingsley and West Africa* (London: Guilford Press, 1994).

Boardman, R., 'The Manchester Tactical Society: Gaming in Nineteenth-Century Britain', *Political Studies*, 17 (1969), 226–7.

Bobbitt, P., *The Shield of Achilles: War, Peace and the Course of History* (London: Penguin, 2003).

Boone, J., 'Vacation Cruises, or the Homoerotics of Orientalism, Homophobia, Masochism', *Diacritics*, 24 (1995), 151–68.

Booth, K., 'Cold Wars of the Mind', in *idem*. (ed.), *Statecraft and Security: The Cold War and Beyond* (Cambridge UK: Cambridge University Press, 1998), 29–55.

Borg, E. L., 'Sharing the Blame for September Eleventh: The Case for a New Law to Regulate the Activities of American Corporations Abroad', *Arizona Journal of International and Comparative Law*, 20 (2003), 607–43.

Borman, A., 'Harold Williams: A British Journalist and Linguist in Russia', *Russian Review*, 28 (1969), 327–37.

Bortnevski, V. G., 'White Administration and White Terror (The Denikin Period)', *Russian Review*, 52 (1993), 132–54.

Boserup, E., *The Conditions of Agricultural Growth; The Economics of Agrarian Change under Population Pressure* (London: George Allen and Unwin, 1965).

Bowler, P., *The Eclipse of Darwinism* (Baltimore MD: Johns Hopkins University Press, 1983).

Bowman, *The New World: Problems in Political Geography* (New York: World Book Company, 1928 [1921]).

—— 'Geography *vs.* Geopolitics', *Geographical Review*, 32 (1942), 646–58.

Bradshaw, Y. W., and J. Huang, 'Intensifying Global Dependency: Foreign Debt, Structural Adjustment, and Third World Underdevelopment', *Sociological Quarterly*, 32 (1991), 321–42.

Bräuniger, T., and T. König, 'Making Rules for Governing Global Commons: The Case of Deep-Sea Mining', *Journal of Conflict Resolution*, 44 (2000), 604–29.

Brecht, B., 'Life of Galileo' [1941], in *idem., Plays Three* (London: Methuen, 1987), 1–121.

—— 'War has been Created by Men' [1950], trans. F. Sharma, 'Bertolt Brecht: Poems on Contemporary Themes', *Revolutionary Democracy*, 9:2 (September 2003) at <http://www.revolutionarydemocracy.org/rdv9n2/poemsbb.htm>, accessed 1 May 2008.

Bremer, P., 'New Risks in International Business', *Viewpoint: The Marsh and McLennan Companies Journal*, 2001:2 at <http://www.bettermanagement.com/library/library.aspx?l=4521&pagenumber=3>, accessed 20 June 2008.

Brennan, T., 'The Subtlety of Caesar', *Transitions*, 5:2 (2003), 200–6.

'Bringing Bigwigs to Justice', *Economist*, 12 January 2008, 51–2.

Brett, N., 'Language Laws and Collective Rights', *Canadian Journal of Law and Jurisprudence*, 4 (1991), 347–60.

Brinkley, G. A., *The Volunteer Army and Allied Intervention in South Russia, 1917–1921* (Notre Dame IN: University of Notre Dame Press, 1966).

Brittan, S., 'Weapons Exports: The Bogus Moral Dilemma', *World Economics*, 4:2 (2003), 39–56.

Brodie, H., E. W. Doherty, J. R. Fernstrom, E. Fischer, D. Kirk, and H. W. Weigert, *Principles of Political Geography* (New York: Appleton-Century-Crofts, 1957).

Brown, S., 'An End to Grand Strategy', *Foreign Policy*, 32 (1978), 22–46.

Brzezinski, Z., *Between Two Ages: America's Role in the Technocentric Era* (New York: Viking Press, 1970).

—— 'Memo to President, December 26, 1979', at <http://edition.cnn.com/SPECIALS/cold.war/episodes/20/documents/brez.carter/>, accessed 20 June 2008.

—— *Game Plan: The Geostrategic Framework for the Conduct of the U.S.–Soviet Contest* (Boston MA: Atlantic Monthly Press, 1986).

—— 'America's New Geostrategy', *Foreign Affairs*, 66:4 (1988), 680–99.

—— 'The Cold War and its Aftermath', *Foreign Affairs*, 71:4 (1992), 31–49.

—— 'The Premature Partnership', *Foreign Affairs*, 73:2 (1994), 67–83.

Brzezinski, Z., 'A Geostrategy for Eurasia', *Foreign Affairs*, 76:5 (1997), 50–64.

—— *The Grand Chessboard: American Primacy and its Geostrategic Imperatives* (New York: Perseus Books, 1997), 38–9.

—— *The Choice: Global Domination or Global Leadership* (New York: Basic Books, 2004).

—— 'Five Flaws in the President's Plan', *Washington Post*, (12 January 2007), A19.

Buchanan, P. J., *A Republic, not an Empire: Reclaiming America's Destiny* (Washington DC: Regency Publishing, 2002 [1999]).

Buckley, S., 'Remaking the World Order: Reflections on Huntington's Clash of Civilizations', *Theory and Event*, 2:4 (1998) at <http://muse.jhu.edu/login?uri = / journals/theory_and_event/v002/2.4buckley.html>, accessed 10 February 2008.

Bulliet, R. W., *The Case for Islamo-Christian Civilization* (New York: Columbia University Press, 2004).

Burton, A., 'Thinking beyond the Boundaries: Empire, Feminism and the Domains of History', *Social History*, 26 (2001), 60–71.

Buruma, I., 'Lost in Translation: The Two Minds of Bernard Lewis', *New Yorker*, 14 June 2004, at <http://www.newyorker.com/archive/2004/06/14/040614crbo_books>, accessed 20 June 2008.

Bush, G. W., 'Remarks by the President; White House Lawn, 16 September 2001' at <http://www.whitehouse.gov/news/releases/2001/09/20010916–2.html>, accessed 23 September 2007.

—— 'Address to a Joint Session of Congress and the American People, 20 September 2001' at <http://www.whitehouse.gov/news/releases/2001/09/20010920–8.html>, accessed 23 September 2007.

—— 'Remarks by the President on Winston Churchill and the War on Terror, Library of Congress, 4 February 2004' at <http://www.whitehouse.gov/news/ releases/2004/02/20040204–4.html>, accessed 14 July 2008.

Cain, P. J., 'J. A. Hobson, Cobdenism, and the Radical Theory of Economic Imperialism, 1898–1914', *Economic History Review*, N.S. 31 (1978), 565–84.

—— 'Empire and the Languages of Character and Virtue in Later Victorian and Edwardian Britain', *Modern Intellectual History*, 4 (2007), 249–73.

Campbell, D., 'Exodus: Where will Iraq go Next', *Harper's Magazine* (April 2008), 50–6.

Campbell, K. M., and C. Johnson Ward, 'New Battle Stations?', *Foreign Affairs*, 82:5 (2003), 95–103.

Cantor, L. M., 'Halford Mackinder: His Contribution to Geography and Education', M.A. thesis, University of London (1960).

Carlton, D., 'Churchill and the Two "Evil Empires" ', *Transactions of the Royal Historical Society*, 11 (2001), 331–51.

Carr, E. H., *The Twenty Years' Crisis 1919–1939: An Introduction to the Study of International Relations* (London: Palgrave, 2001 [1940]).

Carter, J., 'State of the Union Address 1980, January 23, 1980' at http://www. jimmycarterlibrary.org/documents/speeches/su80jec.phtml, accessed 18 June 2008.

Carty, A., 'Marxism and International Law: Perspectives for the American (Twenty-First) Century?', *Leiden Journal of International Law*, 17 (2004), 247–70.

Casement, R., 'The Main Report' [1903], in S. Ó Síocháin and M. O'Sullivan (eds.), *The Eyes of Another Race: Roger Casement's Congo Report and 1903 Diary* (Dublin: University College Dublin Press, 2003), 49–117.

Castells, M., *The Rise of the Network Society* (Oxford UK: Blackwell, 2000).

Chen, M., J. Vanck, F. Lands, and J. Heintz, with R. Jhabvala and C. Bonner, *Progress of the World's Women 2005: Women, Work and Poverty* (New York: United Nations Development Fund for Women, 2005).

Cheney, R., 'Vice President's Remarks at the World Affairs Council of Philadelphia Luncheon Honoring Professor Bernard Lewis', at <http://www.whitehouse.gov/news/releases/2006/05/20060501-3.html>, accessed 20 June 2008.

Chomsky, N., *Radical Priorities* (Montréal: Black Rose Books, 1981).

Christopherson, S. and N. Lillie, 'Neither Global nor Standard: Corporate Strategies in the New Era of Labor Standards', *Environment and Planning A*, 37 (2005), 1919–38.

Churchill, W. S., *The World Crisis: The Aftermath* (London: Thornton Butterworth, 1929).

Churchill, W., *A Little Matter of Genocide: Holocaust and Denial in the Americas, 1492 to the Present* (San Francisco CA: City Lights Books, 1997).

Claeys, G., 'The "Survival of the Fittest" and the Origins of Social Darwinism', *Journal of the History of Ideas*, 61 (2000), 223–40.

Clark, J. P., 'The Dialectical Social Geography of Élisée Reclus', in A. Light and J. M. Smith (eds.), *Philosophy and Geography I: Space, Place and Environmental Ethics* (Lanham MD: Rowman and Littlefield, 1997), 117–42.

Clarke, P., 'Introduction', in J. A. Hobson, *Crisis of Liberalism: New Issues of Democracy* (Brighton: Harvester Press, 1974 [1909]), i–xliii.

Clifford, J., 'Travelling Cultures', in L. Grossberg, C. Nelson, and P. Treichler (eds.), *Cultural Studies* (London: Routledge, 1992), 96–116.

Clover, C., 'Dreams of the Eurasian Heartland: The Reemergence of Geopolitics', *Foreign Affairs*, 78:2 (1999), 9–13.

Coakley, J., 'Approaches to the Resolution of Ethnic Conflict: The Strategy of Non-territorial Autonomy', *International Political Science Review*, 15 (1994), 297–314.

Cockburn, P., 'Revealed: Secret Plan to Keep Iraq Under US Control', *Independent*, 5 June 2008, at <http://www.independent.co.uk/news/world/middle-east/revealed-secret-plan-to-keep-iraq-under-us-control-840512.html>, accessed 20 June 2008.

Cohen, J., and C. Sabel, 'Extra Rempublicam Nulla Justitia?', *Philosophy and Public Affairs*, 34 (2006), 147–75.

Colás, A., *Empire* (Cambridge UK: Polity, 2007).

A Collection of Reports on Bolshevism in Russia: Abridged Edition of Parliamentary Paper, Russia no. 1, 1919 (London: Stationery Office, 1919).

Collingsworth, T., *The Alien Torts Act—A Vital Tool for Preventing Corporations from Violating Fundamental Human Rights* (Washington DC: International Labor Rights Fund, 2003).

Connolly, W. E., 'The New Cult of Civilizational Superiority', *Theory and Event*, 2:4 (1998) at <http://muse.jhu.edu/login?uri=/journals/theory_and_event/v002/2.4connolly.html>, accessed 10 February 2008.

Conrad, J., 'Geography and Some Explorers' [1924], in *idem.*, *Last Essays* (New York: Doubleday, Page, and Co., 1926), 1–21.

Cooley, A., 'U.S. Bases and Democratization in Central Asia', *Orbis*, 52 (2008), 65–90.

Cooper, R., *The Postmodern State and the World Order* (London: Demos, 2000).

—— 'Why We Still Need Empires', *Observer*, 7 April 2002, 27.

—— *The Breaking of Nations: Order and Chaos in the Twenty-First Century* (London: Atlantic Books, 2003).

Copulus, M. R., *America's Achilles Heel, the Hidden Costs of Imported Oil: A Strategy for Energy Independence* (Washington DC: National Defense Council Foundation, 2003).

—— 'Testimony before the Senate Foreign Relations Committee March 30, 2006', at <http://www.evworld.com/article.cfm?storyid=1003>, accessed 20 July 2008.

Cornell, S. E., 'The United States and Central Asia: In the Steppes to Stay?', *Cambridge Review of International Affairs*, 17 (2004), 239–54.

Cornwell, J., *Hitler's Scientists: Science, War, and the Devil's Pact* (London: Viking, 2003).

Cortright, D., *Gandhi and Beyond: Non-violence for an Age of Terrorism* (Boulder CO: Paradigm, 2006).

Cosgrove, D., *Apollo's Eye: A Cartographic Genealogy of the Earth in the Western Imagination* (Baltimore MD: Johns Hopkins University Press, 2001).

Crampton, A., and G. Ó Tuathail, 'Intellectuals, Institutions and Ideology: The Case of Robert Strausz-Hupé and "American Geopolitics" ', *Political Geography*, 15 (1996), 533–55.

Creagh, R., 'Critique: Badouin, A.; Reclus Colonialiste?', at <http://raforum.info/reclus/spip.php?article106&lang=fr>, accessed 22 December 2007.

Crouch, D., and D. Ward, *The Allotment: Its Landscape and Culture* (London: Faber, 1988).

Cunningham, H., 'Jingoism in 1877–78', *Victorian Studies*, 14 (1971), 419–53.

Cunningham, W., 'English Imperialism', *Atlantic Monthly*, 84:501 (1899), 1–7.

Currie, R., 'The Arts and Social Studies, 1914–1939', in B. Harrison (ed.), *The History of the University of Oxford. Volume VIII. The Twentieth Century* (Oxford UK: Clarendon Press, 1994), 109–38.

Curtis, M., *Web of Deceit: Britain's Real Role in the World* (London: Vintage, 2003).

Curzon, G. N., *Russia in Central Asia in 1889 and the Anglo-Russian Question* (London: Longmans, Green and Co., 1889).

—— 'The Transcaspian Railway', *Proceedings of the Royal Geographical Society*, N.S. 11 (1889), 273–95.

—— 'The Karun River and the Commercial Geography of South-West Persia', *Proceedings of the Royal Geographical Society*, N.S. 12 (1890), 509–32.

—— *Persia and the Persian Question. Volume 1* (London: Longmans, Green and Co., 1892).

—— *Persia and the Persian Question. Volume 2* (London: Longmans, Green and Co., 1892).

—— *Frontiers* (Oxford UK: Clarendon Press, 1907).

Daalder, I. H., and J. M. Lindsay, *America Unbound: The Bush Revolution in Foreign Policy* (Washington DC: Brookings Institution Press, 2003).

Dagan, H., *Enquête sur l'Antisémitisme* (Paris: P.-V. Stock, 1899).

Dalby, S., 'Ecological Politics, Violence, and the Theme of Empire', *Global Environmental Politics*, 4:2 (2004), 1–11.

Dalley, P., The Black Hole: Money, Myth and Empire (London: FigTree, 2006).

Daniels, S., and C. Nash, 'Lifepaths: Geography and Biography', *Journal of Historical Geography*, 30 (2004), 449–58.

Darwin, C. R., *On the Origin of Species by Means of Natural Selection, or the Preservation of Favoured Races in the Struggle for Life* (London: John Murray, 1859).

Dasgupta, P., *An Inquiry into Well-being and Destitution* (Oxford UK: Clarendon Press, 1993).

Davies, N., 'Lloyd George and Poland, 1919–20', *Journal of Contemporary History*, 6 (1971), 132–54.

Davis, S. H., 'Executive Summary', in *idem* (ed.), *Indigenous Views of Land and the Environment* (Washington DC: World Bank, 1994), ix–xi.

Davis, W. M., 'The Geographical Cycle', *Geographical Journal*, 14 (1899), 481–504.

Dawson, M. H., 'The Many Minds of Sir Halford J. Mackinder: Dilemmas of Historical Editing', *History in Africa*, 14 (1987), 27–42.

de Waal, A., *Famine Crimes: Politics and the Disaster Relief Industry in Africa* (Oxford UK: James Currey, 1997).

—— and O. Khin, 'Against Gunboat Diplomacy', *Prospect*, June 2008, 18–19.

'The Ded Unkunpi Projects', at <http://web.mac.com/alliesms/Allies/Ded_Unkunpi.html>, accessed 20 July 2008.

der Derian, J., 'The Simulation Syndrome: From War Games to Game Wars', *Social Text*, 24 (1990), 187–92.

Deudney, D., 'Geopolitics as Theory: Historical Security Materialism', *European Journal of International Relations*, 6 (2000), 77–107.

—— 'Greater Britain or Greater Synthesis? Seeley, Mackinder, and Wells on Britain in the Global Industrial Era', *Review of International Studies*, 27 (2001), 187–208.

Deuel, W. R., *People under Hitler* (New York: Harcourt Brace, 1942).

Dickenson, J., 'The Naturalist on the River Amazons and a Wider World: Reflections on the Centenary of Henry Walter Bates', *Geographical Journal*, 158 (1992), 207–14.

Diner, D., *Beyond the Conceivable: Studies on Germany, Nazism, and the Holocaust* (Berkeley CA: University of California, 2000).

Dodds, K. J., 'Eugenics, Fantasies of Empire and Inverted Whiggism: An Essay on the Political Geography of Vaughan Cornish', *Political Geography*, 13 (1994), 85–99.

Dodge, T., *Inventing Iraq: The Failure of Nation Building and a History Denied* (New York: Columbia University Press, 2003).

Dower, N., 'Against War as a Response to Terrorism', *Philosophy and Geography*, 5 (2002), 29–34.

Doyle, M. W., *Empires* (Ithaca NY: Cornell University Press, 1986).

Drezner, D. W., 'Globalization and Policy Convergence', *International Studies Review*, 3:1 (2001), 53–78.

Driver, F., 'Geography's Empire: Histories of Geographical Knowledge', *Environment and Planning D: Society and Space*, 10 (1992), 23–40.

—— *Geography Militant: Cultures of Exploration in the Age of Empire* (Oxford UK: Blackwell, 2001).

Du Bois, W. E. B., *Darkwater: Voices from Within the Veil* (New York: Dover Publications, 1999 [1920]).

Duffield, M., 'War as a Network Enterprise: The New Security Terrain and its Implications', *Cultural Values*, 6 (2002), 153–65.

Dugin, A., 'The Great War of Continents' (1992) at <http://www.gnosticliberation-front.com/The Great War of Continents A.Dugin.htm>, accessed 14 January 2008.

—— *Osnovy Geopolitiki: Geopoliticheskoe Budushchee Rossii* [The Foundations of Geopolitics: Russia's Geopolitical Future] (Moscow: Arktogeya, 1997).

Dunbar, G. S., *Élisée Reclus: Historian of Nature* (Hamden CT: Archon Books, 1978).

Earl of Ronaldshay, *Life of Lord Curzon; being the Authorized Biography of George Nathaniel Marquess Curzon of Kedleston, K.G.* [Volume One] (London: Ernest Benn, 1928).

Earle, C., 'Beyond the Appalachians, 1815–1860', in T. F. McIlwraith and E. K. Mueller (eds.), *North America: The Historical Geography of a Changing Continent*, second edition (Lanham MD: Rowman and Littlefield, 2001), 165–88.

Edwards, M., 'The New Great Game and the New Great Gamers: Disciples of Kipling and Mackinder', *Central Asian Survey*, 22 (2003), 83–102.

Eichner, H., 'The Rise of Modern Science and the Genesis of Romanticism', *PMLA* (Publications of the Modern Languages Association), 97 (1982), 8–20.

Eland, I., *The Empire Strikes Out: The 'New Imperialism' and its Fatal Flaws. Policy Analysis no. 459* (Washington DC: Cato Institute, 2002).

Elcock, H. J., 'Britain and the Russo-Polish Frontier, 1919–1921', *Historical Journal*, 12 (1969), 137–54.

Ellis, R. J., 'A Geography of Vertical Margins: Twentieth-Century Mountaineering Narratives and the Landscapes of Neo-Imperialism', Ph.D. thesis, University of Colorado-Boulder (1990).

Elster, J., 'On Majoritarianism and Rights', *East European Constitutional Review*, 1:3 (1993), 19–24.

Emmanuel, A., *Unequal Exchange: A Study of the Imperialism of Trade* (London: New Left Books, 1972 [1969]).

Energy Information Administration, 'Official Energy Statistics from the U.S. Government', at <http://www.eia.doe.gov/basics/quickoil.html>, accessed 20 July 2008.

Enloe, C., *Bananas, Beaches and Bases: Making Feminist Sense of International Politics* (Berkeley CA: University of California Press, 1989).

—— *Maneuvers: The International Politics of Militarizing Women's Lives* (Berkeley CA: University of California Press, 2000).

Evenett, S. J., and M. Meier, 'An Interim Assessment of the US Trade Policy of "Competitive Liberalization" ', *World Economy*, 31 (2008), 31–66.

'Excerpts From Pentagon's Plan: "Prevent the Re-Emergence of a New Rival" ', *New York Times*, (8 March 1992), 14a.

'The Expedition to Mount Kenya', *Geographical Journal*, N.S. 14 (1899), 564.

Farber, P. L., *Finding Order in Nature: The Naturalist Tradition from Linnaeus to E. O. Wilson* (Baltimore MD: Johns Hopkins University Press, 2000).

Farmer, P., 'Never Again? Reflections on Human Values and Human Rights', in G. B. Peterson (ed.), *Tanner Lectures on Human Values, Vol. 26* (Salt Lake City UT: University of Utah Press, 2006), 139–88.

—— and N. Gastineau Campos, 'Rethinking Medical Ethics: A View from Below', *Developing World Bioethics*, 4 (2004), 17–41.

Ferguson, N., *Empire: How Britain Made the Modern World* (London: Penguin, 2002).

Ferguson, N., *Empire: The Rise and Demise of the British World Order and the Lessons for Global Power* (New York: Perseus Books, 2003).

—— 'Biography' (n.d.) at <http://www.niallferguson.org/bio.html>, accessed 14 February 2008.

Fettweis, C. J., 'Sir Halford Mackinder, Geopolitics, and Policymaking in the 21st Century', *Parameters, US Army War College Quarterly*, (Summer 2000) at <https://carlisle-www.army.mil/usawc/Parameters/00summer/fettweis.htm>, accessed 1 January 2008.

—— 'Revisiting Mackinder and Angell: the Obsolescence of Great Power Geopolitics', *Comparative Strategy*, 22:2 (2003), 109–29.

Fifield, R. H., and G. E. Pearcy, *Geopolitics in Principle and Practice* (Boston MA: Ginn, 1944).

Figes, O., 'The Red Army and Mass Mobilization during the Russian Civil War, 1919–1921', *Past and Present*, 129 (1990), 168–211.

Fleming, M., *The Geography of Freedom: The Odyssey of Élisée Reclus* (Montréal: Black Rose Books, 1988).

Fleure, H. J., 'Régions Humaines', *Annales de Géographie*, 26 (1917), 161–74.

—— 'Sixty Years of Geography and Education', *Geography*, 38 (1953), 231–64.

Foster, J. B., 'The New Geopolitics of Empire', *Monthly Review*, 57:8 (2006), 1–18.

Foucault, M., *Archaeology of Knowledge* (New York: Pantheon, 1972 [1969]).

—— *The History of Sexuality: An Introduction* (London: Penguin, 1981 [1976]).

—— 'Security, Territory, Population, Lecture 11' [1978], in *idem, Security, Territory, Population. Lectures at the Collège de France, 1977–1978* (London: Palgrave Macmillan, 2007), 285–310.

Frank, J. A., *Bush on the Couch: Inside the Mind of the U.S. President* (London: Politico's, 2006 [2004]).

Frank, K., *The Voyage Out: The Life of Mary Kingsley* (London: Hamish Hamilton, 1987).

Frankel, G., 'U.S. Mulled Seizing Oil Fields in '73: British Memo Cites Notion of Sending Airborne to Mideast', *Washington Post Foreign Service*, 1 January 2004, A01.

Frederick, S. Y., 'The Anglo-German Rivalry, 1890–1914', in W. R. Thompson (ed.), *Great Power Rivalries* (Columbia SC: University of South Carolina Press, 1999), 306–36.

Freeden, M., 'Eugenics and Progressive Thought: A Study in Ideological Affinity', *Historical Journal*, 22 (1979), 645–71.

Freeman, J., 'Collaborative Governance in the Administrative State', *UCLA Law Review*, 45 (1997), 1–98.

Freshfield, D., and W. L. J. Wharton (eds.), *Hints to Travellers* (London: Royal Geographical Society, 1893).

Friedman, T. L., *The World is Flat: A Brief History of the Twenty-First Century* (New York: Farrar, Straus and Giroux, 2005).

Fromkin, D., *A Peace to End All Peace: The Fall of the Ottoman Empire and the Creation of the Modern Middle East* (New York: Henry Holt, 1989).

Frum, D., and R. Perle, *An End to Evil: How to Win the War on Terror* (New York: Ballantine Books, 2004).

Fry, D., *Beyond War: The Human Potential for Peace* (Oxford UK: Oxford University Press, 2007).

Fukuyama, F., 'The End of History?', *National Interest*, 16 (Summer 1989), 3–18.

—— *The End of History and the Last Man* (London: Penguin, 1992).

Fulford, T., D. Lee, and P. J. Kitson, *Literature, Science, and Exploration in the Romantic Era* (Cambridge UK: Cambridge University Press, 2004).

Funnell, W., 'National Efficiency, Military Accounting and the Business of War', *Critical Perspectives on Accounting*, 17 (2006), 719–51.

Gaddis, J. L., *The Long Peace: Inquiries into the History of the Cold War* (New York: Oxford University Press, 1987).

—— 'A Grand Strategy of Transformation', *Foreign Policy*, 133 (2003), 50–7.

Gallagher, J., and R. Robinson, 'The Imperialism of Free Trade', *Economic History Review*, N.S. 6 (1961), 1–15.

Gallie, W. B., 'Essentially Contested Concepts', *Proceedings of the Aristotelian Society*, 56 (1956), 167–98.

Garten, J. E., 'Business and Foreign Policy', *Foreign Affairs*, 76:3 (1997), 67–79.

Garvin, T., 'The Anatomy of a Nationalist Revolution: Ireland, 1858–1928', *Comparative Studies in Society and History*, 28 (1986), 468–501.

George, H., *Historical Geography of the British Empire* (London: Oxford University Press, 1904).

George, S., *Another World is Possible if . . .* (London: Verso, 2004).

Gershoni. I., and J. P. Jankowski, *Egypt, Islam and the Arabs: The Search for Egyptian Nationhood, 1900–1930* (Oxford UK: Oxford University Press, 1986).

Giblin, B., 'Élisée Reclus: Un Géographe d'Exception', *Hérodote*, 117 (2005), 11–28.

—— 'Élisée Reclus et les Colonisations', *Hérodote*, 117 (2005), 135–52.

Gibson-Graham, J. K., *The End of Capitalism (As We Knew It): A Feminist Critique of Political Economy* (Oxford UK: Blackwell, 1996).

—— 'Enabling Ethical Economies: Cooperativism and Class', *Critical Sociology*, 29:2 (2003), 123–61.

Gilbert, E. W., 'The Right Honourable Sir Halford Mackinder, P.C., 1861–1947', *Geographical Journal*, 110 (1947), 94–9.

—— 'Introduction', in *idem.* (ed.), *'The Scope and Methods of Geography' and 'The Geographical Pivot of History' by Sir Halford J. Mackinder* (London: Royal Geographical Society, 1951).

—— *British Pioneers in Geography* (London: David and Charles, 1972).

Gilmour, D., *Curzon: Imperial Statesman* (London: John Murray, 1994).

Gleditsch, N. P., P. Wallensteen, M. Eriksson, M. Sollenberg, and H. Strand, 'Armed Conflict 1946–2001: A New Dataset', *Journal of Peace Research*, 39 (2002), 615–37.

Godden, L., 'The Invention of Tradition: Property Law as a Knowledge Space for the Appropriation of the South', *Griffith Law Review*, 16 (2007), 375–410.

GoGwilt, C., *The Fiction of Geopolitics: Afterimages of Culture from Wilkie Collins to Alfred Hitchcock* (Stanford CA: Stanford University Press, 2000).

Goldman, L., *Dons and Workers: Oxford and Adult Education since 1850* (Oxford UK: Oxford University Press, 1995).

Goodhand, J., *Aiding Peace? The Role of NGOs in Armed Conflict* (Rugby UK: IDG Publishing, 2006).

Gorman, D., 'Lionel Curtis, Imperial Citizenship, and the Quest for Unity', *Historian*, 66 (2004), 67–96.

Gottmann, J., 'The Background of Geopolitics', *Military Affairs*, 6 (1942), 197–206.

Goudie, A. S., 'George Nathaniel Curzon: Superior Geographer', *Geographical Journal*, 146 (1980), 203–9.

Graham, P., T. Keenan, and A.-M. Dowd, 'A Call to Arms at the End of History: A Discourse-Historical Analysis of George W. Bush's Declaration of War on Terror', *Discourse and Society*, 15 (2004), 199–221.

Gray, C. S., *The Geopolitics of the Nuclear Era: Heartland, Rimlands and the Technological Revolution* (New York: Crane, Russak, 1977).

—— *The Geopolitics of Super Power* (Lexington KY: University Press of Kentucky, 1988).

—— 'In Defence of the Heartland: Sir Halford Mackinder and his Critics a Hundred Years On', in B. W. Blouet (ed.), *Global Geostrategy: Mackinder and the Defence of the West* (Abingdon UK: Frank Cass, 2005), 17–35.

Green, E. H. H., *The Crisis of Conservatism: The Politics, Economics and Ideology of the British Conservative Party, 1880–1914* (London: Routledge, 1995).

Green, J., *Engels: A Revolutionary Life* (London: Artery Publications, 2008).

Greenblatt, S., *Marvellous Possessions: The Wonders of the New World* (Chicago IL: University of Chicago Press, 1991).

Greenlee, J. G., 'Imperial Studies and the Unity of the Empire', *Journal of Imperial and Commonwealth History*, 7 (1979), 321–35.

Gregory, D., *Geographical Imaginations* (Oxford UK: Blackwell, 1994).

Griffin, E., *Blood Sport: Hunting in Britain since 1066* (New Haven CT: Yale University Press, 2007).

Guelke, J., 'The Political Morality of the Neo-conservatives: An Analysis', *International Politics*, 42 (2005), 97–115.

Guha, A. C., *First Spark of Revolution: The Early Phase of India's Struggle for Independence, 1900–1920* (Bombay India: Orient Longman, 1971).

Gurr, T. R., 'Ethnic Warfare on the Wane', *Foreign Affairs*, 79:3 (2000), 52–64.

Guterl, M. P., 'The New Race Consciousness: Race, Nation, and Empire in American Culture, 1910–1925', *Journal of World History*, 10 (1999), 307–52.

Gyorgy, A., 'The Geopolitics of War: Total War and Geostrategy', *Journal of Politics*, 5 (1943), 347–62.

Hajjar, S. G., *U.S. Military Presence in the Gulf: Challenges and Prospects* (Carlisle PA: US Army War College, 2002).

Halim, C., 'The Clash of Civilizations Revisited: A Confucian Perspective', in S. Rashid (ed.), *"The Clash of Civilizations?" Asian Responses* (Dhaka, Bangladesh: The University Press, 1997), 109–25.

Hallam, A., *Great Geological Controversies*, second edition (Oxford UK: Oxford University Press, 1989 [1983]).

Halliday, F., *Islam and the Myth of Confrontation: Religion and Politics in the Middle East* (New York: St. Martin's Press, 1996).

Hansen, P. H., 'Albert Smith, the Alpine Club, and the Invention of Mountaineering in Mid-Victorian Britain', *Journal of British Studies*, 34 (1995), 300–24.

Haraway, D. J., 'Teddy Bear Patriarchy: Taxidermy in the Garden of Eden, New York City, 1908–36', in A. Kaplan and D. Pease (eds.), *Cultures of United States Imperialism* (Durham NC: Duke University Press, 1993), 237–91.

Harbom, L., and P. Wallensteen, 'Armed Conflict and its International Dimensions', *Journal of Peace Research*, 42 (2005), 623–35.

Hardt, M., and A. Negri, *Empire* (Cambridge MA: Harvard University Press, 2000).

Harris, C., 'How did Colonialism Dispossess? Comments from an Edge of Empire', *Annals of the Association of American Geographers*, 94 (2004), 165–92.

Harrison, B., 'Politics', in *idem* (ed.), *The History of the University of Oxford. Volume VIII. The Twentieth Century* (Oxford UK: Clarendon Press, 1994), 377–412.

Harvey, D., *The Condition of Postmodernity* (Oxford UK: Basil Blackwell, 1989).

—— *Justice, Nature, and the Geography of Difference* (Oxford UK: Blackwell, 1996).

—— *The New Imperialism* (Oxford UK: Oxford University Press, 2003).

—— *A Brief History of Neoliberalism* (Oxford UK: Oxford University Press, 2005).

Hathaway, J., 'Why Refugee Law Still Matters', *Melbourne Journal of International Law*, 8:1 (2007), 88–104.

'Haushofer's Heritage', *Time*, 25 March 1946.

Haushofer, K., 'Defense of German Geopolitics' [1945], in E. A. Walsh, *Total Power, a Footnote to History* (Garden City NY: Doubleday, 1948), 344–53.

Hawken, P., *Blessed Unrest: How the Largest Movement in the World Came into Being and Why No One Saw it Coming* (New York: Viking Press, 2007).

Hayek, F. A., 'The London School of Economics', *Economica*, N.S. 13 (1946), 1–31.

Hechter, M., *Internal Colonialism: The Celtic Fringe in British National Development, 1596–1966* (London: Routledge and Kegan Paul, 1975).

Heffernan, M., 'The Limits of Utopia: Henri Duveyrier and the Exploration of the Sahara in the Nineteenth Century', *Geographical Journal*, 155 (1989), 342–52.

—— '*Fin de Siècle, Fin du Monde?* On the Origins of European Geopolitics, 1890–1920', in K. Dodds and D. Atkinson (eds.), *Geopolitical Traditions: A Century of Geopolitical Thought* (London: Routledge, 2000), 27–51.

Heggie, V., 'Lies, Damn Lies, and Manchester's Recruiting Statistics: Degeneration as an "Urban Legend" in Victorian and Edwardian Britain', *Journal of Medicine and Allied Sciences*, 63:2 (2008), 178–216.

Heimer, C., *Reactive Risk and Rational Action: Managing Moral Hazard in Insurance Contracts* (Berkeley CA: University of California Press, 1985).

Held, D., et al., *Debating Globalization* (Cambridge UK: Polity Press, 2005).

Henry, C. M., 'The Clash of Globalizations in the Middle East', *Review of Middle East Economics and Finance*, 1:1 (2003), 3–16.

Hepple, L. W., 'The Revival of Geopolitics', *Political Geography Quarterly*, 5 supplement (1986), 79–90.

—— 'South American Heartland: The Charcas, Latin American Geopolitics and Global Strategies', *Geographical Journal*, 170 (2004), 359–77.

Herb, G. H., *Under the Map of Germany: Nationalism and Propaganda* (London: Routledge, 1996).

Hernig, H. H., '*Geopolitik*, Haushofer, Hitler, and *Lebensraum*', in C. S. Gray and G. Sloan (eds.), *Geopolitics, Geography, and Strategy* (London: Frank Cass, 1999), 218–42.

Herod, A., 'The Practice of International Labor Solidarity and the Geography of the Global Economy', *Economic Geography*, 71 (1995), 341–63.

Heske, H., 'Karl Haushofer: His Role in German Geopolitics and in Nazi Politics', *Political Geography Quarterly*, 6 (1987), 135–44.

Hewitt, J., 'Between Pinochet and Kropotkin: Terrrorism, Human Rights and the Geographers', *Canadian Geographer*, 45 (2001), 338–55.

Hinchcliffe, T., *North Oxford* (New Haven CT: Yale University Press, 1992).

Hinde, H. B., *The Masai Language* (Cambridge UK: Cambridge University Press, 1901).
Hinde, S. L., 'Three Years Travel in the Congo Free State', *Geographical Journal*, 6 (1895), 426–62.
—— *The Fall of the Congo Arabs* (London: Methuen, 1897).
—— and H. Hinde, *The Last of the Masai* (London: Heinemann, 1901).
Hirst, P., *Space and Power: Politics, War and Architecture* (Cambridge UK: Polity, 2005).
—— and G. Thompson, *Globalization in Question: The International Economy and the Possibilities of Governance* (Cambridge UK: Polity, 1996).
Hitchens, C., 'Against Rationalization', *Nation*, 273:10 (8 October 2001), 8.
—— 'Holy Writ', *Atlantic Monthly*, 291:3 (April 2003), 93–9.
Hobsbawm, E., 'The United States: Wider Still and Wider', *Le Monde Diplomatique*, June 2003, at <http://mondediplo.com/2003/06/02hobsbawm>, accessed 11 January 2008.
—— *Globalisation, Democracy and Terrorism* (London: Little, Brown, 2007).
Hobson, J. A., *The War in South Africa* (London: Nisbet, 1900).
—— 'Socialistic Imperialism', *International Journal of Ethics*, 12:1 (1901), 44–58.
—— *The Psychology of Jingoism* (London: Grant Richards, 1901).
—— *Imperialism: A Study* third edition (London: Unwin Hyman, 1988 [1938]; first edition, 1902).
—— 'The Scientific Basis of Imperialism', *Political Science Quarterly* 17 (1902), 460–89.
—— *The Crisis of Liberalism: New Issues of Democracy* (Brighton UK: Harvester, 1974 [1909]).
—— *Work and Wealth* (New York: Macmillan, 1922 [1914]).
—— *Towards International Government* (London: Allen and Unwin, 1915).
—— *Richard Cobden: The International Man* (London: Unwin, 1918).
—— *Confessions of an Economic Heretic: The Autobiography of J. A. Hobson* (Brighton UK: Harvester, 1976 [1938]), 59–60.
Hoganson, K., *Fighting for American Manhood: How Gender Politics Provoked the Spanish–American and Philippine–American Wars* (New Haven CT: Yale University Press, 1998).
Hogarth, D. G., *The Nearer East* (London: Heinemann, 1902).
Holdich, T., *India* (London: Oxford University Press, 1904).
Hooper, C., *Manly States: Masculinities, International Relations and Gender Politics* (New York: Columbia University Press, 2001).
Horsman, R., *Race and Manifest Destiny: The Origins of American Racial Anglo-Saxonism* (Cambridge MA: Harvard University Press, 1981).
Hottes, R., 'Walter Christaller', *Annals of the Association of American Geographers*, 73 (1983), 51–4.
'How Geography Can be Made Interesting', *Transactions and Twenty-Third Report of the Council of the Liverpool Geographical Society* (Liverpool UK: Liverpool Geographical Society, 1914), 7–8.
Howard, M., 'The World According to Henry: From Metternich to Me', *Foreign Affairs*, 73:3 (1994), 132–40.

Howe, A., *Free Trade and Liberal England, 1846–1946* (Oxford UK: Clarendon Press, 1997).

Howe, S., *Ireland and Empire: Colonial Legacies in Irish History and Culture* (Oxford UK: Oxford University Press, 2000).

Hudson, B., 'The New Geography and the New Imperialism, 1870–1918', *Antipode*, 9 (1977), 12–19.

Human Security Centre, *Human Security Report 2005: War and Peace in the Twenty-First Century* (Oxford UK: Oxford University Press, 2005).

Huntington, S. P., 'The United States', in M. J. Crozier, S. P. Huntington, and J. Watanuki (eds.), *The Crisis of Democracy: Report on the Governability of Democracies to the Trilateral Commission* (New York: New York University Press, 1995), 59–118.

—— 'The Clash of Civilizations?', *Foreign Affairs*, 72:3 (1993), 22–49.

—— *The Clash of Civilizations and the Remaking of World Order* (New York: Simon and Schuster, 1997).

—— *Who are We? The Challenges to America's National Identity* (New York: Simon and Schuster, 2004).

Huxley, T. H., 'The Struggle for Existence in Human Society' [1888], in P. Kropótkin (ed.), *Mutual Aid: A Factor of Evolution* (Boston MA: Extending Horizons Books, n.d.), 329–41.

Hyndman, J., *Managing Displacement: Refugees and the Politics of Humanitarianism* (Minneapolis MN: University of Minnesota Press, 2000).

Ignatieff, M., *Empire Lite: Nation Building in Bosnia, Kosovo, and Afghanistan* (London: Vintage, 2003).

Ignotus, M., 'Seizing Arab Oil, *Harper's Magazine*, March 1975, 45–62.

Ikenberry, G. J., 'Is American Multilateralism in Decline?', *Perspectives on Politics*, 1 (2003), 533–50.

Jackson, R., *The Global Covenant: Human Conduct in a World of States* (Oxford UK: Oxford University Press, 2000).

Jacobson, P. D., 'Rosebery and Liberal Imperialism, 1899–1903', *Journal of British Studies*, 13 (1973), 83–107.

Janiewski, D. E., 'Engendering the Invisible Empire: Imperialism, Feminism and US Women's History', *Australian Feminist Studies*, 36 (2001), 279–93.

Jaska, M. F., 'Putting the "Sustainable" Back in Sustainable Development: Recognizing and Enforcing Indigenous Property Rights as a Pathway to Global Environmental Sustainability', *Journal of Environmental Law and Litigation*, 21 (2006), 157–205.

Jauvert, V., 'Les révélations d'un ancien conseiller de Carter', *Le Nouvel Observateur*, 1732 (15 January 1998), 76.

Jay, P., 'Regionalism as Geopolitics', *Foreign Affairs*, 58:3 (1979), 485–514.

Jenkins, R., *Churchill* (London: Macmillan, 2001).

Jesse, N. G., and K. P. Williams, *Identities and Institutions: Conflict Reduction in Divided Societies* (Albany NY: State University of New York Press, 2005).

Johnson, C., *The Sorrows of Empire: Militarism, Secrecy and the End of the Republic* (New York: Metropolitan Books, 2004).

Johnson, F. A., *Defence by Committee: The British Committee of Imperial Defence, 1885–1959* (London: Oxford University Press, 1960).

Johnston, W., 'E. H. Carr's Theory of International Relations: A Critique', *Journal of Politics*, 29 (1967), 861–84.

Jones, M., 'The Rise of the Regional State in Economic Governance: "Partnerships for Prosperity" or New Scales of State Power', *Environment and Planning A*, 33 (2001), 1185–211.

Joxe, A., *Empire of Disorder* (New York: Semotexte, 2002).

Kadish, L., *The Oxford Economists of the Late Nineteenth Century* (Oxford UK: Oxford University Press, 1982).

Kagan, R., *Paradise and Power: America and Europe in the New World Order* (London: Atlantic Books, 2004 [2003]).

Kamat, S., 'NGOs and the New Democracy: The False Saviors of International Development', *Harvard International Review*, 25 (2003), 65–9.

Kaplan, A., 'Romancing the Empire: The Embodiment of American Masculinity in the Popular Historical Novel of the 1890s', *American Literary History*, 2 (1990), 659–90.

Kaplan, R., *Warrior Politics: Why Leadership Demands a Pagan Ethos* (New York: Random House, 2000).

Karkkainen, B. C., 'Post-Sovereign Environmental Governance', *Global Environmental Politics*, 4:1 (2004), 72–96.

Kearney, R., 'The Irish Mind' [1985], in *idem, Navigations: Collected Irish Essays 1976–2006* (Dublin: Lilliput Press, 2006), 17–31.

Kearns, G., 'Closed Space and Political Practice: Frederick Jackson Turner and Halford Mackinder', *Environment and Planning D: Society and Space*, 2 (1984), 23–34.

—— 'Fin-de-Siècle Geopolitics: Mackinder, Hobson and Theories of Global Closure', in P. Taylor (ed.), *Political Geography of the Twentieth Century* (London: Belhaven Press, 1993), 9–30.

—— 'The Imperial Subject: Geography and Travel in the Work of Mary Kingsley and Halford Mackinder', *Transactions of the Institute of British Geographers*, N.S. 22 (1997), 450–72.

—— 'The Virtuous Circle of Facts and Values in the New Western History', *Annals of the Association of American Geographers*, 88 (1998), 377–409.

—— 'Ireland after Theory', *Bullán: An Irish Studies Journal*, 6 (2002), 107–14.

—— 'The Moral Economy of Migration', paper given to the Conference on 'Migrations, Nations, and Citizenship', Cambridge, July 2004, at <www.crassh.cam.ac.uk/events/2003–4/KearnsPaper.pdf>, accessed 4 January 2008.

—— 'Naturalising Empire: Echoes of Mackinder for the Next American Century?', *Geopolitics*, 11 (2006), 74–98.

—— 'The History of Medical Geography after Foucault', in S. Elden and J. Crampton (eds.), *Space, Knowledge and Power: Foucault and Geography* (Aldershot UK: Ashgate Press, 2007), 205–22.

—— 'The Geography of Terror', *Political Geography*, 27 (2008), 360–3.

—— 'Progressive Geopolitics', *Geography Compass*, 2:8 (2008), 1599–1620.

—— and S. Reid-Henry, 'Vital Geographies: Luck, Longevity and the Human Condition', *Annals of the Association of American Geographers*, (in press).

Kellner, D., *From 9/11 to the Terror War: The Dangers of the Bush Legacy* (Lanham MD: Rowman and Littlefield, 2003).

Keltie, J. S., *Geographical Education: Report to the Council of the Royal Geographical Society* (London: John Murray, 1885).

—— 'Miss Kingsley on West Africa', *Geographical Journal*, 9 (1897), 324.

—— 'Obituary. Prince Kropótkin', *Geographical Journal*, 57 (1921), 316–19.

Kendle, J. E., *Colonial and Imperial Conferences: A Study in Imperial Organization* (London: Longman, 1967).

Kenez, P., *Civil War in South Russia 1919–1920: The Defeat of the Whites* (Berkeley CA: University of California Press, 1977).

Kennedy, P., *The Rise and Fall of the Great Powers: Economic Change and Military Conflict from 1500 to 2000* (New York: Random House, 1987).

Killoran, G., '45 minutes or 45 days is not the issue', *Chartist*, November 2003, at <http://chartist.org.uk/articles/intpol/nov03killoran.htm>, accessed 14 January 2008.

Kindelberger, C. P., 'The Rise of Free Trade in Western Europe', in J. A. Frieden and D. A. Luke (eds.), *International Political Economy: Perspectives on Global Power and Wealth*, fourth edition (London: Routledge, 2000), 73–9.

King, N., 'Obama Tones Foreign-Policy Muscle', *Wall Street Journal*, 5 September 2007, at <http://online.wsj.com/public/article/SB118895877299317784.html?mod=blog>, accessed 14 June 2008.

Kingsley, M., *Travels in West Africa: Congo Français, Corisco and Cameroons* (London: Macmillan, 1897).

—— *West African Studies*, second edition (London: Macmillan, 1901 [1899]).

Kinvig, C., *Churchill's Crusade: The British Invasion of Russia 1918–1920* (London: Hambledon Continuum, 2006).

Kiss [Kish], G., 'Political Geography into Geopolitics', *Geographical Review*, 32 (1942), 632–45.

Kissinger, H., *The White House Years* (Boston MA: Little, Brown, and Co., 1979).

—— *Diplomacy* (New York: Touchstone, 1995 [1994]).

Kjellén, R., 'Studier öfver Sveriges Politiska Gränser' [Studies of Sweden's Political Borders], *Ymer*, 19 (1899), 283–331.

—— *Stormakterna: Konturer Kring Samtidens Storpolitik* [Great Powers: The Form of Modern International Relations] (Stockholm: Hugo Gerbers, 1905).

—— *Stormakterna och Världskrisen* [The Great Powers and the World Crisis] (Stockholm: Hugo Gerbers, 1920).

Klare, M., 'The New Geopolitics', *Monthly Review*, 55 (2003), 51–6.

Klein, N., 'Downsizing in Disguise', *Nation*, 23 June 2003, at <http://www.thenation.com/doc/20030623/klein>, accessed 18 June 2008.

—— *The Shock Doctrine: Rise of Disaster Capitalism* (London: Penguin, 2007).

Kleveman, L., *The New Great Game: Blood and Oil in Central Asia* (New York: Atlantic Books, 2003 [2002]).

Koehl, R. L., *RKFDV: German Resettlement and Population Policy, 1939–1945; a History of the Reich Commission for the Strengthening of Germandom* (Cambridge MA: Harvard University Press, 1957).

Koot, G. M., *English Historical Economics, 1870–1926: The Rise of Economic History and Neomercantilism* (Cambridge UK: Cambridge University Press, 1988).

Kozul-Wright, R., and P. Rayment, *The Resistible Rise of Market Fundamentalism: Rethinking Development Policy in an Unbalanced World* (London: Zed Books, 2007).

Kramer, P. A., 'Empires, Exceptions, and Anglo-Saxons: Race and Rule between the British and United States' Empires, 1880–1910', *Journal of American History*, 88 (2002), 1315–53.

Krauthammer, C., 'The Unipolar Moment', *Foreign Affairs*, 70:1 (1991), 23–33.

Kristol, W., and R. Kagan, 'National Interest and Global Responsibility', in I. Stelzer (ed.), *Neo-conservatism* (London: Atlantic Books, 2004).

Kropótkin, P., 'What Geography Ought to Be', *Nineteenth Century*, 18 (1885), 940–56.

—— *Words of a Rebel* (Montréal: Black Rose Books, 1992 [1885]).

—— 'What Revolution Means' [1886], in N. Walter and H. Becker (eds.), *Act for Yourselves: Articles from 'Freedom' 1886–1907 by Peter Kropótkin* (London: Freedom Press, 1988), 24–37.

—— *In Russian and French Prisons* (New York: Schocken Books, 1971 [1887]).

—— 'Parliamentary Rule' [1887], in N. Walter and H. Becker (eds.), *Act for Yourselves: Articles from 'Freedom' 1886–1907 by Peter Kropótkin* (London: Freedom Press, 1988), 37–41.

—— 'Revolution and Famine' [1887], in N. Walter and H. Becker (eds.), *Act for Yourselves: Articles from 'Freedom' 1886–1907 by Peter Kropótkin* (London: Freedom Press, 1988), 66–70.

—— 'Rocks Ahead' [1888], in N. Walter and H. Becker (eds.), *Act for Yourselves: Articles from 'Freedom' 1886–1907 by Peter Kropótkin* (London: Freedom Press, 1988), 71–4.

—— 'The Conquest of Bread' [1892], in M. S. Shatz (ed.), *Kropotkin: 'The Conquest of Bread' and Other Writings* (Cambridge UK: Cambridge University Press, 1995), 1–202.

—— 'On the Teaching of Physiography', *Geographical Journal*, 2 (1893), 350–9.

—— 'Mutual Aid amongst Ourselves', *Nineteenth Century*, 39 (1896), 914–36.

—— *The State: Its Historic Role* (London: Freedom Press, 1969 [1896]).

—— *Anarchism: Its Philosophy and Ideal* (San Francisco CA: Free Society, 1898) at http://dwardmac.pitzer.edu/Anarchist_Archives/Kropótkin/philandideal.html, accessed 16 July 2003.

—— *Fields, Factories and Workshops Tomorrow* (London: George Allen and Unwin, 1974 [1899]).

—— *Memoirs of a Revolutionist* (London: The Cresset Library, 1962 [1899]).

—— *Mutual Aid: A Factor of Evolution* (Boston MA: Extending Horizons Books, n.d. [1902]).

—— *Modern Science and Anarchism* (London: Freedom Press, 1912 [1904]).

—— 'The Dessication of Eur-Asia', *Geographical Journal*, 23 (1904), 722–34 (and discussion, 734–41).

—— '1886–1907: Glimpses into the Labour Movement in this Country' [1907], in N. Walter and H. Becker (eds.), *Act for Yourselves: Articles from 'Freedom' 1886–1907 by Peter Kropótkin* (London: Freedom Press, 1988), 114–21.

—— 'Anarchism' [1910], in M. S. Shatz (ed.), *Kropotkin: 'The Conquest of Bread' and Other Writings* (Cambridge UK: Cambridge University Press, 1995), 233–47.

—— 'The Direct Action of Environment on Plants', *Nineteenth Century and After*, 68 (1910), 58–77.

—— 'The Theory of Evolution and Mutual Aid' [1910], in *idem*, *Evolution and Environment* (Montréal: Black Rose Books, 1995), 117–38.

—— 'The Direct Action of Environment and Evolution', *Nineteenth Century and After*, 85 (1919), 70–89.

—— *Ethics Origin and Development* (New York: Tudor Publishing, 1947 [1922]).

Krugman, P., 'Battlefield of Dreams', *New York Times*, 4 May 2004, at <http://query.nytimes.com/gst/fullpage.html?res=9B03E5DA103DF937A35756C0A9629C8B63&sec=&spon=&pagewanted=1>, accessed 18 June 2008.

Kruszewski, C., 'The Pivot of History', *Foreign Affairs*, 32 (1954), 388–401.

Kunitz, S. J., 'Globalization, States, and the Health of Indigenous Peoples', *American Journal of Public Health*, 90 (2000), 1531–9.

Kurlansky, M., *Nonviolence: Twenty-five Lessons from the History of a Dangerous Idea* (New York: Modern Library, 2006).

Lacoste, Y., 'Elisée Reclus, un très large conception de la géographicité et une bienveillante géopolitique', *Hérodote*, 117 (2005), 29–52.

Laity, P., *The British Peace Movement 1870–1914* (Oxford UK: Oxford University Press, 2001).

Lambert, D., and A. Lester, 'Introduction: Imperial Spaces, Imperial Subjects', in *idem* (eds.), *Colonial Lives Across the British Empire: Imperial Careering in the Long Nineteenth Century* (Cambridge UK: Cambridge University Press, 2006), 1–31.

Larson, J., 'Not without a Plan: Geography and Natural History in the Late Eighteenth Century', *Journal of the History of Biology*, 19 (1986), 447–88.

Laruelle, M., *Aleksandr Dugin: A Russian Version of the European Radical Right? Kennan Institute Occasional Paper 294* (Washington DC: Woodrow Wilson International Center for Scholars, 2006).

—— 'Alexandre Dugin: A "Eurasionist" View on Chechnya and the North Caucasus', *Chechnya Weekly*, 8:6 (6 February 2007) at <http://www.jamestown.org/chechnya_weekly/article.php?articleid=2372693>, accessed 1 April 2008.

le Billon, P., 'The Geopolitical Economy of "Resource Wars" ', *Geopolitics*, 9 (2004), 1–29.

le Carré, J., *The Mission Song* (New York: Little, Brown and Company, 2006).

Lee, R., 'Moral Money? LETS and the Social Construction of Economic Geographies in Southeast England', *Environment and Planning A*, 28 (1996), 1377–94.

Lee, Y. W., *The Japanese Challenge to the American Neoliberal World Order* (Palo Alto CA: Stanford University Press, 2008).

Lehmann, V., 'Patent on Seed Sterility Threatens Seed Saving', *Biotechnology and Development Monitor*, 35 (1998), 6–8.

Leighten, P., 'The White Peril and L'Art nègre: Picasso, Primitivism, and Anticolonialism', *Art Bulletin*, 72 (1990), 609–30.

Lemann, N., 'The Next World Order', *New Yorker*, 1 April 2002, 42–8.

Lenin, V. I., *Imperialism, the Highest Stage of Capitalism: A Popular Outline* (New York: International Publishers, 1939 [1917]).

Lewis, B., 'The Roots of Muslim Rage', *Atlantic Monthly*, 266:3 (1990), 47–60.

Leyshon, A., R. Lee, and C. C. Williams (eds.), *Alternative Economic Spaces* (London: Sage, 2003).

Liauzu, C., 'Les Sociétés musulmanes dans l'Oeuvre d'Élisée Reclus', *Hérodote*, 117 (2005), 123–34.

Liberman, P., 'The Spoils of Conquest', *International Security*, 18 (1993), 125–53.

Lind, M., 'The Tragic Costs of Bush's Iraq Obsession', *Financial Times*, 5 September 2005 at <http://www.newamerica.net/publications/articles/2005/the_tragic_costs_of_bushs_iraq_obsession>, accessed 11 January 2008.

Lindqvist, S., 'Bombing the Savages', *Transition*, 87 (2001), 48–64.

Lippmann, W., *U.S. Foreign Policy: Shield of the Republic* (Boston MA: Little, Brown, 1943).

Little, A., *The Far East* (Oxford UK: Clarendon Press, 1905).

Livingstone, D. N., 'Natural Theology and Neo-Lamarckism: The Changing Context of Nineteenth-Century Geography in the United States and Great Britain', *Annals of the Association of American Geographers*, 74 (1984), 9–28.

—— *The Geographical Tradition: Episodes in the History of a Contested Enterprise* (Oxford UK: Blackwell, 1992).

Lloyd, T., 'Africa and Hobson's Imperialism', *Past and Present*, 55 (1972), 130–53.

'London School of Economics Mackinder Centre for the Study of Long Wave Events', at <http://www.lse.ac.uk/collections/mackinderCentre/>, accessed 20 June 2008.

Long, D., *Towards a New Liberal Internationalism: The International Theory of J. A. Hobson* (Cambridge UK: Cambridge University Press, 1996).

Lorimer, D. A., 'Science and the Secularization of Victorian Images of Race', in B. Lightman (ed.), *Victorian Science in Context* (Chicago IL: University of Chicago Press, 1997), 212–35.

Lossau, J., 'Politische Geographe und Geopolitik', *Eerdkunde*, 56 (2002), 73–80.

Lucas, E., *The New Cold War: Putin's Russia and the Threat to the West* (London: Bloomsbury, 2008).

MacGillis, A., 'Brzezinski Backs Obama', *Washington Post*, 25 August 2007, A3.

MacKenzie, D., 'Eugenics in Britain', *Social Studies of Science*, 6 (1976), 499–532.

MacKenzie, J. M., (ed.), *Imperialism and Popular Culture* (Manchester UK: Manchester University Press, 1986).

'Mackinder Forum, Earlier Meetings', at <http://www.mackinderforum.org/mission_earlier.htm>, accessed 10 June 2008.

'Mackinder Forum, Mission Statement, The Geopolitical Challenge', at <http://www.mackinderforum.org/mission_statement.htm>, accessed 18 June 2008.

'Mackinder Forum, Mission, What We Do', at <http://www.mackinderforum.org/mission_what.htm>, accessed 18 June 2008.

Mackinder, H. J., *A Syllabus of a Course of Lectures on the New Geography* (Oxford UK: Oxford University Extension Lectures, 1886).

—— 'The Scope and Methods of Geography', *Proceedings of the Royal Geographical Society*, N.S. 9 (1887), 141–60 (and discussion, 160–74).

—— 'The Physical Basis of Political Geography', *Scottish Geographical Magazine*, 6 (1890), 78–84.

—— 'Reclus' "Universal Geography" ', *Geographical Journal*, 4 (1894), 158–60.

—— 'Modern Geography, German and English', *Geographical Journal*, 6 (1895), 367–79.

—— 'The Diary of Halford John Mackinder' [1899], in K. M. Barbour (ed.), *H. J. Mackinder: The First Ascent of Mount Kenya* (London: Hurst, 1991), 27–251.

Mackinder, H. J., 'A Journey to the Summit of Mount Kenya, British East Africa', *Geographical Journal*, 15 (1900), 453–80.

—— 'The Ascent of Mount Kenya', *Alpine Journal*, 148 (1900), 102–10.

—— 'The Great Trade Routes. (Their Connection with the Organization of Industry, Commerce and Finance.)', *Journal of the Institute of Bankers*, 21 (1900), 1–6, 137–55, and 266–73.

—— *Britain and the British Seas* (London: Heinemann, 1902).

—— 'The Development of Geographical Teaching out of Nature Study', *Geographical Teacher*, 2 (1904), 191–7.

—— 'The Geographical Pivot of History', *Geographical Journal*, 23 (1904), 421–37 (and discussion, 437–44).

—— 'Man-Power as a Measure of National and Imperial Strength', *National and English Review*, 15 (1905), 136–45.

—— *Money-Power and Man-Power: The Underlying Principles rather than the Statistics of Tariff Reform* (London: Simpkin Marshall, 1906).

—— *Our Own Islands: An Elementary Study in Geography, Part I*, fourth edition (London: George Philip and Son, 1910 [1906]).

—— *Our Own Islands: An Elementary Study in Geography, Part II* (London: George Philip and Son, 1906).

—— *Lands Beyond the Channel: An Elementary Study in Geography*, sixth edition (London: George Philip and Son, 1912 [1908]).

—— *The Rhine: Its Valley and History* (London: Chatto and Windus, 1908).

—— 'Geographical Conditions Affecting the British Empire. I. The British Islands', *Geographical Journal*, 33 (1909), 462–76.

—— *Seven Lectures on the United Kingdom for Use in India; Reissued for Use in the United Kingdom* (London: Visual Instruction Committee of the Colonial Office, 1909).

—— *Distant Lands: An Elementary Study in Geography*, fifth edition (London: George Philip and Son, 1913 [1910]).

—— *India: Eight Lectures Prepared for the Visual Instruction Committee of the Colonial Office* (London: George Philip and Son, 1910).

—— *The Nations of the Modern World: An Elementary Study in Geography*, fourth edition (London: George Philip and Son, 1915 [1911]).

—— 'The Teaching of Geography from an Imperial Point of View, and the Use which Could and Should be Made of Visual Instruction', *Geographical Teacher*, 6 (1911), 79–86.

—— *The Modern British State: An Introduction to the Study of Civics*, second edition (London: George Philip and Son, 1922 [1914]).

—— 'Some Geographical Aspects of International Reconstruction', *Scottish Geographical Magazine*, 33 (1917), 3–11.

—— *Democratic Ideals and Reality: A Study in the Politics of Reconstruction* (London: Constable, 1919).

—— 'The Sub-Continent of India', in E. J. Rapson (ed.), *The Cambridge History of India. Volume I. Ancient India* (Cambridge UK: Cambridge University Press, 1922), 1–36.

—— *The World War and After: A Concise Narrative and Some Tentative Ideas* (London: George Philip and Son, 1924).

—— 'The English Tradition and the Empire: Some Thoughts on Lord Milner's Credo and the Imperial Committees', *United Empire*, 16 (1925), 724–35.

Mackinder, H. J., 'Comment on Wooldridge and Smetham: The Glacial Drifts of Essex and Hertfordshire, and their Bearing upon the Agricultural and Historical Geography of the Region', *Geographical Journal*, 73 (1931), 266–9.

—— 'The Human Habitat', *Scottish Geographical Magazine*, 47 (1931), 321–35.

—— 'Progress of Geography in the Field and in the Study during the Reign of His Majesty King George the Fifth', *Geographical Journal*, 86 (1935), 1–16.

—— 'The Round World and the Winning of the Peace', *Foreign Affairs*, 21 (1943), 595–605.

—— 'Speech on Receiving the Patron's Medal of the RGS', *Geographical Journal*, 105 (1945), 230–2.

—— and M. E. Sadler, *University Extension: Past, Present, and Future*, third edition (London: Cassell, 1891 [1890]).

Macmillan, M., *Peacemakers: Six Months that Changed the World* (London: John Murray, 2001).

Maddison, A., *The World Economy* (Paris: OECD Publications, 2006).

Maddox, G., 'The "Crusade" Against Evil: Bush's Fundamentalism', *Australian Journal of Politics and History*, 49 (2003), 398–411.

Maddrell, A. M. C., 'Empire, Emigration and School Geography: Changing Discourses of Imperial Citizenship, 1880–1925', *Journal of Historical Geography*, 22 (1996), 373–87.

Magdoff, H., *Imperialism Without Colonies* (New York: Monthly Review Press, 2003).

Maguire, K., and A. Lines, 'Exclusive: Bush Plot to Bomb his Arab Ally', *Daily Mirror* (22 November 2005) at <http://www.mirror.co.uk/news/tm_objectid= 16397937&method=full&siteid=94762&headline=exclusive–bush-plot-to-bomb-his-arab-ally-name_page.html>, accessed 14 July 2008.

Mahan, A. T., *The Influence of Sea Power upon History, 1660–1783* (Boston MA: Little, Brown, 1918 [1890]).

Malik, C., 'Independence: Reality and Myth', in B. Ward, T. P. Whitney, R. Strausz-Hupé, and C. Malik (eds.), *The Legacy of Imperialism* (Pittsburgh PA: Chatham College, 1960), 69–94.

'Maps ETC' at <http://etc.usf.edu/maps/pages>, accessed 1 April 2008.

Markham, C., 'The Field of Geography', *Geographical Journal*, (1898), 1–15.

Marks, S., 'Empire's Law', *Indiana Journal of Global Legal Studies*, 10 (2003), 449–66.

Marsden, W. E., ' "All in a Good Cause": Geography, History and the Politicization of the Curriculum in Nineteenth and Twentieth Century England', *Journal of Curriculum Studies*, 21 (1989), 509–26.

—— 'Rooting Racism into the Educational Experience of Childhood and Youth in the Nineteenth- and Twentieth-Centuries', *History of Education*, 19 (1990), 333–53.

Marsh, P. T., *Bargaining on Europe: Britain and the First Common Market* (New Haven CT: Yale University Press, 2000).

Marshall, M. G., and J. Goldstone, 'Global Report on Conflict, Governance, and State Fragility', *Foreign Policy Bulletin*, 17:S01 (2007), 3–21.

Marx, D., *International Shipping Cartels* (Princeton NJ: Princeton University Press, 1953).

Marx, K., 'Inaugural Address of the International Working Men's Association' [1864], in *idem, The First International and After: Political Writings, Volume 3* (Harmondsworth UK: Penguin, 1973), 73–81.

Mattern, J., *Geopolitik: Doctrine of National Self-Sufficiency and Empire* (Baltimore MD: Johns Hopkins University Press, 1942).

Mayer, H., and P. Knox, 'Slow Cities: Sustainable Places in a Fast World', *Journal of Urban Affairs*, 28 (2006), 321–34.

Mazrui, A. A., 'Racial Conflict or Clash of Civilizations? Rival Paradigms for Emerging Fault-Lines', in S. Rashid (ed.), *"The Clash of Civilizations?" Asian Responses* (Dhaka, Bangladesh: The University Press, 1997), 27–37.

McCoubrey, H., and J. Morris, *Regional Peacekeeping in the Post-Cold War Era* (The Hague: Kluwer Law International, 2000).

McDonough, T., (ed.), *Was Ireland a Colony? Economics, Politics, and Culture in Nineteenth-Century Ireland* (Dublin: Irish Academic Press, 2005).

McEwan, C., 'How the "Seraphic" became "Geographic": Women Travellers in West Africa, 1840–1915', Ph.D. thesis, Loughborough University of Technology (1995).

—— 'Cutting Power Lines within the Palace? Countering Paternity and Eurocentrism in the "Geographical Tradition" ', *Transactions of the Institute of British Geographers*, N.S. 23 (1998), 371–84.

—— *Gender, Geography and Empire: Victorian Women Travellers in West Africa* (Aldershot UK: Ashgate, 2000).

McFarlane, C., 'Crossing Borders: Development, Learning and the North–South Divide', *Third World Quarterly*, 27 (2006), 1413–37.

McGovern, R., 'Bush, Oil, and Moral Bankruptcy', *Counterpunch*, 27 September 2007, at <http://www.counterpunch.org/mcgovern09272007.html>, accessed 14 July 2008.

McIntosh, M., S. Waddock, and G. Kell (eds.), *Learning to Talk: Corporate Citizenship and the Development of the UN Global Compact* (Sheffield UK: Greenleaf Publishing, 2004).

McKenzie, C., 'The British Big-Game Hunting Tradition, Masculinity and Fraternalism with particular reference to "The Shikar Club" ', *Sports Historian*, 20 (2000), 70–96.

McNamara, P., *A Catholic Cold War: Edmund A. Walsh, S.J., and the Politics of American Anticommunism* (New York: Fordham University Press, 2005).

Mearsheimer, J., *The Tragedy of Great Power Politics* (New York: W. W. Norton and Co., 2001).

—— 'Hans Morgenthau and the Iraq War: Realism versus Neo-Conservatism', *Open Democracy*, 19 May 2005, at <http://www.opendemocracy.net/democracy-americanpower/morgenthau_2522.jsp>, accessed 23 September 2007.

—— and S. Walt, *The Israel Lobby and U.S. Foreign Policy* (New York: Farrar, Straus and Giroux, 2007).

Megoran, N., 'Revisiting the "Pivot": The Influence of Halford Mackinder on Analysis of Uzbekistan's International Relations', *Geographical Journal*, 170 (2004), 347–58.

Mehta, U. S., *Liberalism and Empire: A Study in Nineteenth-Century British Liberal Thought* (Chicago IL: University of Chicago Press, 1999).

Meiksins Wood, E., *Empire of Capital* (London: Verso, 2005 [2003]).

Meinig, D. W., *The Shaping of America: A Geographical Perspective on 500 Years of History. Volume 1. Atlantic America, 1492–1800* (New Haven CT: Yale University Press, 1986).

—— *The Shaping of America: A Geographical Perspective on 500 Years of History. Volume 3. Transcontinental America 1850–1915* (New Haven CT: Yale University Press, 1998).

—— *The Shaping of America: A Geographical Perspective on 500 Years of History. Volume 4. Global America, 1915–2000* (New Haven CT: Yale University Press, 2005).

Metcalf, P., *James Knowles: Victorian Editor and Architect* (Oxford UK: Clarendon Press, 1982).

Metz, S., (ed.), *Revising the Two MTW Force Shaping Paradigm* (Carlisle PA: Strategic Studies Institute, 2001).

Michel, S., 'Defining Hydrocommons Governance along the Border of the Californias; A Case Study of Transbasin Diversions and Water Quality in the Tijuana–San Diego Metropolitan Region', *Natural Resources Journal*, 40 (2000), 931–69.

Mill, H. R., *The Realm of Nature: An Outline of Physiography* (London: W. A. Knight, 1892).

—— *An Autobiography* (London: Longmans Green, 1951).

Miller, M., 'Introduction', in *idem.* (ed.), *P. A. Kropótkin, Selected Writings on Anarchism and Revolution* (Cambridge MA: MIT Press, 1970), 1–44.

Mills, S., *Discourses of Difference: An Analysis of Women's Travel Writing and Colonialism* (London: Routledge, 1991).

Mitchell, T., *Colonising Egypt* (Berkeley CA: University of California Press, 1988).

Mladineo, S. V., 'Introduction', in H. J. Mackinder, *Democratic Ideals and Reality*, new edition (Washington DC: National Defense University Press, 1996 [1919]), xvi–xxii.

Monshipouri, M., C. E. Welch, and E. T. Kennedy, 'Multinational Corporations and the Ethics of Global Responsibility: Problems and Possibilities', *Human Rights Quarterly*, 25 (2003), 965–89.

'Monthly Record', *Geographical Journal*, 103 (1944), 132.

Moore, J., *The Post-Darwinian Controversies* (Cambridge UK: Cambridge University Press, 1979).

Moravcsik, A., 'Reassessing Legitimacy in the European Union', *JCMS: Journal of Common Market Studies*, 40 (2002), 603–24.

Morris, C., *Winston's Cumulative Encyclopaedia, Vol. 9* (Philadelphia PA: John C. Winston Co., 1919).

Morris, J., *Pax Britannica: The Climax of an Empire* (London: Faber, 1968).

Morrissey, J., 'Basing and Biopolitics: US Juridical Warfare in the War on Terror', in D. Grondin (ed.), *War Beyond the Battlefield* (in press).

Moseley, H. N., *Notes by a Naturalist on the "Challenger", Being an Account of Various Observations Made During the Voyage of H.M.S. "Challenger" Round the World in the Years 1872–1876* (London: Macmillan, 1879).

'Mr. Mackinder on Geography-Teaching', *Science*, 14 (13 December 1889), 408–9.

Mulvaney, D. J., 'Spencer, Sir Walter Baldwin (1860–1929)', in *Australian Dictionary of Biography. Volume 12* (Melbourne: Melbourne University Press, 1990), 33–6.

Munck, R., 'Neoliberalism, Necessitarianism and Alternatives in Latin America: There is No Alternative (TINA)?', *Third World Quarterly*, 24 (2003), 495–511.

Murphy, D. T., *The Heroic Earth: Geopolitical Thought in Weimar Germany, 1918–1933* (Kent OH: Kent State University Press, 1997).

Murphy, G., *Hemispheric Imaginings: The Monroe Doctrine and Narratives of the U.S. Empire* (Durham NC: Duke University Press, 2005).

Myers, G., 'Colonial Geography and Masculinity in Eric Dutton's "Kenya Mountain" ', *Gender, Place and Culture*, 9 (2002), 23–38.

Myers Jaffe, A., and R. Soligo, 'Re-evaluating US Strategic Priorities in the Caspian Region: Balancing Energy Resource Initiatives with Terrorism Containment', *Cambridge Review of International Affairs*, 17 (2004), 255–68.

'The Mysteries of Geopolitics', *Time*, 11 January 1943.

Nagel, J., 'Masculinity and Nationalism: Gender and Sexuality in the Making of Nations', *Ethnic and Racial Studies*, 21 (1998), 242–69.

Nash, D., 'The Boer war and its Humanitarian Critics', *History Today*, 49:6 (1999), 42–9.

Nation, R. C., 'Regional Studies in a Global Age', in J. B. Bartholomees, Jr. (ed.), *U.S. Army War College Guide to National Security and Policy* (Carlisle PA: Strategic Studies Institute, 2004), 51–65.

'National Material Capabilities (v3.02)' at <http://www.correlatesofwar.org/COW2 Data/Capabilities/nmc3–02.htm>, accessed 1 January 2008.

The National Security Strategy of the United States of America (17 September 2002) at <http://www.whitehouse.gov/nsc.nssall.html>, accessed 7 January 2008.

National Defense Strategy of the United States of America, March 2005 (Washington DC: Department of Defense, 2005).

Natter, W., 'Geopolitics in Germany, 1919–45', in J. Agnew, K. Mitchell, and G. Toal (eds.), *A Companion to Political Geography* (Oxford UK: Blackwell, 2003), 187–203.

Newman, D. W., 'Theorizing Collective Indigenous Rights', *American Indian Law Review*, 31 (2006), 273–89.

Newton-Small, J., 'Obama's Foreign-Policy Problem', *Time*, 18 December 2007, at <http://www.time.com/time/nation/article/0,8599,1695803,00.html?xid=feed-cnn-topics>, accessed 14 June 2008.

'Niall Ferguson: Biography' at <http://www.niallferguson.org/bio.html>, accessed 1 January 2008.

Nimocks, W., *Milner's Young Men: The 'Kindergarten' in Edwardian Imperial Affairs* (Durham NC: Duke University Press, 1968).

Ninkovich, F., *Modernity and Power: A History of the Domino Theory in the Twentieth Century* (Chicago IL: University of Chicago Press, 1994).

Nonini, D. M., 'Introduction: The Global Idea of the Commons', in *idem.* (ed.), *The Global Idea of 'The Commons'* (New York: Berghahn Books, 2007), 1–25.

Norton, A., *Leo Strauss and the Politics of American Empire* (New Haven CT: Yale University Press, 2004).

'Notes from the Editors', *Monthly Review*, 55:8 (2004), 1–2.

Nworah, K. D., 'The Aborigines' Protection Society, 1889–1909: A Pressure-Group in Colonial Policy', *Canadian Journal of African Studies*, 5 (1971), 79–91.

Obama, B., 'Renewing American Leadership', *Foreign Affairs*, 86:4 (2007), 2–16.

—— 'Remarks at AIPAC Policy Conference, June 4, 2008', at <http://my.barack obama.com/page/community/post/HQblog/gG5CKp>, accessed 20 June 2008.

O'Brien, P. K., 'Imperialism and the Rise and Decline of the British Economy, 1688–1989', *New Left Review*, 238 (1999), 48–80.

Office of Management and Budget, *Budget of the United States Government: Fiscal year 2008* (Washington DC: Office of Management and Budget, 2007) at <http://www.whitehouse.gov/omb/budget/fy2008/budget.html>, accessed 14 April 2007.

Office of the United Nations High Commissioner for Refugees, *The State of the World's Refugees: Human Displacement in the New Millennium* (Oxford UK: Oxford University Press, 2006).

Officer, L. H., 'What Was the U.K. GDP Then?' (Chicago IL: MeasuringWorth. Com, 2007) at <http://www.measuringworth.com/datasets/ukgdp/result.php>, accessed 2 January 2008.

O'Hara, S. L., 'Great Game or Grubby Game: The Struggle for Control of the Caspian', *Geopolitics*, 9 (2004), 138–61.

—— M. Heffernan, and G. Endfield, 'Halford Mackinder, the "Geographical Pivot", and British Perceptions of Central Asia', in B. W. Blouet (ed.), *Global Strategy: Mackinder and the Defence of the West* (London: Frank Cass, 2005), 90–106.

Ohmae, K., *The Borderless World* (New York: Harper Business, 1990).

Orford, A., *Reading Humanitarian Intervention: Human Rights and the Use of Force in International Law* (Cambridge UK: Cambridge University Press, 2003).

Osaghae, E. E., 'The Ogoni Uprising: Oil Politics, Minority Agitation and the Future of the Nigerian State', *African Affairs*, 94 (1995), 325–44.

Osterhammel, J., 'Britain and China, 1842–1914', in W. R. Louis, A. M. Low, and A. Porter (eds.), *The Oxford History of the British Empire. Volume III. The Nineteenth Century* (Oxford UK: Oxford University Press, 1998), 146–69.

Ó Síocháin, S., and M. O'Sullivan, 'Introduction', in S. Ó Síocháin and M. O'Sullivan (eds.), *The Eyes of Another Race: Roger Casement's Congo Report and 1903 Diary* (Dublin: University College Dublin Press, 2003), 1–44.

Ó Tuathail [Toal], G., *Critical Geopolitics: The Politics of Writing Global Space* (Minneapolis MN: University of Minnesota Press, 1996).

—— 'Thinking Critically about Geopolitics', in G. Ó Tuathail, S. Dalby, and P. Routledge (eds.), *The Geopolitics Reader* (London: Routledge, 1998), 1–12.

—— 'Part I. Introduction', in G. Ó Tuathail, S. Dalby, and P. Routledge (eds.), *The Geopolitics Reader* (London: Routledge, 1998), 15–25.

—— 'Understanding Critical Geopolitics: Geopolitics and Risk Society', *Journal of Strategic Studies*, 22:2/3 (1999), 107–24.

—— 'Spiritual Geopolitics: Fr. Edmund Walsh and Jesuit Anti-communism', in K. Dodds and D. Atkinson (eds.), *Geopolitical Traditions: A Century of Geopolitical Thought* (London: Routledge, 2000), 187–210.

Owens, M. T., 'In Defense of Classical Geopolitics', *Naval War College Review*, 52:4 (1999), 59–76.

Padover, S. K., 'Japanese Race Propaganda', *Public Opinion Quarterly*, 7 (1943), 191–204.

Pak, C. Y., *Korea and the United Nations* (The Hague: Kluwer Law International, 2000).

Pakenham, T., *The Boer War* (New York: Random House, 1979).

—— *The Scramble for Africa* (London: Weidenfeld and Nicolson, 1991).

Parker, W. H., *Mackinder: Geography as an Aid to Statecraft* (Oxford UK: Clarendon Press, 1982).

Partsch, J., *Central Europe* (London: Heinemann, 1903).

Patnaik, U., *The Republic of Hunger, and Other Essays* (Monmouth, Wales: Merlin Press, 2007).

Paye, J.-C., *Global War on Terror* (New York: Telos Press, 2007 [2004]).

Pearce, A. J., 'Introduction', in H. J. Mackinder, *Democratic Ideals and Reality*, new edition (New York: Norton, 1962 [1919]), ix–xxiv.

Pearce, R. D., *Mary Kingsley: Light at the Heart of Darkness* (Oxford UK: Kensal Press, 1990).

Peel, J. D. Y., *Herbert Spencer: The Evolution of a Sociologist* (London: Heinemann Educational, 1971).

Pelfrey, W., *Billy, Alfred, and General Motors: The Story of Two Unique Men, a Legendary Company, and a Remarkable Time in American History* (New York: AMACOM/American Management Association, 2006).

Pels, P., 'A Prehistory of Ethical Codes in Anthropology', *Current Anthropology*, 40 (1999), 101–114.

Phillips, K., *American Theocracy: The Perils and Politics of Radical Religion, Oil, and Borrowed Money in the Twenty-First Century* (London: Penguin, 2006).

Phillips, R., *Mapping Men and Empire: A Geography of Adventure* (London: Routledge, 1997).

Pickering, A., 'Cyborg History and the World War II Regime', *Perspectives in Science*, 3 (1995), 1–49.

Pieterse, J. N., 'Neoliberal Empire', *Theory, Culture and Society*, 21:3 (2004), 119–40.

Pinochet Ugarte, A., *Introduction to Geopolitics* (Santiago: Editorial Andrés Bello, 1981 [1968]).

Pitts, J., *A Turn to Empire: The Rise of Imperial Liberalism in Britain and France* (Princeton NJ: Princeton University Press, 2005).

Ploszajska, T., 'Representations of Imperial Landscapes and Peoples in Popular Geography Texts, 1870–1944', in M. Naish (ed.), *Values in Geography Education* (London: Institute of Education, 1998), 29–34.

Porter, A., 'Sir Roger Casement and the International Humanitarian Movement', *Journal of Imperial and Commonwealth History*, 29 (2001), 59–74.

Porter, B., *Critics of Empire: British Radical Attitudes to Colonialism in Africa, 1895–1914* (London: Macmillan, 1968).

—— *The Absent-Minded Imperialists: Empire, Society, and Culture in Britain* (Oxford UK: Oxford University Press, 2004).

—— 'We Don't Do Empire', *History Today*, 55:3 (2005), 31–3.

Potter, S. R., 'Peter Alexeivich Kropótkin, 1842–1921', in T. W. Freeman (ed.), *Geographers: Bibliographical Studies, Volume 7* (London: Mansell, 1983), 63–9.

Pratt, M. L., *Imperial Eyes: Travel Writing and Transculturation* (London: Routledge, 1992).

Proctor, R., *Racial Hygiene: Medicine under the Nazis* (Cambridge MA: Harvard University Press, 1988).

Puder, J., 'Bernard Lewis Credits Bush on Iraq', *Frontpage Magazine*, 11 May 2007, at <http://www.frontpagemag.com/Articles/ReadArticle.asp?ID=28255>, accessed 20 June 2008.

Pynchon, T., 'Foreword', in G. Orwell, *1984* (New York: Plume, 2003 [1949]), vii–xxvi.

—— *Against the Day* (New York: Penguin, 2006).

Pynchon, T., '[Promotional blurb for *Against the Day*, posted briefly at Amazon. com]' (2006), at http://against-the-day.pynchonwiki.com/wiki/index.php?title- =Against_the_Day_description, accessed 1 June 2008.

Ramonet, I.,'Servile States', *Le Monde Diplomatique*, October 2002, at <http://mondediplo.com/2002/10/01servile>, accessed 8 January 2008.

Rangsimaporn, P., 'Interpretations of Eurasianism: Justifying Russia's Role in East Asia', *Europe-Asia Studies*, 58:3 (2006), 371–89.

Rashid, A., *Taliban: Militant Islam, Oil and Fundamentalism in Central Asia* (London: I. B. Tauris, 2000).

Ratzel, F., *Anthropogeographie. 2. Teil. Die geographische Verbreitung der Menschen* [Anthropogeography. Part 2. The Geographical Distribution of Humankind] (Stuttgart: J. Engelhorn, 1891).

—— *History of Mankind. Vol. 1* (London: Macmillan, 1896 [1894]).

—— 'Der Lebensraum: Eine biogeographische Studie' [Living-space: A Biogeographical Study], in K. Bücher, K. V. Fricker, F. X. Funck, G. v. Mandry, G. v. Mayr, F. Ratzel, *Festgaben für Albert Schäffle zur siebensigen Widerkehr seines Geburtstages am 24. Februar 1901* (Tübingen: H. Laupp, 1901), 103–89.

—— *Die Erde und das Leben: Eine vergleichende Erdkunde, I* [Earth and Life: A Comparative Geography. I] (Leipzig: Bibliographisches Institut, 1901).

—— *Politische Geographie oder die Geographie der Staaten, des Verkehrs und des Krieges* [Political Geography, or the Geography of States, Commerce, and War] (Munich: R. Oldenbourg, 1903).

Raustiala, K., 'The Geography of Justice', *Fordham Law Review*, 73 (2005), 2501–60.

Reclus, *Voyage à la Sierra Nevada de Sainte-Marthe: Paysages de la Nature tropicale* (Paris: Hachette, 1861).

—— 'L'Homme et la Nature: De l'Action humaine sur la Géographie physique', *Revue des Deux Mondes*, 54 (1864), 762–71.

—— 'Du Sentiment de la Nature dans les Sociétés modernes', *Revue des Deux Mondes*, 63 (1866), 352–81.

—— La Terre: Description des Phenomènes de la Vie du Globe. I. Les Continents [The Earth: A Descriptive History of the Phenomena of the Life of the Globe. I. The Continents] (Paris: Hachette, 1868).

—— *Histoire d'un Ruisseau* (The Story of a Stream) (Paris: J. Hetzel, 1869).

—— La Terre: Description des Phénomènes de la Vie du Globe. II. L'Atmosphére, L'Océan, La Vie [The Earth: a Descriptive History of the Phenomena of the Life of the Globe. II. Atmosphere, Ocean and Life] (Paris: Hachette, 1869).

—— *The Earth and its Inhabitants. I. Europe, Vol. I. Greece. Turkey in Europe, Rumania, Servia, Montenegro, Italy, Spain and Portugal*, ed. E. G. Ravenstein (New York: D. Appleton and Co., 1883 [1876]).

—— *The Earth and Its Inhabitants. VI. Asia, Vol. I. Asiatic Russia*, ed. E. G. Ravenstein and A. H. Keane (New York: D. Appleton and Co., 1884 [1881]).

—— *Nouvelle Géographie universelle: La Terre et Les Hommes. VI. Asie. Livre VI. L'Asie Russe* (Paris: Hachette, 1881).

—— *The Earth and its Inhabitants. VIII. Asia, Vol. IV. India and Indo-China*, ed. A. H. Keane (New York: D. Appleton and Co., 1885 [1884]).

—— 'East and West', *Contemporary Review*, 66 (1894), 475–87.

—— 'The Progress of Mankind', *Contemporary Review*, 70 (1896), 761–83.

—— 'Pages de Sociologie préhistorique', *L'Humanité Nouvelle*, 2:8 (1898), 129–43.

—— 'On Vegetarianism' [1901], in *idem, On Vegetarianism, and The Great Kinship of Humans and Fauna* (Petersham North NSW, Australia: Jura Media, 1996), 1–6.

—— 'On Spherical Maps and Reliefs', *Geographical Journal*, 22 (1903), 290–3 (and discussion, 294–9).

Reclus, É., 'Preface', in J. Grave (ed.), *Patriotisme–Colonisation* (Paris: Les Temps Nouveaux, 1903).

—— *L'Homme et la Terre, I. Les Ancêtres, Histoire ancienne* (Paris: Librairie Universelle, 1905).

—— *L'Homme et la Terre, V. Histoire moderne (suite); Histoire contemporaine* (Paris: Librairie Universelle, 1905).

—— *L'Homme et La Terre. VI. Histoire contemporaine (suite)* (Paris: Librairie Universelle, 1908).

—— *Correspondance II. Octobre 1870–Juillet 1889* (Paris: Schleicher Frères, 1914).

—— *Correspondance III. Septembre 1889–Juillet 1900* (Paris: Alfred Costes, 1925).

Redfield, P., 'Doctors, Borders, and Life in Crisis', *Current Anthropology*, 20 (2005), 328–61.

Reining, C. C., 'A Lost Period of Applied Anthropology', *American Anthropologist*, 64 (1962), 593–600.

Remy, S. P., *The Heidelberg Myth: The Nazification and Denazification of a German University* (Cambridge MA: Harvard University Press, 2002).

R[eynolds], J. R., 'Review of Mackinder, "Seven Lectures on the United Kingdom for Use in India" ', *Geographical Teacher*, 6 (1911), 73.

Rhodes James, R. (ed.), *Winston S. Churchill: His Complete Speeches, 1897–1963* (New York: Chelsea House Publishers, 1974).

Rice, C., 'Promoting the National Interest', *Foreign Affairs*, 79:1 (2000), 45–62.

Richards, R. J., *The Romantic Conception of Life: Science and Philosophy in the Age of Goethe* (Chicago IL: University of Chicago Press, 2002).

Ricoeur, P., *Time and Narrative, Volume 3* (Chicago IL: University of Chicago Press, 1988 [1985]).

Riddell, R. C., S.-E. Kruse, T. Kyllönen, S. Ojanpera, and J.-L. Vielajus, *Searching for Impact and Methods: NGO Evaluation Synthesis Study. A Report Produced for the OECD/DAC Expert Group on Evaluation* (Helsinki: Department for International Development Cooperation, Ministry of Foreign Affairs, 1997).

Riedi, E., 'Women, Gender, and the Promotion of Empire: the Victoria League, 1901–1914', *Historical Journal*, 45 (2002), 569–99.

Rishikof, H., 'Juridical Warfare: The Neglected Legal Instrument', *Joint Force Quarterly*, 48 (2008), 11–13.

Ritchie, J., 'Travels with Jean' at <http://beki.typepad.co.uk/travels_with_jean/>, accessed 18 June 2007.

Robbins, K. G., 'Lord Bryce and the First World War', *Historical Journal*, 10 (1967), 255–78.

Roberts, C., *The Unnatural History of the Sea* (Washington DC: Island Press, 2007).

Roberts, P., *The End of Oil* (New York: Houghton Mifflin, 2004).

Robertson, G., *Crimes Against Humanity: The Struggle for Global Justice*, third edition (London: Penguin, 2006 [1999]).

Robinson, J., *Ordinary Cities: Between Modernity and Development* (London: Routledge, 2006).

Rodriguez-Garavito, C. A., 'Global Governance and Labor Rights: Codes of Conduct and Anti-Sweatshop Struggles in Global Apparel Factories in Mexico and Guatemala', *Politics and Society*, 33 (2005), 203–33.

Rodríguez-Pose, A., 'Growth and Institutional Change: The Influence of the Spanish Regionalization Process on Economic Performance', *Environment and Planning C: Government and Policy*, 14 (1996), 71–87.

Rokke, E. J., 'Preface', in H. J. Mackinder, *Democratic Ideals and Reality*, new edition (Washington DC: National Defense University Press, 1996), vii.

Romm, J. R., *The Edges of the Earth in Ancient Thought: Geography, Exploration, and Fiction* (Princeton NJ: Princeton University Press, 1992).

Rose, G., *Feminism and Geography: The Limits of Geographical Knowledge* (Cambridge UK: Polity, 1993).

Rosecrance, R. N., and A. A. Stein (eds.), *No More States? Globalization, National Self-Determination, and Terrorism* (Lanham MD: Rowman and Littlefield, 2006).

Rosencranz, A., and D. Louk, 'Doe v. Unocal: Holding Corporations Liable for Human Rights Abuses on Their Watch', *Chapman Law Review*, 8 (2005), 135–52.

Rössler, R., ' "Area Research" and "Spatial Planning" from the Weimar Republic to the German Federal Republic: Creating a Society with a Spatial order under National Socialism', in M. Renneberg and M. Walker (eds.), *Science, Technology and National Socialism* (Cambridge UK: Cambridge University Press, 1994), 126–38.

—— 'Geography and Area Planning under National Socialism', in M. Szöllösi-Janze (ed.), *Science in the Third Reich* (Oxford UK: Berg, 2001), 59–78.

Rotberg, R. I., and M. F. Shore, *The Founder: Cecil Rhodes and the Pursuit of Power* (Oxford UK: Oxford University Press, 1988).

Rowbotham, S., ' "Travellers in a Strange Country": Responses of Working Class Students to the University Extension Movement, 1873–1910', *History Workshop Journal*, 12 (1981), 62–95.

Roxby, P. M., 'Mr. Mackinder's Books on the Teaching of Geography and History', *Geographical Teacher*, 7 (1914), 404–7.

—— 'Sixty Years of Geography and Education: A Retrospect of the Geographical Association', *Geography*, 38 (1953), 231–64.

Royal Commonwealth Society. Fisher Collection. Catalogue (Cambridge UK: Cambridge University Library, unpublished, n.d.).

'Royal Geographical Society', *Quarterly Review*, 46 (1831), 55.

Rudolph, J. R., Jr, 'Ethnic Sub-states and the Emergent Politics of Tri-level Interaction in Western Europe', *Western Political Quarterly*, 30 (1977), 537–57.

Rumley, D., J. V. Minghi, and F. M. Grimm, 'The Content of Ratzel's "Politische Geographie" ', *Professional Geographer*, 25 (1973), 271–7.

'Rumsfeld and His Crew', *Current Concerns*, 2000:11 (November 2001) at <http://www.currentconcerns.ch/archive/20011106.php>, accessed 14 January 2008.

Russell, G., 'Alfred Thayer Mahan and American Geopolitics: The Conservatism and Realism of an Imperialist', *Geopolitics*, 11 (2006), 119–40.

Russell, I. C., *North America* (London: Oxford University Press, 1904).

Ryan, J. R., 'Visualizing Imperial Geography: Halford Mackinder and the Colonial Office Visual Instruction Committee, 1902–11', *Ecumene*, 1 (1994), 157–76.

—— 'Photography, Geography and Empire, 1840–1914', Ph.D. thesis, Royal Hollo-
way and Bedford College, University of London (1994).

—— *Picturing Empire: Photography and the Visualization of the British Empire*
(Chicago IL: University of Chicago Press, 1997).

Said, E., *Orientalism* (Harmondsworth UK: Penguin, 1985 [1978]).

Sampson, G., ' "Trouble Spots": Projects, Bandits, and State Fragmentation',
in J. Friedman (ed.), *Globalization, the State, and Violence* (Walnut Creek CA: Rowman
Altamira, 2003), 309–42.

Sangtin Writers Collective and Richa Nagar, *Playing with Fire: Feminist Thought and
Activism through Seven Lives in India* (Minneapolis MN: University of Minnesota
Press, 2006).

Scahill, J., 'Did Bush Really Want to Bomb Al Jazeera?', *Nation* (23 November 2005)
at <http://www.thenation.com/doc/20051212/scahill>, accessed 14 July 2008.

Scargill, D. I., 'The RGS and the Foundations of Geography at Oxford', *Geographical Journal*, 142 (1976), 438–61.

Schafft, G. E., *From Racism to Genocide: Anthropology in the Third Reich* (Chicago
IL: University of Illinois Press, 2004).

Schama, S., *Landscape and Memory* (London: HarperCollins, 1995).

Scheiber, H. N. (ed.), *Law of the Sea: The Common Heritage and Emerging Challenges*
(Dordrecht: Martinus Nijhoff, 2000).

Schell, J., *The Unconquerable World: Power, Non-violence, and the Will of the People*
(London: Allen Lane, 2003).

—— 'The Moral Equivalent of Empire', *Harper's Magazine*, 316 (February 2008),
9–13.

Schiavo-Campo, S., and M. Judd, *The Mindanao Conflict in the Philippines: Roots,
Costs, and Potential Peace Dividend. Conflict Prevention and Reconstruction Unit.
Working Paper 24* (Washington DC: World Bank, 2005).

Schmitt, C., *The "Nomos" of the Earth in the International Law of the "Jus Publicum
Europaeum"* (New York: Telos Press Publishing, 2003 [1950]).

Schumacher, F., 'The American Way of Empire: National Tradition and Transatlantic Adaptation in America's Search for Imperial Identity, 1898–1910', *GHI Bulletin*,
31 (2002), 35–50.

Schweder, R. A., 'George W. Bush and the Missionary Position', *Daedalus*, 133:4
(2004), 26–36.

Searle, G. R., *The Quest for National Efficiency: A Study in British Politics and
Political Thought, 1899–1914* (Oxford UK: Blackwell, 1971).

Sedgwick, M., *Against the Modern World: Traditionalism and the Secret Intellectual
History of the Twentieth Century* (Oxford UK: Oxford University Press, 2004).

Seeley, J. R., *The Expansion of England: Two Courses of Lectures* (London: Macmillan, 1883).

Seelye, J., *War Games: Richard Harding Davis and the New Imperialism* (Amherst
MA: University of Massachusetts Press, 2003).

Seiple, C., 'Revisiting the Geo-Political Thinking of Sir Halford Mackinder: United
States–Uzbekistan Relations, 1991–2005', Ph.D. thesis, Fletcher School of Law of
Law and Diplomacy (2006).

Seldon, A., *Blair: The Biography* (London: Free Press, 2004).

Semmel, B., 'Sir Halford Mackinder: Theorist of Imperialism', *Canadian Journal of Economics and Political Science*, 24 (1958), 554–61.
—— *Imperialism and Social Reform: English Social–Imperial Thought, 1895–1914* (London: Allen and Unwin, 1960).
Sempa, F. P., *Geopolitics: From the Cold War to the 21st Century* (New Brunswick NJ: Transaction, 2002).
Semple, E.C., *American History and its Geographic Conditions* (Boston MA: Houghton, Mifflin, 1903).
—— *Influences of Geographic Environment, on the Basis of Ratzel's System of Anthropo-geography* (New York: Henry Holt and Co., 1911).
Sen, A., *Identity and Violence: The Illusion of Destiny* (New York: W. W. Norton and Co., 2006).
Sennett, R., and J. Cobb, *The Hidden Injuries of Class* (New York: Knopf, 1972).
Shapiro, M. J., 'Samuel Huntington's Moral Geography', *Theory and Event* 2:4 (1998) at <http://muse.jhu.edu/login?uri = /journals/theory_and_event/v002/2.4shapiro. html>, accessed 10 February 2008.
Sheppard, E., 'Constructing Free Trade: From Manchester Boosterism to Global Management', *Transactions of the Institute of British Geographers*, N.S. 30 (2005), 151–72.
Shiva, V., *Stolen Harvest: The Hijacking of the Global Food Supply* (Cambridge MA: South End Press, 2000).
Shlapentokh, D., 'Dugin Eurasianism: A Window on the Minds of the Russian Elite or an Intellectual Ploy?', *Studies in East European Thought*, 59 (2007), 215–36.
Shulzinger, R. D., 'The Naïve and Sentimental Diplomat: Henry Kissinger's Memoirs', *Diplomatic History*, 4:3 (1980), 303–16.
Simons, G., *Iraq: From Sumer to Sudan* (London: St. Martins Press, 1994).
Singer, J. D., 'Reconstructing the Correlates of War Dataset on Material Capabilities of States, 1816–1985', *International Interactions*, 14 (1987), 115–32.
Singer, J. D., S. Bremer, and J. Stuckey, 'Capability Distribution, Uncertainty, and Major Power War, 1820–1965', in B. Russett (ed.), *Peace, War, and Numbers* (Beverly Hills CA: Sage, 1972), 19–48.
Sivanandan, A., 'Race, Terror and Civil Society', *Race and Class*, 47:3 (2006), 1–8.
Sklar, H. (ed.), *Trilateralism: The Trilateral Commission and Elite Planning for World Government* (Cambridge MA: South End Press, 1980).
Slater, D., *Geopolitics and the Post-colonial* (Oxford UK: Blackwell, 2004).
Sloan, G., and C. S. Gray, 'Why Geopolitics?', in C. S. Gray and G. Sloan (eds.), *Geopolitics, Geography, and Strategy* (London: Frank Cass, 1999), 1–11.
Sloan, P. R., ' "The Sense of Sublimity": Darwin on Nature and Divinity', *Osiris*, 16 (2001), 251–69.
Smith, G., 'The Masks of Proteus: Russia, Geopolitical Shift and the New Eurasianism', *Transactions of the Institute of British Geographers*, N.S. 24 (1999), 481–94.
Smith, J., 'Response to Wallerstein: The Struggle for Global Society in a World System', *Social Forces*, 83 (2005), 1279–85.
—— 'Social Movements and Multilateralism', in E. Newman, R. Thakur, and J. Tirman (eds.), *Multilateralism Under Challenge? Power, International Order, and Structural Change* (New York: United Nations University Press, 2006), 385–421.
Smith, J. M., 'State Formation, Geography, and a Gentleman's Education', *Geographical Review*, 86 (1996), 91–100.

Smith, M., 'Anatomy of a Rumour: Murder Scandal, the Muscavat Party and Narratives of the Russian Revolution in Baku, 1917–20', *Journal of Contemporary History*, 36 (2001), 211–40.

Smith, N., *American Empire: Roosevelt's Geographer and the Prelude to Globalization* (Berkeley CA: University of California Press, 2003).

—— *The Endgame of Globalization* (New York: Routledge, 2005).

Smith, R., *The Utility of Force: The Art of War in the Modern World* (London: Allen Lane, 2005).

Smith, W. D., 'Friedrich Ratzel and the Origins of Lebensraum', *German Studies Review*, 3:1 (1980), 51–68.

Smith-Rosenberg, C., and C. Rosenberg, 'Female Animal: Medical and Biological Views of Woman and Her Role in Nineteenth-Century America', *Journal of American History*, 60 (1973), 332–56.

Smyth, W. J., *Map-Making, Landscapes and Memory: A Geography of Colonial and Early Modern Ireland, c.1530–1750* (Cork: Cork University Press, 2006).

Soloway, R. A., *Birth Control and the Population Question in England 1877–1930* (Chapel Hill NC: University of North Carolina Press, 1982).

—— 'Counting the Degenerates: The Statistics of Race Deterioration in Edwardian England', *Journal of Contemporary History*, 17 (1982), 137–64.

Spencer, H., *The Principles of Biology. Volume I*, revised and enlarged edition (London: Williams and Norgate, 1898 [1864]).

—— *The Principles of Sociology. Volumes I–III* (London: Williams and Norgate, 1876–96).

'Spottiswoode Family Archive' at <http://www.jsasoc.com/Family_archive/Archive/>, accessed 20 October 2007.

Spykman, N. J., *The Geography of the Peace* (New York: Harcourt, Brace, 1944).

Stamatopoulou, E., 'Indigenous Peoples and the United Nations: Human Rights as a Developing Dynamic', *Human Rights Quarterly*, 16 (1994), 58–81.

Stavrianakis, A., '(Big) Business as Usual: Sustainable Development, NGOs, and UK Arms Export Policy', *Conflict, Security, and Development*, 5 (2005), 45–67.

Stephens, B., 'The Amorality of Profit: Transnational Corporations and Human Rights', *Berkeley Journal of International Law*, 20 (2002), 45–90.

Stockholm International Peace Research Institute, *SIPRI Yearbook 2006: Armaments, Disarmament and International Security* (Oxford UK: Oxford University Press, 2006).

Stocking, G. W., 'What's in a Name? The Origins of the Royal Anthropological Institute', *Man*, N.S. 6 (1971), 369–90.

Stoddart, D. R., (ed.), *Geography, Ideology, and Social Concern* (Oxford UK: Blackwell, 1981).

—— *On Geography: And its History* (Oxford UK: Basil Blackwell, 1986).

—— 'Geography and War: The "New Geography" and the "New Army" in England, 1899–1914', *Political Geography*, 11 (1992), 87–99.

Stolle, D., M. Hooghe, and M. Micheletti, 'Politics in the Supermarket: Political Consumerism as a Form of Political Participation', *International Political Science Review*, 26:3 (2005), 245–69.

Strausz-Hupé, R., *Geopolitics: The Struggle for Space and Power* (New York: Putnam's, 1942).

Suleri, S., *The Rhetoric of English India* (Chicago IL: Chicago University Press, 1992).

Summers, A., 'Militarism in Britain before the Great War', *History Workshop Journal*, 2 (1976), 104–23.

Sundberg, J., 'NGO Landscapes: Conservation and Communities in the Maya Biosphere Reserve, Peten, Guatemala', *Geographical Review*, 88 (1998), 388–412.

Suskind, R., 'Faith, Certainty and the Presidency of George W. Bush', *New York Times. Magazine*, 17 October 2004, at http://www.nytimes.com/2004/10/17/magazine/17BUSH.html?ex=1255665600&en=890a96189e162076&ei=5090&partner=rssuserland, accessed 14 May 2008.

Swaisland, C., 'The Aborigines Protection Society, 1837–1909', in H. Temperley (ed.), *After Slavery: Emancipation and its Discontents* (London: Routledge, 2000), 265–80.

Symonds, R., *Oxford and Empire: The Last Lost Cause?* (New York: St. Martin's Press, 1986).

Tabb, W. K., 'Globalization is *an* Issue, the Power of Capital is *the* Issue', *Monthly Review*, 49:2 (1997), 20–30.

Takeuchi, K., 'The Japanese Imperial Tradition, Western Imperial and Modern Japanese Geography', in A. Godlewska and N. Smith (eds.), *Geography and Empire* (Oxford UK: Blackwell, 1994), 188–206.

—— 'Japanese Geopolitics in the 1930s and 1940s', in K. Dodds and D. Atkinson (eds.), *Geopolitical Traditions: A Century of Geopolitical Thought* (London: Routledge, 2000), 72–92.

Taylor, E. G. R., *Tudor Geography 1485–1583* (London: Methuen, 1930).

—— *Late Tudor and Early Stuart Geography 1583–1650* (London: Methuen, 1934).

Taylor, P. J., 'The New Geography of Global Civil Society: NGOs in the World City Network', *Globalizations*, 1 (2004), 265–77.

Teggart, F. J., 'Geography as an Aid to Statecraft: An Appreciation of Mackinder's "Democratic Ideals and Reality" ', *Geographical Review*, 8:4/5 (1919), 227–42.

Telford, T., 'The Nuremberg War Crimes Trials: An Appraisal', *Proceedings of the Academy of Political Science*, 23 (1949), 19–34.

Tétreault, M. A., 'The Sexual Politics of Abu Ghraib: Hegemony, Spectacle, and the Global War on Terror', *NWSA Journal*, 18:3 (2006), 33–50.

Thackeray, D. A., 'The Crisis of the Tariff Reform League and the Division of "Radical Conservatism", c. 1913–1922', *History*, 91 (2006), 45–61.

Thompson, A. S., 'Tariff Reform: An Imperial Strategy, 1902–1913', *Historical Journal*, 40 (1997), 1022–54.

—— 'The Language of Imperialism and the Meanings of Empire: Imperial Discourse in British Politics, 1895–1914', *Journal of British Studies*, 36:2 (1997), 147–77.

Thompson, E. P., *Customs in Common* (London: Merlin Press, 1991).

Thompson, J., 'Modern Britain and the New Imperial History', *History Compass*, 5 (2007), 455–62.

Thorndike, J., 'The Lurid Career of a Scientific System which a Briton Invented, the Germans Used and the Americans Need to Study', *Life*, 23 December 1941, 106–15.

Thornton, A. P., *The Imperial Idea and its Enemies: A Study in British Power* (London: Macmillan, 1959).

Thornton, R., *American Indian Holocaust and Survival: A Population History since 1492* (Norman OK: University of Oklahoma Press, 1987).

Thrift, N., 'A Hyperactive World', in R. J. Johnston, P. J. Taylor, and M. Watts (eds.), *Geographies of Global Change: Remapping the World in the Late Twentieth Century* (Oxford UK: Blackwell, 1995), 18–35.

Tickner, J., 'Gendering a Discipline: Some Feminist Methodological Contributions to International Relations', *Signs: Journal of Women in Culture and Society*, 30 (2005), 2173–88.

Tompkins, E. B., *Anti-imperialism in the United States: The Great Debate, 1890–1920* (Philadelphia PA: University of Pennsylvania Press, 1970).

Townshend, J., *J. A. Hobson* (Manchester UK: Manchester University Press, 1990).

Traub, J., *The Best Intentions: Kofi Annan and the UN in the Era of American Power* (London: Bloomsbury, 2006).

Trumpbour, J., 'The Clash of Civilizations: Samuel P. Huntington, Bernard Lewis, and the Remaking of the Post-Cold War World Order', in E. Qureshi and M. A. Sells (eds.), *The New Crusades: Constructing the Muslim Enemy* (New York: Columbia University Press, 2003), 88–130.

Tsogas, G., *Labor Regulation in a Global Economy* (London: M. E. Sharpe, 2001).

Tuhuwai Smith, L., *Decolonizing Methodologies: Research and Indigenous Peoples* (London: Zed Books, 1999).

Tunander, O., 'Swedish–German Geopolitics for a New Century: Rudolf Kjellén's "The State as a Living Organism" ', *Review of International Studies*, 27 (2001), 451–63.

Turner, S., 'Suspended Spaces—Contesting Sovereignties in a Refugee Camp', in T. B. Hansen and F. Stepputat (eds.), *Sovereign Bodies: Citizens, Migrants, and States in the Postcolonial World* (Princeton NJ: Princeton University Press, 2005), 312–32.

Turrell, R. V., ' "Finance … The Governor of the Imperial Engine": Hobson and the case of Rothschild and Rhodes', *Journal of Southern African Studies*, 13 (1987), 417–32.

Tyler, J. E., *The Struggle for Imperial Unity, 1868–1895* (London: Longmans, Green, 1938).

Tyler, P. E., 'U.S. Strategy Plan Calls for Insuring No Rivals Develop', *New York Times*, 8 March 1992, 1f.

Ullman, R. H., *Anglo-Soviet Relations, 1917–1921. Volume 2. Britain and the Russian Civil War, November 1918–February 1920* (Princeton NJ: Princeton University Press, 1968).

Unger, C., *The Fall of the House of Bush: The Untold Story of How a Band of True Believers Seized the Executive Branch, Started the Iraq War, and Still Imperils America's Future* (New York: Scribner, 2007).

United Nations Development Programme, *Human Development Report 2007/2008: Fighting Climate Change: Human Solidarity in a Divided World* (New York: United Nations Development Programme, 2007).

Urquhart, B., 'Limits on the Use of Force', in C. A. Croker, F. O. Hampson, and P. Hall (eds.), *Leashing the Dogs of War: Conflict Management in a Divided World* (Washington DC: United States Institute of Peace Press, 2007), 265–76.

Vagts, A., 'Geography in War and Geopolitics', *Military Affairs*, 7:2 (1943), 79–88.

Virilio, P., 'The State of Emergency' [1977], in J. der Derian (ed.), *The Virilio Reader* (Oxford UK: Blackwell, 1998), 46–57.

von Clausewitz, C., *Vom Kriege* [On War] (Berlin: Dummlers Verlag, 1832).

Walford, R., *Geography in British Schools, 1850–2000* (London: Taylor & Francis, 2005).

Wallach, L., and P. Woodall, Public Citizen, *Whose Trade Organization? A Comprehensive Guide to the WTO* (New York: New Press, 2004).

Walsh, E. A., 'Geopolitics and International Morals', in H. W. Weigert and V. Stefansson (eds.), *Compass of the World: A Symposium on Political Geography* (London: Harrap, 1946), 12–39.

—— *Total Power: A Footnote to History* (Garden City NY: Doubleday, 1948).

Walt, S. M., 'The Case for Finite Containment: Analyzing U.S. Grand Strategy', *International Security*, 14 (1989), 5–49, 9.

Wanklyn, G., *Friedrich Ratzel: A Biographical Memoir and Bibliography* (Cambridge UK: Cambridge University Press, 1961).

Wapner, P., *Environmental Activism and World Civic Politics* (New York: City University of New York Press, 1996).

Warner, G., 'Nixon, Kissinger and the *Rapprochement* with China, 1969–1972', *International Affairs*, 83:4 (2007), 763–81.

Watts, M. J., *Silent Violence: Food, Famine, and Peasantry in Northern Nigeria* (Berkeley CA: University of California Press, 1983).

—— 'Righteous Oil? Human Rights, the Oil Complex, and Corporate Social Responsibility', *Annual Review of Environment and Resources*, 30 (2005), 373–407.

Weidhorn, M., 'A Contrarian's Approach to Peace', in J. W. Muller (ed.), *Churchill as Peacemaker* (Cambridge UK: Cambridge University Press, 1997), 24–53.

Weigert, H. W., 'German Geopolitics: A Workshop for Army Rule', *Harper's Magazine*, November 1941, 586–97.

—— *Generals and Geographers: The Twilight of Geopolitics* (New York: Oxford University Press, 1942).

—— 'Haushofer and the Pacific', *Foreign Affairs*, 20:4 (1942), 732–42.

Weinreich, M., *Hitler's Professors: The Part of Scholarship in Germany's Crimes against the Jewish People* (New York: Yiddish Scientific Institute, 1946).

Welch, M., *Scapegoats of September 11th: Hate Crimes and State Crimes* (Piscataway NJ: Rutgers University Press, 2006).

Wheeler, N. J., *Saving Strangers: Humanitarian Intervention in International Society* (Oxford UK: Oxford University Press, 2000).

White, H., *The Content of Form: Narrative Discourse and Historical Representation* (Baltimore MD: Johns Hopkins University Press, 1987).

Whitfield, S., *Life Along the Silk Road* (Berkeley CA: University of California Press, 2001).

Whittlesey, D., *German Strategy of World Conquest* (London: Robinson, 1944).

Wilkinson, S., *Thirty-Five Years, 1874–1909* (London: Constable, 1953).

Williams, C. C., *A Commodified World? Mapping the Limits of Capitalism* (London: Zed Books, 2005).

Williams, W. W., 'United States and the Debate over Philippine Annexation: Implications for the Origins of American Imperialism', *Journal of American History*, 66 (1980), 810–31.

Williamson, J., 'What Washington Means by Policy Reform', in *idem* (ed.), *Latin American Adjustment: How Much Has Happened?* (Washington DC: Institute for International Economics, 1990), 7–20.

Wills, J., 'Taking on the CosmoCorps? Experiments in Transnational Labor Organization', *Economic Geography*, 74 (1998), 111–30.

Wilson, K. (ed.), *A New Imperial History: Culture, Identity, and Modernity in Britain and the Empire, 1660–1840* (Cambridge UK: Cambridge University Press, 2004).

—— 'Old Imperialisms and New Imperial Histories: Rethinking the History of the Present', *Radical History Review*, 95 (2006), 211–34.

Winlow, H., 'Anthropometric Cartography: Constructing Scottish Racial Identity in the Early Twentieth Century', *Journal of Historical Geography*, 27 (2001), 507–28.

—— 'Mapping Moral Geographies: W. Z. Ripley's Races of Europe and the United States', *Annals of the Association of American Geographers*, 96 (2006), 119–41.

Wise, M. J., 'The Scott Keltie Report 1885 and the Teaching of Geography in Great Britain', *Geographical Journal*, 152 (1986), 367–82.

—— 'The First Half Century, 1895–1945', typescript of lecture given at LSE, 7 July 1995, at <www.lse.ac.uk/collections/geographyAndEnvironment/research/Researchpapers/rp60.pdf>, accessed 1 January 2008.

Withers, C. W. J., D. Finnegan, and R. Higgitt, 'Geography's Other Histories? Geography and Science in the British Association for the Advancement of Science, 1831–c.1933', *Transactions of the Institute of British Geographers*, N.S. 31 (2006), 433–51.

Wittfogel, K., 'The Hydraulic Civilizations', in W. L. Thomas (ed.), *Man's Role in Changing the Face of the Earth* (Chicago IL: University of Chicago Press, 1956), 152–64.

Wolf, N., *The End of America: Letter of Warning to a Young Patriot* (White River Junction VT: Chelsea Green Publishing, 2007).

Wolfowitz, P. D., 'Clinton's First Year', *Foreign Affairs*, 73:1 (1994), 28–43.

Womack, J. P., D. T. Jones, and D. Roos, *The Machine that Changed the World: The Story of Lean Production* (New York: HarperPerennial, 1991).

Wonders, K., 'Hunting Narratives of the Age of Empire: A Gender Reading of their Iconography', *Environment and History*, 11 (2005), 269–91.

Woodcock, G., and I. Avakumović, *The Anarchist Prince: A Biographical Study of Peter Kropótkin* (New York: Schocken Books, 1971 [1950]).

Woodward, E. L., *Great Britain and the German Navy* (Oxford UK: Clarendon Press, 1935).

Woodward, R., 'From Military Geography to Militarism's Geographies: Disciplinary Engagements with the Geographies of Militarism and Military Activities', *Progress in Human Geography*, 29 (2005), 718–40.

Woodward, R., *State of Denial: Bush at War, Part III* (New York: Simon and Schuster, 2006).

'World Affairs Council "Islam and the West" Conference Explores Critical Topics in Middle East Relations', *Philadelphia* (*Business Wire*), 1 May 2006, at <http://www.businesswire.com/portal/site/google/index.jsp?ndmViewId = news_view&newsId = 20060501005557&newsLang = en>, accessed 20 June 2008.

'World Wide Military Deployments' at <http://www.globalsecurity.org/military/world/deploy.htm>, accessed 17 April 2008.

Wright, D., 'Curzon and Persia', *Geographical Journal*, 153 (1987), 343–50.

Yamin, F., 'NGOs and International Environmental Law: A Critical Evaluation of their Roles and Responsibilities', *Review of European Community and International Environmental Law*, 10 (2001), 149–62.

Yergin, D., *The Prize: The Epic Quest for Oil, Money, and Power* (New York: Random House, 1991).

Young, R., *White Mythologies: Writing History and the West* (London: Routledge, 1990).

Zacharias, U., 'Legitimizing Empire: Racial and Gender Politics of the War on Terrorism', *Social Justice*, 30:2 (2003), 123–32.

Zeleny, J., 'Obama, in Miami, Calls for Engaging with Cuba', *New York Times*, 24 May 2008, A15.

Zimmern, A., *The American Road to World Peace* (New York: E. P. Dutton, 1953).

Zunes, S., 'The Influence of the Christian Right in the U.S. Middle East Policy', *Middle East Policy*, 12 (2005), 73–8.

REFERENCES

Primary Sources

Bodleian Library, University of Oxford
Bryce Papers.
Milner Papers.
Sadler Papers.

Cambridge University Library
Benjamin Kidd Correspondence and Papers.
A. H. Fisher Letters.

Churchill College, Cambridge
Churchill Papers.

London School of Economics Archives
Wilson Woolley, M., 'The Philosophy of Sir Halford J. Mackinder', unpublished MS; Mackinder M 1856 (1).

National Archives, Kew
Cabinet Papers.
Foreign Office Papers.
Mackinder Papers.

Rhodes House Library, University of Oxford
Mackinder's Kenya Notebooks; Mss. Afr. r.11–30.

Royal Geographical Society, London
Kropótkin Correspondence.
Mackinder Correspondence.
H. R. Mill Correspondence.
Royal Geographical Society Council Minutes.

School of Geography, University of Oxford
Gilbert Papers.
Mackinder Papers.

West Sussex Record Office, Chichester
Maxse Collection.

Newspapers and Periodicals
Kelly's Directory of Oxfordshire 1895 (London: Kelly, 1895).
The Parliamentary Debates, 4th Series (February 1892 to December 1908).
The Official Report, House of Commons, 5th Series (January 1909 to March 1981).
Times (London).

INDEX